In the Wake of the Mongols

HARVARD-YENCHING INSTITUTE MONOGRAPH SERIES 116

In the Wake of the Mongols

*The Making of a New Social Order in
North China, 1200–1600*

Jinping Wang

Published by the Harvard University Asia Center
Distributed by Harvard University Press
Cambridge (Massachusetts) and London 2020

The Harvard-Yenching Institute, founded in 1928, is an independent foundation dedicated to the advancement of higher education in the humanities and social sciences in Asia. Headquartered on the campus of Harvard University, the Institute provides fellowships for advanced research, training, and graduate studies at Harvard by competitively selected faculty and graduate students from Asia. The Institute also supports a range of academic activities at its fifty partner universities and research institutes across Asia. At Harvard, the Institute promotes East Asian studies through annual contributions to the Harvard-Yenching Library and publication of the *Harvard Journal of Asiatic Studies* and the Harvard-Yenching Institute Monograph Series.

Library of Congress Cataloging-in-Publication Data

Names: Wang, Jinping, 1979– author.
Title: In the wake of the Mongols : the making of a new social order in North China, 1200–1600 / Jinping Wang.
Other titles: Harvard-Yenching Institute monograph series ; 116.
Description: Cambridge, Massachusetts : Published by the Harvard University Asia Center, 2018. | Series: Harvard-Yenching Institute monograph series ; 116 | Includes bibliographical references and index.
Identifiers: LCCN 2017060073 | ISBN 9780674987159 (hardcover : alk. paper) ISBN 978-0674-24789-5 (pbk : alk. paper)
Subjects: LCSH: Social structure—China—History. | Mongols—China—History. | China—Social conditions—960–1644. | China—History—960–1644.
Classification: LCC DS750.66 .W36 2018 | DDC 951/.102—dc23 LC record available at https://lccn.loc.gov/2017060073

Index by Stephen Ullstrom
First paperback edition 2020

♾ Printed on acid-free paper

Last figure below indicates year of this printing
29 28 27 26 25 24 23 22 21 20

To two great teachers who both changed my life:
Deng Xiaonan and Valerie Hansen

Contents

Maps, Figures, Plates, and Tables

Maps

Figures

Plates *(following p. 165)*

Tables

Acknowledgments

This book is the product of a decade-long study of north China. My academic advisors, friends, and colleagues have continuously provided me generous help and support, without which I could easily have gotten lost on this long journey.

Above all, I owe my deepest gratitude to my two greatest teachers: Deng Xiaonan from Peking University and Valerie Hansen from Yale University. Each is a role model for me as a scholar, teacher, and person. This book is dedicated to them. Deng Xiaonan was the first teacher who showed me the path to becoming a historian. Sitting in her enlightening lectures on imperial China in spring 1998 changed my life, and ever since then I have been fascinated by the history of premodern China. She was also the one who suggested that I begin to focus my study on long-term social change in north China. The rigorous academic training I experienced under her supervision at Peking University will be a lifelong treasure. More importantly, she has shown me by example what integrity and responsibility mean for a scholar.

Valerie Hansen, my advisor at Yale, deserves more appreciation than I could ever express in words. I can honestly say that without her, this book would never have taken shape. Valerie's ultimate dedication to her students truly deserves emulation. Even after my graduation, she has continued to read and comment on every chapter of this book with critical shrewdness and affection. Her thorough and thoughtful comments have influenced virtually every page of this book. Since 2004, Valerie has taken up the role as my teacher of academic English, both spoken and written. She painstakingly corrected my grammatical errors, relentlessly changed my bad writing habits, and patiently explained to me why one word or expression is better than another. After I gave a talk on this book at Yale in April 2017, Valerie told me that she felt both happy and "sad" that she now had little to correct in my English. I took this as an affectionate compliment to me and an acknowledgment of my sincere filial repayment of my debt to her.

Indeed, Valerie has been more than just an academic advisor for me. She and two other Yale professors—Phyllis Granoff and Koichi Shinohara—have been my loving academic parents, supporting me and guiding me step by step as I faced numerous challenges in graduate school, the job market, the workplace, and life itself. Over these years, the three of them have shown me by word and deed what really matters in life and how we can work efficiently and live happily. Because of them, New Haven is my second home in my heart.

In addition to my great mentors, my three dearest friends—Blake Atwood, Tomoyasu Iiyama, and Xiaowei Zheng—have provided me with endless intellectual inspiration and emotional support along the journey. One of the luckiest things that happened to me after graduating from Yale has been meeting Blake, a brilliant scholar of Iranian and Middle Eastern films. Since the two years we both worked at the University of Pennsylvania, we have shared a passion for teaching and have become each other's most important intellectual interlocutor. As a great writer and a sharp thinker himself, Blake edited the entire book and provided numerous valuable suggestions and comments. Many of my breakthrough moments in writing the book happened during long intense discussions we had in Philadelphia, Austin, Singapore, and Kuala Lumpur. Tomo, also a historian of north China, has generously shared many fieldwork materials with me and answered my numerous queries with his characteristic erudition and patience. In 2014 we managed to conduct fieldwork together to investigate Jin-Yuan steles in northern Shanxi. With great enthusiasm, we read and discussed many steles mentioned in this book at their original locations. These were some of the most exciting and intellectually satisfying moments of my scholarly life. I am most grateful for Xiaowei's twenty years of loyal friendship and unceasing faith in me.

During our numerous conversations over the phone or via Skype, Xiaowei always offered me much-needed comfort and encouragement when I doubted my work or when my research hit a bottleneck. Her insights on the transformations of China in the modern period have also inspired me to see premodern China in a different light.

This book would not have been possible without the support of two great research institutes and my wonderful colleagues there. A postdoctoral fellowship in the Department of East Asian Languages and Civilizations and the Humanities Forum, both at the University of Pennsylvania, opened the broader world of religious studies and intellectual history to me. I thank my mentor Paul Goldin for his strong support in my early career and his eye-opening insights on Confucianism, which have completely changed my view of this influential Chinese philosophy. I also thank my colleague Nancy Steinhardt for sharing her incredible knowledge on architectural and temple murals in north China in the Mongol-Yuan era. I had two great years at Penn, thanks also to the kindness of Brian Vivier, Ayako Kano, Linda H. Chance, Victor Mair, David Spafford, and many other colleagues. My home institution, the Department of History at the National University of Singapore, has provided a friendly and supportive environment. I am deeply grateful for the abundant research grants that university has provided and for my department's generosity in allowing me to take two nonteaching semesters so that I could focus on writing the book. My warmest thanks go to my caring colleagues in both the Department of History and the Department of Chinese Studies.

Several scholars have read the manuscript of this book in whole or in part and shared their insightful comments with me. I owe Joseph McDermott innumerable debts for the countless hours he put in helping me revise both the conclusion of the book and a journal article that grew from one section of chapter 3. I first met Joe in June 2014 at the first Harvard University conference on Middle-Period China. Since then I have benefited profoundly from his deep knowledge of and insights into village society in China over numerous joyful conversations via e-mail and phone and over drinks. Mark Halperin's constructive suggestions greatly helped me revise chapter 3, and my discussion of irrigation society in chapter 4 was refined thanks to critical comments by Christian

Lamouroux, Peter Perdue, and Ling Zhang. Sarah Schneewind and Koh Khee Heong provided important comments on an early version of chapter 5, helping me fix mistakes in my description of Ming China. Thomas Dubois read early versions of the introduction and conclusion of the book and offered some very valuable suggestions for revision.

Many other scholars, colleagues, and friends around the world provided me with helpful feedback and other forms of support for this project at its different stages and on various occasions. For their generous support, my gratitude goes to Christopher Atwood, Bettine Berge, Timothy Bernard, Marcus Bingenheimer, Peter Bol, Beverly Bossler, Cynthia Brokaw, Haydon Cherry, Wonhee Cho, Hilde De Weerdt, Kenneth Dean, Michael Feener, Siyen Fei, Jan Fitter, Eric Greene, Mia Lee, Steven Teiser, and Maitrii-Aung Thwin, and to Fang Chengfeng, Funada Yoshiyuki, Gao Keli, Hsu Ya-hwei, Huang Kuan-Chung, Iguro Shinobu, Kang Peng, Kang Yi, Li Yiwen, Liu Chen, Liu Ching Cheng, Lu Xiqi, Luo Xin, Morita Kenji, Ong Chang Woei, Kishimoto Mio, Liu Wei, Rong Xinjiang, Wu Ya-ting, Xie Shi, Xu Lanjun, Xu Man, Yamamoto Meishi, Yi Sumei, Zhang Junfeng, and Zheng Zhenman. At the National University of Singapore I have had the privilege of teaching graduate students who have taught me a lot in return. Huang Yanjie, Lü Shuang, and Wang Feifei, in particular, have contributed to my thinking as the project progressed. And Zhao Jiemin offered much assistance in making maps and illustrations for this book.

I want to thank the publishers of *East Asian Publishing and Society* and the *Journal of International Asian Studies* for allowing me to reproduce here parts of two articles I published in those journals. The book also benefited greatly from the constructive suggestions of two readers for the Harvard University Asia Center and the efforts of its wonderful editors. The reader's report from Robert Hymes was enormously helpful. I am very grateful for his meticulous chapter-by-chapter comments and his warm encouragement. Suggestions by a second anonymous reader helped me articulate the arguments in my conclusion more precisely. I am also grateful to Robert Graham, who has been an unfailingly supportive editor and has answered my numerous manuscript-related e-mails with patience and encouragement.

Finally, I am eternally indebted to my loving parents, Wang Huichang and Chen Xiuyun. Although they received little education because of the Cultural Revolution, they have always made my education a high priority, for which they made huge sacrifices in my childhood. Although they understand very little of what I do as a historian, they have never stopped believing in me and have tried their utmost to support all the choices I have made in my career and life. I only hope that this book will make them proud.

Preface

Just as they had finished their morning chanting, we came upon them, more than a dozen middle-aged women with short hair. They were not wearing any jewelry or wedding rings. It was past 10:00 a.m., and they had already finished their morning ritual practice. But they kindly made an exception and put their Buddhist robes back on so that they could perform their regular rites for us to see (see plate 1).

Every morning and evening, these women gathered at the temple to chant Buddhist texts and perform rituals with their monk master. At other times of the day, most of them simply went home to their families, but a few remained at the temple.

It was August 9, 2006, and together with participants in a historical anthropology workshop, I was visiting a temple to Guandi at Cuizhuang village in Shanxi province, about 500 kilometers southwest of Beijing. Guandi refers to Guan Yu 關羽 (160–220), a Shanxi native and a famous general in the Three Kingdoms period. Later, he was worshipped by the Chinese as the most popular god of war and wealth, commonly known as Emperor Guan (*Guandi* 關帝). To our great surprise, this temple had become a Buddhist institution called the Monastery of Awakened Wisdom (*Jüehui si* 覺慧寺). Since 2001, the monk master and women from Cuizhuang and neighboring villages had been meeting and reciting Buddhist texts in the temple.

On the day of our visit, the master happened to be absent, but the village women gladly shared their stories with us. They were Buddhist disciples of the monk, whom they had invited to their temple from Mt. Wutai, one of the four sacred Buddhist mountains, some 300 kilometers northwest of Beijing. The women were very proud that their monk master had taken them to Mt. Wutai to receive some Buddhist precepts.

This modern Buddhist group has much in common with the thirteenth-century Quanzhen (Complete Realization) Daoist groups who play such an important part in this book. Like this small temple, the Quanzhen Daoist convents provided a community for powerless women. While Quanzhen nuns sought wartime shelter from the violence and chaos of the Mongol conquest, these contemporary Buddhist women, all middle-aged and some illiterate, sought peacetime shelter, for a few hours a day, from domestic violence, divorce, poverty, and profound loneliness (most of their children had left to study or work in cities). One of the women had run from her abusive family and come to this temple. This Buddhist community, just like the Quanzhen convents centuries ago, supplemented and even replaced the families who had failed these village women.

The male master and some of his female disciples in Cuizhuang lived and slept in the same temple, a phenomenon I was initially surprised to find mentioned in inscriptions about the thirteenth-century Quanzhen communities, too. This practice irritated many local villagers, who believed that men and women should not live in the same place unless they were members of the same family. Later, when I conducted fieldwork in other parts of Shanxi, I realized that living together was a common, though controversial, practice in many local monasteries. The Quanzhen Daoists also permitted men and women to live in the same space. This practice broke with the conventional separation between monks and nuns that had become widespread among both Buddhists and Daoists since at least the Tang dynasty (618–907).

In another echo of the past, just like the Quanzhen clergy before them, the village women in Cuizhuang relied on official recognition by the state to avoid persecution and resist social pressure. The Quanzhen clergy in the thirteenth century, as I will show in this book, constantly erected steles with imperial edicts that recorded patronage from the Mongol rulers. Materials like this make it possible to tell the story of how Buddhism and Daoism flourished in north China from the point of view of ordinary Chinese people. For the Cuizhuang Buddhist women, a red silk banner hanging on the wall of the Guandi temple (seen at the top left in the photograph), played a role similar to the historical steles. The banner, issued by the government-affiliated Buddhist Association of Zezhou county in 2005, recognized the temple as an "advanced unit" (*xianjin danwei* 先進單位) for "propagating the dharma, benefiting sentient beings, loving the state, and loving the teaching" (*hongfa lisheng, aiguo aijiao* 弘法利生, 愛國愛教).

The fusion of Buddhist doctrine with state-promoted patriotism provided Cuizhuang Buddhist women with a strong ideological justification. During our visit, local villagers, often male, complained that the Buddhist women neglected housework and their familial obligations to care for their husbands and children. The women defended themselves with the exact language of the banner from the Buddhist Association and argued that their practices fostered the greater good of their families and community.

A few years later, when I began to write about the thirteenth-century Quanzhen Daoist order, memories of my encounter with the Cuizhuang women kept coming back to me. Especially as I immersed myself in historical records from centuries ago, what I saw and heard at the Guandi temple on that hot summer morning has reminded me of the gap between religious doctrines and practice. I have tried to understand, respectfully, the choices people made to survive difficult situations, even if their choices upset others in their society.

Equally important, the Cuizhuang experience, as well as my other fieldwork trips in Shanxi, deepened my interest—on both a personal and an intellectual level—in the great diversity among Chinese regional cultures. Growing up in a village of the lower Yangzi delta in Jiangsu province, I never saw any old temples in my own or neighboring villages; most had been destroyed during World War II and the Cultural Revolution. Thus, I had quite a shock in Shanxi villages, where I encountered many Buddhist monasteries, Daoist abbeys, temples of local deities, and even Catholic churches—many of which have survived for centuries. Some continue to serve local communities as religious spaces where people can gather, offer incense, pray to deities, and organize temple festivals. And still others, like the Guandi temple in Cuizhuang village, have become centers for new, locally organized religious groups that have mushroomed in the relatively free religious environment in China since the 1980s.

During the past decade, the questions that came out of my fieldwork experiences have mingled with other questions emerging from historical materials to shape this book, which explains the formation of a strong regional culture in Shanxi since the year 1200. It is also a study of numerous northern men and women who, after the devastating Mongol invasion of China in the early thirteenth century, struggled to overcome both crises in their lives and political upheavals through religious practice.

Abbreviations

DQ	*Sanjin shike daquan* 三晉石刻大全
JL	*Hongtong Jiexiu shuili beike jilu* 洪洞介休水利碑刻輯錄
JS	*Jinshi* 金史
JSK	*Dingxiang jinshi kao* 定襄金石考
JSL	*Daojia jinshi lüe* 道家金石略
QJ	*Yuan Haowen quanji* 元好問全集
QSXB	*Jin Yuan Quanzhenjiao shike xinbian* 金元全眞教石刻新編
QYW	*Quan Yuan wen* 全元文
SFJ	*Zhongguo difangzhi jicheng: Shanxi fuxianzhi ji* 中國地方志集成: 山西府縣志輯
SSXB	*Shike shiliao xinbian* 石刻史料新編
YDZ	*Yuan dianzhang* 元典章
YS	*Yuanshi* 元史
ZB	*Hongtong xian shuili zhi bu* 洪洞水利志補

A Note to the Reader

For the citation of lengthy inscription titles in footnotes, I have provided the full title in romanization and Chinese characters when citing it the first time and used a short-format title thereafter.

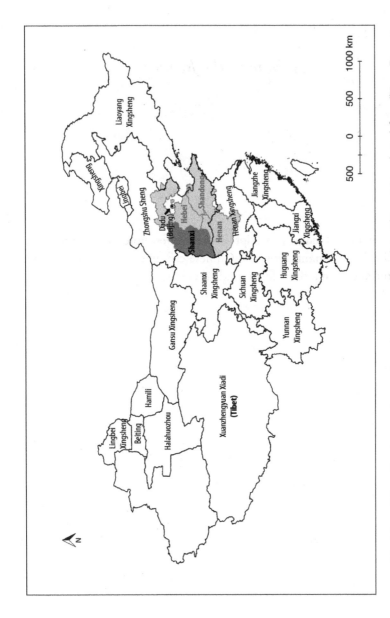

MAP 1 The Mongol-Yuan Empire superimposed on the territory of modern China. Map adapted from "Yuan Dynasty Provincial Boundaries in 1290," downloaded from https://worldmap.harvard.edu/data/geonode:yuan_dynasty_provincial _boundaries_in_12_ia2. Harvard CHGIS.

INTRODUCTION

Like many young men in prominent northern Chinese families, Zhou Xianchen (1188–1262) studied hard through his early years. He hoped to follow in his older brother's footsteps and pass the civil service examinations. As a boy, Xianchen attended school in his home county—Dingxiang in the northern part of Shanxi province. Dingxiang is located just south of the Yanmen Pass, one of the major passes in the Great Wall. On the other side of the Great Wall stretched the grasslands of the Mongolian steppes, where in 1206 Chinggis Khan (ca. 1162–1227) was forming a powerful confederation after being named leader of all the people in tents, who would be soon known by the entire Eurasian world as the Mongols. As a young man in his twenties, Xianchen knew little about what was happening on the steppes. He continued to study for the exams.

Then in 1216 the Mongols attacked his hometown, and Xianchen gave up his hope of becoming a civil official. He first organized a local militia to fight the Mongols and defended his relatives and fellow townsmen, but the Mongol troops, riding powerful steeds and using lethal weapons, overwhelmed the Chinese. The Mongols shot what were then the world's most advanced compound bows with uncanny accuracy and used large-scale siege weaponry such as catapult-propelled gunpowder shells to break through the walls of well-guarded cities and towns.[1] Xianchen and his fellow townsmen surrendered. An experienced martial artist, Xianchen

1. Morgan, *The Mongols*, 80.

switched sides and joined the Mongol armies, which went on to conquer all of north China (*huabei* 華北) by 1234. His military service to the Mongols earned him the most prestigious social status of Hereditary Vassal (*shihou* 世侯), which allowed him and his family to monopolize the local government of Dingxiang through subsequent decades. In a few short years, Xianchen transformed himself from an examination candidate to a local warlord, and his family from a scholar-official one to a military one.

These transformations resulted from more than good luck and military prowess. Like many other strongmen who rose up in the military under the Mongols, Xianchen chose to work with clergy of Complete Realization Daoism (*Quanzhen dao* 全眞道).[2] Quanzhen Daoism was the most powerful religious movement in north China at the time. Xianchen and the Quanzhen Daoists worked together to rebuild the postwar social order, which subsequently consolidated his family's new power. During a military campaign in southern Shanxi province, about three hundred kilometers from his home in Dingxiang, Xianchen met Guo Shouwei, a Quanzhen nun famed for her devotion. Xianchen repeatedly and earnestly invited her to his native village and eventually convinced her to relocate. There, they established the new Xuanyuan Abbey under Shouwei's supervision. This abbey helped local villagers recover from their losses and rebuild community solidarity.

Two texts carved into stone recount the lives of this man and woman. In the early twentieth century, a scholar from Dingxiang collected local inscriptions including the two texts.[3] One of the steles, installed on Xianchen's grave by his family members, recorded his biography; it still stands there today. The other stele, no longer extant, was installed at the

2. Scholars often translate the term *zhen* as "perfected," "perfection," "authenticity," or "realization." See Marsone, "Accounts of the Foundation of the Quanzhen Movement," 95–96; Komjathy, *Cultivating Perfection*, 9–17. However, the question remains open whether the word *zhen* has a single meaning in Quanzhen teachings. The term's meaning—referring to "perfection," "realization," or "authenticity"—varies in different contexts and it seems to me that the name Complete Realization (Quanzhen) Daoism best captures the sense of the term.

3. Wang Liyong 王利用, "Gu zuofuyuanshuai quan sizhou duyuanshuai xuanshou zhengxing qianhu Zhouhou shendaobei" 故左副元帥權四州都元帥宣授征行千戶周侯神道碑, *JSK*, 2.40a–45a; Zhou Rouzhong 周柔中, "Xuanyuan guan ji" 玄元觀記, *JSK*, 2.13b–15b.

Xuanyuan Abbey by Xianchen and his younger brother. It documented how Shouwei built the abbey and worked with local villagers. These two texts preserve significant information on the alliance between the warlord and the nun. That alliance was typical of the times. Hundreds of similar local inscriptions tell similar stories of difficult conditions in north China during the Mongol conquest and of a new world that subsequently emerged.

This book is about that new world, in which men like Xianchen and women like Shouwei exercised power in local society. It tells the stories of many northern Chinese like Xianchen and Shouwei who under Mongol rule gave up one life path and consciously chose to lead a new kind of life, especially a religious one.

Chinese society experienced multiple devastating invasions by various foreign conquerors, yet none was as catastrophic as the Mongol conquest of north China in the early thirteenth century. In just two decades following the Mongols' first attack in 1211, Mongol troops systematically ravaged every city, town, and village that refused to surrender and ruthlessly killed countless inhabitants. In 1207, before the Mongol invasion, census-takers registered about fifty-three million people in the territory controlled by the Jin dynasty (1115–1234); by the time the war ended in 1234, that number had dropped by two-thirds.[4] Wiping out more than half of the population and ruining much of the farmland and communities, the Mongols caused the old social order to collapse.

This book poses two key questions: How did northern Chinese men and women rebuild their society after the devastation of the Mongol

---

4. There are no accurate records or any scholarly studies of the death rate in north China during the Mongol conquest, but the few available statistics are suggestive. According to the official histories of the Jin and Yuan dynasties, when the Jin government took the last national census in 1207, the government registered 7,618,438 households and 53,532,151 individuals. The population in this year reached its Jin-dynasty peak in north China (*JS* 46.1036). In 1235 and 1236 the Mongol government registered about two million households in the Hebei, Shanxi, and Shandong regions. Although there were problems of unregistered households, changes in the average size of a household, and geographic variation, the dramatic population loss during the Jin-Mongol war was clear. For studies on the household categories and problems with those numbers, see Otagi, "Mongurujin seiken shita no kanchi ni okeru hanseki no mondai" 蒙古人政権下の漢地における版籍の問題, in his *Tōyō shigaku ronshū*, 4: 212–59; Wu Songdi, *Zhongguo renkou shi*, 379–84; Zhang Boquan and Wu Yuhuan, "Jindai de renkou."

conquest? How did their efforts alter social and economic forces in the succeeding centuries? These questions highlight the short- and long-term impacts of the Mongol conquest on north China. Although largely unknown, a surprisingly large number of existing inscriptional sources—such as the two texts about Xianchen and Shouwei—provide sufficient evidence to answer these questions.

Based on these fascinating local materials, this book recounts a remarkable, yet previously untold, story of how northern Chinese men and women resiliently adapted to the unprecedented circumstances of the Mongol conquest and created a radically new social order under the leadership of Daoists and Buddhists. In this new social order, Quanzhen Daoism and Buddhism led northerners to form new social groups so that they could survive the Mongol invasion and rebuild communities after the war and other disasters. More impressively, both religious orders created new networks that circulated and distributed resources and wealth in the north. The Quanzhen Daoist and Buddhist orders also took in people of diverse motivations and then deployed them in a wide variety of intellectual, religious, social, and economic projects. The orders' clergy acted as the social and even political elite at the local level, translating initiatives of the Mongol rulers and the imperial state so that they served local interests.

This book documents the making of this distinctive social order during the Mongol era in the northern province of Shanxi, and its unmaking after the Mongols left in 1368. It sheds light on the fundamental ruptures in Chinese society caused by the Mongol conquest and argues that there was a distinctive northern path of social transformation featuring clergy activism. The Mongol era was not the only period in Chinese history when the clergy were influential.[5] It was, however, the only time after the eleventh century during which organized religions served as institutional anchors in the remaking of the social order down to the village level.

---

5. Before the Mongol era, powerful religious orders in Chinese history included the Celestial Masters Movement during the Han dynasty (206 BCE–220 CE), Kou Qianzhi's state-backed version of Celestial Masters Daoism in the sixth century, and the Buddhist order during the Tang dynasty (618–907).

This book's geographic focus, north China, includes today's Shandong, Shanxi, Hebei, and Henan provinces as well as the Beijing and Tianjin areas (see map 1). Between the twelfth and the seventeenth centuries, this region experienced four dynastic transitions alternating between foreign and Chinese rule. In 1127, the Jurchen, an originally forest-dwelling people in modern Manchuria, defeated the Northern Song dynasty (960–1127) and established a dynasty in north China named Jin (金, "gold," which referred to the name of a river in their original territory). The Mongols defeated the Jin in 1234. The early Mongol khans ruled north China as part of the Great Mongol State (*Yeke Monggol Ulus*, or *Damenggu guo* 大蒙古國 in Chinese). In 1271 Khubilai Khan (r. 1260–94), grandson of Chinggis Khan, broke away from the unified Mongol empire. He borrowed from Chinese tradition to create a dynasty, which he named "the Great Yuan" (元, "prime"), a term taken from the Chinese classic *Book of Changes*.[6] Yuan rule in China ended in 1368, when the Chinese peasant and former Buddhist monk Zhu Yuanzhang 朱元璋 (1328–98) led an army that drove the Mongols out of Beijing and established the Ming (明, "bright") dynasty (1368–1644). In the seventeenth century, Han Chinese rule again gave way to foreign rule when the Manchus—descendants of the Jurchen—conquered the Ming and ruled China as the Qing (清, "pure") dynasty (1644–1911).

If we compare the Mongols to the other two foreign dynasties, the Jin and the Qing, we can understand better what made them unique. The Jurchen and the Manchus largely retained and even consolidated a Chinese model of social order that had been fully established in the Northern Song dynasty. The Confucian literati (*shi* 士 or *shidafu* 士大夫, which more often than not refers to scholar-officials), a social group whose members specialized in learning, spearheaded the creation and understanding of this model, in which literary skill and scholarly learning were the major qualifications for entrance into officialdom via civil service examinations testing knowledge of Confucian classics. During the Northern Song, civilian rule underpinned this literati-centered social order, and political power rested in the alliance between the emperor and the bureaucracy

6. In doing so, the Mongols started a new tradition, and following dynasties chose names that referred to their fundamental trait instead of the founding family's name or origin.

run by scholar-officials.[7] The Jin and the Qing continued this model of social order.[8] The Mongols did not: they introduced new systems of governance that drew heavily on steppe traditions and bypassed many Confucian political norms, resulting in structural changes throughout Chinese society. Their rule departed so radically from the Northern Song–Jin model that they created a uniquely decentralized political order. This is the immediate historical context for the new social order that is the subject of this book.

The Transformation of the Political Order under Mongol Rule

To understand why the social changes in north China were unique, we must first understand the profoundly transformative nature of Mongol rule. Destructive as they were, the Mongol invasions were just the beginning of this transformation. Six subsequent generations of northern Chinese would live under and adapt to a political and social system that was unlike anything China had ever experienced before.

Above all, the Mongol-Yuan regime created a whole new system of social stratification by classifying its subjects according to their "ethnic" and professional identity as defined by the Mongols. The Mongols divided all people into four ethnic groups in a descending order of legal status: the Mongols, the *Semu* 色目 people (that is, the "various categories" of Central and Western Asian peoples), the Han people (*hanren* 漢人), and the Southerners (*nanren* 南人). The Han people referred to residents of

7. The establishment of this political order of civilian rule, as Deng Xiaonan has amply demonstrated, was also the outcome of a long-term ideological enterprise of shaping a powerful Song political culture known as "the 'Ancestors' Family Instructions," which was originally formulated by the Song literati and constantly used by the emperor and his officials to stabilize the political order. See Deng, *Zuzong zhifa*. A concise English version of this important work is available in Deng and Lamouroux, "The 'Ancestors' Family Instructions.'"

8. Scholarship of the New Qing history has demonstrated that the Manchus applied different ways of governance in the empire's frontier regions where Han Chinese were not the majority population. See Elliot, *The Manchu Way*.

the previous Jin territory, regardless of their actual ethnic identity preceding the conquest. Similarly, the Southerners referred to residents of the previous territory of the Southern Song dynasty (1127–1279). Along with redefining "ethnic" identity, the Mongols established a complex household system that organized people into eighty-three hereditary household categories.[9] The ethnic four-rank system was fundamentally a form of political stratification. It often came into play when the government handed out offices and other state honors. In contrast, the household system was a form of rigid social stratification. It had more impact on people's social and economic life.

Meanwhile, unlike their immediate predecessors, the Mongols did not base their administrative models only on the traditions of earlier dynasties. They freely borrowed from multiple historical models and traditions of the nomadic steppes, Islamic and Central Asian regimes, and Chinese dynastic institutions. As a result, the Mongol-Yuan state created multiple centers of legitimate political power and established varied routes to these centers of power. Many of these new power centers and routes were alien to Song or even Jin scholar-officials.

To begin with, the Mongol-Yuan state extended the prerogatives of the emperor to the entire royal family. In doing so, it formalized alternative centers of political power held by Mongol princes, empress dowagers, imperial sons-in-law, and even distinguished generals. The Mongols, as Peter Jackson has pointed out, regarded their conquests "not as the possessions of the emperor or Great Khan but as the joint property of the imperial family as a whole, including female members."[10] Provision thus had to be made for all imperial family members. Chinese practices since the Tang and Song dynasties had located most imperial descendants in the capital and afforded them an affluent lifestyle but little political power.[11] The Mongol rulers, in contrast, continued the nomadic customs of patrimonialism to give fiefs to princes and other nobles.

The Mongols' fiefs were of two basic types: *"ulus"* (*ulus* is a Mongolian term meaning "realm, people under one ruler"), mainly on the steppes;

9.   On the distinctive household system under Mongol rule, see Huang Qinglian, *Yuandai huji zhidu yanjiu*.

10.   Jackson, "From Ulus to Khanate: The Making of the Mongol State c. 1220–c. 1290," 12.

11.   Chaffee, *Branches of Heaven*, 8.

and "appanage" ("*touxia*" 投下 in Chinese sources, meaning "shares of population, lands, and booty") in settled areas. While *ulus* holders directly controlled their domain and people, appanage holders did so indirectly. In theory, officials answerable to the great khan governed the appanages, but control was often highly contested. From the time Ögödei Khan (r. 1229–41) distributed appanages in north China in 1236, Mongol nobles appointed overseers (*darughachi*) and judges (*jarghuchi*) in their appanages; some even had their private representatives collect taxes directly. Appanage holders had their representatives in the central government and drew on government resources to reward their retainers (*kesig* in Mongolian; *quexue* 怯薛 in Chinese sources) or to patronize religious establishments.[12] As emperor, Khubilai Khan created a special type of appanage known as "fiefs of stationed princes": the princes and their descendants inherited positions as the highest military leaders in their fiefs—often in strategically important frontier regions—and shared administrative power with local civil governments.[13] The Mongol appanage system resulted in multiplicity in the political structure of Yuan China. Unlike the Chinese imperial system that concentrated all state power in the hands of the emperor and his bureaucracy, the Mongol khan co-ruled with his entire imperial clan.

While the Mongol rulers did draw on Chinese institutional models to create a bureaucracy, the Yuan administration was fundamentally based on a key Mongol tradition: recruitment practice favored hereditary transmission.[14] The dozens of families who had "*huja'ur*" status monopolized almost all high-ranking positions.[15] *Huja'ur* is a Mongolian term (*genjiao* 根脚 in Chinese) indicating personal connections, family background, and seniority. In the Mongol-Yuan political context, *huja'ur* referred particularly to an individual's or family's historical connections to Chinngis Khan and his descendants. The *huja'ur* families received special recogni-

---

12. Endicott-West, *Mongolian Rule in China*, 73–79; Atwood, *Encyclopedia of Mongolia*, 18–19; Li Zhi'an, *Yuandai fenfeng zhidu yanjiu*, 53–154 and 247–51.

13. Li Zhi'an, *Yuandai fenfeng zhidu yanjiu*, 183–205.

14. Chinggis Khan first established the policy of ensuring that all of the 90–120 captains of the "thousand" military units would receive a hereditary share in government authority and revenues, and this tradition of hereditary transmission soon spread to all levels. See Atwood, "Mongols," 242 and 245.

15. Funada, "Semuren yu Yuandai zhidu shehui," 166.

tion for the loyalty that bound Mongol rulers to their subjects. When later Mongol rulers appointed civil and military officials, they gave priority to men from families with *huja'ur* connections. The earlier those connections had been established, the more prestigious the family, and the higher the ranks its male members could receive.[16]

While the majority of *huja'ur* families were Mongols or *Semu* people, about twenty ethnically Chinese families also achieved *huja'ur* status. These were the families of the most powerful Chinese Hereditary Vassals, who governed territories with tens of cities and commanded armies with tens of thousands of soldiers.[17] Almost all *huja'ur* families originated from military leaders who had joined early Mongol khans in the wars of conquest—men like Zhou Xianchen, whose story opened this book. Descendants of these military elites inherited their ancestors' privileged positions. They formed the upper and middle classes of the governing elite in the Mongol-Yuan regime. The regime thus brought back a style of government based on aristocracy (which had vanished in China during the tenth century) by creating a hereditary status group with guaranteed legal privileges and access to office.[18]

The Mongol tradition of hereditary transmission explains early Mongol rulers' indifference to the Chinese system of civil service examinations, the defining meritocratic institution of the Chinese Confucian state since the Northern Song. Also, as the Mongols traditionally valued technicians over scholars, early Mongol rulers expressed no interest in employing the services of Confucian-educated scholars.[19] Although Khubilai Khan and his successors used Confucian cultural heritage as a means of reinforcing their political legitimacy in China, they established no civil service examinations until 1313, when they announced the restoration of the

16. Xiao, "Yuandai sida menggu jiazu" 元代四大蒙古家族, in his *Nei beiguo*, 511.

17. Xiao, "Yuandai jige hanjun shijia de shihuan yu hunyin" 元代幾個漢軍世家的仕官與婚姻, in his *Nei beiguo*, 278.

18. For the disappearance of the aristocracy during the Tang-Song transition, see Tackett, *Destruction*.

19. As Elizabeth Endicott-West has pointed out, the Mongols' disdain for Confucian-educated scholars derived not so much from any hostility to the Confucian tradition but rather from the ease with which the Mongols recognized the utility of practical endeavors such as record keeping and military skills (*Mongolian Rule in China*, 113).

examinations on a triennial basis.[20] Yet they recruited only twenty-five
holders of *jinshi* 進士 ("presented scholar," the highest degree for imperial civil service examinations in Chinese history) from each of the four
legally defined ethnic groups. This meant they recruited no more than
fifty adult Chinese males in a given exam year, compared to the many
hundreds who were recruited every three years during the Song and the
Jin. Moreover, the *jinshi* degree holders, who accounted for a mere
4.3 percent of all government officials in the last fifty years of the Yuan,
never earned the respect of the Yuan rulers. The degree holders' political
status was not only much inferior to that of men from *huja'ur* families
but even lower than that of those who entered officialdom through the
route of clerkship, a path the literati of the Song and Jin had despised.[21]
The Mongol-Yuan political world thus marginalized the Confucian
literati.

Among the Chinese population in north China, job performance and
personal connections replaced literary skill and Confucian learning as the
major qualifications for entrance to and promotion within Mongol-Yuan
officialdom. Four occupational groups benefited most from the Mongols'
recruitment standard of job performance, as Iiyama Tomoyasu points out:
members of the military, clerks, members of specialist households, and
religious leaders. Many northern Chinese men were drawn to military
service by the prospect of rapid promotion and an extraordinary privilege that was seldom granted to their civilian counterparts: they could
transmit their office to their heirs. Many educated men, on the other
hand, were attracted to careers as clerks, due to the possibility of promotion into officialdom.[22] However, the clerical route to office was a long
and tedious journey for such men: they had to work their way up through
unranked or low-ranking clerical positions to attain a ranked, salaried
position as a local official, and thirty years of service in a prefectural government merited promotion into officialdom only at the low rung of the

20. The Mongol-Yuan regime continued to worship Confucius as the supreme sage
of state orthodoxy in temples devoted to him and supported the establishment of Confucian temple-schools from the metropolis down to the county level to accommodate
members of Confucian households.

21. Xiao, "Yuandai keju yu jingying liudong: yi yuantong yuannian jinshi wei
zhongxin" 元代科舉與菁英流動: 以元統元年進士為中心, in his *Nei beiguo*, 187–90.

22. Iiyama, "Genealogical Steles in North China," 164.

seventh of nine grades. By the time they became local officials, most men had reached a relatively advanced age. Only a few could achieve high-ranking positions before retirement, and those who did so often had secured patronage from Mongol princes or other nobles.[23] So although the Mongol-Yuan regime offered some institutional routes for Chinese men to enter the bureaucratic government, the rewards were few.

By Chinese standards, the most peculiar and unorthodox recruitment measure was the elevation of specialist households and religious leaders. In the complex household system, the specialist households were those whose members had proficiency in a specific skill, such as craftsmanship, medical knowledge, divination, or animal handling. The Yuan government created specific bureaucratic agencies to administer specialist households separately from the ordinary commoner households (*minhu* 民戶). It also assigned specialist households to permanent and hereditary service to *ulus* and appanage holders, who set up private agencies to oversee them. Talented men from specialist households, if judged to be particularly skilled by the Mongol ruling elite, could gain access to official positions in those agencies by rising through the ranks to become heads of their industry in a particular region.[24] Since the *ulus* and appanage holders directly appointed officials to staff their private agencies, personal connections played an important role for specialist-household men seeking promotion. In these ways, the social group of craftsmen and other manually skilled people gained official status for the first time in Chinese society.

Religious leaders, on the other hand, gained power through a distinctive system of separate government bureaucracies for each recognized religion.[25] These religious bureaucracies held civilian jurisdiction through

---

23. For examples, see Iiyama, "A Career between Two Cultures."

24. Li Zhi'an, *Yuandai fenfeng zhidu yanjiu*, 162–82; Iiyama, "Genealogical Steles in North China," 164–65.

25. The Mongols recognized four major religions: Buddhism, Daoism, Islam, and Nestorian Christianity. In the 1280s, the Yuan regime created three different court bureaucracies to administer religious communities, the *Xuanzheng Yuan* 宣政院 for Buddhism, the *Jixian yuan* 集賢院 for Daoism, and the *Chongfu si* 崇福司 for Christianity (*YS* 87.2192–94 and 89.3273). Although Islam was one of the four religions recognized by the Mongols, no central Muslim organization was founded in Yuan China. This was likely due to Islam's fall from favor in Khubilai's reign. See Atwood, "Buddhists as Natives."

the controversial system of joint courts (*yuehui* 約會), which allowed their representatives, together with other authorities, to settle legal cases that involved religious communities.[26] Given the overwhelming influence of Buddhism and Daoism as two native religions in China, the religious bureaucracies under Mongol rule were often referred to as "Buddhist and Daoist government offices" (*sengdao yamen* 僧道衙門) in Chinese sources.

In this system of religious administration, the Buddhist bureaucracy reigned supreme. After Khubilai became the great khan of the Mongol empire in 1260, he established Tibetan Lamaist Buddhism as the state religion. Imperial patronage of Buddhism continued until 1368, and the Buddhists became the most powerful religious group in Yuan China.[27] Paralleling the civil bureaucracy from the central court to regional and local governments, the Buddhist bureaucracy formed a semiautonomous power center on both the national and local levels. The Mongol state even granted Buddhist officials ranks and honors in the same way as it did for civil officials. The Mongols thus made religious service a prominent route to government office, opening up new access to power, status, and wealth.

Even before 1260, the Mongols had granted clergy extraordinary social and economic privileges. The Mongols subscribed to a unique political theology which, as Christopher Atwood argues, assumed that the religions the Mongols favored—including Buddhism and Daoism—all prayed to the same God, who had blessed Chinggis Khan with victories in war and continued to respond to human prayers by granting favors to the dynasty. To secure God's blessings through prayer, the Mongols gave their favored religions extensive tax exemptions and patronage. While early Mongol rulers did not collect any taxes from the religious orders, Khubilai tried to curtail their religious privileges by ordering them to pay land and commercial taxes, but his successors revoked his policy.[28] In general, the level of tax exemption and autonomy the Mongols granted to the clergy as a whole was far greater than that in earlier or later dynasties. The Quanzhen Daoists, benefiting from their master's early personal connections to Chinggis Khan, were the first Chinese religious group that took advantage of this policy, and the Buddhists quickly followed suit.

26. Cho, "Beyond Tolerance."
27. Franke, *From Tribal Chieftain to Universal Emperor*, 58.
28. Atwood, "Validation by Holiness or Sovereignty," 252.

In sum, the political system of the Mongol-Yuan regime marked a genuine departure from the meritocratic civilian rule established in the Northern Song dynasty. The Jin state had partially inherited this Song tradition. It concentrated its military power among the Jurchen but continued to bring Chinese literati into the civil bureaucracy via the civil service examination system. The Mongol-Yuan regime, in contrast, adopted a policy of strong decentralization and a steppe-style aristocracy. Mongol rulers allocated legitimate political power to multiple centers within and beyond the regular bureaucracy and allowed both institutional and personal access to those power centers. They also created a hereditary status group to constitute the bulk of the upper and middle classes of governing elite and preferred people with either personal connections or inherited positions, in spite of any other recruitment criteria.

This novel political milieu under Mongol rule bred a new social environment in north China. Many Chinese individuals and families readjusted their career choices and sought to take advantage of whatever connections they could foster with powerful patrons. Careers in the military, clerical positions, or specialist households all relied heavily on the authority of the state. Only the religious route provided not just relatively easy access to powerful patrons but also access to ideological and institutional clout outside the government. Underpinned by their unprecedented political, social, and economic power, Buddhist and Daoist orders established their institutions in almost every city, town, and village throughout north China. The clergy and their institutions, serving as critical indigenous agents in negotiating with the Mongol state, provided northern Chinese with new, but effective, means of navigating the perils and uncertainties of Mongol rule.

A focus on religious institutions and clergy leads to the two inherently connected issues examined in this book: the social institutions that dominated local society and the social elites whose members ran those institutions. These institutions and elites often played important roles in the social reorganization caused by dynastic transition, political reform, and natural disaster. The process of social reorganization, in turn, revealed major changes in power dynamics as institutions and individuals vied for political clout, social status, and material wealth. The existing scholarship on social elites and their institutions has largely focused on south China, and it forms the most relevant intellectual context for this study to engage with. Focusing on north China allows this book to show the workings of a local society quite different from that in the south.

The South-Centered Narrative of Social Change in Middle-Period China

According to the traditional Confucian ideal, the family provided a time-less model for ruling elites to organize society and govern the state. A passage from *The Great Learning* (*Daxue* 大學), one of the Confucian *Four Books*, articulates the prevailing Confucian ideology about the relation among self, family, state, and the world: "Those of antiquity who wished that all people throughout the empire would let their inborn luminous virtue shine forth put governing their states well first; wishing to govern their states well, they first established harmony in their households; wishing to establish harmony in their households, they first cultivated themselves" (古之欲明德於天下者，先治其國。欲治其國者，先齊其家。欲齊其家者，先修其身).[29] This Confucian ideal of political governance and social arrange-ment, as Anthony Yu argues, posits that there is a fundamental unity between the realms of ethics and politics based on family and state.[30] The family was the basic unit of society, and no intermediary institutions existed in the social space between family and state.

Early Confucian teachings thus provided little instruction to the rul-ing elite on how to establish leadership in society beyond managing their own households and serving virtuously in government. Instead, religious Daoism and Buddhism, increasingly important after the second century CE, provided the first intermediary institutions in Chinese history to link the family to society and the state. Religious Daoism posed the first chal-lenge to Confucian ideology but recognized the importance of family. Buddhism, on the other hand, rejected the Chinese family system and valorized a celibate clergy. Daoist and Buddhist monasteries flourished and by the tenth century provided nongovernmental public space, edu-cation, and community.[31]

29. *The Four Books*, 4–5.
30. A. Yu, *State and Religion in China*, 96.
31. Gernet, *Buddhism in Chinese Society*; Dien, *Six Dynasties Civilization*, 387–423.

In the late tenth century, the Northern Song dynasty began a new era of social change in terms of dominant social elites and institutions. On the one hand, Song China, as Robert Hymes argues, saw a strong new tendency of "laicization of religion" driven by the growth of a commercial market in religion. The balance of power and initiative shifted from the clergy toward the laity. While the laity provided demand, the clergy offered services catering to the laity's needs, often for payment.[32] On the other hand, accompanying the new rebalancing of lay-clerical relations was a full-fledged Confucian revival. The Northern Song fully established the civil service examination system, which granted Confucian literati both a chance to hold government office and a privileged legal status. Benefiting from their elite status, literati created new literati-centered institutions based on kinship. On a broader scale, they also formed non-kin networks based on social connections and mutual recognition as fellow literati. Using these networks, Song literati drew on preexisting dyadic ties of friendship, shared student status, student-teacher relationships, and shared local origin to form poetic or intellectual societies.[33] In this period, the literati-centered social transformation occurred in both north and south China.

The year 1127 marked a watershed in Chinese history. In the century that followed the Jurchen conquest of the Northern Song, China was divided, with the south under the Southern Song and the north under the non-Chinese rule of the Jin dynasty. In the past few decades, historians of middle-period China have enthusiastically responded to the influential hypothesis proposed by Hymes and Robert Hartwell, which posits that there was a localist shift in the Song literati after 1127. According to this hypothesis, the Southern Song literati developed new locally oriented strategies and self-definition as well as new patterns of elite life and elite-state relations that continued in southern China down to the Qing dynasty.[34] In demonstrating how political office continued to be appreciated as an indication of the literati's place in the Southern Song, Beverly Bossler recognizes the localist shift but emphasizes that the change was gradual and more continuous than disruptive in the Northern and Southern Song

---

32. Hymes, "Sung Society and Social Change," 596.
33. Ibid., 631–32.
34. Hartwell, "Demographic, Political, and Social Transformations of China"; Hymes, *Statesmen and Gentlemen*.

periods.[35] In his recent work, Hymes stresses that in the Southern Song, the sons of prominent families—both those who had not yet achieved office and those who had reached high office—adopted this localist strategy, but he cautions us not to misunderstand the "localist strategy" construct as "dissociation from the state or the complete abandonment of national-level aspirations by Southern Song elites."[36]

Intellectual historians have emphasized the relationship between the localist shift and the contemporary Neo-Confucian intellectual movement of the Learning of the Way (*Daoxue* 道學), led by Zhu Xi 朱熹 (1130–1200). Highlighting localism and voluntarism as two major features, Peter Bol argues that the Neo-Confucian Movement in the Southern Song suited a social elite whose members had developed considerable independence from the state and did not always hold office. The same centuries saw the rise both of the southern literati as an independent social force and of Neo-Confucianism as a literati ideology.[37]

In the 2003 volume *The Song-Yuan-Ming Transition in Chinese History*, scholars argue that the Jiangnan 江南 region of the lower Yangzi River basin was the only region that continued the earlier trend of social transformation—particularly the localist turn of literati elite—after the Mongol conquest of the south in the 1270s. Although their exclusive emphasis on Jiangnan is problematic, these scholars importantly show that the Southern Song pattern of local literati social centrality continued in the Yuan.[38]

35. See Bossler, *Powerful Relations*. Her argument has been echoed by Huang Kuanchong's case studies of several elite families, which demonstrate that both Northern and Southern Song elite families based their social networks on local society and aimed at office in the central government (*Songdai de jiazu*).

36. Hymes, "Sung Society and Social Change," 631, see also 627–58.

37. Bol, *Neo-Confucianism in History*. While accepting Bol's view in general, Hymes also argues that the Learning of the Way Movement was not only a reflection of what he called "the *shih*-oriented culture" but also "a considered and critical response to it" ("Sung Society and Social Change," 658).

38. Smith and von Glahn, eds., *The Song-Yuan-Ming Transition*. See particularly the introduction, chapter 1, and chapter 7. Christian Lamouroux points out the necessity of studying other regions first before jumping to these conclusions, especially the assumption that the Jiangnan experience represented the general trajectory of historical development for most other regions in late imperial China (review of *The Song-Yuan-Ming Transition*).

In the literati-centered society of south China in the Southern Song and Yuan, local literati elites indeed created their own institutions. They not only established a new model of inclusive local lineages.[39] Southern literati, especially Neo-Confucians, also created private academies as institutional bases to form networks. To offset the great influence of Buddhist and Daoist devotional societies among commoners, literati elites created charitable granaries and community compacts. They hoped that these would absorb non-literati families into reconstituted local communities under the leadership of literati families.[40] Meanwhile, by supporting Buddhist and Daoist monasteries as well as the temples of local cults, southern literati families expanded their influence into the religious realm.[41]

The increasing influence of literati-centered institutions, as Hymes argues, contributed to the continued laicization under the Mongols.[42] The southern laity held more power than they had earlier, and the clergy were more inclined to try to accommodate the interests of the laity. This phenomenon reached well beyond the elite level to encompass the popular level. Consider Barend ter Haar's innovative study of lay devotional societies in the Song and Yuan periods. These societies, which often did not have clerical leadership, demonstrated a capacity for lay religious achievement.[43]

This South-based narrative represents the prevailing approach to middle-period Chinese history in general and to state-society relations in particular, with an almost exclusive focus on the literati. This approach is appropriate for the south. The south developed the strongest literati culture of all Chinese regions after the eleventh century, and it was in the south that the influential Neo-Confucian Movement arose after the twelfth century. As this book shows, however, this model does not apply to the north, which underwent more than two hundred years of foreign

39. See Clark, *Portrait of a Community*; Hymes, "Sung Society and Social Change," 656–57.

40. Bol, *Neo-Confucianism in History*, 229–56.

41. Hymes, *Way and Byway*, chapter 5, and "Sung Society and Social Change," 600.

42. Hymes, "Sung Society and Social Change," 618–21.

43. Ter Haar, *The White Lotus Teachings*, 1–113.

rule after 1127.[44] The leading historians of the Song and Yuan dynasties, including Xiao Qiqing, Li Zhi'an, and Hymes, have all called attention to regional discrepancies between the north and the south in economic, cultural, and political traditions after 1127.[45] The north and the south indeed followed very different paths of social transformation, particularly in their responses to Mongol rule.

A Different Path: The Social Dominance of Religious Institutions

A wide range of local sources will show that as far as north China was concerned, religious institutions functioned as critical building blocks. Meanwhile, northern Confucian literati and their institutions were much weaker than their southern counterparts. Even after the Mongols unified the two regions in 1279, the Confucian literati as a distinctive social group remained strong only in the south. The Mongol government placed the Chinese literati under the category of Confucian households (*ruhu* 儒户) and granted them exemptions from the duty of labor service similar to what Buddhists and Daoists enjoyed. But unlike the clergy, Confucian households did not receive tax exemptions because the Mongol rulers did not see Confucianism as a religion.[46] Also, although men of Confucian households continued to study Confucian texts in public school, mastery of those texts no longer led to political office. The Mongols excluded both northern and southern scholars from political power. Nevertheless, southern literati suffered much less from the Mongol invasion than their northern counterparts did, and the southerners' institutions

---

44. Two studies have discussed north China but still focus on literati. See Ong, *Men of Letters*; Koh, *A Northern Alternative*.

45. Xiao, "Zhongguo jinshi qianqi nanbei fazhan de qiyi yu tonghe: Yi Nansong Jin Yuan shiqi de jingji shehui wenhua wei zhongxin" 中国近世前期南北发展的歧异与统合：以南宋金元时期的經濟社會文化爲中心, in his *Yuandai zuqun wenhua*, 1–22; Li Zhi'an, "Liangge Nanbeichao"; Hymes, "Sung Society and Social Change," 658–61.

46. Khubilai issued two edicts (in 1284 and 1285) specifying that Confucian households would be exempted from labor service but not from paying land and commercial taxes. *YDZ*, 2:1090–91.

remained relatively intact. After 1279 most former Song literati families in the south continued to thrive; they controlled positions in private academies and official schools, developed lineage organizations, and played leading roles in organizing local militia, water control and relief efforts, and even religious affairs.[47]

In contrast, the influence of northern literati remained almost negligible. Confucian households in the north accounted for about 0.167 percent of the entire population of north China, whereas in the south the number was close to 1 percent.[48] Men from the northern Confucian households studied or taught in official schools, as there were few private academies in the north. They spent decades holding different positions as schoolteachers or government clerks before finally being promoted to an office of the lowest rank—if they were lucky. Moreover, while 80–100 percent of the counties in the south had official schools, only 10–25 percent of the counties in the north did.[49]

Northern elites included the families of those who had secured government or extragovernment appointments in the regular civil bureaucracy, military service, the separate administration of specialist households, or Mongol nobles' appanages. Indeed, as Hymes rightly suspects, northern elites were more dependent on offices and the state than their southern counterparts were.[50] Among the northern elites, families of Hereditary Vassals such as General Zhou Xianchen attained the most prestige.[51] These families exerted great influence in local society. They commonly put up genealogical steles in ancestral graveyards to confirm

47. Walton, "Song-Yuan zhuanbian de hanren"; Su, *Yuandai difang jingying*.
48. According to Xiao's estimates, northern Confucian households in 1276 numbered 3,890, constituting only 0.61 percent of the total number of military and civilian households (2,320,000). Li Xiusheng has pointed out the mistake in Xiao's calculation and argued that the correct percentage should be about 0.167 percent. See Xiao, "Yuandai de ruhu: Rushi diwei yanjinshi shangde yizhang" 元代的儒户：儒士地位演進史上的一章, in his *Yuandai shi xintan*, 15; Li Xiusheng, "Yuandai de ruhu," 2–7.
49. Chaffee, *The Thorny Gates of Learning*, 136–37.
50. Hymes, "Sung Society and Social Change," 659.
51. There is a rich body of scholarship on hereditary lords in the Mongol and Yuan periods, mostly in Japanese and Chinese. For a review of this literature and the most recent study, see Fu, *Yuandai Hanren shihou qunti*. For a study in English, see De Rachewiltz, "Personnel and Personalities."

their kinship solidarity and claim elite social status.[52] They also inter-
married with other powerful families. Still, their power did not reach
very far. General Zhou's family, for instance, exercised influence in only
a few neighboring villages. Also, unlike southern literati families, the
new elite families in the north focused on their own descent groups and
rarely incorporated non-kin into their networks.

Religious institutions, in contrast, brought the northerners together.
Again, as General Zhou Xianchen's fellowship with the nun Guo Shouwei
shows, northern elite families had to rely on powerful religious institutions to help them create and strengthen community solidarity. In a
war-torn society, religious organizations proved most successful in nurturing community sentiment among people with different surnames and
from different localities.

When the Mongol conquest destroyed vast numbers of villages, ordinary northern Chinese, especially powerless peasants, had a difficult
time rebuilding their communities. Many of them turned for protection
to powerful Buddhist and Daoist monasteries, which often had massive
landholdings. These monasteries enjoyed tax exemptions that allowed
them to accumulate both wealth and property. Buddhists and Daoists
participated in agricultural production and the building of infrastructure and so helped rebuild postwar village communities. It was a popular
practice among northern villagers—not just local governors like General
Zhou Xianchen—to invite monks and nuns into their village communities
to serve as abbots of local hermitages or temples. Villagers also organized
associations of lay believers attached to those temples. To avoid paying
land taxes, many villagers "donated" their farmland to large Buddhist or
Daoist monasteries and affiliated themselves with the monasteries as
"tenants."

Buddhist and Daoist institutions were in general much more powerful than Confucian ones under the Mongols. Buddhist and Daoist orders
even linked family and state in the Mongols' distinctive household system. Under Mongol rule, three types of households paralleled the Three
Teachings (*sanjiao* 三教) in Chinese tradition: Confucian, Buddhist, and
Daoist. Confucian scholar-officials worried that Buddhist and Daoist
households outnumbered them in the empire as a whole. In 1271, a scholar-

52.   Iiyama, "'Sonkōryō hikokugun,'" 157–59.

official named Wei Chu presented a memorial to Khubilai seeking an imperial order to allow the Hanlin Academy to function as an office in charge of Confucian households' affairs. Wei argued that because the government had specific bureaus for Daoist and Buddhist households, and even for households of musicians, it was urgent to set up an office to take care of Confucian households.[53] Yuan Confucians such as Wei clearly understood that their teaching had a critical weakness compared to Buddhism and Daoism: the lack of strong institutional ties among its followers.

Buddhists and Daoists parlayed their material wealth, monastic establishments, patronage networks, and religious bureaucracies into genuine political and social influence. Their impressive monastic networks, including thousands of monasteries in cities, towns, and villages throughout China, contributed to expansive connections among their members—including both the clergy and lay followers—at a level Confucians could not match. The Buddhist and Daoist orders became the dominant social institutions in stabilizing and rebuilding postwar society. Eventually, it took more than a dynastic transition and changes in state policies for the two religions to lose that influence in the late imperial period.

The Setting, Sources, and Chapter Outline

This book focuses on Shanxi because that province provides a perfect regional context for exploring long-term social change in north China. From ancient times, the province has been a coherent geographical unit. It is bounded by the Taihang Mountains in the east, and one of its two historical names is *Shanxi* 山西, meaning "west of the mountains." The Lüliang Mountains and the Yellow River create a natural border between Shanxi and Shaanxi province to the west; Shanxi's other historical name is *Hedong* 河東, meaning "east of the river." The province is bounded on the south by the Yellow River and on the north by the Yin Mountains and steppe. Two-thirds of the province lies in the eastern part of the loess plateau. Hilly lands occupy the province's eastern and

---

53. Wei Chu 魏初, "Qing yi hanlin guan ruhu" 請以翰林管儒戶, in *Yuandai zouyi jilu*, 1:177.

western sections, and a string of river basins lie in the middle along its biggest river, the Fen.

Shanxi maintained a high degree of continuity in administrative structure across the various dynasties after the thirteenth century. The province includes three major regions from north to south: Datong 大同, Taiyuan 太原, and Pingyang 平陽 (map 2). In the Yuan dynasty, for the first time in history, these three regions were integrated into one regional administrative unit under the name of the Pacification Commission of Hedong Shanxi (*Hedong shanxi dao xuanwei si* 河東山西道宣慰司), which was under the direct administration of the Central Secretariat (*Zhongshusheng* 中書省), the central government's chief administrative agency. In the Ming these three regions became Shanxi province. This study mainly focuses on the regions of Taiyuan and Pingyang, which jointly bore the name Hedong from the Northern Song dynasty on.[54] The region of Datong is excluded from this study because it inherited culture and population from the Liao dynasty (907–1123) instead of the Northern Song. Also, unlike Taiyuan and Pingyang, in the Jin dynasty the Datong region was a gathering point for Jurchen nobles, who owned much of the local land.[55] After 1127, exemplifying the common experience of north China, communities in Taiyuan and Pingyang underwent many periods of large-scale social disruption because of wars, raiding by nomads, and natural disasters. The recurrent fragmentation of local society resulted in the reshuffling of local power structures.

This study also focuses on Shanxi because of the province's rare abundance of available local sources from numerous religious establishments. Throughout history the region has developed strong traditions of religious belief and practice. The scarcity of water contributes to the popularity of rainmaking rituals and water deity worship. Often seen as a cradle of ancient Chinese civilization, Shanxi had an extraordinarily rich collection of famous mythical and historical figures, many of whom developed into local tutelary deities known for bringing rain or water resources. It was

54. The administrative units in the Taiyuan area in the Jin, Yuan, and Ming dynasties were, respectively, the northern circuit of Hedong, Taiyuan circuit (Ji'ning circuit after 1305), and Taiyuan prefecture; the units in the Pingyang area were the southern circuit of Hedong, Pingyang circuit (Jinning circuit after 1305), and Pingyang prefecture.

55. Liu Pujiang, *Liao Jin shilun*, 219.

MAP 2 Places in Shanxi province mentioned in this book. Map adapted from "Provinces of China (Circa 1997)," downloaded from https://worldmap.harvard.edu/data /geonode:Provinces_1997. Harvard CHGIS.

also home to several important sacred sites for the organized religions of Buddhism and Daoism. Mt. Wutai, in northern Shanxi, became a Buddhist pilgrimage site as early as the eighth century, while the Palace of Eternal Joy (*Yongle gong* 永樂宮), built by the Quanzhen Daoist School in southern Shanxi, developed into a national Daoist center in the thirteenth century.

From the eleventh century on, Shanxi villagers formed community worship associations (*she* 社) to hold regular religious ceremonies—often featuring theatrical performances—in temples dedicated to various local deities. This practice continued for a thousand years. Even in the early twentieth century, the traditional community worship associations still conducted religious ceremonies and hired theatrical troupes. Many of these activities died out in the early years of Communist rule, but they have since reemerged. Geographical isolation and strong religious traditions helped many temples and inscriptions carved on stone steles to survive during World War II and the Cultural Revolution, when similar sources were largely destroyed in other provinces.

These materials made this study possible. Recent publications, as well as extensive archeological excavations in Shanxi, have produced a body of newly discovered primary sources touching on all aspects of life in north China before the seventeenth century: inscriptions on stone steles, temple murals, epitaphs of local leaders, irrigation documents on stone, and tomb carvings.[56] The main sources for this study are stele inscriptions. During my fieldwork in Shanxi between 2006 and 2014, I collected more than a hundred unpublished inscriptions from the Jin, Yuan, and Ming periods, especially those on the reverse sides of the steles that give the names, occupations, and villages of the donors. Many of these steles remain in their original temples and shrines. Some of them still lie in farm fields, and others have been moved to local museums. I have transcribed many of these unpublished inscriptions and used them

---

56. This study has greatly benefited from a provincewide project in the past decade that has published stele inscriptions from all counties and cities in the series A Complete Collection of Steles in Shanxi (*Sanjin shike daquan* 三晉石刻大全). The series now includes more than forty volumes, and more are on the way. Unfortunately, however, many of the inscriptions published in it are not accompanied by information about the donor.

in this study (appendix 1). This book also draws on a wide range of other local sources, especially local gazetteers and literary anthologies.

The nature of existing local sources reflects the north-south divergence between 1200 and 1600. In south China, a large number of sources on paper survive in the forms of manuscript and printing. These include anthologies, genealogies, contracts, and miscellaneous notes. They have enabled social historians to write in-depth accounts of social change in regions like the lower Yangzi delta, the Pearl River delta, and Fujian province.[57] In contrast, printing—especially for private and commercial purposes—was much less common in the north, and cultural expression on paper was also less important. As in other northern regions, the most distinctive local sources in Shanxi are stele inscriptions. As this study will show, the exceptional abundance of stele inscriptions in north China, particularly in the Mongol-Yuan period, is not an accident. Steles were the most common way for northern individuals and institutions to express their social power. For this reason, steles are not just a source material. They also reveal the nature of the social performance the actors—including those who installed the steles, wrote the inscriptions for the steles, and read the steles—had in mind in the past.

Five chapters structured by time period and topic follow. This study focuses on the Mongol-Yuan period and provides partial coverage of the Jin and Ming dynasties for context. In the Jin dynasty, the group with the most social prestige was the literati, who received a Confucian education in state-sponsored public schools and entered Jin officialdom through civil service examinations. Tracing the life experiences of the well-known scholar Yuan Haowen (1190–1257), who witnessed the flourishing of a Confucian social order based on examination ties, chapter 1 provides the baseline for northern Chinese society before the Mongol conquest.

The next three chapters consider the social, political, and economic dimensions of the religious institutions that created the distinctive social order in north China under Mongol rule. The Quanzhen Daoist order assumed a quasi-governmental role and organized the postwar social reconstruction from 1234 to 1281 (chapter 2). The order accommodated

57. Szonyi, *Practicing Kinship*; D. Faure, *Emperor and Ancestor*; Dean and Zheng, *Ritual Alliances of the Putian Plain*; McDermott, *The Making of a New Rural Order*.

destitute former Jin literati, provided northerners with alternative education, promoted the activities of women outside their families, and helped urban and rural residents use Quanzhen ideological ties to bind fragmented communities together. Chapter 3 analyzes the powerful new Buddhist order centering at Mt. Wutai. Elite Wutai monks creatively used their connections to the Mongol rulers and their official positions in the powerful new Buddhist bureaucracy to bring wealth and prestige to their lay families. The new Buddhist order challenged traditional norms: people came to see Buddhist monks as both filial sons and reliable husbands. Buddhist and Daoist clergy extended their influence beyond the monastery and established extensive socioeconomic ties in local society. Buddhists and Daoists penetrated irrigation associations, locally powerful and exclusive village institutions for water management and allocation (chapter 4). They participated in developing irrigation projects, acted as heads of local irrigation associations, and rebuilt rural infrastructure after the devastating earthquakes of 1303.

In 1368, the Chinese overthrew the Mongols and placed a Chinese emperor on the throne. The Ming dynasty reinstated the civil service examinations and suppressed organized religions, both Buddhist and Daoist. The distinctive Yuan-type social order changed and within two hundred years vanished in Ming Shanxi. As chapter 5 will show, this long history of unmaking the old order reveals the legacy of Mongol rule in late imperial China.

In short, Mongol rule had a much deeper and longer lasting impact on local society than the previous wave of Jurchen conquest. For three decades after the Jurchen conquest of north China in 1127, the Jin state borrowed Northern Song institutions to promote Confucianism and recruited Chinese literati to the civil bureaucracy. The northern literati retained their status as the political and social elite under Jurchen rule. State patronage and the lack of competition from southern literati resulted in by far the highest number of degree holders that north China ever produced.

The Mongols, however, transformed both the political and the social order in north China, excluding Confucian literati from government office and bringing previously marginalized social groups to the forefront. Meanwhile, the Chinese people—both literati and non-literati—showed great flexibility and creativity in their reaction to the unexpected crises of foreign rule. They did not exclusively follow the prescriptions of some literati elites. More remarkably, religion provided the most dynamic ideological and institutional resources. Northern Chinese men and women developed innovative strategies and practices that allowed them to survive and succeed in the unfamiliar world under Mongol rule. Although the Yuan dynasty brought political unity to China and facilitated north-south communications after conquering the Southern Song in 1279, north China continued to differ significantly from the south. These differences persisted after the collapse of Mongol rule in 1368. After that date, northern and southern China had different historical trajectories partly because of their very different experiences of Mongol rule.

CHAPTER I

Yuan Haowen and the Degree-Holder Society in the Jin Dynasty

In 1203, a scholar-official named Yuan Ge 元格 took his fourteen-year-old adopted son Yuan Haowen 元好問 (1190–1257) to Lingchuan county, Shanxi, in north China, then under Jurchen rule.[1] There Yuan Haowen spent the next five years studying with a teacher his father had carefully chosen for him: Hao Tianting 郝天挺 (1161–1217), a local *jinshi* degree holder who was teaching in the county school. In the Jin dynasty's central capital, Zhongdu 中都 (now Beijing), while waiting to be appointed to his next position, Yuan Ge had consulted with all his relatives and friends about where to find a good tutor to prepare his beloved son for the civil service examinations. Those consulted all recommended Zezhou subprefecture (now Jincheng, Shanxi), because it had been famous for producing excellent scholars since the Northern Song dynasty. Giving priority to his son's education, Ge took a position as magistrate of Lingchuan, a county in Zezhou subprefecture.

This story, told by Yuan Haowen three decades later in the funeral biography of his teacher Hao Tianting, illustrates the functioning of the typical Chinese examination-based society after the Northern Song. In this society, the civil service examination system functioned as the major mechanism for placing Confucian literati in government, and participation in the exams was the most important state-associated marker of

---

1. Yuan Haowen's biological father was Ge's older brother, Yuan Deming 元德明, who entrusted Haowen to the childless Ge.

literati status. Yuan Haowen first saw this society flourish in north China in the middle Jin dynasty and then saw it completely dissolve after the Mongol conquest, which started in 1211.

Yuan Haowen was one of the Jin scholars whose lives were dramatically changed by the Mongol conquest in the early decades of the thirteenth century.[2] He stands out as our best informant on the sea change in northern Chinese society during the Jin-Yuan transition, particularly as it concerned literati. First, as a well-known scholar who lived through the late Jin and the early Mongol periods, Yuan Haowen traveled widely and associated with an extraordinarily large number of people, both literati and non-literati (map 3).

Second, Yuan Haowen left the richest body of surviving materials about late Jin literati, politics, and society. After the demise of the Jin state in 1234, Yuan Haowen decided to write a history of the Jin state and people. For the rest of his life, he devoted himself to this massive historical writing project. Some of his books have been lost over time, but many others survive.[3] Yuan built the Pavilion of Unofficial History (*yeshiting* 野史亭) for his history-writing project next to the ancestral graveyard of his family in his native village of Hanyan, in Xiurong county (now Xinzhou, Shanxi). The graveyard of the Yuans has survived and is a famous historical site in Xinzhou today (see plate 2). People pay respectful visits and make offerings to a modern statue of Yuan Haowen in the graveyard (fig. 1.1).

2.   Yuan's given name Haowen, which literally means "fond of learning," refers to a passage in *Lunyu* 論語 (5.21). The translation is from Confucius, *The Analects of Confucius*, 22. Yuan Haowen's literary name was Yuzhi 裕之, and his pseudonym was Yishan 遺山.

3.   His record of the siege of Kaifeng, *Miscellaneous Notes in the Year Renchen, 1232* (*Renchen zabian* 壬辰雜編), was lost. His surviving writings have been compiled and edited by modern scholars into *The Collected Works of Yuan Haowen* (*Yuan Haowen quanji*, hereafter *Q J*). This includes materials from the original *Collected Works of Yishan* (*Yishan ji* 遺山集), *Anthology of the Central Region* (*Zhongzhou ji* 中州集), and *The Record of the Listener Continued* (*Xu yijian zhi* 續夷堅志). Its appendix includes several introductions to the *Collected Works of Yishan*, the primary sources related to Yuan Haowen written by his contemporaries, and a year-by-year chronology of his life compiled by the modern scholar Miao Yue 繆鉞. Because the *Q J* omits poems by Jin literati originally preserved in Yuan Haowen's *Zhongzhou ji*, I will cite the complete version of the *Zhongzhou ji* when quoting those poems.

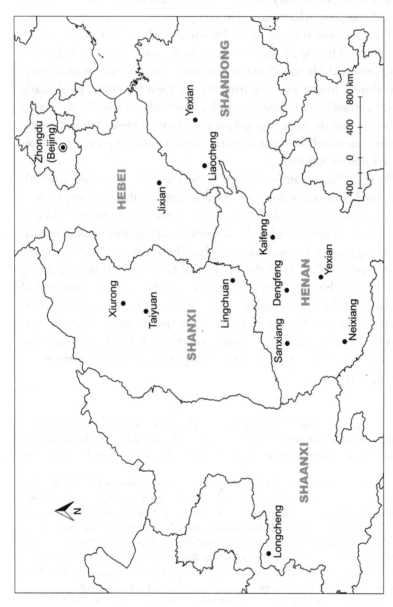

MAP 3 Places Yuan Haowen visited in 1190–1234. Map adapted from "Provinces of China (Circa 1997)," downloaded from https://worldmap.harvard.edu/data/geonode:Provinces_1997. Harvard CHGIS.

FIGURE I.I A statue of Yuan Haowen, Yuan family graveyard, Xinzhou, Shanxi province. This statue, probably dating to the 1980s or 1990s, portrays Yuan Haowen as a scholar by placing a brush in one hand and a book in the other. Yuan Haowen's writings are a crucial source about the Jin and Yuan occupation of north China. Author photo.

Using Yuan Haowen as the major source, this chapter describes the Jin examination-based society to establish a baseline for the discussion in the following chapters of the profound social transformation in north China under Mongol rule. In Jin society, Confucian literati, especially degree holders (who had passed the exams), held the status of a political and social elite among the Han population under Jurchen rule.[4] This type of literati-centered social order had taken shape in north China during

4.   A large number of modern Chinese and Japanese studies have greatly furthered our understanding of the Jin literati's political roles in Jin history, literary achievements, and intellectual culture. See Liu Pujiang, *Ershi shiji liaojinshi*, 242–60 and 323–24.

the Northern Song. Beginning with the third Jurchen emperor, Xizong (r. 1135–50), the Jin reserved military power to the Jurchen elite recruited from the Jurchen social-military units of battalions (*meng'an* 猛安) and companies (*mouke* 謀克), while entrusting the management of the civil bureaucracy to Chinese Confucian elites recruited through civil service examinations. Military power ranked above civilian.[5] Yet under Jurchen rule civil service examinations functioned as a major way for Chinese literati families to maintain their social status and as a ladder for non-literati families to move upward. The distinction between degree holders and others also separated the elite from the nonelite. This means that Jin literati elites remained largely dependent on the state. To this extent, the Jin examination-based society probably could be better described as a degree-holder society, in which literati who passed civil service examinations dominated elite society.

As we will see, the dramatic expansion of the Jin examination system and the increasing imperial patronage of Chinese literati culture after the 1160s greatly consolidated the literati-centered social order in north China. State-sponsored Confucian schools functioned as the institutional centers for literati learning and education for taking exams. The schools also provided the literati with a social space for circulating political and social information and forming extra ties, such as marriage alliances and friendships. Importantly, the lands of state schools that were allocated by the Jin state to support teachers and students enjoyed tax exemption, marking the prestigious social status of Chinese literati under Jurchen rule.

Examination candidates, teachers and students of state schools, and scholar-officials constituted the social group of literati, whose members enjoyed the most favorable social status among the Han under Jurchen rule. These men identified with each other based on their common experiences in civil service examinations and, for those who gained degrees, in Jin officialdom. Yuan Haowen was born in the golden age of the Jin literati, and during his childhood and youth (from 1190 to 1211), he witnessed and participated in the flourishing examination society in north China. His adult years (from 1211 to 1234) saw the gradual dissolution of that society following the first Mongol invasion. And in the last two de-

5. Schneider, "The Jin Revisited," 369–72.

cades of his life, Yuan Haowen struggled to adapt to a completely different world—one that had discarded civil service examinations and marginalized him and his literati peers.

Yuan Haowen in the Degree-Holder Society before the Mongol Invasion

When the Northern Song fell to the Jurchen in 1127, the majority of northern literati families moved south, and a number of local schools were destroyed. However, Chinese literati as a distinctive social group survived in north China, as the Jurchen government continued to recruit Chinese scholars as officials. Yuan Haowen frequently mentioned three crucial conditions for becoming a scholar. As he explains in one essay,

> The creation of a scholar depends on state education, family origins of his father and elder brothers, and group study with teachers and friends. All of these three elements are absolutely necessary. It is like the beautiful women in the world. Most of them are nurtured in wealthy and well-known families. Of course there are famous beauties in the villages. Yet when those women become wives of officials, their posture and manners are not even as good as servant-girls of elite families. The reason is the same. Accordingly, education is necessary to cultivate talented people.[6]

Note that the value that Yuan sees in the "family origins of his father and elder brothers" is not notable pedigree or blood descent but training: learning how to be a scholar and gentleman. In this way origins are absolutely parallel to "state education" and "study with teachers and friends." But the key element that held these three conditions together was the civil service examination system.

Unlike the Northern Song government, which recruited most officials through the civil service examinations, the Jin government recruited Chinese through the examinations but recruited Jurchen and members of other non-Han ethnic groups—including Khitan, Bohai, and Xi

---

6. Yuan Haowen, "Xinan shilao Xin Yuan" 溪南詩老辛愿, *QJ*, 41.957.

people—through protection (*yin* 廕), hereditary selection, and transfer from military service. Moreover, the Jin government always reserved the most important military positions and top civil positions for Jurchen officials.[7] After Emperor Shizong 世宗 (r. 1161–89) established the Jurchen *jinshi* degree examinations in 1170, a few Jurchen, particularly poor commoners, also took the exams to achieve upward social mobility.[8]

In theory, Chinese scholar-officials could receive appointment to high-ranking and even ministerial posts, but they had to pass through more posts before receiving such an appointment than did their Jurchen counterparts. Most Chinese officials started in county-level positions after receiving their *jinshi* degrees and spent their political careers in local government.[9] For example, Yuan Haowen's father, Yuan Ge, had been a county official in 1194 and was still a county magistrate when he died, in 1210.[10]

The flourishing society centered on degree-holders that Yuan Haowen witnessed early in his life was the product of a prospering civil culture supported by the imperial government under the reigns of two Jurchen emperors—Shizong and Zhangzong 章宗 (r. 1190–1208). These emperors, as Peter Bol argues, favored the idea that a civil order, to which Chinese literati were philosophically and practically committed, was a social good of universal value and could serve the imperial interest.[11] Even the promotion of Jurchen-language schools and examinations by the two emperors reflected, as Xin Wen demonstrates, the transformation of Jurchen identity in the direction of literary culture instead of "Jurchenization," as historians have traditionally believed.[12] Shizong and Zhangzong showed

---

7. Liu Pujiang, *Liaojinshi lun*, 77–82.

8. Iiyama, *Kin Gen jidai*, 140–44.

9. Tao, "Jindai de zhengzhi jiegou" and "Political Recruitment in the Chin Dynasty."

10. For the development of the Jin examination system and the Han Chinese literati's involvement in the examinations, see Mikami, "Kin no kakyo seido to sono seiji teki sokumen" 金の科挙制度とその政治的側面, in his *Kinshi kenkyu III*, 268–320.

11. Bol, "Seeking Common Ground," 491–92.

12. Wen, "The Road to Literary Culture." For a comprehensive review of historians' debate about Shizong's efforts to revive the Jurchen traditions, see Schneider, "The Jin Revisited," 343–62. Schneider also rejects the argument that Shizong initiated a "Jurchen nativistic movement" and emphasizes that he merely tried to strengthen the Jurchen forces politically and socially in Jin society to consolidate the legitimacy of the government (393, see also 382–95).

great interest in Chinese learning, raised the quotas for recipients of Chinese *jinshi* degrees, and most importantly, gave preference to officials with *jinshi* degrees. Their reigns marked a golden era for Chinese literati. As Yuan Haowen remarks, "The government recruited the literati through examinations on rhyme prose (*cifu* 詞賦) and the classics (*mingjing* 明經). Many students who passed those examinations reached high-ranking positions. Since the examinations were an easy path to officialdom, people competed to take them. A civil order attained harmony, and the sound of students reciting books was heard in community and family schools."[13] Imperial patronage of literati prompted enthusiasm for learning and education. While the lack of competition from southern literati helped literati families in the north succeed, northern Chinese literati also had a better chance of receiving degrees than did their counterparts in the south. The number of examination candidates during Zhangzong's reign held steady at 30,000 to 40,000 in any given examination year, and about one-fifth of candidates passed the department examinations. In contrast, during the late Northern Song only 10,000 to 20,000 students from north China took the examinations in a single year.[14] And the passing rate in the Song was only one-tenth to one-fourteenth on average.[15]

In the same year that Yuan Haowen was born (1190), Emperor Zhangzong ascended the throne. Yuan Haowen regarded Zhangzong's reign—the period in which he grew up—as the best time for literati. As he put it: "In the Cheng'an (1196–1200) and Taihe (1201–1208) periods, civil culture flourished brightly. Among literati who were born at that time, nine-tenths of those who came from poor families benefited from their fathers' and elder brothers' learning and grew up from students to be famous and capable scholar-officials."[16] Here again, Yuan Haowen

---

13. Yuan Haowen, "Shouyang xianxue ji" 壽陽縣學記, *QJ*, 32.674.

14. Iiyama, *Kin Gen jidai*, 158–59. It is worth pointing out, though, that northern exam-takers in the Northern Song already had a better chance than southern ones, because the Song state used lower standards for northerners to guarantee that a significant number of them would pass the exams and enter office.

15. Araki, *Sōdai kakyo seido kenkyū*, 102–27 and 223–35. Also the average number of successful candidates per examination in the Northern Song and Southern Song was about 457.8 and 446.4 respectively, whereas under the Jin during the period 1167–1187 the average was 500, and during the period 1188–1199 it was 677.7. See Tao, "Political Recruitment in the Chin Dynasty," 28–29.

16. Yuan Haowen, "Zhangjun muzhiming" 張君墓誌銘, *QJ*, 24.537.

wants to highlight the importance of family origins and education in creating a successful scholar. But the narrative suggests that a larger number of successful examination students than before came from humble literati families that had not previously produced officials. A rough survey of data in the *Anthology of the Central Region*—a collection of Jin literati biographies and poems compiled by Yuan Haowen after 1233—shows that among the literati who received their education or earned *jinshi* degrees during and after Shizong's reign, the majority indeed came from literati families. Among sixty-three individuals for whom family background information is listed and who received *jinshi* degrees or became officials, only three were reported to have come from peasant or poor families, and only one from a clerk family.

The ability of elite families to maintain their prestigious status shows the critical importance of examination success for northern Chinese in the Jin dynasty. Many former elite families in north China abandoned the choice of military career and turned to the civil service examination route.[17] Yuan Haowen's great-grandfather was a military officer in the late Northern Song. During the Jin, when civil service examinations became the only route to officialdom for Han Chinese, the men of the Yuan family tried to shift their identity from the military elite to the literati elite. Starting with Yuan Haowen's grandfather, who gained a *jinshi* degree in 1157 and served in the Jin local government, three generations of Yuan men took the examinations; some succeeded, while others failed. Yuan Haowen's father Yuan Ge earned the *jinshi* degree, possibly in the early 1190s; Yuan Haowen later mentioned that as a child, he accompanied his father to take up his position as a local official in Ye county (now Licheng, Shandong) around 1194.[18] Yuan Haowen's great uncle, biological father, and elder brother all failed at the prefectural examinations and ended up spending their lives in their native village of Hanyan, either farming or teaching local students.[19] Yuan Haowen's uncle, Yuan Sheng 元升, was the only one who kept to the military route, yet he was unable to obtain military office due to the lack of a recommendation from

17. Iiyama identified ninety-one individuals from northern Shanxi who held the *jinshi* degree in the Jin dynasty, but only seventeen during the Five Dynasties and the Northern Song (see *Kin Gen jidai*, 107–26, particularly 113 and 118–19).

18. Yuan Haowen, "Jinan xingji" 濟南行紀, *QJ*, 34.713.

19. *QJ*, 37.775, 39.823, 41.967, and 53.1263.

a senior military official, which was required at that time.[20] Yuan Sheng's experiences illustrate the difficulties Chinese had in being appointed to military offices, which were mostly monopolized by the Jurchen and members of other ethnic groups. As a result, most Chinese elite families tried to educate their young men in Confucian learning, particularly in exam learning.

Yuan Haowen received his early education from family members. His mother, Lady Zhang, was his first teacher. He states in a funeral biography for the famous Jin scholar-official Wang Huanghua 王黄華, "From the time I began to talk, my mother taught me to recite Mr. [Wang]'s poems."[21] After he entered elementary school at the age of seven, Yuan Haowen started to study Confucian texts, beginning with the *Classic of Filial Piety*.[22] He later vividly described in a poem his experience of learning the text:

我昔入小學	When I had just entered elementary school,
首讀仲尼居	I first read "Zhongni [Confucius] Stayed at Home Idly" [the first chapter of the *Classic of Filial Piety*].
百讀百不曉	I read it aloud one hundred times and still did not understand;
但有唾成珠	Only my spittle formed pearls [meaning that he recited the poem numerous times].[23]

Although he mocked himself for not understanding what the Confucian text meant, from his childhood, Yuan Haowen was no doubt talented in learning. In an introduction to the Yuan clan genealogy that he later wrote, he explains, "I began to read books at the age of four and to learn composing poems at the age of eight."[24] At the time, Yuan Haowen— together with Yuan Haogu 元好古 the older son of his biological father, Yuan Deming—probably studied composing poems with Deming, who

20. Yuan Haowen, "Chengfeng Henan Yuangong muming" 承奉河南元公墓銘, *QJ*, 25.539.
21. Yuan Haowen, "Wang Huanghua mubei" 王黄華墓碑, *QJ*, 16.395.
22. Yuan Haowen, "Guyi ershou" 古意二首, *QJ*, 1.12.
23. Yuan Haowen, "Qufu jixing shishou" 曲阜紀行十首, *QJ*, 2.45.
24. Yuan Haowen, *Nanguanlu yin* 南冠錄引, *QJ*, 37.774.

taught at a community school in the countryside and was particularly fond of poetry.[25]

Yet even within the same literati kin group, young men's opportunities to receive a good education differed, depending on their family's wealth and even on birth order. Haogu never left his hometown, possibly because Deming did not have enough money to afford Haogu's tour to study. Yuan Haowen tells us that Deming led a very simple life because he had not inherited much from his father and also because he cared little about making a living.[26] As a result, besides studying with his father, Yuan Haogu seemed to associate only with several local literati friends. Yuan Haowen, however, had the opportunity to study with various literati while accompanying his adoptive father to civil-administration positions in different regions. When Yuan Ge was serving in the local government of Jizhou (now Jixian, Hebei) in 1200, Lu Duo 路鐸—a well-known local scholar-official—taught the eleven-year-old Haowen to compose essays.[27]

In north China under Jurchen rule, it was mainly the state schools that prepared students for civil service examinations. Notably, there were almost no private schools there like the private academies (*shuyuan* 書院) in the south that on the one hand prepared students for participation in the exams and on the other hand claimed to offer an education less oriented to a career.[28] The state school system in the north expanded a great deal along with the expansion of the civil service examinations during the reigns of Shizong and Zhangzong, who established a nationwide state education network paralleling the hierarchical administrative system from the capital to central regional cities. By 1190, in addition to six capital schools that had a combined enrollment of 795, twenty-four prefectural schools and sixty subprefectural schools—representing about half of the 174 Jin prefectures and subprefectures—had been established with government-allocated funds to accommodate about 1,800

25.   Yuan Haowen, "Xian dafu shi" 先大夫詩, *Q J*, 41.967. Haogu was four years older than Haowen and his name (Haogu means "fond of the past"), like Haowen's, refers to a passage in *The Analects of Confucius*. See Confucius, *The Analects of Confucius*, 31.

26.   Yuan Haowen, "Xian dafu shi," *Q J*, 41.967.

27.   Hao Jing 郝經, "Yishan xiansheng muming" 遺山先生墓銘, *Q J*, 53.1263.

28.   For the academy movement in Southern Song China, see Chaffee, "Chu-hsi and the Revival"; Chen Wenyi, *You guanxue dao shuyuan*.

students collectively. Each of these schools had one professor selected from those who either had taken the civil service examinations five times (without passing) or held a *jinshi* degree but were over age fifty (and therefore too old to embark on an official career).[29] The government supervised state schools by controlling their funding, teaching positions, and enrollment quotas, indicating strong ties between the Jin state and literati education. At least two-thirds of 683 Jin counties also had schools.[30] These public schools, often called "temple schools" (*miaoxue* 廟學) because they combined a school and a Confucian temple, functioned as institutional centers for Jin scholars and examination students.[31] Some regional state schools developed reputations for producing a number of scholar-officials. For instance, the Taiyuan prefectural school became famous among Jin literati after seven students from the school passed the *jinshi* degree examinations in 1191, and one of them attained the highest ranking of Number One Scholar (*Zhuangyuan* 狀元).[32]

State schools appealed to the Jin literati because all students in those schools were exempted from the duty of labor service and received regular stipends from the government.[33] According to the law titled "Supporting Schools and Educating Students" (*Shanxue yangshi fa* 贍學養士法), which was promulgated in 1201, each regional school student received annually thirty *shi* (about sixty kilograms) of millet from 60 *mu* 畝 (approximately 4 hectares) of state land cultivated by tenant farmers, and each National University (*taixue* 太學) student received all of the income from 108 *mu* (approximately 7 hectares) of land that was assigned to him.[34] Additionally, some regional schools also received financial support from

29. The enrollment in prefectural schools was limited to 20 to 60 students, and that in subprefectural schools to 10 to 30. See *JS*, 10.229 and 51.1132–33. See also Tao, "Public Schools in the Chin Dynasty." According to Tao, the official history's description of the school system is reliable.

30. Tao, "Public Schools in the Chin Dynasty," 54; *JS*, 24.550.

31. Most local official schools included Confucian temples, yet not every local Confucian temple was combined with a school. See Zhang Fan, "Jindai difang guanxue," 87–88.

32. Zhao Feng 趙沨, "Taiyuan fuxue wenmiao bei" 太原府學文廟碑, in *Quan Liao Jin wen*, 2:1755–56; Yuan Haowen, "Zhang Daizhou Dajie" 張代州大節, *QJ*, 41.911.

33. On the system of labor service in the Jin dynasty, see Chan, "Organization and Utilization of Labor Service."

34. *JS*, 11.257.

powerful local literati families. According to Yuan Haowen, a Lady Chuan, the widow of a high-ranking official from Jizhou, used a large amount of money to buy 2,000 *mu* (approximately 133 hectares) of good land, which she donated to the Jizhou subprefectural school to support its students.[35] In the Jin, school lands were exempted from taxes. The land Lady Chuan gave to the school could support three hundred or more students.

Supporting public schools was a good way for literati families to improve their prestige, both in local society and in the national literati circle. Soon after Lady Chuan's donation to the school, the prefect reported the event to the court, and Emperor Shizong granted Lady Chuan the honorific title of Lady Sublime Virtue (*chengde furen* 成德夫人). Since the Northern Song, the image of virtuous women had largely focused on support for the education of their male relatives.[36] This image continued to shape the Jin literati's view of the social values of women in elite families.

Given the material and intellectual advantages of state schools, Yuan Ge might have wanted Haowen to study in the Jizhou subprefectural school or, even better, at the National University while Ge was in the capital in 1203. Yet a strict admission qualification prevented Haowen from attending the subprefectural school, let alone the National University. State schools gave priority to the family members of officials with official ranks above at least the sixth grade, but Ge's official rank as a Jin magistrate was only 7b. According to state policy, prefectural and subprefectural schools also reserved one-third of their spots (up to twenty) for the sons and grandsons of lower-ranking officials, but they required recommendations from the prefectural government and had to pass entrance examinations.[37] Haowen was still young at the time and had not started studying for the civil service examinations; even if he had taken the entrance examinations, he might not have been able to pass them.

Yuan Ge chose instead to send Haowen to county schools, which had much looser requirements because of their half-official and half-local nature. Emperor Zhangzong had made it clear that the government would not allocate funds to support county schools but encouraged local offi-

35.   Yuan Haowen, "Lu Jizhou Zhongxian" 路冀州仲顯, *QJ*, 41.910.
36.   Bossler, *Powerful Relations*, 12–24.
37.   *JS*, 51.1130.

cials and populations to build and support these institutions.[38] Due to a lack of resources, many county magistrates cooperated with local literati or powerful families to raise money for school construction and education. The educational quality of a given county school, then, reflected the region's cultural level. This is why Yuan Ge focused on finding the best place for Haowen to study.

Yuan Ge's relatives and literati friends in the capital all recommended Zezhou subprefecture. Shanxi ranked among the top educational regions in the Jin cultural landscape. As Yuan Haowen would later state proudly, "The deities that take charge of the fortune of literary composition have favored Hedong for one hundred years."[39] Scholars from both the southern and northern parts of Shanxi achieved their greatest success in the examinations during Zhangzong's reign.[40] Within Zezhou, Lingchuan county had a particularly good reputation because several prominent local literati families had produced successful scholars who placed first in the national examinations; in fact, two families had produced five top candidates between them. In total, more than eighty people who earned the *jinshi* degree in the Jin dynasty came from Zezhou, about thirty-two of whom were from Lingchuan.[41] The success of local literati heightened local enthusiasm for education while attracting many students from other regions.

---

38.   Zhao Bingwen 趙秉文, "Jiaxian wenmiao chuangjian jiangtang ji" 郟縣文廟創建講堂記, *Jinwen zui*, 14.133.

39.   Yuan Haowen, "Ti Li Tingxun suocang *Yajitu* ershou" 題李庭訓所藏雅集圖二首, *QJ*, 12.303.

40.   Iiyama's solid study of the regional distribution of Jin degree holders shows that before Shizong's reign, only eighteen scholars from northern Shanxi and eleven from southern Shanxi had earned *jinshi* degrees in the first four decades of the Jin dynasty. During Shizong's reign, three *jinshi* degree holders came from northern Shanxi, and fourteen came from the south. In Zhangzong's reign, twenty-five *jinshi* degree holders came from northern Shanxi, and forty-nine came from the south. See Iiyama, *Kin Gen jidai*, 75.

41.   According to the local gazetteer, Wu Mingfu came in first in the national rhyme prose examinations in 1154. His nephew Wu Tianyou did the same in 1199, forty-five years later. In the Zhao family, Zhao Anrong and Zhao Anshi obtained the honor in 1140 and 1160, respectively. In 1203 Wu Tianhe, Wu Tianyou's younger brother, ranked first in the classics examinations. Another Wu family member earned the *jinshi* degree. See *Lingchuan xianzhi* [1779], 21.7b and 10a–12b.

When Yuan Ge brought Haowen to Lingchuan in 1203, Hao Tianting—Haowen's future teacher—was teaching in the county school. The history of Hao's clan reveals how a single scholarly family dominated literati education in Lingchuan. The Hao family migrated from Taiyuan to Zezhou at the end of the Northern Song dynasty. They became a well-known scholarly family in Zezhou society after the career of Tianting's uncle, Hao Zhen 郝震, who studied at the National University in the capital and later taught in the countryside. The Haos established a family rule to prevent their undivided family, which often included a hundred people, from falling apart. The family rule stipulated that the Hao men would work in different fields according to their individual talents: some as farmers, some as businessmen, and some as scholars. Subsequently, the whole family became wealthy enough to support more family members in careers as scholars. Hao Tianting and two of his nephews all took the palace examinations, and Tianting earned the *jinshi* degree. When Tianting's older brother Hao Yuan 郝源 became the head of the family, he made a new rule that one of his younger brothers or nephews must teach in the county school, suggesting that the Haos monopolized teaching positions there.[42]

The ability to support county schools demonstrated a family's leading role within local society. Since instructors in county schools did not receive a regular salary from the government, only people like the Hao family scholars, who had solid economic support within their own kinship group, could afford to teach in county schools. When new magistrates came to Lingchuan, they often visited the Haos, and the Haos had a close relationship with Yuan Ge when he was serving as magistrate. At the county school, Yuan Haowen studied under Hao Tianting alongside Tianting's son, Hao Siwen 郝思溫, who was the same age as Haowen. When Yuan Ge ended his tenure as magistrate and left Lingchuan in 1206, he entrusted Haowen's education completely to the Haos.

Yuan Ge expected Hao Tianting to prepare Haowen for the civil service examinations. Yet Hao believed that a real scholar should learn much more than what the examinations tested, so he taught Haowen to compose poems, a skill not important for passing the exams. When someone criticized Hao for not preparing the magistrate's son for the exami-

---

42. Hao Jing, "Xianbo dafu muming" 先伯大父墓銘, *QYW*, 4: 446–47.

nations, Hao replied: "Precisely. I do not want him to be an examination candidate!"[43] The Lingchuan county school's semiofficial and semiprivate nature and the fact that it was supported by private wealth made it resemble a southern private academy in that it was oriented by the head teacher's choice toward something broader than exam training. Even so, most students still saw exam taking as their primary reason for learning. Yuan Haowen never gave up his hope of passing the examinations. In 1205, at the age of sixteen, he traveled to Taiyuan to take the prefectural examinations for the first time, but he failed to pass. Nevertheless, he clearly learned poetry well from Hao Tianting. During this trip, on hearing a story about a wild goose that committed suicide after its mate was shot by a hunter, Yuan Haowen bought the two geese from the hunter, buried them, and wrote one of the most celebrated lyrics on romantic love in Chinese classical poetry.[44]

Hao Tianting's relatives claimed that they had inherited their educational philosophy directly from adherents of the Northern Song Neo-Confucian scholar Cheng Hao 程灝 (1032–85), who had served as magistrate of neighboring Jincheng county in Zezhou and taught local scholars there. We do not know whether or not Hao Tianting taught Yuan Haowen about Cheng Hao's learning, as Jin exams did not test students' knowledge of Neo-Confucianism. But Hao did teach his son Siwen about Cheng Hao's learning, and Siwen subsequently taught his son Hao Jing 郝經 (1223–75), who became a famous northern Neo-Confucian scholar and a student of Yuan Haowen.[45] As for Yuan Haowen, he shared Hao Tianting's view of poetry but disliked Neo-Confucianism throughout his life.

Yuan Haowen's six years in Lingchuan, from 1203 to 1208, were a period of peace and happiness for him. This was also the period when he began to establish and expand his personal social network in the Jin literati world. Apart from studying, he started to gather with his county school classmates and other literati to drink, compose poems, and enjoy the local landscape. Yuan tells us that three days before Tomb-Sweeping

43. Quoted in Yuan Haowen, "Hao xiansheng muming" 郝先生墓銘, *QJ*, 23.518.

44. Yuan Haowen, "Mo yu'er (Hen renjian, qing shi hewu)" 摸魚兒 (恨人間，情是何物), *QJ*, 42.987.

45. Hao Jing, "Xian zengshu dafu dongxuan laoren muming" 先曾叔大父東軒老人墓銘, *QYW*, 4:444–45.

Day (the *Qingming* 清明 festival) in 1205, he went on an excursion with five or six literati friends to a temple dedicated to the Two Immortals—two popular local goddesses. They visited the temple, enjoyed the view of a local stream, and composed poems. Yuan's poem, which was inscribed on the wall of the temple and is still visible today, states that nothing made him happier than looking at the beauty of differently shaped hills in the mild spring air.[46] Yuan also associated with a local literati family surnamed Qin. He and Qin Lüe 秦略, who was a member of Yuan's father's generation, became friends, drinking and composing poems together.

In this period, Yuan Haowen established a marriage alliance with the powerful Zhang scholar-official family in his hometown, which exemplifies how such alliances strengthened the Jin literati's social networks. In 1207, at the age of eighteen, Yuan temporarily returned to his rural home in Xiurong county to marry the daughter of the high-ranking official Zhang Han 張翰, also a Xiurong native. The Zhangs were even more successful than the Yuans in local society. Zhang Han had earned the *jinshi* degree in 1188 and was a junior assistant at the Ministry of Revenue (ranked 6b) in 1208. His younger brother Zhang Shu 張俅 had passed the *jinshi* exam in 1200 and later reached the position of associate commander-in-chief of Northern Hedong circuit (ranked 4b).[47] Establishing a marriage alliance with the Zhang family offered Yuan Haowen a stronger elite family background. During the marriage preparations Yuan Ge instructed Haowen about civil administration to prepare him for future official positions like that of magistrate.[48] Yuan Ge had done everything necessary for his adoptive son's success in the intellectual and political world, yet Haowen had to pass the *jinshi* degree examinations to reach the pinnacle of the Jin degree-holder society.

After marrying, Yuan Haowen returned to Linchuan to complete his studies with Hao Tianting. In 1208 Yuan Haowen left Lingchuan and moved to Longcheng county in Shaanxi to be near his father, who was the magistrate there at that time. Yuan Haowen continued to concentrate

---

46.   Yuan Haowen, "Xixi erxianmiao tiliu" 西溪二仙廟題留, *QJ*, 14.372.

47.   Later, Zhang Han's nephew Zhang Tianyi passed the *jinshi* degree examinations in 1212, and his son Zhang Tianren held the position of assistant commissioner of the palace attendants service (ranked 6b). See Yuan Haowen, "Zhang hubu Han" 張戶部翰, *QJ*, 41.916.

48.   Yuan Haowen, "*Nanguanlu* yin," *QJ*, 37.775.

on examination learning, associating with other literati, and taking the exams. His life did not change much until the spring of 1210, when Yuan Ge died of an ulcer in Longcheng. In that year, at the age of twenty-one, Yuan Haowen ended a decade of studying away from home and took his adoptive father's coffin to Hanyan village for burial in their ancestral graveyard.

After Yuan Ge died, Haowen and his immediate family—including his mother, wife, and their first daughter, Yuan Zhen 元真, born in 1209—lived a comfortable life in their rural home supported by wealth and property Haowen had inherited from his father, and Haowen continued to study for the examinations.[49] Yuan Haowen must have passed the prefectural exams in the fall of 1212, since he traveled to the capital in the spring of 1213 for the next round of departmental examinations. In Yuan Haowen's time, a student needed to take three rounds of triennial examinations—at the prefectural, departmental, and palace levels. The prefectural examinations were often held at a regional examination site during the fall, and the next two rounds were held in the capital the following spring.[50] After failing the exams in the capital, Yuan Haowen returned to stay in the Taiyuan prefectural school for the summer. He could be admitted to a prefectural school without taking the entrance examinations by virtue of a government policy aimed at showing benevolence to examination candidates who had passed prefectural examinations but failed departmental examinations.[51]

Yuan Haowen's experience in the Taiyuan prefectural school reveals the important role state schools played for literati trying to establish helpful social networks in Jin society. State schools provided both room and board to students and allowed them to study together intensively every day and develop relationships with each other—as acquaintances, friends, rivals, or even enemies—that would shape their future lives intellectually and politically. In the Taiyuan prefectural school, Yuan organized a study group (*xiake* 夏課) with two students from Jiaocheng, Shanxi, who were living in the same dormitory as he was.[52] The study group was a

49. About Yuan Zhen's birth year, see the textual analysis in Shi, *Yuan Yishan nianpu*, 40.

50. There were national examinations in 1213. See Xue, *Jindai keju*, 185–88.

51. *JS*, 51.1131.

52. Yuan Haowen, "Shiqishi mengqiu xu" 十七史蒙求序, *QJ*, 36.754–55.

distinctive way for literati, and examination students in particular, to interact socially. Many of these groups, as Iiyama Tomoyasu has pointed out, were originally designed so students could share books, due to the lack of books in the early Jin period.[53] Students in the same study group also gathered for parties and banquets. According to a ghost story that Yuan recorded, an examination candidate once organized a study group whose members dined together every ten days. After one member died, on the next date designated for a party the others set a place for the deceased student to commemorate him. After the food was served, the spoon and chopsticks at the seat for the dead student rose into the air as if the student were using them. Everyone sobbed and could not eat.[54] Yuan included this anecdote in the book of tales *The Record of the Listener Continued*, an important source for this chapter.[55]

In addition to literati gatherings, state schools also provided space for Jin examination students to collectively imagine a distinctive spiritual world reflecting their own lives and literati culture. For instance, in one tale that Yuan Haowen heard from a school instructor, set sometime between 1161 and 1189, several students were studying together late at night in the Taiyuan prefectural school. After midnight, someone suddenly heard the sound of a person walking outside the window. A female ghost— who, according to the tale, was a concubine of a Northern Song official buried near the school—entered the dormitory and lightly tapped those

53.   Iiyama, *Kin Gen jidai*, 79.
54.   Yuan Haowen, "Xunhui zhi yi" 旬會之異, *QJ*, 48.1147.
55.   In a tomb inscription for the Daoist Yu Zixu written in 1238, Yuan mentions that a few illiterate people were capable of composing thoughtful hymns, which he had included in *The Record of Listener Continued* that he was writing (*QJ*, 31.645). Clearly he had at least already started to write the book in 1238. The latest date mentioned in the book was 1251, suggesting that Yuan finished this book late in life. The period of writing *The Record of Listener Continued* paralleled Yuan's historical writing project after the Jin fell in 1234, indicating that *The Record of Listener Continued* might be part of Yuan's massive project to write the history of the Jin state and Jin people. The title and literary genre of the book follow the model of *The Record of the Listener* (*Yijian zhi* 夷堅志), written by Southern Song scholar Hong Mai 洪邁 (1123–1202). Like Hong Mai, Yuan collected tales from various sources: some recorded events that he witnessed or experienced, and some he heard from relatives, friends, colleagues, and others. The majority of his informants were literati, and about one-fifth of the 207 tales are about people in his social network. On Hong Mai's book, see Hansen, *Changing Gods in Medieval China*, 17–23, and Ter Haar, "Newly Recovered Anecdotes."

who were asleep, murmuring, "this person will receive the *jinshi* degree, and this person will not." The three students she tapped performed exactly as she had foretold.[56]

Constructing, circulating, and recording these anecdotes were part of the Jin literati's social and cultural life beyond studying for the exams. Many of the anecdotes that Yuan Haowen collected about Jin literati in *The Record of the Listener Continued* were very similar to those in a large body of examination stories that had circulated in Song society about omens, prophecies, and dreams concerned with foretelling examination success.[57] The fact that Yuan was able to collect so many anecdotes about examination students is in itself evidence of the constant circulation of such information within the active social networks of Jin literati.

At the Taiyuan prefectural school, Yuan Haowen and his literati peers must have discussed important political and social news as well, especially news about the earthshaking Mongol attacks along the Jin border, which began in 1211 and grew more threatening over the next two years. Yuan likely had heard the news early. His home subprefecture, Xinzhou— which included Xiurong and Dingxiang as subordinate counties—was close to the Jin border that Mongol troops attacked, and local people spoke of the possibility of a nomadic invasion from the north as early as 1209.[58] Yet local literati did not seem to realize how serious the Mongol threat was. Even in the eighth month of 1213, after the Jin western capital (Datong, in modern-day Shanxi) had fallen to the Mongols, Yuan Haogu, Haowen's elder biological brother who never left his hometown, still met literati friends in Xinzhou to enjoy the mid-autumn festival, drinking and composing poems. Local literati life continued unaffected until early 1214.[59]

---

56. Yuan Haowen, "Yu'er" 玉兒, *QJ*, 48.1133.

57. For examination stories in the Song, see Chaffee, *The Thorny Gates of Learning*, 177–81.

58. Yuan wrote in *The Record of the Listener Continued* that as early as 1209 some Xinzhou natives had fled to Taiyuan on hearing about the northern nomadic attack on the Jin border, and in 1213 a local family started to recite a Buddhist Marishiten incantation in pursuit of spiritual protection from incoming disasters. See Yuan Haowen, "Wang Wanzhong" 王萬鍾 and "Molizhitian zhou" 摩利支天咒, *QJ*, 41.898 and 49.1162.

59. Yuan Haowen, "Minzhi xiong shichen" 敏之兄詩讖, *QJ*, 48.1131.

The Fall of Areas North of the Yellow River

The year 1214 marked a seismic shift in Yuan Haowen's life: his earlier comfortable days as the son of a well-off literati family came to an end, and an unsettling two years as a wartime fugitive began. In the spring of that year, Mongol troops appeared in Shanxi, ravaging every city, town, and village in their path and killing large numbers of people. The devastation was unprecedented. Li Junmin 李俊民 (1176–1260) described a destroyed Zezhou in the spring of 1214: "On the first day of the second month, the capital city of the prefecture fell. The violent fire set the sky ablaze. The city walls were destroyed, buildings burned down, and marketplaces turned into ruins. The surrounding region for one thousand miles became completely desolate. There was no trace of human presence."[60] A similar scene occurred in Xinzhou. After breaching the prefectural city wall on April 14, the Mongols slaughtered more than 100,000 residents.[61] Yuan Haowen's brother Haogu, then twenty-nine, was killed in that massacre. Yuan Haowen and his family survived the turbulence by hiding in the local mountains.[62]

The war caused massive migration, the deaths of many literati and commoners, the destruction of schools, the suspension of civil service examinations, and ultimately the unraveling of literati activities in areas north of the Yellow River. Many Zezhou scholars—including Li Junmin and Hao Tianting—fled their hometowns to escape the war, and the active local literati communities that Yuan Haowen had witnessed a decade ago disappeared amid the devastating population loss.[63] Local schools were abandoned, too. As Yuan later lamented, "The survival of the temple

---

60.   Li Junmin, "Zezhou tuji" 澤州圖記, *QYW*, 1:51.

61.   Yuan Haowen, "Wang Wanzhong," *QJ*, 41.898.

62.   Yuan Haowen, "Bibing Yangqu beishan zhi yanggu ti shikan" 避兵陽曲北山之羊谷題石龕, *QJ*, 14.345.

63.   Li Junmin later recorded that the population of Zezhou dropped to 973 households after the war ended in 1235 (Li Junmin, "Zezhou tuji," *QYW*, 1:51). And from a 1209 inscription, we learn that Xiangling county in southern Shanxi alone had had more than 20,000 households on the eve of the Mongol conquest. See Kong Tianjian, "Xiangling xian chuangxiu miaoxue ji" 襄陵縣創修廟學記, *Quan Liao Jin wen*, 2:1932.

school was utterly hopeless. . . . The people in power were mostly military leaders who did not care about the school, which gradually fell into disrepair due to damage by rain and wind."[64]

In the summer of 1214 the Jurchen Emperor Xuanzong 宣宗 (r. 1213–24) abandoned the central capital (now Beijing), crossed the Yellow River, and moved his court to the southern capital (now Kaifeng), an event euphemistically dubbed the southern crossing (*nandu* 南渡) by contemporary literati. From then on examinations were mostly given only in areas south of the Yellow River, particularly Henan and Shaanxi—the only two intact regions under state control after 1214. In that year, students were excused from taking the prefectural exams and allowed to go directly to the departmental examinations in the central capital and Kaifeng. Some nine thousand men participated, and about one-tenth of the candidates passed.[65] Although still seeking refuge in Shanxi, Yuan Haowen managed to travel to Kaifeng for the examinations, yet he failed once again.

The loss of literati life, the ruins of public schools, and the suspension of civil service examinations all marked the disappearance of critical institutions that had sustained the Jin degree-holder society in the areas north of the Yellow River before 1214. In such chaos, the Yuan family needed to decide whether to remain in northern Shanxi or flee. They had been on the move since the spring of 1214. In 1216 Mongol troops attacked Xinzhou a second time. The Yuans hastily hid their collection of fine books and artifacts inside their house and then fled again to the nearby mountains. After the Mongol army withdrew, in light of the frequent raids in northern Shanxi, the Yuans decided to join three to four million other northern Chinese and move south to the territory that—at least for the time being—was still held by the Jin state.[66] They entrusted some books to their relatives in Taiyuan and buried their inkstones at their rural villa, hoping that they would someday return and retrieve this treasured family property.[67] They packed two carts of selected

64. Yuan Haowen, "Zhaozhou xue ji" 趙州學記, *QJ*, 32.673.
65. *JS*, 51.1139–40.
66. Wu Songdi, *Zhongguo renkou shi*, 383.
67. Yuan Haowen, "Guwu pu" 故物譜, *QJ*, 39.823.

materials to go south with them, including a thousand books, manuscripts hand-copied by their ancestors, and a hundred paintings.

Not every literati family chose to flee south. Instead, some families, like that of Zhou Xianchen (mentioned at the beginning of this book), remained in their locales. Many shifted from maintaining a literati identity to engaging in military service. Even within a single family, individual choices could differ. Zhou Xianchen's elder brother, Zhou Dingchen, who was a friend of Yuan Haowen, chose a different path than the one his brother took. According to Zhou Dingchen's funeral biography, written by Yuan Haowen, the two men met in Kaifeng during the summer of 1214 when both took the departmental examinations. While Yuan Haowen failed, Dingchen passed the *jinshi* examinations and received an appointment as vice magistrate of Wutai county, Shanxi. In 1216, when Mongol troops under the leadership of Mukhali launched the attack on northern Shanxi, Xianchen traveled to Yangqu county next to Dingxiang county, where Dingchen was serving as the magistrate, to consult with his elder brother about what he should do in the face of the upcoming calamity. Dingchen told his younger brother to do whatever was necessary to protect their family and fellow villagers in Dingxiang, but Dingchen, as a loyal Jin official, had decided to die at his post with his wife and children. The two brothers did what they had chosen: one surrendered to the Mongols and successfully elevated their natal family to Hereditary Vassal status, and the other died for the old regime and preserved his own moral integrity as a loyal Confucian official.[68]

Yuan Haowen's Harsh New Life as a Farmer in Henan

After Yuan Haowen and his family finally arrived in Henan in the summer of 1216, he found many literati gathering there, including two old friends—Liu Angxiao 劉昂霄 from Lingchuan county and Zhao Yuan 趙元 from Dingxiang county. Yuan Haowen had been friends with Zhao since childhood and had met Liu ten years earlier, when they took the

---

68. Yuan Haowen, "Yangqu ling Zhoujun mubiao" 陽曲令周君墓表, *QJ*, 22.497–98.

prefectural examinations in Taiyuan.[69] With the help of Liu and Zhao, Yuan temporarily settled in Sanxiang county (now Yiyang county, in Henan province) and quickly joined local literati communities. In one instance, Yuan met a scholar, Xin Yuan 辛愿, who led the life of a poor peasant after being bullied by local clerks.[70] While living in Sanxiang county, Yuan, Liu, Zhao, and Xin occasionally visited local temples, composed and exchanged poems, and met new people, such as the Chan Buddhist Master Ying 英禪師, a monk-poet from Baoying Monastery in Luoxi. Master Ying was originally an examination candidate in Liaodong and had moved to Henan in 1213.[71] Association with other scholars meant the continuation of a literati life that these men had all once enjoyed. As Zhao explained in a poem for Yuan, "Catching a glimpse of associated friends makes any place one's hometown."[72]

Yet their lives were no longer the same, and tremendous losses had accompanied their migration. Many northern scholars who moved to Henan after 1214 lost all their property and were plunged into poverty. Yuan Haowen described his situation: "In this year [1217] I temporarily stayed in Sanxiang county. In the tenth month the northern army conquered the Tong Pass, and we took refuge at Mount Nüji in Santan. When we went down the mountain, we lost almost everything in the flames of war."[73] He was unable to keep most of his books, paintings, inkstones, and fine artifacts. The tangible loss of property accompanied the intangible loss of a formal system of social support. When Yuan's teacher Hao Tianting moved to Henan with his wife and children, they lost substantial support from their kinship networks—including material support, job opportunities, and social prestige. No one from the outside helped them. Hao lived in poverty and eventually died of illness.[74]

With their circumstances so dramatically changed in Henan, many literati families like the Yuans had to earn a living.[75] The duty of supporting

69. Yuan Haowen, "Yuxuan jushi Zhao Yuan" 愚軒居士趙元, *QJ*, 41.878–79.
70. Yuan Haowen, "Xinan shilao Xin Yuan," *QJ*, 41.956–57.
71. Yuan Haowen, "*Mu'an shiji* xu" 木庵詩集序, *QJ*, 37.773.
72. Zhao Yuan, "Ji Yuzhi ershou" 寄裕之二首, *QJ*, 54.1275.
73. Yuan Haowen, "Guwu pu," *QJ*, 39.823.
74. Yuan Haowen, "Hao xiansheng muming," *QJ*, 23.518.
75. When the Yuans first arrived in Henan, to earn some income, Yuan Haowen's uncle Yuan Sheng, who used to support himself by farming, applied for a government

the family now fell to Yuan Haowen, who had his mother, wife, and three young daughters to feed. His first daughter, Yuan Zhen, had been born in 1209; the third daughter, Axiu 阿秀, was born in 1219; and the second, Yuan Yan, was born sometime in between. In 1218, for the sake of security, Yuan Haowen moved his home to Dengfeng, a mountainous and isolated county in front of Mount Song—the Central Sacred Peak. To solve the urgent problem of food supplies, Yuan turned to farming. According to him, members of other formerly well-known official families did the same after moving to Henan.[76]

Agricultural life was very difficult for men like Yuan Haowen, who had so little experience. As his friend Zhao Yuan, who also had to live as a farmer, once told him, "In terms of working the land, old peasants are my true teachers."[77] Both men acquired agricultural knowledge from experienced peasants. After a year in Dengfeng, Yuan realized that it was not an ideal place for farming. Long-lasting drought followed by damaging rain destroyed much of the crop, and the harvest in the fall was not enough to feed his whole family.[78] Yuan decided to find better land elsewhere.

In the winter of 1218, shivering in an unlined garment in a cold northerly wind, Yuan Haowen traveled alone to neighboring areas, and in 1219 he ultimately found land in Kunyang (an ancient name for what was then Ye county (now Yexian county in Henan). He was very satisfied with the land in Kunyang, stating that "the lower land was good for either sorghum or rice. I have dug a long ditch to plant water chestnuts and learned how to plant red ginger from an experienced vegetable grower."[79] He built a hut near this parcel of land at Kunyang to live in while growing crops and left his household in Dengfeng. As a result, he had to travel frequently between Dengfeng and Kunyang, 150 kilometers away.

---

position under the shadow privilege of his brother Yuan Ge. Yet Yuan Sheng died of disease soon after receiving an appointment. See Yuan Haowen, "Chengfeng Henan Yuangong muming," *QJ*, 25.539.

76.   Yuan Haowen, "Gaomen guan" 高門關, *QJ*, 4.78.

77.   Zhao Yuan, "Shuhuai ji Yuan di Yuzhi yun sishou" 書懷寄元弟裕之韻四首, *QJ*, 54.1274.

78.   Yuan Haowen, "Ji Zhao Yizhi" 寄趙宜之, *QJ*, 5.101.

79.   Yuan Haowen, "Xuehou zhao linshe Wang Zan Zixiang yin" 雪後招鄰舍王贊子襄飲, *QJ*, 3.65–66.

In a new place, it was naturally easier for Yuan Haowen to associate with his peers first and only later with unfamiliar local peasants. A hospitable neighbor who was a reclusive scholar and also liked to compose poems apparently liked Yuan's company; he even tried to convince Yuan to move his family to Kunyang. Yuan used the excuse that his horse was sick to explain his decision not to move. Perhaps it was too risky to exhaust all the family savings building a new home there, because he did not own the land. Or he might simply not have been able to afford a second move. His experience of associating with a landlord several years later confirmed that he had no money to buy land or hire laborers. As he explains in the poem "Sighing for Wheat,"

借地乞麥種	I rented a piece of land and borrowed wheat seeds;
徼倖今年秋	I expected a good fortune this fall.
乞種尚云可	I could tolerate begging for seeds;
無丁復無牛	But I have neither strong laborers nor oxen.
田主好事人	The landlord is a warmhearted man who likes to help others;
百色副所求	He gave me anything I asked for.[80]

Yuan Haowen's dependence on the landlord suggests a new type of literati-peasant connection formed by the literati's engagement in farming, which demanded a lot of time and energy. This new connection demonstrates a dramatic decrease both in the available income that had provided the material foundation for literati life and in the leisure time that permitted literati to concentrate on studying and associating with peers.

Meanwhile, associating with peasants gave literati new awareness of social problems and perspectives on social customs that differed from what they had been used to learning from texts. Daily life as farmers allowed literati to share peasant anxieties that were new to them, such as concern about the weather. In the poem that follows, Yuan Haowen complained of his misfortune in farming because of a severe drought, using the metaphor of the Drought Mother:

| 四月草不青 | The shoots were not green in April; |
| 吾種良漫投 | My seeds have been sown in vain. |

80.   Yuan Haowen, "Mai tan" 麥歎, *QJ*, 1.18.

田間一太息	I stood in the fields and sighed;
此歲何時周	When could I ever have a harvest this year?
向見田父言	I once heard from farmers;
此田本良疇	This land had been fertile.
三歲廢不治	It has not been cultivated for three years;
種則當備收	The gain should be doubled once it has been farmed.
如何落吾手	How could it happen that in my hands,
羊年變雞猴	The Year of the Sheep became the Year of the Chicken or of the Monkey?
身自是旱母	I myself [might] be the Drought Mother;
呫呫將誰尤	I cannot blame anyone else.[81]

The metaphor of the Drought Mother likely came from a story Yuan heard from local peasants and later recorded in *The Record of the Listener Continued*. According to Yuan, a severe drought occurred in the Luoyang area during 1213. In Dengfeng local people circulated a rumor of a demon that brought the drought. Since they believed that the drought demon would often accompany fire, when a peasant's house caught fire one evening, local people instructed teenagers to beat the fire with big sticks to drive off the demon.[82]

The personal experience of farming allowed men like Yuan Haowen to truly understand the hardship of peasants. He wrote a poem describing his joy while standing in the rain in Ye county, where he was cultivating his Kunyang land—rain that he happily attributed to a dragon deity.[83] When he later served as a magistrate of Neixiang county in Henan, Yuan Haowen accepted the locals' request to pray for rain from a dragon deity when a drought had lasted more than three months. The peasants built a new temple for the dragon deity to thank it for bringing rain. In the record Yuan wrote of the event, instead of describing peasants' behavior as unorthodox and labeling their deities without government sanction as licentious, he expressed a deep understanding of the significance of rain and dragon worship for peasants.[84]

81.   Ibid., 1.18–19.

82.   Yuan Haowen, "Gaocheng hanba" 告成旱魃, *Q J*, 48.1132.

83.   Yuan Haowen, "Ye xian yuzhong" 葉縣雨中, *Q J*, 8.168.

84.   Yuan Haowen, "Changqing quan xinmiao ji" 長慶泉新廟記, *Q J*, 32.679. On the licentious cults, see Hansen, *Changing Gods in Medieval China*, 84–95.

Peasant culture and village customs became new topics of conversation among the late Jin literati who had gathered in Henan. *The Record of the Listener Continued* by Yuan Haowen includes many stories about such topics from Henan. Three anecdotes from the same Hantou village in the south of Pingyu county describe peasant beliefs in taboos, the afterlife, and reincarnation, as well as villagers' lawsuit practices.[85] Yuan heard some stories in person and some from local officials and literati.

More importantly, their agricultural experiences reflected the literati's declining political and socioeconomic status. For example, the family of Yuan Haowen's friend Zhao Yuan fell down the social ladder from scholar-officials to impoverished peasants. Zhao depicts his rural life as a farmer in the poem "Learning to Sow Grain":

不堪炊煮一箱書	I have a box of books, which are not enough for fuel to cook a meal;
十口東西若可糊	How can I feed ten mouths?
食祿已慚中隱吏	The salary I received was small enough to shame retired clerks;
墾山聊作下農夫	I reclaimed mountain lands and now work as a lowly peasant.
藁遺場圃無多積	Coming away from the threshing ground, I accumulated little;
子入官倉困遠輸	And I had trouble delivering the crop seeds to a remote official granary.
近日愚軒睡眠少	Recently I have had little sleep,
打門時復有追胥	Because clerks coming to collect taxes have repeatedly knocked at my door.[86]

Zhao had served as a vice magistrate before his eyesight deteriorated and he had to retire from the post. His comment about his salary suggests the insufficient wages for low-ranking Jin scholar-officials and their low political status: they ranked below the clerks who were usurping the power of civil officials. Indeed, after 1214 clerks at both the local and central levels gained considerable power and were often promoted faster than

---

85.　Yuan Haowen, "Zhengsou fan tujin" 鄭叟犯土禁, "Zhangtong ruming" 張童入冥, "Fan Yuanzhi jue niusong" 范元質決牛訟, *QJ*, 48.1122–23 and 1165.

86.　Zhao Yuan, "Xue jia" 學稼, *Zhongzhou ji*, 5.268.

holders of the *jinshi* degree.[87] In the eyes of local clerks, Zhao was no different from other peasants after he withdrew from the government and started cultivating land.

The declining social and economic position of the Zhao family affected the choice of occupation for the next generation. Zhao told Yuan Haowen that "I have a son who has abandoned reading books and diligently cultivates land in the mountains."[88] When Yuan later mentioned Zhao Yu 趙顒—the son of Zhao Yuan—in Zhao Yuan's biography, instead of discussing Zhao Yu's poems or scholarly achievements, he said only that Zhao Yu had integrity as a recluse, hinting at Zhao Yu's lack of literati education.

Yuan Haowen's generation of literati now struggled not only to adjust themselves to a harsh new life in Henan but also to maintain their literati identity. They did not choose to farm; they had no other option. The famous poet Tao Qian 陶潛 (365–427; more commonly known as Tao Yuanming 陶淵明) claimed to have withdrawn from the world to lead a peaceful hermit life as a farmer, and Chinese literati often invoked Tao's model and presented farming and reading (*gengdu* 耕讀) as an ideal lifestyle.[89] However, in a poem he sent to his friend Han Junxi in Qinzhou subprecture in Shanxi province, for Han's hall of Farming and Reading, Yuan Haowen rejected Tao's model:

讀書與躬耕	Reading books and farming land in person,
兀兀送殘年	One quietly passes the last days of life.
淵明不可作	Yuanming could not be imitated;
尚友乃爲賢	Yet it is wise to associate with virtuous friends.
田家豈不苦	Aren't farmers suffering—
歲功聊可觀	A year's harvest is so little?
讀書有何味	What is the meaning of reading books?
有味不得言	The meaning is hard to say.[90]

87. Tillman, "An Overview of Chin History and Institutions," 37.
88. Zhao Yuan, "Shu huai ji Yuan di Yuzhi yun sishou," *QJ*, 54.1274.
89. For a late Ming example, see Spence, *Return to Dragon Mountain*, 156–57 and 224–27.
90. Yuan Haowen, "Ji ti Qinzhou Han Junxi gengdu xuan" 寄題沁州韓君錫耕讀軒, *QJ*, 2.56–57.

From his own experience as a poor farmer, Yuan Haowen knew all too well that being a farmer meant having not an idyllic time but a hard, exhausting, and anxious daily life. Although he asked a rhetorical question about the meaning of reading, for Yuan and his peers, reading was a symbol of their literati identity, something that differentiated them from ordinary farmers.

Yuan Haowen's Political Career and the Collapse of the Jin State

As the Jin government continued to recruit Chinese officials through the civil service examinations, many literati in areas south of the Yellow River, like Yuan Haowen, continued to try to find positions in the government. After he moved to Henan, in addition to associating with local literati friends, Yuan tried to make his name known in the literati circles of the capital, particularly among established scholar-officials like Zhao Bingwen 趙秉文 (1159–1232), the leader of the Jin intellectual world at the time.[91] Yuan visited Zhao to present him with two poems in 1217. After Zhao praised Yuan's poems highly and introduced him to other established scholar-officials, such as Yang Yunyi 楊雲翼 (1170–1228), Yuan—now nicknamed Gifted Scholar Yuan (Yuan *caizi* 元才子)—immediately gained fame in the literati world of Kaifeng. Yuan Haowen later regarded Zhao and Yang as his intellectual and political role models. When Zhao was the chief examiner in 1221, Yuan finally passed the civil service examinations, after six failed attempts in the preceding sixteen years, and gained the highest degree of *jinshi* at the age of thirty-two. But he was accused by others of having improper ties to examiners like Zhao, Yang, Lei Yuan 雷淵 (1186–1231), and Li Xianneng 李獻能 (1192–1232)—scholar-officials with whom Yuan had indeed associated frequently.[92] Behind this incident was a heated factional conflict at the Jin court between scholar-officials with *jinshi* degrees and officials who had

91.   Bol, "Chao Ping-wen" and "Seeking Common Ground," 502–12.
92.   Yuan Haowen, "Zhao Xianxian zhenzan" 趙閑閑眞贊, *QJ*, 38.798.

been promoted from positions as clerks.[93] Outraged by the accusations, Yuan refused to accept a government appointment and returned to Deng-feng county to farm.

In the following three years, while continuing to farm his Kunyang land to support his family, Yuan Haowen devoted himself to poetry and associating with his literati peers, especially in their efforts to search for enduring values in the Chinese cultural tradition and to enable Jin lite-rati to claim authority over that tradition. Taking the Northern Song literati Su Shi 蘇軾 (1037–1101) as a model for literati learning, these late Jin literati, under the leadership of Zhao Bingwen, emphasized literary composition—in particular, writing poetry—as a key method of master-ing the cultural tradition.[94] Fully committed to this idea, Yuan wrote many fine poems during his frequent meetings with old and new literati friends. His poems circulated widely among contemporary literati, some via letters and others by word of mouth. According to Hao Jing, who studied with Yuan and later wrote his teacher's funeral biography, Yuan's poetry became so popular in these years that everyone was reciting lines of his poems in villages and on the road. "It was almost like Su Shi and Huang Tingjian had been reborn!" Hao commented, invoking the mem-ory of two famous eleventh-century poets.[95]

Yuan Haowen's literary fame brought him another chance to obtain a position in the government. The deteriorating political environment in the 1220s, however, made government service increasingly hard to endure for scholar-officials who tried to hold on to Confucian moral integrity. In 1224, after passing the special degree examinations for recruiting ex-traordinary literary talent, Yuan received his first official appointment as a junior compiler in the Historiography Academy (*Guoshi yuan* 國史院).

93. Takahashi, "Gen Yisan to tōsō."
94. Bol, "Seeking Common Ground," 495–520. In his reexamination of the late Jin intellectual movement, Qiu Yihao claims that Bol mistakenly believed that the shared pursuit of pure literature brought the Jurchen rulers and Han literati together to see "this culture of ours" as their common ground. This is a misrepresentation of Bol's argument. But Qiu is right that the late Jin intellectual revival was the literati's response not just to the development of literati culture but to the interaction of all three teachings—Confucianism, Buddhism, and Daoism. In particular, the literati wanted to offset the increasing influence of new Daoist schools by establishing the literati's cultural identity in Confucianism and by allying with Buddhists. See Qiu Yihao, "Wudao," 87–88.
95. Hao Jing, "Yishan xiansheng muming," *QJ*, 53.1263.

Yet in the sixth month of the next year, Yuan declined the position and returned to Dengfeng again. In a poem he composed upon his departure from the capital, Yuan explained that he could neither bear a crowded urban life nor endure the stress of a political career.[96] What caused his stress was most likely corrupt and complicated court politics. The last Jin emperor, Aizong (r. 1224–34), was a weak and indecisive ruler who constantly yielded to the poor advice of sycophants and recalcitrant Jurchen military officials. Meanwhile, despite the increasing menace from the Mongols, the Jin court was caught in a bitter, self-perpetuating power struggle between military officials and other Jurchen and Chinese scholar-officials.[97] In Yuan's eyes, the political world was decaying, but even more devastating was the decline of Confucian teaching. In a poem he wrote in 1226 Yuan lamented that "the Sacred Teaching had difficulty achieving success."[98]

After witnessing the degeneration of court politics and Confucian teaching, from 1226 to 1228 Yuan Haowen served three terms in local government as a magistrate and one as a prefectural secretary. He now found himself watching a local society also on the verge of collapse yet unable to do anything about it. The scenes that Yuan saw were indeed terrible: tyrannical officials and clerks, heavy taxation and requisitions of extra military supplies, and frequent local riots all drove peasants to despair. Other than accepting local peasants' request to pray for rain to the dragon deity, as mentioned above, Yuan was unable to help peasants reduce their suffering. In a 1227 poem recounting a conversation he had had with local peasants, Yuan sadly expressed his limited power. As he explained, he could forbid clerks to harass ordinary people, but he could do nothing to relieve the burden of military taxes. He could only tell the peasants not to evade them, for otherwise they could suffer whippings or even execution.[99] He knew, however, that it was impossible for peasants who had already been devastated by increasing land taxes and the duty of labor services to offer more grain to support the armies. Where could Yuan raise enough grain to fulfill his county's tax quota? Sitting in a

96. Yuan Haowen, "Chujing" 出京, *QJ*, 1.9.
97. Chan, "From Tribal Chieftain to Sinitic Emperor," 128–31.
98. Yuan Haowen, "Yinjiu wushou" 飲酒五首, *QJ*, 1.15–16.
99. Yuan Haowen, "Su Jutan" 宿菊潭, *QJ*, 1.23.

studio alone on a quiet night, anxious about his inability to either raise the taxes needed or help ordinary people, Yuan once again thought of retiring.[100]

The political and social environments grew worse and worse for Jin literati. In 1228, upon his mother's death, Yuan Haowen left his position as magistrate and declined an appointment offered by a Jurchen military strongman. Later he agreed to serve in that strongman's office, but soon left. Yuan's repeated withdrawals from office indicated that he shared the feelings of many contemporary scholar-officials who had been deeply disappointed by the political world and were frustrated by their powerlessness to alter the situation. Yuan argued that the custom of favoring personal profit had become so strong that any effort to change it was doomed. Literati could do nothing but reject such customs first and then influence others by behaving like gentlemen.[101] In reality, literati could not even save their own lives in a world full of extreme violence. As warfare continued, military strongmen monopolized power both at court and in regional governments. Some literati found jobs in the offices of regional strongmen, who often had the power of life and death over their subordinates. Yuan's friend Li Fen recommended himself to the powerful general Wu Xian and served as an assistant in Wu's branch secretariat until the general had him murdured.[102]

In 1231, Yuan Haowen moved to Kaifeng for a new position in the central government. This was, unfortunately, the beginning of even greater tragedy in his personal life. Mongol troops attacked Kaifeng in April 1231, but the solid fortifications of the city prevented it from being conquered immediately. The Mongol troops reacted by launching a yearlong siege, which eventually caused the capital, and the Jin state as a whole, to collapse irreversibly. By the end of that year, the situation inside Kaifeng had grown desperate. On March 24, 1232, Yuan's third daughter, Axiu, died of sickness at the age of fourteen, and Yuan himself became very ill.[103] In June and July, a devastating epidemic swept the city, claiming the lives of more than 900,000 residents.[104] As food supplies dwindled, rice prices

---

100. Yuan Haowen, "Neixiang xianzhai shushi" 內鄉縣齋書事, *QJ*, 8.173.
101. Yuan Haowen, "Fengzhi Zhaojun mujieming" 奉直趙君墓碣銘, *QJ*, 22.500.
102. Yuan Haowen, "Li Jiangyi Fen" 李講議汾, *QJ*, 41.959.
103. Yuan Haowen, "Xiaonü Axiu muming" 孝女阿秀墓銘, *QJ*, 25.546.
104. *JS*, 17.387.

skyrocketed to two taels of silver per liter, plunging the people into an abyss of misery. Yuan saw men sell their wives for just one meal.[105] In the worst cases, according to an eyewitness, the starving stripped the dead of their flesh, ate children, and killed people who walked alone at night and then ate them.[106]

Conditions in Kaifeng deteriorated even further in the spring of 1233 and led to the fall of the capital in early summer. In January, Emperor Aizong fled the capital to Caizhou (Runan county, in Henan), where he ended his own life a year later.[107] On March 3 Cui Li 崔立, one of four generals in charge of defending Kaifeng, rebelled. He slaughtered the leading civilian ministers, enthroned a puppet prince regent, and then surrendered to the Mongols. Cui and his followers killed any official at court who disobeyed them.[108] Tragically for Yuan Haowen, his controversial involvement in erecting a notorious stele for Cui endangered his reputation among his peers.[109] A few days after the Mongols took over the city, they sent former Jin officials—including Yuan—to Liaocheng county in Shandong in the custody of Mongol troops and their Chinese allies.

On June 1, 1233, two days after Kaifeng fell, Yuan Haowen sent a letter to Yelü Chucai 耶律楚材 (1189–1243), the Mongol's secretariat director, who was in charge of administrative affairs in the conquered part of north China. In the letter, Yuan asked Yelü to protect northern Chinese literati. He listed fifty-four Jin literati, calling them "the best people in the empire," who could be helpful to the new government but were still in danger.[110] The purpose of Yuan's letter has been debated: Did he use it to introduce himself to the Mongol authorities, or was he trying to protect traditional Chinese culture? Did his behavior reflect a lack of personal integrity?[111] The letter's effect was minimal, in any case: only a few

---

105. Yuan Haowen, "Nie xiaonü muming" 聶孝女墓銘, *QJ*, 25.545.

106. Liu Qi, *Guiqian zhi*, 11.126.

107. *JS*, 18.395–403.

108. Yuan Haowen, "Nie Yuanji muzhiming," *QJ*, 21.491.

109. Yang Qingchen, "Yiwei zhijian."

110. Yuan Haowen, "Ji Zhongshu Yelü gong shu" 寄中書耶律公書, *QJ*, 39.804–5.

111. For the scholarly debate about Yuan's intentions, see Yao Congwu, "Yuan Haowen duiyu baoquan zhongyuan"; Han Zhiyuan, "Yuan Haowen zai Jin Yuan."

of the listed scholars were hired.[112] All fifty-four men had gathered in Henan after 1214 and fled to areas north of the Yellow River in the early 1230s, before the Mongols besieged Kaifeng. Yuan's list of their names and native places indicates his broad circle of associates. Among those fifty-four scholars, nineteen were natives of Shanxi. Yet none of Yuan's close friends appeared on the list, because they had all died.

The violent and chaotic final four years of the Jin state, 1231–1234, saw the nearly complete extinction of the entire literati class. As Yuan Haowen later lamented, "Most descendants of scholars with illuminating virtues and marvelous fame were dead, and most families that had produced high-ranking officials had gone. Less than one-tenth of them survived. Among those still alive, countless became homeless, fell into slavery, and could not preserve themselves from cold and hunger."[113] In addition to the decimation of the northern literati and the disappearance of literati families, most Confucian schools were abandoned, and more importantly, the civil service examinations were suspended. As a result, all the institutional mechanisms that had sustained the degree-holder society in north China disintegrated.

The lives of the small number of literati survivors, such as the fifty-four scholars on Yuan Haowen's list and Yuan himself, now largely relied on the mercy of the Mongol rulers and the new governing elites. Yuan counted on Yelü Chucai to help the fifty-four scholars. But it was a group of non-literati warlords—the Han Chinese Hereditary Vassals—that protected Yuan for the rest of his life. Many other Jin literati found refuge in the religious communities of Quanzhen Daoism. Military strongmen and Quanzhen Daoists became the new political and social elites among the northern Chinese population under Mongol rule. Quanzhen Daoists, who acted in cooperation with the Mongol rulers and Mongol-appointed governors and local officials, now made a spectacular entrance onto the historical stage and played unprecedented leading roles in reorganizing and integrating the war-torn society in north China after 1234.

112.	De Rachewiltz, "Ye-lü Chu-ts'ai," 205.

113.	Yuan Haowen, "Longshan zhaoshi xinying zhi bei" 龍山趙氏新塋之碑, *QJ*, 30.627.

CHAPTER 2

The Quanzhen Daoist Order and Postwar Social Reconstruction, 1234–1281

Fighting finally ended after the Mongols completed their seizure of north China in 1234. The following spring Yuan Haowen moved north to Shandong province at the invitation of Zhao Tianxi 趙天錫, who had been appointed governor of Guanshi county by the new Mongol state. Zhao asked Yuan to compose a brief history of a Quanzhen Daoist abbey, which the governor had renovated on behalf of his aged mother. Throughout north China the Quanzhen Daoist order drew many different social groups, in addition to former Jin literati, together to play leading roles in rebuilding the shattered local society after the Jin-Mongol war. These groups ranged from the Mongols and local governors in the upper classes to peasants and craftsmen in the lower classes. Most remarkably, a large number of women—like Zhao's mother, who studied Quanzhen Daoist teachings with a male master—also participated in the new Quanzhen order that emerged rapidly to dominate the social space between state and family after 1234. Yuan Haowen could not help wondering why Quanzhen Daoism appealed to so many different people at the time. He attempted to account for the success of the movement in this inscription:

> Sometime after the Zhenyuan [1153–55] and Zhenglong [1156–60] periods the Quanzhen School came into being. Wang Zhongfu [Wang Zhe 王喆, 1112–70], a native of Xianyang [in Shaanxi province], founded the school,

and others including Tan, Ma, Qiu, and Liu followed him.[1] Their teachings originate in the learning of the deep and quiet yet are free from the deluded Daoist priests' rituals of purification and the seeking of fortune. They borrow from Chan Buddhist practices of meditation yet avoid the mortification of the Dhūta [Toutuo 頭陀, "Renunciant"].[2] The Quanzhen devotees farm land and dig wells. They support themselves and give their surplus to others. Their lives appear to be easy compared with those in the chaotic world. As a result, lazy and powerless people opt to follow them.

South to the Huai region, north to the desert, west to Shaanxi, and east to the sea, from mountains to cities, Quanzhen buildings are everywhere. Their communities number from ten to one hundred, they pass their teachings down one on one, and their power is unstoppable.

Fearing rebellions like the Five Pecks of Rice led by Zhang Jue [d. 184], the authorities prohibited the school. Yet, at the same time, some generals and ministers supported the Quanzhen School. As a result, it survived and became even more prosperous after a temporary decline.

Now, fifty to seventy years later, it seems as though the school cannot be challenged. After the disorder of the Zhenyou period [1213–16], all discipline and civil order have been gone. Ordinary people have nothing to hold on to. The only teaching that has offered them guidance is the Quanzhen School. Today one-fifth of the Chinese in the north have succumbed to the Quanzhen teaching.[3]

Thus Yuan Haowen portrays the Quanzhen teaching as a new religion that particularly appealed to powerless people because of its religious simplicity, economic self-reliance, and charitable practices. His account pinpoints the profound social depression that made possible the deep penetration of the Daoist order into Chinese society in the first half of the thirteenth century. When neither rulers nor kinship organizations offered protection from violence and misery, only the Quanzhen Daoists

---

1. "Tan, Ma, Qiu, and Liu" refer to Wang Zhe's four major disciples: Tan Chuduan 譚處端 (1122–85), Ma Yu 馬鈺 (also known as Ma Danyang 馬丹陽; 1122–83), Qiu Chuji 丘處機 (1148–1227), and Liu Chuxuan 劉處玄 (1146–1203).

2. For the relationship between the Quanzhen Daoists and the Buddhist movement of Dhūta, see Marsone, "Daoism under the Jurchen Jin Dynasty," 1138–40.

3. Yuan Haowen, "Ziwei guan ji" 紫微觀記, *QJ*, 35.740–41.

were able to provide the necessary social services.[4] It was unusual, yet reasonable given the circumstances, for a scholar like Yuan to admit that Quanzhen Daoism had replaced Confucianism as the provider of moral and cultural authority for his contemporaries. But the Quanzhen Daoist order offered more than this and showed extraordinary institutional strength and innovation as an organized religion.

The Strength and Innovation of the Quanzhen Daoist Order

The Quanzhen Daoist order provided syncretic teachings and a new social lifestyle that appealed to numerous northerners. The order's founder, Wang Zhe (an unsuccessful degree candidate) urged his followers to read the Confucian text *The Classic of Filial Piety* (*Xiaojing* 孝經) and the Buddhist text *The Heart Sutra* (*Xinjing* 心經), in addition to the Daoist *Classic of the Way and Integrity* (*Daodejing* 道德經). In the late 1160s, when Wang established multiple societies in Shandong to organize his followers, he labeled these societies with the exact term of "three teachings" (*sanjiao* 三教), emphasizing that his teaching reconciled Daoism, Buddhism, and Confucianism. Wang instructed his disciples to pursue an austere lifestyle, including celibacy, vegetarianism, and meditation, to gain health, longevity, and inner peace, with the ultimate goal of gaining immortality. The Seven Perfected (*qizhen* 七眞)—seven well-known disciples of Wang Zhe, particularly Qiu Chuji—further emphasized the importance of establishing a monastic order.[5] Borrowing from Buddhism, Quanzhen masters encouraged their followers to establish as many Quanzhen institutions as possible to help devotees survive the chaos of their times.

---

4. Yuan's account of the popularity of the Quanzhen teaching was echoed in many other inscriptions composed by literati or scholar-officials in the thirteenth century. See, for example, "Tongxuan guan ji" 通玄觀記 (composed by an early Yuan official named Song Dao 宋道), *QSXB*, 132–33.

5. For major studies of Wang Zhe and the Seven Perfected, see Hachiya, *Kindai Dōkyō no kenkyū*, and *Kin Gen jidai no Dōkyō*. Marsone has suggested that the tradition of the Seven Perfected was constructed by Wang Chuyi 王處一 (1142–1217), one of the Seven Perfected ("Accounts of the Foundation of the Quanzhen Movement," 96).

This was particularly important given that about one-third of the northern Chinese population had become impoverished refugees during the Jin-Mongol war.[6]

More remarkably, the Quanzhen Daoist order bridged the traditional gender gap and attracted a large number of women both as clergy and as sponsors. The Quanzhen communities accepted female disciples from the very beginning. The Seven Perfected included one woman, Sun Bu'er 孫不二 (1119–82), who had been married to Ma Yu. The couple separated when they became Wang's disciples, and Sun eventually became a role model for all Quanzhen nuns.[7] Because Confucian teachings offered little guidance for girls and widows whose families could no longer support them, countless homeless women who lost their husbands or natal families in the disorder found a haven in Quanzhen communities. Some Quanzhen institutions were built for women—in particular, for widows and orphaned girls. And women in the Quanzhen order could freely associate with members of the opposite sex.

In addition to its doctrinal and social appeal, the rapid institutional development of Quanzhen Daoism owed much to Mongol imperial patronage. Before the Mongol invasion, Quanzhen Daoism had received varying degrees of imperial support from the Jin court, but it was closely watched by the Jin government and lacked a strong organization. Early Quanzhen masters attracted followers through the use of ascetic practices. During the Jin-Mongol war, Qiu Chuji, as a religious leader, successfully suppressed local revolts in Shandong and engaged in relief work, which won him great popularity among local people. His ability to mobilize mass support brought the Quanzhen Daoist communities into the international spotlight. In 1219 the rulers of competing states—the Jin, the Southern Song, and the Mongols—all invited Qiu Chuji to their courts as they fought to gain control of the Shandong region.[8] After weighing his political options, Qiu Chuji chose the Mongols. He and eighteen disciples traveled across the steppes to meet Chinggis Khan in the mountains

6. Chen Gaohua, "Yuandai de liumin wenti."
7. For the most comprehensive study of Sun Bu'er, see Komjathy, "Sun Buer."
8. The Jurchen Emperor Xuanzong (r. 1213–23) and the Southern Song Emperor Ningzong (r. 1195–1224) summoned Qiu Chuji in 1216 and 1219, respectively. Chinggis Khan sent his envoy to summon Qiu to his court in Central Asia in 1219.

south of the Hindu Kush, and the journey to the meeting lasted three years in 1220–22.[9]

Their trip bore handsome dividends: Chinggis issued two edicts recognizing Qiu Chuji as the leader of all Daoists and exempting his disciples from taxes and the duty of labor service.[10] At that time Mongol troops were taking many northern Chinese captive, and after returning to Yanjing (now Beijing), Qiu sent his disciples to distribute Daoist ordination certificates among the prisoners of war to redeem more than twenty thousand of them from Mongol custody. According to Chingghis's edicts, one only needed to be a disciple of Qiu to regain one's freedom.[11] The Quanzhen church gained the unusual right to issue ordinations, a right that had been reserved for the state since the Tang dynasty. In addition, in contrast to the situation in the Northern Song and Jin periods, when all religious communities needed to receive legitimate monastic plaques from the government, the Mongol rulers gave Quanzhen leaders the privilege of granting monastic plaques themselves.[12] This marked a turning point for Quanzhen Daoism, which was transformed from a semiautonomous ascetic religious movement into a systematically institutionalized monastic order.[13]

The anarchic and chaotic political conditions continued in the three decades after the fall of the Jin, facilitating the rapid spread of the Quanzhen order throughout north China. The Mongol empire's capital between 1234 and 1260 was Karakorum, on the Mongolian steppes, and the Mongols were preoccupied with their continuing wars of conquest. In this early stage of Mongol rule in China, the Mongol khans were happy to outsource significant administrative responsibility to local groups or organizations that they felt were competent and reliable. North China at

9. De Rachewiltz and Russell, "Ch'iu Ch'u-chi."

10. Tao-chung Yao, "Ch'iu Ch'u-chi and Chinggis Khan."

11. Yao Sui 姚燧, "Changchun gong beiming" 長春宮碑銘, in *JSL*, 671–72.

12. Granting official monastic plaques and issuing ordination certificates were two important strategies used by the Song and Jin governments to control organized religion. In the Jin dynasty, the imperial court occasionally sold Buddhist and Daoist monastic plaques to offset wartime expenditures. Early Quanzhen masters also bought monastic plaques to protect their institutions from government suppression. See Keika, "Kindai no jikan meigaku"; Tao-chung Yao, "Buddhism and Taoism under the Chin," 158–67.

13. Komjathy, *Cultivating Perfection*, 33–62.

the time was in practice under the decentralized rule of many Chinese Hereditary Vassals who pledged allegiance to the Mongols' administrative agency, headquartered in Yanjing, but who had considerable autonomy in their own domains. Almost all the powerful Hereditary Vassals sought the help of Quanzhen masters for their governance of territories.

For instance, Hereditary Vassals throughout Shanxi competed with each other to invite Qiu's disciple, the acting Quanzhen Patriarch Yin Zhiping 尹志平 (1169–1251), to perform offering rituals (*jiao* 醮) to soothe the souls of local residents who had died in warfare and to stabilize postwar society in the regions they governed. The performance of offering rituals became a typical observance that connected local governors and Quanzhen masters.[14] In 1235 and 1237 Yin met with several Shanxi governors, who in return granted Yin a large number of local abbeys and convents.[15] As we will see, the Quanzhen order, authorized by the Mongol state and recognized by regional Hereditary Vassals, assumed many governmental functions, including organizing relief work and building infrastructure.

The social and political environments in the thirteenth century were favorable to Quanzhen Daoism. In addition, as Vincent Goossaert has pointed out, the religious order was unprecedented in several ways. First, while the majority of earlier religious institutions in north China had been controlled by lay organizations such as local families and territorial temple associations that had limited access to the clergy, the Quanzhen Daoist institutions were thoroughly controlled by the clergy. Second, all other new religious movements in north China that also received Mongol patronage managed to build monastic networks over only a few counties or prefectures, whereas the Quanzhen order proved able to implant itself all over north China, with several thousand abbeys and convents.[16] Third, the Quanzhen Daoists invented several identity-building mechanisms—

14. By the late twelfth century, the offering rituals had become regarded as an efficacious way of exorcising troublesome ghosts and restoring the order of the human world. See S. Huang, "Summoning the Gods."

15. Fujishima, "Zenshinkyō no tenkai."

16. The other new religious movements included the Teaching of the Great Unity (*Taiyi jiao* 太一教) and the True Great Way (*Zhenda dao* 真大道). For studies of these movements, see Chen Yuan, *Nansong chu hebei xindaojiao kao*; Chen Zhichao, "Jin Yuan Zhendadao."

such as the lore of ascetic life, a symbolic name system, and practices of clerical travel and assemblies—to tie monks and nuns together and to induce lay people to recognize the order.[17]

Moreover, the Quanzhen monastic order was tightly interrelated with the Quanzhen Daoist lineages (*zongmen* 宗門 or *zongpai* 宗派), which identified themselves through their discipleship with the Seven Perfected. Quanzhen Daoists built dense cross-regional monastic networks—each surrounding the main monastery of a specific religious lineage, where the ancestral tablet of the lineage's founder was honored. Quanzhen Daoists often carved detailed lists of temples and monasteries belonging to this lineage on the reverse side of steles commemorating their founder or the construction of the main monastery; one extant list includes 242 such Quanzhen establishments.[18] All these lineage-based Quanzhen institutions were integrated within an organized church under the centralized leadership of the Quanzhen patriarch (*Quanzhen jiaozhu* 全真教主) at the Palace of Everlasting Spring (*Changchun gong* 長春宮), in Yanjing. The Mongol ruler recognized and officially appointed the Quanzhen patriarch as the supreme head of the Quanzhen church.[19]

The size of the Quanzhen population also attested to the remarkable institutional strength of the Quanzhen order. Yuan Haowen's estimate that one-fifth of the northern population became Quanzhen followers was no exaggeration. Goossaert estimates that under Mongol rule in the Yuan dynasty more than twenty thousand northerners registered as Quanzhen Daoists.[20] However, a contemporary scholar reported in 1286 that male and female Daoists numbered 300,000, which seems likely since a large number of Quanzhen Daoists did not receive official ordination.[21] And this number of Daoists is much higher than in any other dynasty.[22]

---

17. Goossaert, "The Invention of an Order."

18. Ibid., 115–16.

19. For the Quanzhen patriarch system and the inheritance of fourteen Quanzhen patriarchs under Mongol rule, see Zhang Guangbao, *Jin Yuan Quanzhenjiao shi*, 112–72.

20. Goossaert, "The Invention of an Order," 112.

21. Hu Zhiyu 胡祗遹, "Jizhen guan bei" 集真觀碑, in *JSL*, 328–32.

22. On the demography of Daoist populations in Chinese history, see Bai Wengu, "Lidai sengdao renshu kaolun," 1–6.

Equipped with alluring doctrine, powerful political connections, and effective centralized leadership, the Quanzhen communities used their extraordinary institutional prowess to embark on an unprecedented social mission: rebuilding the war-torn local society. We can best see the Quanzhen Daoist order's importance in social reconstruction in Shanxi after the Jin-Mongol war concluded in 1234. The residents of postwar Shanxi confronted drought, plagues of locusts, countless exposed corpses, ruined communities, the atrocities of Mongol troops, and ruthless exploitation by Mongol nobles and hereditary governors. All this brought untold suffering to people without power or resources.

During these difficult times, as this chapter will show, the new Quanzhen Daoist order organized people from different social groups to undertake novel tasks that no one had thought possible before 1234. The new tasks included recruiting former Jin literati to print a new Daoist canon and provide an alternative Quanzhen school education, encouraging Quanzhen nuns to establish convents that sheltered homeless women and children (even at the village level), and cooperating with local residents to build large-scale pilgrimage sites. These functions combined the social undertaking of postwar community building and the Quanzhen ambition of nationwide institutional expansion. The order's operations efficiently mobilized massive human and material resources and exhibited creative ways in which the Quanzhen clergy, as new social elites, consolidated their status and power under Mongol rule.

Accommodating Former Jin Literati

Literati had served as patrons for clergy—both Buddhists and Daoists—for much of China's history. In the north, however, patronage relations between literati and Daoists were reversed in the first half of the thirteenth century, when Quanzhen Daoists provided physical shelter for former Jin literati who were now destitute and homeless. A southern Shanxi scholar recorded that thousands of scholar-officials and other men from scholarly families became slaves of Mongolian soldiers after the Mongol invasion. Many of them entered the Quanzhen Daoist order to regain their freedom and become exempted from labor service and taxation.[23] More importantly, the Quanzhen Daoist order attracted literati by creating distinctive jobs for them, such as essay writing, text editing, and monastic lecturing. Scholars in the Quanzhen order also tried to resolve the tensions between Confucian and Quanzhen ideals in education and daily life.

National political unrest and social turmoil had motivated some Jin literati to join Quanzhen Daoist communities as early as in the 1210s. For instance, a friend of Yuan Haowen in Henan chose to become a Quanzhen Daoist in 1217 after suffering political persecution.[24] A second major wave of conversion occurred in the early 1230s, when the Mongols launched decisive campaigns to conquer Shaanxi and Henan, the last two regions under Jin control. Many Henan residents joined the Quanzhen order after fleeing to areas already controlled by the Mongols and their Chinese followers.

As a firm adherent of Confucianism, Yuan Haowen did not join the Quanzhen order, but his personal network included many Quanzhen Daoists—such as friends and relatives who became Quanzhen monks and nuns, and people who asked him to compose inscriptions.[25] In an inscription for a Daoist abbey written in 1243, Yuan confessed, "Ever since the Northern Crossing [in 1233], I have associated with many Quanzhen Daoists."[26] Indeed, most of his writings about Quanzhen Daoism were composed after 1234. His second daughter, Yuan Yan, became a Daoist nun after her husband's death around 1230.[27]

In the fall of 1238, with funding from Zhao Tianxi and Zhao's superior Yan Shi 嚴實 (1182–1240), a powerful regional warlord in Shandong, Yuan Haowen brought his family home to northern Shanxi. On their way, they passed Wangwu Mountain, where Yuan's relative Mingdao, who had become a Quanzhen Daoist, resided. Mingdao introduced

23. Duan Chengji 段成己, "Chuangxiu Qiyun guan ji" 創修棲云觀記, *QSXB*, 134.

24. Yuan Haowen, "Sun Boying muming" 孫伯英墓銘, *QJ*, 31.642.

25. As early as 1234, when Yuan was still in Mongol custody, a Quanzhen Daoist traveled from Henan to Shandong to ask him to write an inscription for the Daoist's residential abbey. See Yuan Haowen, "Qingzhen guan ji" 清真觀記, *QJ*, 35.741–46.

26. Yuan Haowen, "Taigu guan ji" 太古觀記, *QJ*, 35.739.

27. Li Suping, "Nüguan Yuan Yan kao."

Yuan to a local Daoist who asked him to write an inscription.[28] Although Yuan never explicitly acknowledged it, when he was living at home in the countryside and during his frequent travels in Shanxi, Hebei, and Shandong, writing inscriptions for others—including Quanzhen institutions and priests—became an important source of income for him.[29]

While living at home, Yuan Haowen also associated with local Quanzhen Daoists. In 1244 he traveled to a neighboring county to visit a local abbey where the retired former Jin official Wang Chunfu 王純甫 was staying and studying Daoist cultivation practices. In four days of climbing two mountains with Wang and other friends, Yuan stayed in three Daoist abbeys, drank with his friends, and heard from an elderly Daoist the local myth of a legendary Quanzhen patriarch. Although Yuan expressed doubts about the story's authenticity, he pointed out that the loss of books in the Mongol conquest meant that the living were the only ones who could claim to know the history of Daoist communities in the mountains.[30]

Yuan Haowen and Qin Zhi'an 秦志安 (1188–1244)—both Shanxi natives—represented two different ways in which former Jin literati connected with the Quanzhen Daoist order in the Great Mongol State. Among the many Quanzhen Daoists that Yuan knew, Qin was one of his closest friends. The two men had met each other in the first decade of the thirteenth century when Yuan was studying in Lingchuan county and was associated with the Qins, a prestigious local scholarly family. After the two men both fled to Henan and lived in the same area, they exchanged poems. While Yuan eventually passed the exams and became a scholar-official, Qin completely lost interest in the secular world after failing the exams many times, and he joined the Quanzhen order. As an outsider and an insider, respectively, Yuan and Qin provide in their personal experiences and writings an unprecedentedly sharp image of the literati's active and profound presence in the Quanzhen Daoist order during the Jin-Yuan transition.

28. Yuan Haowen, "Tongxian guan ji" 通仙觀記, *QJ*, 35.744–46.

29. For other Quanzhen inscriptions Yuan Haowen wrote after 1234, see *QJ*, 31.646–47, 649–50, and 651–52 and 35.736–38, 741–42, and 746–47.

30. Yuan Haowen, "Liangshan xing ji," 兩山行記 *QJ*, 34.719–22.

FIGURE 2.1 Daoist caves in Dragon Mountain, about twenty kilometers southwest of Taiyuan, the capital of Shanxi province. These are the largest existing Daoist caves in China. When Song Defang came to the site in 1234, he found two caves and dug out five more to hold statues of Daoist deities. One was dedicated to Song himself (see fig. 2.2). The site's size reflects the success of Quanzhen Daoism in the 1200s. Author photo.

In 1233 Qin Zhi'an fled the chaos in Henan and returned to his native area in Zezhou subprefecture, where he met the Quanzhen master Song Defang 宋德方 (1183–1247) and became his disciple. Thus, at age forty-five, Qin embarked on a new career as a "literati Daoist" and devoted the rest of his life to Quanzhen Daoist projects.[31] He first received instruction in Daoist talismans, registers, and rituals from Song and assisted his teacher in carving Daoist caves in Dragon Mountain near Taiyuan between 1234 and 1237 (figs. 2.1 and 2.2).[32]

31.   In this book I use *literati Daoist* as an analytical term to refer to the group of Quanzhen Daoists who had been Confucian literati before entering the Quanzhen order.

32.   Jing, "The Longshan Daoist Cave."

FIGURE 2.2 The Daoist cave in Dragon Mountain dedicated to Song Defang. Song's statue is on the central platform; there are also statues of two attendants, one on each side of Song. The attendants, not shown in this photo, are Song's two major disciples, Qin Zhi'an and Li Zhiquan. Inscriptions inside the cave written by Qin and Li are dated 1238 and 1239. The heads of the statues were removed sometime after 1920. The marks left by the decapitation process are visible and indicate careful removal, perhaps to preserve the heads' value on the art market. Author photo.

After completing the caves in 1237, Song Defang and Qin Zhi'an were invited by a local governor to perform an offering ritual, and they traveled to the Pingyang area (now Linfen city, in Shanxi), which had been a major printing center in north China since the twelfth century.[33] There Song decided to begin carving woodblocks to print a new Daoist canon, later called the *Treasured Canon of Mysterious Capital* (*Xuandu baozang* 玄都寶藏).[34] Because of Qin's extensive learning, Song

33.   Zhang Xiumin, *Zhongguo yinshua shi*, 174 and 200–201.

34.   Scholars of Daoism have documented well the compilation and printing of, and bibliographical changes in, this Daoist canon. See Chen Guofu, *Daozang yuanliu kao*, 161–74; Schipper and Verellen, *Taoist Canon*, 1131–33. Surviving fragments of the canon consist of a number of chapters of two Daoist texts: the *Seven Slips from the Book-*

entrusted him with editing a complete set of Daoist texts. Qin devoted his remaining years to overseeing the publication of the Daoist canon and to writing hagiographies of Quanzhen masters in Pingyang city's Daoist Abbey of Mysterious Capital (*Xuandu guan* 玄都觀, also called *Changchun guan* 長春觀), which was the headquarters of the canon project.[35] The project became an important way for Song and Qin to expand Quanzhen institutions in southern Shanxi as well as to recruit former Jin literati. When Qin died in 1244, soon after completion of the canon's printing, his disciples asked Yuan Haowen to compose an epitaph for him.[36]

This epitaph documents Qin Zhi'an's role in the canon project as well as a distinctive institutional network that Qin Zhi'an and Song Defang established to sponsor the carving of the woodblocks for the canon. Yuan wrote:

> Qin Zhi'an asked Song Defang's permission to read anything he liked in the Daoist canon.
>
> Song said, "After the disorder, many Daoist texts were scattered and lost. Only the Daoist canon in Guanzhou subprefecture [now Jingle county, in Shanxi] is preserved.[37] I intend to revive the lost tradition by printing and publishing the canon. Yet I am not up to the task. Rather than cultivating yourself, why don't you share your knowledge with the world?"
>
> Qin Zhi'an bowed twice and replied, "Understood."
>
> Qin Zhi'an then established twenty-seven offices and hired more than five hundred laborers. Qin himself worked as editor-in-chief at the Abbey

bag in the Clouds (*Yunji qiqian* 雲笈七籤) and the *Scripture of Great Clarity in Wind and Dews* (*Taiqing fenglu jing* 太清風露經). These fragments are now preserved in the National Library in Beijing.

35. Hou, "Yuan kan *Xuandu baozang*."

36. Yuan Haowen, "Tongzhenzi mujieming" 通眞子墓碣銘, *QJ*, 31.647–48.

37. The Daoist canon mentioned here refers to the version of the *Great Jin Treasured Canon of Mysterious Capital* (*Dajin xuandu baozang* 大金玄都寶藏) that was printed by the Jin government in 1190. Song might have received the copy from his senior colleague Yin Zhiping. A funeral biography of Yin mentions that in 1234 Ögödei Khan's empress gave Yin a copy of the Daoist canon, which might have been the Guanzhou version. See Yi Gou 弋彀, "Xuanmen zhangjiao qinghe miaodao guanghua zhenren Yin zongshi beiming bing xu" 玄門掌教清和妙道廣化眞人尹宗師碑銘幷序, *JSL*, 568.

of Mysterious Capital in Pingyang. He contributed much to correcting
the more than eight thousand fascicles of Daoist texts in the categories of
Three Grottos and *Four Supplements*.[38]

Qin Zhi'an's career change typifies the experience of literati who turned
from studying Confucian classics and historical and literary texts for examinations to learning Daoist rituals, editing Daoist texts, and writing
about Quanzhen institutions. Before 1234 many former Jin literati like
Qin would most likely have become government officials or teachers at
Confucian schools; with the suspension of the examinations after 1234,
they could be neither. Joining the Quanzhen Daoist order and working
on the canon project thus became an appealing option for many destitute literati.

In addition to its headquarters in Pingyang, the canon project accelerated the expansion of Quanzhen Daoist institutions in Shanxi by
establishing twenty-seven branch offices in different Daoist abbeys—
thirteen in Shanxi province, nine in neighboring Shaanxi province to the
west, and five in Henan province to the east.[39] Each branch office, staffed
with scholars, collected texts that were categorized according to the divi-
sions of the Daoist canon and carved new wood printing blocks. For instance, Song Defang entrusted his disciple He Zhiyuan 何志淵—a former
Jin examination student—with supervising the seven branch offices in
Taiyuan that compiled the section "All Heavens" (*Juntian* 均天).[40]

Qin Zhi'an and Song Defang recruited many former Jin literati to
work on the project, particularly in 1237–38, when the Mongol government under the leadership of Yelü Chucai in Yanjing held a one-time
special examination in north China for those seeking the honor of being
a "Confucian household." Those so designated could serve as clerks in
the government and gain exemption from labor service just as Buddhists

38. Yuan Haowen, "Tongzhenzi mujieming," *QJ*, 31.647–48.

39. The branch offices in Shanxi were under the direct leadership of Song's Daoist
lineage, while others were operated through the coordination between that lineage and
other Quanzhen lineages based in Henan and Shaanxi. See Jinping Wang, "A Social
History of the *Treasured Canon*," 12–16.

40. Du Siwen 杜思問, "Chongxiu Shuigu Lequan guan ji" 重修水谷樂全觀記,
JSL, 652.

and Daoists did.[41] Pingyang was a main examination site. All former Jin literati, including those who had been captured by Mongol soldiers during the war and had become the latter's slaves, were allowed to take the exam. According to Makino Shūji, at least one-fourth of the four thousand-odd literati who officially received the status of Confucian household by passing the exam had been prisoners or slaves. Their liberation was by no means unconditional; instead, a ransom was often required for their freedom,[42] and not all captured literati had family members or friends to ransom them. In contrast, becoming a Quanzhen Daoist guaranteed immediate freedom, a privilege extended from Chinggis Khan's edicts to Qiu Chuji. As a result, some successful candidates, such as He Zhiyuan, did not take the title of Confucian household and became a Quanzhen Daoist instead.[43]

Even after gaining Confucian household status, some former Jin literati still joined the Quanzhen order out of concern for their own personal safety. The evidence of a famous literati Daoist named Li Daoqian 李道謙 (1219–96), who became a canon complier at a branch office in Shaanxi, is compelling. After the 1237–38 examinations, Li was registered as a member of a Confucian household. Because his family was very wealthy, he had none of the economic difficulties faced by many destitute former Jin literati. However, he still chose to become a Daoist because of continuing social instability in north China during the Mongols' war against the Southern Song dynasty. Many senior Quanzhen masters competed with each other to make Li a disciple due to his well-known

---

41. Many northern Chinese Confucian scholars made their living by farming, teaching in local schools, and serving the government in lower-ranking offices. The Lingchuan scholar Li Ping, for example, took the examinations, received the status of Confucian household, and was exempted from labor service. From then on, he lived by farming and taught his sons to read. His sons later worked as instructors in state schools. See Li Tingshi 李庭實, "Li shangshu zhuifeng Longxi junhou shendaobei" 李尚書追封隴西郡侯神道碑, in *Lingchuan xianzhi* [1779], 25.23b–27a.

42. Makino, "Transformation of the *Shi-jên*."

43. Some, such as Yuan Haowen's friend Ma Ge 麻革, chose to work as compilers in the Office of Literature (*Jingji suo* 經籍所) established by Yelü Chucai in Pingyang; this office of the central government took charge of editing and publishing books under official sponsorship. See Ma Ge, "You Longshan ji" 游龍山記, appendixed in *Guiqian zhi*, 151.

learning.[44] Li's case implies that at the time, the Quanzhen order was more able than a better-off family to shield individuals from military violence. More importantly, when state institutions like Confucian schools and civil service examinations no longer provided literati with ways to realize their intellectual values, the Quanzhen order did.

Another recruit to the canon project was Song Defang's important disciple Li Zhiquan 李志全 (1191–1261).[45] Li was the son of a former Jin *jinshi* degree holder and had once studied for the civil service examinations. During the turmoil of the Mongol conquest in the 1220s, Li became a Quanzhen Daoist after visiting the Quanzhen Patriarch Qiu Chuji. Li was practicing Daoist cultivation in the mountains of northern Shanxi when Song recruited him to join the printing project.[46]

We do not know the precise number of scholars who worked on the canon project, but considering the tremendous workload of editing around eight thousand fascicles of Daoist texts and the large geographical coverage of the project, many people must have been involved. And those who performed physical labor—including transporting wood, making paper, carving blocks, and actually printing individual sheets of paper—clearly outnumbered those who edited texts. While Yuan Haowen put the number at five hundred, another inscription reports that three thousand or so participated, which is more likely.[47]

Song Defang and many of his followers raised funds to print the canon. During his travels in north China to seek texts and sponsors, Song repaired and established hundreds of Daoist abbeys and recruited thousands of disciples.[48] An inscription about Song credits him with provid-

44. Song Bo 宋渤, "Xuanming wenjing tianle zhenren Ligong daoxingming xu" 玄明文靖天樂眞人李公道行銘序, *JSL*, 714.

45. Li Wei 李蔚, "Dachao gu jiangshi Lijun muzhiming" 大朝故講師李君墓誌銘, *JSL*, 581.

46. Another source mentions that Li Zhiquan became a Quanzhen Daoist under the influence of his relative named Li Zhitian 李志田, who had been a farmer before becoming a Quanzhen Daoist. See "Sanlao tonggong bei" 三老同宮碑 (author unknown), *JSL*, 560–61.

47. Li Ding 李鼎, "Xuandu zhidao piyun zhenren Song tianshi citang beiming bing xu" 玄都至道披云眞人宋天師祠堂碑銘并序, *JSL*, 547.

48. Shang Ting 商挺, "Xuandu zhidao chongwen minghua zhenren daoxing zhi bei" 玄都至道崇文明化眞人道行之碑, *JSL*, 614; Li Ding, "Xuandu zhidao piyun zhenren," *JSL*, 547.

ing all of the cloth, food, and other articles of everyday use that participants needed.[49] He obtained such supplies in several ways: by using his
personal network to appeal to Mongol officials and local governors, sending his followers to beg for donations, and taking resources from Daoist
institutions that he controlled.[50] At the beginning of the project, Song
received 1,500 taels of silver from Governor Hu Tianlu 胡天祿 in Pingyang and instructed one follower, who had been a farmer and a soldier,
to take charge of providing supplies for the Golden Lotus branch office
(*Jinlian ju* 金蓮局).[51] Song's Daoist lineage controlled more than two hundred Daoist abbeys across Shanxi, Shaanxi, Henan, Hebei, Shandong,
and Gansu provinces.[52] In many of these local abbeys, Song's disciples ac-
cumulated monastic property by farming land, operating watermills, and
running shops.[53] Daoists at one abbey gained sufficient wealth to make
high-quality paper for printing the Daoist canon, which also suggests
that some Quanzhen Daoist communities functioned as papermaking
workshops and were active in the printing business.[54] Clearly, the Quanzhen social and monastic networks at the time functioned as a new
mechanism for generating and redistributing wealth, which provided
literati with new means of acquiring a living.

Thanks to support from the Daoist communities, scholars like Qin
Zhi'an, He Zhiyuan, and Li Zhiquan did not experience disturbance and
poverty. More importantly, they were able to concentrate on textual studies and writing—the preferred lifestyle for literati. But they were not
isolated from the rest of world. They established new social support systems within Daoist communities bound by master-disciple relations and
religious fellowship. For instance, in 1248 Qin Zhi'an's six disciples and
other colleagues who had once worked on the canon project gathered to
erect a stone inscribed with Yuan Haowen's epitaph for Qin in front of
Qin's tomb.[55]

49. Li Ding, "Xuandu zhidao piyun zhenren," *JSL*, 547.

50. "Sanlao tonggong bei," *JSL*, 560–61.

51. Ibid., 560–61.

52. Jing, *Daojiao quanzhenpai gongguan*, 117–24.

53. Yan Fu 阎复, "Xuandu wanshou gong bei" 玄都萬壽宮碑, *JSL*, 656.

54. Li Zhiquan, "Jiyuan Shifang longxiang wanshou gong ji" 濟源十方龍祥萬壽宮
記, *JSL*, 507.

55. Yuan Haowen, "Tongzhenzi mujieming" 通眞子墓碣銘, *JSL*, 487.

The Daoist canon also attracted the attention of other literati, who did not join the Quanzhen communities but became associated with Daoists and wrote for the canon or for those who were involved in producing it. As we have seen, Yuan Haowen wrote the epitaph for Qin Zhi'an. And Yuan's close friend Li Ye 李冶 (1192–1279)—a well-known Confucian scholar and mathematician—wrote a preface for the canon.[56] The Quanzhen Daoist order in the first half of the thirteenth century affected almost every scholar in north China, either personally or indirectly.

The publication of the canon gave rise to new teaching positions for literati Daoists in new Daoist-style schools that temporarily replaced the Confucian schools of Jin times, most of which had been destroyed during the Jin-Mongol war. This was not the first time in Chinese history that Daoist schools had been established. Emperor Xuanzong of the Tang 唐玄宗 (r. 712–57) first established schools to promote and teach Daoism, and Emperor Huizong of the Song 徽宗 (r. 1101–25) created a Daoist school system in 1116 and incorporated Daoist schools into the local public school system two years later.[57] In contrast to these earlier Daoist schools, which were sponsored and governed by the state, Quanzhen Daoists completely controlled their schools.

After he finished editing Daoist texts, Song Defang organized six offices to print more than a hundred copies of the canon and distributed them to well-known Daoist institutions, where he established new lectureships. Song appointed literati Daoists, including Qin Zhi'an and He Zhiyuan, to lecture on Daoist knowledge and accounts of ancient sages. The lay disciple Li Ding explained what his master Song did: "For each copy of the canon, the Master appointed scholars who were familiar with Daoist teachings to occupy a lectureship and ordered them to teach accounts of how sages became the sages recorded in Daoist texts. . . . Among those scholars, some extended their lectures and exemplified the great value of Confucius's idea that in instruction there is no separation into categories (*youjiao wulei* 有教無類).[58] Lecturers did not ask whether those who came to listen to the lectures belonged to the Daoist order."[59]

56. Li Ding, "Xuandu zhidao piyun zhenren," *JSL*, 547.

57. Chao, "Daoist Examinations and Daoist Schools."

58. The term *youjiao wulei* refers to Confucius's words in a passage in *The Analects*. See Confucius, *The Analects of Confucius*, 39.

59. Li Ding, "Xuandu zhidao piyun zhenren," *JSL*, 547.

These lectures also attracted nonreligious listeners who sought an education at the Daoist schools, since many of the lecturers were scholars skilled in teaching. Yuan Haowen's epitaph for Qin Zhi'an emphasizes in particular that no other lecturers could match him in popularity: students from different regions came to Pingyang to study Daoist and Confucian texts with Qin.[60]

Contemporary literati recognized the lectureships that Song Defang established as a route for scholars to achieve fame, an otherwise impossible goal in those troubled times. The experience of Li Zhiquan, one of Song's major disciples, is typical.[61] Li developed a reputation as an erudite scholar among senior Quanzhen leaders after spending ten years editing Daoist texts and serving as a lecturer at a Daoist abbey in the Qinzhou subprefecture of Shanxi. Later, he was appointed superintendent of a Daoist School of Mysterious Learning (*xuanxue* 玄學) in Yanjing by the third Quanzhen patriarch, Li Zhichang 李志常 (1193–1256)—who was originally a Confucian literatus. In the funeral biography of Li Zhiquan, the author Li Wei, a state school official, discussed how Li Zhiquan had benefited from the Quanzhen order in establishing his reputation among his contemporaries:

> Literati agreed that the high level of Li Zhiquan's scholarship would have brought him a *jinshi* degree. The world was in confusion and the areas north of the Yellow River were particularly chaotic. In protecting himself, he had no spare time [for study]. Days passed like years. His robust ambitions declined, and he was content to bury himself in the real world. Undoubtedly he might have died without anyone knowing his worth. Yet once he entered the Daoist order and received recommendation and praise from Quanzhen masters, he became an Exalted Scholar (*gaoshi* 高士).[62]

The Quanzhen order offered literati an alternative route to fame—not through success in the civil service examinations or literary achievements,

60. Yuan Haowen, "Tongzhenzi mujieming," *QJ*, 31.648.

61. Other examples found in extant sources include Zhao Xiyan 趙希顏, a disciple of Song, and a Daoist named He Zhiqing 賀志慶. See Chen Defu 陳德福, "Qingxu gong Beijing" 清虛宮碑銘, *JSL*, 790–91; "Qiyuan zhenren menzhong bei" 樓元真人門眾碑, *QSXB*, 173.

62. Li Wei, "Dachao gu jiangshi Lijun," *JSL*, 581.

as would have been true in the Northern Song and Jin, but through their accomplishment in Daoist enterprises, such as printing and teaching the Daoist canon.

This was true not just in Shanxi: literati Daoists were strongly present in the nationwide Quanzhen Daoist order, particularly in the Quanzhen education system. The Quanzhen Schools of Mysterious Learning staffed by literati Daoists were established in all circuits in north China. Several literati Daoists who had participated in the canon project and lectured on the canon at such schools later became abbots of important Daoist monasteries.[63] Quanzhen Daoists extended their educational enterprise even beyond Quanzhen monasteries. The Mongol rulers entrusted Patriarch Li Zhichang and another literati Daoist, Feng Zhiheng 馮志亨 in Yanjing, with leadership of the Mongol National University (*Guozi xue* 國子學), which educated young men from politically elite Mongol and Chinese families. Feng acted as the instructor-in-chief at the university, teaching both Confucian and Daoist classics to Mongolian students.[64]

Literati Daoists even supported each other in seeking important positions in the Quanzhen order, ranging from the highest position of patriarch to middle-level positions like abbots of large Daoist monasteries. For instance, Feng Zhiheng supported his close friend Li Zhichang in his bid to be patriarch, and Li later promoted Feng to be the chief Daoist registrar and acting patriarch, the second highest rank in the Quanzhen leadership. There was a rumor at the time that the two men helped each other because they both had been Confucians.[65] Feng and Li indeed favored the integration of Confucian and Daoist teachings in Quanzhen education.

63.   Li Daoqian and his colleague Shi Zhijian 石志堅 were typical examples. Both of them once lectured at the Daoist school in the Ancestral Hall on Mount Zhongnan. Li later became the abbot of the Ancestral Hall and the leader of all Quanzhen communities in the Shaanxi and Sichuan regions; Shi became the abbot of the Daoist Palace of Modeling on Sages (*Zongsheng gong* 宗聖宮), a lower temple of the Ancestral Hall. See Song Bo, "Xuanming wenjing tianle zhenren," *JSL*, 714; Li Daoqian, "Zhongnanshan Zongsheng gongzhu Shigong daoxing ji" 終南山宗聖宮主石公道行記, *JSL*, 637.

64.   For the roles of Quanzhen Daoists in the Mongol National University, see Jinping Wang, "Rujia zi, daozhe shi," 70–73.

65.   Zhao Zhu 趙著, "Zuoxuan jizhao dashi Fenggong daoxing beiming" 佐玄寂照大師馮公道行碑銘, *JSL*, 521–22.

The increasing influence of literati Daoists and the importance of education in the Quanzhen order reinforced each other. Together, they advanced the Quanzhen shift toward emphasizing book learning, which had been ignored by early Quanzhen masters. By compiling Quanzhen sources and writing Quanzhen books, many literati Daoists—such as Qin Zhi'an in Shanxi and Li Daoqian in Shaanxi—helped give the Quanzhen community the scholarly authority to write its own history. Quanzhen Daoists used this history as propaganda in creating a unique Quanzhen identity and promoting an established Quanzhen order throughout north China.[66]

Contemporary literati felt a tension between their old educational traditions and the new religious teachings, yet they were unable to alter the latter. Yuan Haowen witnessed the decline in Confucian education for children in northern Shanxi. In an inscription for a Quanzhen abbey that he composed in 1244, Yuan reported that Quanzhen Daoists had penetrated so deeply into the Taizhou region of northern Shanxi, where most people were Buddhists, that even children learned Quanzhen Daoism. Not a single person, he felt, was teaching children Confucian texts.[67]

The tension between Quanzhen and Confucian ideals also appeared in daily life. Quanzhen monastic rules, like Buddhist monastic rules for monks and nuns, or the *vinaya*, required celibacy. This requirement inevitably resulted in conflicts between the clergy and the lay families they left behind when they joined the Quanzhen order, especially when wives and children suffered from the loss of a breadwinning husband and father. Yuan Haowen's student Hao Jing wrote a letter in 1238 to criticize his maternal uncle Xu Dehuai 許德懷, who had abandoned his wife and son to become a Quanzhen Daoist. After reading Hao's letter, Xu eventually gave up his religious practice and returned to his family.[68] Still, not all families had such happy reunions.

Many literati Daoists who clung to monastic life worried that they could not fulfill their obligation to their ancestors to produce an heir, as the Confucian family order required. Who would carry on their family

66. Katz, "Writing History, Creating Identity"; Jinping Wang, "A Social History of the *Treasured Canon*," 8–10 and 26–29, and "Rujia zi, daozhe shi," 74–82.

67. Yuan Haowen, "Mingyang guan ji" 明陽觀記, *QJ*, 35.746–47.

68. Hao Jing 郝經, "Qing jiushi Xu daoshi chu huandu shu" 請舅氏許道士出圜堵書, *QYW*, 4:149–52.

lines? And who would care for their ancestral tombs? Li Zirong 李子榮, a former examination student from Luzhou subprefecture in southeastern Shanxi, faced this dilemma. Li joined a local Daoist abbey to live a simple life after giving up his political career with the Mongols, possibly in the late 1210s.[69] Most of his lineage members died during the war, leaving Li the only surviving member of his family. Having no children, Li wondered who would tend his family graveyard, where his distinguished ancestors were buried.

Li Zirong's creative solution typified the new social order of the day. He transformed the house of his secular family into a Daoist hermitage and asked his disciples to live there and keep a careful watch on the graveyard of the Li lineage. He also donated land that had belonged to his family to provide food for the Daoists living in the hermitage. After the hermitage was completed, to gain official recognition, he applied to the government for a monastic plaque and received one with the name Abbey of Jade Emptiness (*Yuxu guan* 玉虛觀). Still, his mind was not at ease. Sending a letter to his friend, the scholar Song Zizhen, Li asked that Song compose a record to inform later managers and residents of the hermitage about its origin and voice Li's hope that they would burn a stick of incense to his ancestors at important festivals.[70]

Li Zirong's strategy of entrusting religious communities to take care of a family's ancestral graveyard appeared common among the clergy at the time, both Quanzhen Daoists and Buddhists.[71] We can understand the uniqueness of this practice by comparing it to the slightly earlier institutions of the merit cloister (*gongde yuan* 功德院) or tomb monastery (*fensi* 墳寺) of the Northern Song, which also took charge of caring for a family's ancestral graveyards and performing rituals of ancestral worship. The merit cloisters first arose out of the wish of high-ranking officials of the Northern Song and their families to preserve their ancestral tombs and property, especially when they had to spend most of their life in government posts far from home. Thus, merit cloisters initially came with an official stamp of approval. For the Northern Song families, merit clois-

---

69. Song Zizhen 宋子貞, "Yuxu guan ji" 玉虛觀記, *QYW*, 1:179–80.

70. Ibid., 1:179.

71. For a Buddhist example, see Wang Liyong 王利用, "Kuangong anzhu tuoji zuxian gongde ji" 寬公庵主托祭祖先功德記, *DQ: Hongtong*, 54–55.

ters served not just as a marker of prestige but also as tax shelters, because landholdings attached to the cloister were exempt from taxation. Although monks were invited to reside in and care for the merit cloisters, the Northern Song families usually retained control over the cloisters as their private property.[72] In the case of Quanzhen institutions, the initiative and authority was in the hands of the clergy, who extended their respect for their master to the latter's extinct natal family. At the time when so many kinship groups were fragmented or even eliminated, the Quanzhen order provided an effective monastic strategy to address the social anxiety related to ancestral worship.

All the northern Chinese who joined the Quanzhen communities had to face the challenges arising from their former roles and obligations in families. The Confucian values so deeply embedded in their minds did not just fade away at the moment they decided to enter a Quanzhen monastery. The same was true for women, another important social group that made its mark in the Quanzhen Daoist order and whose members brought with them the concerns of their former secular lives.

Promoting Women's Activities

In the Confucian-dominated society of the Jin, women spent most of their lives at home fulfilling their family obligations as daughters, wives, daughters-in-laws, and mothers. After 1234, however, women with Quanzhen ties played important outside roles. They were able to assume leadership positions in public arenas, including religious organizations, local society, and even government building projects. Highborn Jurchen women entered the Quanzhen order and helped attract the support of local authorities. Ordinary women initiated the construction of convents for widows and orphaned girls. Some elite Chinese women—mothers and wives of officials—became Quanzhen nuns to enjoy an alternative lifestyle, and others took direct charge of Daoist projects under the supervision of women in the Mongol imperial family.

72. Chikusa, *Chūgoku bukkyō shakaishi kenkyū*, 111–43.

Among numerous northern women who joined the Quanzhen monastic order, a few highborn Jurchen women stood out, not only because they had distinctive ethnic backgrounds but also because they played important roles in the development of Quanzhen institutions and female Quanzhen networks. Highborn Jurchen women in the Jin already had a tradition of joining religious orders after their husbands died. Some of them did so to escape the restrictions placed on widows in Jurchen tradition, such as following their husbands in death or levirate remarriage.[73] Quanzhen masters welcomed such special disciples, who helped the early Quanzhen community appeal to imperial patrons and survive the government persecution in 1190.[74] During the Jin-Yuan transition, many highborn Jurchen women—not just widows but also unmarried girls—traveled throughout north China, propagating Quanzhen teaching and building social networks with political authorities to develop Quanzhen institutions in new regions.

Two Jurchen nuns named Aodun Miaoshan 奥敦妙善 (1198–1275) and Wole Shoujian 斡勒守堅 (1181–1251) are good examples. After becoming Quanzhen nuns, they both obtained financial support from ethnically non-Chinese governors who had surrendered to the Mongols. Miaoshan and Shoujian were the two women's religious names; their secular names are unknown. As Goossaert points out, from the beginning of the thirteenth century to the end of the Yuan dynasty, well over 95 percent of Quanzhen names follow a very simple rule: the first character in a monk's name was one of the three possibilities: *zhi* 志 ("devotion"), *dao* 道 ("the way"), or *de* 德 ("virtue"). Similarly, the first character in a nun's name was chosen from the following three possibilities: *miao* 妙 ("wonderful"), *shou* 守 ("moral integrity"), and *hui* 慧 (or 惠) ("clever" or "kind").[75] The second character in the given name could be anything.

Miaoshan's experience demonstrates that some Quanzhen nuns attracted followers through the display of asceticism, much as male Quanzhen Daoists did. Quanzhen teachings made no clear distinction between

73. L. Johnson, *Women of the Conquest Dynasties*, 154. Most of these women entered Buddhist orders and spent the rest of their lives in Buddhist monasteries. A few others became interested in Quanzhen Daoism in the late Jin period. For an example, see Ma Yu 馬鈺, "Man ting fang" 滿庭芳, *JSL*, 435.

74. Zhang Qiaogui, "Daojiao chuanbo," 104–5.

75. Goossaert, "The Invention of an Order," 130.

male and female practitioners, and the order allowed monks and nuns to communicate with each other freely. Miaoshan studied with Qiu Chuji when she was young and stayed in a meditation enclosure (*huandu* 環堵) for more than ten years.[76] After leaving the enclosure, she wore paper clothing, ate just one meal a day (of fruit only), and allegedly did not sleep for several years.[77] In addition to these common Quanzhen ascetic practices, also followed by male Quanzhen Daoists, Miaoshan cut her hair and disfigured her face, actions typically reserved for women aiming to rid themselves of the external symbols of femininity—an important goal for female Quanzhen Daoists pursuing self-realization.[78] A military governor also surnamed Aodun heard about her asceticism, was deeply impressed, and invited her to his headquarters. Like Miaoshan, many Quanzhen nuns practiced asceticism with male masters.[79] However, some women, such as a woman named Ma from southern Shanxi, did so well that they in turn became masters for male Quanzhen monks.[80]

Miaoshan's Quanzhen career peaked after she gained the favor of the Mongol rulers, especially royal women in the Mongol palace. In 1255, after being invited by several Quanzhen nuns to take charge of a convent at Kaifeng, she became so famous that the Mongol leader Möngke Khan (r. 1251–59) ordered a Mongol official to be her patron. In 1271 Khubilai Khan summoned her to pray for the protection of the imperial palace. Miaoshan even successfully built an extensive female Quanzhen network that connected nuns of her convent directly with powerful imperial ladies through the worship of the Sage Mother (*shengmu* 聖母), the mother of Laozi and the major Daoist deity enshrined in the convent.[81]

76. In her childhood, Miaoshan had lived in a Daoist abbey in Beijing with her mother (who also became a Daoist nun), and she might have met Qiu Chuji when the Jurchen Emperor Shizong summoned Qiu to Beijing in 1188 and accommodated him in a prestigious Daoist abbey in the capital.

77. On Quanzhen ascetic practices including sleep deprivation, see Yoshikawa, "Waki wa seki ni"; Eskildsen, *The Teachings and Practices*, 39–56.

78. For the Quanzhen practices specifically for women, see Eskildsen, *The Teachings and Practices*, 83–84.

79. Bao Zhikuan 包志寬, "Chuangjian shenqing an ji" 創建神清庵記, *JSL*, 618.

80. Wang Feng 王鳳, "Xiu huixian an bei" 修會仙庵碑, *QSXB*, 39.

81. Ren Zhirun 任志潤, "Nü lianshi xuanzhen tongming zhenren Aodun jun daoxingji" 女煉師玄眞通明眞人奧敦君道行記, *JSL*, 686–87.

Wole Shoujian's case shows that female clergy, especially those from prestigious family backgrounds, used their connections with the mothers and wives of powerful officials to help attract local authorities as sponsors of Quanzhen Daoist communities. Shoujian was the daughter of a middle-ranking official of the Jin dynasty. She had entered the Daoist order at the age of fifteen and received official Daoist ordination in 1196; her earlier religious affiliation is unclear. In 1223 Qiu Chuji, then the Quanzhen patriarch newly appointed as leader of all Daoists by Chingghis Khan, met Shoujian and eventually accepted her as his disciple. Then Qiu Chuji charged her with running the order in the Hebei region, where Quanzhen Daoists aggressively expanded their institutions immediately after Qiu established the Quanzhen headquarters at the Great Palace of Everlasting Spring in 1224 in Yanjing (part of Hebei at the time).[82] It was unusual for Qiu to choose a recently accepted female disciple instead of a capable male disciple to perform such an important missionary task, but Shoujian's success validated his decision.

A Khitan warlord of the Yelü 耶律 clan—the surname of the royal family of the Liao Dynasty (907–1125)—controlled the Hebei region. After Shoujian came to Hebei, Warlord Yelü and his mother enthusiastically welcomed her.[83] They not only constructed a convent to accommodate Shoujian but also sent two young men of their family to study with her. Shoujian ordained dozens of women as Quanzhen nuns. In the autumn of 1238, when he was appointed by the Mongols to govern the Shaanxi region, Yelü brought Shoujian with him to his new post and converted an old temple of a local deity into a Daoist convent to accommodate her.

---

82. The Great Palace of Everlasting Spring was ruined during the war at the end of the Yuan dynasty and was rebuilt as the Abbey of White Clouds (*Baiyun guan* 白雲觀), which is now the center of Daoist institutions in China.

83. Li Jin 李晉, "Longyang guan Yuzhen qingmiao zhenren benxing ji" 龍陽觀玉眞清妙眞人本行記, *JSL*, 542. The inscription writes the surname of the warlord as Yila 移剌, an alternative Chinese transcription of the Khitan term for Yelü, but does not specify his full name. Judging from the warlord's official titles—"Taifu 太傅, Zongling yekenayan 總領也可那延, Puguogong 濮國公"—and his activity of participating in the Mongols' Sichuan campaign mentioned in the inscription, he is most likely Yelü Zhuge 耶律朱哥, who inherited those titles from his father Yelü Buhua 耶律不花. For the biography of Yelü Buhua and his descendents, see *YS*, 149.3532.

Shoujian's close connection to the Yelü family, which became an important patron for the Quanzhen order in Shaanxi, in turn brought her to the attention of famous male Quanzhen masters, including Yin Zhiping, who inherited the position of Quanzhen patriarch after Qiu's death in 1227. In the spring of 1241, when Yin traveled to Shaanxi, he entrusted Shoujian with the supervision of all Daoist women in Shaanxi and appointed her abbess of a local convent, originally built for the Tang Princess Jade Perfected (*Yuzhen gongzhu* 玉真公主), a well-known aristocratic Daoist nun in the late eighth century.[84]

Other women of lesser family backgrounds also contributed to rebuilding postwar local communities. Consider the experience of the Quanzhen nun Zhang Shouwei 張守微, from Zezhou subprefecture in southeastern Shanxi. Born in the countryside of Jincheng county in Zezhou, Shouwei was married to a local man while she was still a child. In the spring of 1214, when Mongol troops ravaged Zezhou, Shouwei and her family fled to northern Shanxi. After her husband died, Shouwei entered a Quanzhen nunnery, possibly together with her five children (she had one son and four daughters). In 1224 she became a disciple of the abbess of a village hermitage in Taiyuan. After the fighting died down, Shouwei returned to Jincheng.

In 1241 Shouwei and her younger brother Dezhong 德忠, who had also survived the war and returned home, decided to rebuild the ruined Abbey of Cultivation (*Xiuzhen guan* 修真觀) in the city of Jincheng. With help from a local Daoist, Shouwei drew up plans for the specific locations of halls, dormitories, a meditation enclosure, a garden, and a well. She first had a Sacred Hall (*shengtang* 聖堂) built as a meditation space, cultivated what had been wasteland, weeded fields, and erected a foot-high wall around the monastic lands. Under the sponsorship of the prefectural governor, Duan Zhengqing 段正卿, and his wife, Lady Wei, Shouwei completed the construction in five months. When the Sacred Hall was finished, Shouwei's younger brother and his wife both became lay Quanzhen followers. In 1242 Governor Duan ordered Li Junmin 李俊民—a local scholar then working as a secretary for Duan—to compose an

---

84. Li Jin, "Longyang guan Yuzhen qingmiao zhenren benxing ji," *JSL*, 542.

inscription about Shouwei's construction work.[85] This is the source of our information about her. Her experience shows how women in the Quanzhen Daoist order were able to take the initiative and to associate with male Daoist clergy, lay followers, local literati, and officials.

Shouwei's experience also addresses the question of what a woman on her own could do in a time of military violence. Apart from instructing women to commit suicide to maintain their chastity and loyalty to male family members, Confucian doctrines offered little practical guidance for northern women living through decades of disorder.[86] As a Quanzhen nun, Shouwei—a widow who had to strive hard to support her refugee family—had access to an extensive social network with more resources than her immediate family could provide. Had Shouwei not joined the Quanzhen order, she and her children could have died of hunger or violence or become wartime captives as they retreated 300 kilometers from Taiyuan to Zezhou.[87] In the 1230s wandering soldiers in Shanxi often attacked ordinary people, stole their property, and killed them.[88] Even if her family had survived such an attack, Shouwei would have had to depend on her younger brother Dezhong—her only living adult male relative—to support her and help raise her children. It was also unlikely that Shouwei, as an ordinary village woman, would have had any chance to associate with the most powerful couple in Zezhou: Governor Duan and his wife. Her identity as a Quanzhen nun not only protected Shouwei from Mongol violence but also gave her access to locally powerful families. With funding from Duan and his wife, Shouwei was able to rebuild the Abbey of Cultivation, which became a new home for her and her children.

We do not know whether Shouwei took in orphans as well. Yet the case of the Convent of Assembled Perfected (*Jizhen guan* 集眞觀), to the

---

85.　Li Junmin, "Chongjian Xiuzhen guan shengtang ji" 重建修眞觀聖堂記, *QYW*, 1:44–45.

86.　Yuan Haowen wrote an epitaph on his own to praise a widow who committed suicide in Kaifeng city after her father was killed by rebel Jin troops in 1233. See Yuan Haowen, "Nie xiaonü muming" 聶孝女墓銘, *QJ*, 25.545.

87.　Many women, including members of the Jin imperial families, became wartime captives during the Jin-Mongol war. They were brought to the northern steppe or sold to other regions. See Chen Gaohua, "Yuandai nüxing de jiaoyou," 83.

88.　Wang Bowen 王博文, "Qizhenzi Li zunshi mubei" 樓眞子李尊師墓碑, *JSL*, 582–83.

east in Henan province, demonstrates that Quanzhen convents often functioned as orphanages, particularly for girls. A woman named Yang Shouhe 楊守和 and her daughter joined the Daoist order after her husband died when she was forty-one. Later, reportedly with funding from ordinary followers, Shouhe bought a piece of land to build the convent and became its first abbess. She took two girls into the convent who would become important disciples: Shouzhen 守真 and Pang Shouzheng 龐守正.[89] Shouhe's convent became an alternative shelter for local orphaned girls like Shouzheng, who came to the convent at the age of seven.

The master-disciple bond between Abbess Shouhe and her disciples resembled a mother-daughter relationship. Shouhe lived to the ripe age of seventy-two and retained her authority in the convent until her death. Before she died she designated Shouzhen and Pang Shouzheng to inherit the position of abbess, successively, and her disciples obeyed. After Shouhe died, her dedication motivated Shouzheng to take care of the tombs of Shouhe's natal family and of her husband's family when both families had no remaining heirs. Shouzheng's behavior echoed what the Quanzhen monk Li Zirong expected of his disciples: taking care of his ancestral tombs. It was not new for women to mind the affairs of their natal families, or for clergy to continue to take care of their aged parents even after joining a religious order (*chujia* 出家).[90] It was, however, innovative that religious disciples in Quanzhen Daoist monastic communities inherited the family obligations of their masters. Even more unusual, many women in the Quanzhen order were also doing these things.

The achievements of Quanzhen nuns also moved male writers to document female accomplishments. Shouhe, Shouzhen, and Shouzheng were all remarkably successful. The well-known scholar-official Hu Zhiyu 胡祗遹 (1227–93) summarized their deeds in a stele inscription written in 1286: "Shouhe initiated a religious lineage and did things that even vigorous men could not achieve. Shouzhen and Shouzheng inherited Shouhe's enterprise without bringing disgrace to her wisdom of choosing

---

89. Catherine Despeux and Livia Kohn maintain that Shouzhen was Shouhe's daughter, yet my impression from the primary sources is that the daughter and the first disciple were two different women. For a discussion of Quanzhen women in Henan, see Despeux and Kohn, *Women in Daoism*, 152–54.

90. Bossler, "'A Daughter Is a Daughter All Her Life.'"

the suitable successors."[91] For him, Shouhe's ability to build up a convent from nothing and to initiate a religious lineage was extraordinary; Shouzhen and Shouzheng's perpetuation of her legacy was also notable. Shouhe and her disciples cared both for homeless orphaned children and for heirless dead ancestors; their convent functioned as a valuable social institution for both the living and the dead. That might be what impressed contemporaries most about Quanzhen women.

For Chinese women from better-off families, the Quanzhen order provided a promising religious alternative to family life. The popularity of Quanzhen Daoism even shaped the emergence of a new image of elite women in northern Chinese society under Mongol rule. In an epitaph for his mother-in-law, Zuo Shoukuan 左守寬, Hu Zhiyu portrayed an ideal woman whose behavior lived up to both Confucian and Daoist norms. Before becoming a Quanzhen Daoist, Shoukuan was defined through her relationship with male family members: a filial daughter, a virtuous wife, a devoted mother, and a chaste widow. After entering the Quanzhen order, Shoukuan was a serious Quanzhen nun practicing asceticism and monasticism.

Shoukuan's pre-Quanzhen experience supporting her only son's education and official career conformed to the image of an ideal widow that had been mainstream in Chinese society since the Northern Song dynasty, though with an important twist that fit the new age of Mongol rule. According to Hu, Shoukuan married a man who rose from being a farmer to magistrate of Zhangde 彰德 county (now Anyang, in Henan province) because of his military achievements during the Jin-Mongol war. When her husband died, Shoukuan was thirty-nine years old and her son and daughter were still young. Vowing not to marry again but to bring up her son to be a successful man, Shoukuan worked on looms along with two or three servant girls and instructed male servants to till farmland. Meanwhile, she taught her son to study and learn horsemanship and archery. Thanks to Shoukuan's efforts, within a few years her son was able to inherit his father's official rank, and her daughter married Hu.[92] Despite the hardships she experienced, Shoukuan man-

---

91. Hu Zhiyu, "Jizhen guan bei," *JSL*, 671–72.

92. Hu Zhiyu, "Shouzhen xuanjing sanren nüguan Zuo lianshi mubei" 守眞玄靜 散人女冠左煉師墓碑, *JSL*, 1123.

aged to run her household effectively amid the chaos of the Jin-Yuan transition.

This image of Shoukuan's earlier secular life clearly bears some similarity to the lives of her Song-dynasty counterparts as portrayed by Song literati.[93] The primary difference was that while ideal Song widows supported their sons in taking the civil service examinations, Shoukuan drew praise for encouraging her son to learn military skills to succeed in the Mongol government. Nevertheless, the preceding description demonstrates the qualities of faithful wife and devoted mother that defined Shoukuan before she entered the Quanzhen order.

Shoukuan's behavior changed dramatically when she decided to enter the order. Hu relates that after her children reached adulthood and her family property increased, Shoukuan invited her relatives and neighbors to her home and gave the following speech: "When one is born as a man, he withdraws from the world after he achieves success and wins recognition. This is the Way of Heaven. Should it not be just as much so for me as a woman? My children, from now on, please don't consult me about family business again."[94] Shoukuan's alleged speech suggests a confident woman who was not only proud of her success as the head of her family but also determined to leave her family behind in her pursuit of individual spirituality. After the speech Shoukuan soon built a meditation cloister in the backyard of the household, donned Daoist clothing, and studied with a prominent Quanzhen monk. A few years later, Shoukuan moved out of her household and constructed an independent Daoist hermitage in another village, where she lived a quiet spiritual life until her death.

In addition to nuns, female patrons also played an important role in extending the influence of the Quanzhen order throughout north China. Mongol rule created a new space for female patrons from powerful warlord families to exercise their influence in public affairs. Some women even achieved leadership roles in supervising Quanzhen projects. The case of the wife of Governor Du Feng 杜豐 in Qinzhou subprefecture—adjacent to Zezhou—is exemplary. On April 10, 1240, the Great Empress Töregene, a wife of Ögödei Khan (r. 1229–41), issued a decree to officials

93. Liu Jingzhen, "Nü wu wai shi"; Bossler, *Powerful Relations*, 17–20.
94. Hu Zhiyu, "Shouzhen xuanjing sanren," *JSL*, 1123.

in southern Shanxi specifying that Governor Du supervise the Daoist canon project. The decree spells out a possible role for Du's wife:

> To *darughachi* and civil officials of Pingyang circuit:[95] Governor Du Feng in Qinzhou subprefecture should assume the position of chief supervisor to oversee the carving of printing blocks for Daoist canon scriptures and other matters, including construction.
>
> [To Dufeng] Should you lack the time to carry it out yourself, your wife may take over.[96]

Töregene wanted the Du couple to supervise printing activities for good reason. The couple was not only well connected to other Shanxi governors but also known as the most active sponsors of the contemporary Quanzhen Patriarch Yin Zhiping, whom Töregene favored.[97] Lucille Chia has suggested that allowing Du's wife to assume responsibility for the project would make this supervisory task less official.[98] But Töregene may simply have been following an accepted Mongol practice: it was actually common among the Mongols for a noble woman to help her husband with his political career. Töregene herself was in firm control of the Mongol court in the later years of Ögödei's reign.[99] Yet it was completely new for the Chinese to assign an official position to a woman, even if her duties were primarily religious. We do not know whether Lady Wang—Du Feng's wife—did, in fact, take over her husband's position as official superintendent, but we do know that another woman, Lady

95. *Darughachi* refers to special officers often selected from among the grand khan's *nököd*—guards under the direct leadership of a khan—to oversee census taking, tax collection, and military recruitment.

96. "Tiantan shifang da ziwei gong yizhi ji jiewa dian ji" 天壇十方大紫微宮懿旨及結瓦殿記, *JSL*, 480. The edict includes both Chinese and Mongolian texts. The Chinese text shifts abruptly from the third to the second person. The Mongolian text has only three lines. For the translation and discussion of this Sino-Mongolian inscription, see Cleaves, "The Sino-Mongolian Inscription of 1240"; De Rachewiltz, "Some Remarks on Töregene's Edict."

97. Jinping Wang, "A Social History of the *Treasured Canon*," 19–21.

98. Chia, "The Uses of Print," 176.

99. For the relatively high position held by women in Mongol society and their important role in political affairs, see Rossabi, "Khubilai Khan and the Women."

Yang Miaozhen 楊妙眞, the wife of a governor in Shaanxi, actually appointed by the Mongol court to supervise the construction of a key Quanzhen institution in Shaanxi province.[100]

As we have seen, ascetic Quanzhen nuns, enthusiastic female missionaries, women devotees from both ordinary and elite families, and powerful female patrons all associated freely with male Quanzhen Daoists and patrons. Unlike Confucian writings, contemporary Quanzhen Daoist texts express no concern about gender separation. Women in the Quanzhen Daoist order enjoyed unprecedented freedom in communicating and working with the opposite sex, which would have been impossible in Confucian families. In highlighting Quanzhen nuns' institutional leadership as founders of convents and charismatic leaders of religious communities, Shin-Yi Chao even characterizes northern women's participation in the Quanzhen order as "good career moves."[101] Yet we should remember that many poor widows like Zhang Shouwei and Yang Shouhe most likely became Quanzhen Daoists because they had no alternative. Extant Quanzhen writings tell of men who abandoned their families for the order. Interestingly, they record no women who did so. Unmarried girls aside, most adult women entered the order as widows. Over time, contemporary male scholars showed increasing displeasure at the departure of women from Confucian norms. Some tried to reconcile the contradiction between traditionally hierarchical gender relations and the relative gender equality demonstrated by Quanzhen nuns, while others reiterated the importance of Confucian female virtues for Quanzhen nuns—particularly filial piety and chastity.[102]

100. Meng Panlin 孟攀麟, "Shifang chongyang wanshou gong ji" 十方重陽萬壽宮記, QSXB, 69. This Lady Yang Miaozhen was not the same person as the better-known Yang Miaozhen, who led a group of local bandits and later was appointed governor of Shandong by the Mongols in the first half of the thirteenth century. For more on that Yang Miaozhen, see Wu Pei-Yi, "Yang Miaozhen."

101. Chao, "Good Career Moves."

102. Liu Minzhong 劉敏中, "Shenxiao wanshou gong ji" 神霄萬壽宮記, JSL, 709; Liu Jiangsun 劉蔣孫, "Bianliang lu Qiyun guan ji" 汴梁路樓云觀記, JSL, 646.

Building the Pilgrimage Center: The Palace of Eternal Joy

Quanzhen Daoist monks and nuns all painstakingly participated in building the infrastructure of the Quanzhen institutional order, which took physical form in Quanzhen temples and steles erected in villages, towns, and cities throughout north China during the thirteenth century; one scholar puts the number of Quanzhen temples at four thousand.[103] The infrastructure of the Quanzhen order contributed to the workings of both the new Mongol state and local Chinese society.

For the Mongol state, the Quanzhen order took on some quasi-governmental functions. In their heyday, Quanzhen Daoists used their rigorous monastic networks to transport local tribute to the Mongol court, a task usually assumed by local governments. According to a 1252 inscription from the Changchun Abbey in Anyi county in southern Shanxi, Quanzhen Daoists there were entrusted by the central government to take care of a vineyard, which produced grapes for making tributary wine. The Quanzhen monks also had the responsibility of transporting the ripe grapes first to the Office of the Daoist Registrar of Pingyang circuit and then to the Palace of Everlasting Spring—the Quanzhen headquarters in Yanjing. From there Quanzhen Daoists handed the grapes over to the central government.[104]

In local Chinese society, Quanzhen Daoists interacted with lay followers in two overlapping undertakings: building Quanzhen institutions and rebuilding postwar communities. While local residents organized associations to support Quanzhen establishments, Quanzhen monks and nuns played active roles in the daily life of local communities, such as rebuilding infrastructure that had been destroyed in wartime, organizing relief supplies, transferring landholdings, and providing ritual services. Moreover, many powerless villagers sought the protection of Quanzhen Daoist monasteries, which had massive landholdings and provided tax shelters. Some of their landholdings were grants from Mongol rulers and nobles or donations of local governors and followers; others came through

103.　Goossaert, "The Invention of an Order," 117.
104.　"Anyi Changchun guan zhafu" 安邑長春觀札付, *JSL*, 512–13.

the Quanzhen clergy's own efforts or appropriation of land that had belonged to others, including Buddhist monasteries. The development of a Quanzhen monastic network that was centered on the Palace of Eternal Joy (*Yongle gong* 永樂宮), a national Quanzhen pilgrimage center, typifies how major Quanzhen institutions integrated postwar community rebuilding in local society.[105]

Quanzhen Daoists built the Palace of Eternal Joy on the grounds of a local temple dedicated to the Daoist immortal Lü Dongbin 呂洞賓 at Yongle, a market town in Ruicheng 芮城 county, in southern Shanxi. Local residents had built the original temple in the late ninth century. Lü, reportedly a Yongle native, was a popular immortal in many of the anecdotes that circulated widely in Song China. Those anecdotes recounted Lü's literary and calligraphic talents, his miraculous powers to foretell the future and convert others, and his close links with the wine trade and prostitutes.[106] Since the late Tang, local literati and ordinary people had developed a tradition of gathering at the temple annually on Lü's birthday to make offerings, drink, and enjoy musical performances for the whole day.[107]

Wang Zhe, the founder of Quanzhen Daoism, identified Lü as his spiritual master, and later Quanzhen thinkers created a new category of Five Patriarchs (*wuzu* 五祖), of whom Lü was one.[108] In 1240 Song Defang made a pilgrimage to the dilapidated temple at Yongle. After local

105. The monastic complex is now often called the Palace of Eternal Joy, although its original name was the Great Palace of Purified Yang and Limitless Longevity (*Da chunyang wanshou gong* 大純陽萬壽宮). It has become one of the most prominent Daoist pilgrimage sites in China, known particularly for its well-preserved mural paintings. During the late 1950s and early 1960s the entire temple complex was moved from Yongle, a market town, to its present location in Ruicheng county to make way for a dam. Most of the buildings and mural paintings remained intact. Considering the often-cited translation of the monastery's name as the Palace of Eternal Joy, I will use that name in this study. For a comprehensive study of the site of the Palace of Eternal Joy, see Katz, *Images of the Immortal*.

106. Baldrian-Hussein, "Lü Tung-pin in Northern Song Literature."

107. Wang E 王鶚, "Chongxiu Da chunyang wanshou gong bei" 重修大純陽萬壽宮碑, *QSXB*, 127.

108. De Rachewiltz and Russell argue that by 1188 Quanzhen Daoists had officially recognized Lü as one of their patriarchs ("Ch'iu Ch'u-chi," 5). Other scholars believe instead that later Quanzhen Daoists constructed this religious lineage in their hagiographical writings, beginning with Qin Zhi'an's *Record of the Orthodox Lineage of*

officials and residents offered the temple to Song, Quanzhen Daoists took charge of it.[109] In the winter of 1244, a fire burned the temple to ashes. Two years later, supported by the Mongol court, many Shanxi officials, and the Quanzhen leaders, a Quanzhen master named Pan Dechong 潘德沖 brought his disciples and colleagues from Beijing to rebuild the site as a new Quanzhen institution: the Palace of Eternal Joy.[110]

By the time Khubilai Khan ordered Wang E, formerly a Jin scholar-official, to compose an essay to celebrate the completion of the Palace of Eternal Joy in 1262, Quanzhen Daoists had already formed a massive monastic network that encompassed the Palace of Eternal Joy, the Palace of the River, the Efficacious Source (*Hedu Lingyuan gong* 河瀆靈源宮), and the Upper Palace of Purified Yang (*Chunyang shanggong* 純陽上宮); more than ten lower temples surrounding the Upper Palace; and dozens of subordinate small abbeys and hermitages in neighboring villages in at least ten counties and prefectures across Shanxi, Shaanxi, and Henan. Local residents in turn organized lay associations (*hui* 會) for worshipping Lü and building monasteries, invited Quanzhen clergy to establish or take charge of Quanzhen hermitages in villages, relied on Quanzhen Daoists for food supplies, and cooperated with them in agricultural production.[111]

In the early phase of the Quanzhen order's penetration into local society, the clergy were outsiders who relied on local people—particularly through lay associations for worshipping Lü Dongbin—to identify suitable sacred places to build Quanzhen shrines. In his account of how he built the Upper Palace, Liu Ruoshui 劉若水 reports that some time before 1244, he met an association head (*huishou* 會首)—a common title for the organizer of a local association. The association head brought him to the remote Nine-Peak Mountain and told him that a particular grotto

---

the *Golden Lotus* (*Jinlian zhengzong ji* 金蓮正宗記), completed in 1241. See Marsone, "Accounts of the Foundation of the Quanzhen Movement," 98–99.

109.   Li Ding, "Xuandu zhidao piyun zhenren," *JSL*, 547.

110.   "Qing Pangong zhuchi shu" 請潘公住持疏, *JSL*, 491–93; Wang E, "Chongxiu Da chunyang," *QSXB*, 126–27.

111.   Lay associations were one important type of social (and more often religious) organization in traditional China that originated in early Daoist assemblies and Buddhist organizations. See Robinet, *Taoism*, 53–62; Zürcher, *The Buddhist Conquest of China*, 1:219–23.

was said to be the place where Lü had meditated and attained enlightenment (see plate 3). The Daoist Liu Ruoshui remained on the mountain, built a hermitage on the site, and later enlarged it to create the Upper Palace of Purified Yang (plate 4). Lü's meditation grotto and the Upper Palace later became a new sacred site where Quanzhen pilgrims came to pay their respects.[112] Some Daoist pilgrims remained on the mountain and built still other hermitages, contributing to the physical expansion of the Quanzhen religious center.[113]

Quanzhen Daoists attracted local residents by providing them with food supplies in hard times. In contrast to the impoverished local people, the Daoists owned large swathes of property. While enlarging the Upper Palace in 1252, Pan Dechong and Liu Ruoshui bought fertile tracts and recruited peasants to farm monastic lands. They also bought various orchards of vegetables and fruit trees and gardens of bamboo and reed to diversify monastic supplies, and they purchased boats, carts, and mills to support various tasks within the monastery. The combination of personal savings, financial support from local authorities, and donations from other lay patrons meant that the Daoists had ample food most of the time.[114] While serving as the abbot of the Palace of Eternal Joy, Pan frequently loaned millet to local people in the winter and early spring when many villagers ran out. The loans totaled tens of thousands of kilograms. In a year when the harvest was poor, even the Daoists in the Palace of Eternal Joy lacked food. Some Daoists wanted to get the loaned food back from local borrowers, but Pan stopped them to show his generosity. Moved by the gesture, local people later organized associations to

112. Liu Ruoshui, "Xuanshou sangong tidian Dongming yuanjing zhenren Liu Ruoshui zixu" 宣授三宮提點洞明淵靜眞人劉若水自序, *Ruicheng xianzhi* [1997], 797.

113. Zhou Deqia 周德洽, "Chuangjian Xuanyi guan bei" 創建玄逸觀碑, *JSL*, 777–78.

114. When Song Defang first came to Yongle in 1240 and assimilated the temple dedicated to Lü Dongbin into the Quanzhen order, he received a donation of thirty *mu* (approximately two hectares) of irrigated land and a mill from two local military officers and other lay followers. See Li Ding, "Xuandu zhidao piyun zhenren," *JSL*, 547. The funerary biography of Pan Dechong mentions that in 1252, the Quanzhen Patriarch Li Zhichang passed by the Palace of Eternal Joy and gave all of his personal savings to support monastic expenditures there. See Tudan Gonglü 徒單公履, "Chonghe zhenren Pangong shendao zhi bei" 沖和眞人潘公神道之碑, *JSL*, 554–56.

provide annual offerings at the Palace of Eternal Joy on the birthday of Lü Dongbin.

Villagers from different backgrounds under the leadership of local lay associations participated in the construction of the Palace of Eternal Joy as well. One 1262 inscription lists the names and occupations of villager participants in addition to the names of the Quanzhen Daoists (plate 5).[115]

Four married women served as association heads, and more than 240 villagers from Yongle and forty-six subordinate villages participated. Eight of those villagers—four of whom came from the same village—had the occupation *tongshi* 通事, the term for interpreters during the Jin and Yuan periods, which suggests that these people may have been interpreters for the Mongols or other non-Chinese.[116] Also, in another group of eight villagers (all from the same village), seven had obviously Mongol-style names. Since contemporary Chinese sometimes adopted Mongol names, the seven were not necessarily all Mongols. Yet we know that many Mongols immigrated to southern Shanxi after 1236, when Ögödei Khan divided the regions of the recently subjugated Jin dynasty among his kindred. The stele listed an additional fifty-nine villagers from eleven other villages in Ruicheng county, and about twenty who came from eight villages in neighboring counties. In this region it was nothing new for villagers to organize associations to support local monasteries. However, the structure of the Quanzhen Daoist order, with its headquarters at the Palace of Eternal Joy and subordinate villages organized under lay associations, was completely new.

The ties of religious lineage strengthened the relationship between the Palace of Eternal Joy and its subordinate villages. The 1262 inscription mentions twelve Daoist abbeys and convents located in local villages and one in Ruicheng city. Among those institutions, we can trace the history of two abbeys—the Abbey of the Jade Capital (*Yujing guan* 玉京觀) and the Abbey of Lustrous Purity (*Zejing guan* 澤淨觀). Both belonged to the

---

115. The published version of the 1262 inscription transcribes Wang E's text on the front of the stele. The text on the back of this stele is unpublished. In June 2009 I visited the Palace of Eternal Joy, took photos, and transcribed the unpublished sections.

116. On interpreters and their role in Yuan China, see Xiao, "Yuandai de tongshi yu yishi" 元代的通事與譯史, in his *Yuanchao shi xinlun*, 324–84.

religious lineage of Song Defang, whose members worshipped Song at the Palace of Eternal Joy.

The Palace of Eternal Joy became the headquarters of Song Defang's religious lineage after the 1250s. Many of his disciples came to Yongle after the printing blocks for the Quanzhen Daoist canon were transferred from the Abbey of Mysterious Capital in Pingyang to the Palace of Eternal Joy in 1250.[117] He Zhiyuan—one of Song's major disciples, who worked on the canon project—assumed the position of superintendent (*tiju* 提舉) of the Palace of Eternal Joy. With the support of many local governors, who provided money, material, and manpower, He Zhiyuan led his colleagues in constructing a new tomb and shrine in the Palace of Eternal Joy for Song, who died in Shaanxi in 1247.[118] In 1254 more than ten thousand Quanzhen Daoists and lay followers gathered at the palace to attend the grand ceremonial reburying of Song.[119] Song's major disciples would gather annually at the grave and the shrine to commemorate him, like a son would do to honor his deceased father.[120] These practices, arguably borrowed from Confucian funeral rites, extended the Confucian notion of filial piety to relations between disciples and their religious masters.[121] Song's sarcophagus, which was decorated with images of the twenty-four tales of filial piety (*ershisi xiao* 二十四孝), underlines the importance of master-disciple ties (figs. 2.3 and 2.4).[122]

Since many of Song Defang's disciples gathered in southern Shanxi after 1250, the Mongol court ordered He Zhiyuan to take charge of all Daoist monks and nuns in Song's lineage in Pingyang circuit. In the years that followed, He and his colleagues repaired and established many Dao-

117. Wang E, "Chongxiu Da chunyang," *QSXB*, 126. Song's disciple Xing Zhiju, who also participated in the canon project, became the abbot of the Abbey of Mysterious Capital after Qin Zhi'an died and built a library to hold the canon. See "Chonghe zhenren daoxing zhi bei bingxu" 沖和真人道行之碑並序 (dated 1261), *DQ: Linfen yaodu*, 36–37.

118. Du Siwen, "Chongxiu shuigu Lequan guan," *JSL*, 653.

119. "Sanlao tonggong bei," *JSL*, 560–61.

120. Li Ding, "Xuandu zhidao piyun zhenren," *JSL*, 548; Shang Ting, "Xuandu zhidao chongwen minghua," *JSL*, 613.

121. Wang Zongyu, "Quanzhenjiao de rujiao chengfen."

122. Song Defang's and Pan Dechong's tombs were excavated at the same time in the late 1950s. Pan's sarcophagus was decorated with the full twenty-four tales of filial piety. See Xu Pingfang, "Guanyu Song Defang he Pan Dechong."

FIGURE 2.3 Song Defang's sarcophagus in the Palace of Eternal Joy. This stone sarcophagus was made by a local craftsman in southern Shanxi and given to Song's disciples by the salt commissioner of Xiezhou subprefecture in 1254. In that year, Song's disciples held a large assembly at the Palace of Eternal Joy to rebury their master, who had originally been buried in Shaanxi. In addition to four tales of filial piety (see fig. 2.4), the sarcophagus was decorated with line engravings depicting a magnificent household and the family life of an upper-class couple. The sarcophagus has a strongly secular appearance, an intriguing contrast with the austere lifestyle of the Quanzhen master who was buried inside. Author photo.

ist abbeys in local villages, including the Abbey of the Jade Capital and the Abbey of Lustrous Purity.[123]

The history of the Abbey of the Jade Capital at Miaoxia village illustrates how local villagers cooperated with Daoist clergy in Song

123.   Other Quanzhen abbeys in local villages in Song's lineage included the Abbey of Eastern Glory (*Donghua guan* 東華觀) at Shangguo village, the Abbey of Enjoying Completion (*Lequan guan* 樂全觀) at the Water Valley, and the Abbey of the Jade Spring (*Yuquan guan* 玉泉觀). See Du Siwen, "Chongxiu shuigu Lequan guan," *JSL*, 652; He Zhiyuan, "Yuquan guan ji" 玉泉觀記, *JSL*, 683.

FIGURE 2.4 Four tales of filial piety on Song Defang's sarcophagus. Carved onto the sarcophagus shown in figure 2.3 are four tales of filial piety: Guo Ju, who planned to kill his son so that he could provide food for his mother (upper right); Dong Yong, who sold himself to earn money to pay for his father's burial and was rewarded by a divine lady (upper left); Wang Xiang, who loosened his clothing and lay on the ice so that it would melt and he could catch carp for his hungry parents (lower right); and Meng Zong, who wept until bamboo shoots sprouted from the soil watered by his tears, which he then fed to his mother (lower left). Drawing by Amelia Sargent from author photos.

Defang's lineage to establish small abbeys, convents, and hermitages. Song's disciple Xue Zhixi 薛志熙 was a native of Miaoxia and came from what was originally a wealthy family. Given the village's desolation after the war, Xue Zhixi followed the Quanzhen approach of building abbeys to help people survive, working for years to construct buildings, expand monastic landholdings, build roads, and plant vegetables and peach trees in the abbey. In 1252 Xue left Miaoxia to join He Zhiyuan, who had resigned from his position at the Palace of Eternal Joy and was working to guide the construction of a Daoist abbey in another village. Later, when the Abbey of the Jade Capital was in disrepair, Miaoxia villagers invited He to repair it and write an inscription about the abbey in the name of completing Xue's unfinished project.[124] The collegiality between Xue and He influenced the villagers' choices of Daoist clergy and provided them with access to Quanzhen resources. Because He was the leader of all Song's disciples in southern Shanxi, he brought other Quanzhen Daoists with him to complete the monastic construction in Miaoxia.

Why did villagers support the establishment of Quanzhen institutions in their communities? In addition to their spiritual needs, they had economic needs. In the economically strapped countryside under Mongol rule, southern Shanxi peasants struggled with a heavy tax burden, particularly after Pingyang circuit became the fief of descendants of Jochi (c. 1181–1227), Chinggis Khan's eldest son.[125] During one year in the 1250s, the scholar Hao Jing—a southern Shanxi native and, as noted above, a student of Yuan Haowen—presented the memorial "Offensive Words about Shanxi" to Khubilai, who was at that time the Mongol prince responsible for governing north China. The memorial describes the extreme poverty of Pingyang circuit due to exploitation by Jochi's descendants, who held the region as their appanage after 1236. They sent their retainers to extract excessive taxes in gold from local people through the Supervisorate-in-Chief of Pingyang Appanage (*Pingyang touxia zongguan fu* 平陽投下總管府), which existed until 1288.[126] In addition to the direct tax levy by appanage holders, local civil governors often extracted wealth from the region they governed and presented it to appanage holders to form favorable personal connections.[127] Local people who could not bear the burden fled their homes, resorted to cannibalism or died.

Since Quanzhen Daoist monastic property was exempt from all taxes, peasants often "donated" their land to Quanzhen abbeys and convents to avoid paying taxes, while continuing to farm the land. Contemporary

---

124. He Zhiyuan, "Miaoxia Yujing guan ming bing xu" 廟下玉京觀銘并序, *JSL*, 633; Du Siwen, "Chongxiu Shuigu Lequan guan," *JSL*, 652.

125. Muraoka, "Mongoru jidai shoki no kasei."

126. Hao Jing, "Hedong zuiyan" 河東罪言, *QYW*, 4: 90–92. For the Supervisorate-in-Chief of Pingyang Appanage and its abolition in 1288, see Cai Meibiao, *Liao Jin Yuan shi kaosuo*, 369–79.

127. See Yao Sui 姚燧, "Dayuan gu Yan'an bingma zongguan Yuan gong shendao-bei ming bing xu" 大元故延安兵馬總管袁公神道碑銘並序, *Linxian guji kao*, 16.7a–9a (*SSXB*, ser.3, 31: 38).

sources do not explicitly refer to such cases, but a close reading of an inscription for a Quanzhen abbey in a village in Ruicheng gives an impression of one case. In 1237 a villager surnamed Li donated a certain amount of land to a few Daoists to build a Daoist abbey; those Daoists later gave the abbey and land to Song Defang. In 1252 Song's disciple He Zhiyuan led other Quanzhen Daoists to repair the abbey. At that time Li's son made a new contract to donate the land again, this time to He. This suggests that, in reality, the Li family might have continued to own the land after the first "donation" in 1237.[128]

The loss of population in Ruicheng county during the Jin-Mongol war was so severe that the county was incorporated into neighboring Pinglu county in 1266, when Khubilai Khan ordered all counties with fewer than a thousand households to be amalgamated with other counties.[129] The extension of Quanzhen Daoist institutions into postwar Ruicheng society helped villagers reconstruct their daily lives after having lost a great deal. When formerly strong and prominent clans dissolved, some clan members entrusted their ancestral temples to Quanzhen Daoists. For instance, of the three ancestral temples of the locally influential Duan clan, two were devastated in periods of disorder, but one survived because Daoists from a nearby abbey had occupied it. One of the Duan clan members later became a Daoist official in the Palace of Eternal Joy and worked with his relatives to repair the temple.[130] At a time when people and money were scarce, the Quanzhen Daoist order had both.

As their organizational power and wealth grew, the Quanzhen Daoists in the monastic system of the Palace of Eternal Joy developed closer economic ties with local peasants, including landlord-tenant relationships. To feed hundreds of Daoist monks and nuns in the Palace of Eternal Joy and its affiliated abbeys and convents, Daoists acquired vast tracts of land over time and engaged in local agricultural production, just as they solicited lay donations. In 1324 Daoists erected a stele to list all lower

128. Du Siwen, "Chongxiu shuigu Lequan guan," *JSL*, 652.

129. In Shanxi three subprefectures and more than twenty counties were amalgamated under Mongol rule, suggesting massive population loss compared to the previous Jin period. See Wu Songdi, *Zhongguo renkou shi*, 449–51.

130. Duan Xi 段禧, "Chongxiu Duan Ganmu xiansheng citang ji" 重修段干木先生祠堂記, *QSXB*, 142; Wang Yi 王沂, "Jin yuanshuai Duangong beiming" 金元帥段公碑銘, *Ruicheng xianzhi* [1764], 12.12–13.

temples, monastic lands, and permanent monastic households (*changzhu hu* 常住戶) affiliated with the Palace of Eternal Joy.[131] As recorded, the monastic lands were in more than forty places in Ruicheng county, and the monastic property included dozens of lower temples (some in neighboring counties), graveyards for monks and nuns, gardens, and watermills. The inscription specifies that in the case of one watermill, which Daoists from the Palace of Eternal Joy built together with a village leader, Daoists could use the water for fourteen days each month.[132]

In addition to human and material resources, the Quanzhen order, as demonstrated by inscriptions from neighboring regions, also provided ideological and ritual resources that villagers could use to form new social bonds in a fragmented society. In 1260, upon initiating the construction of a temple in a village in Wenxi county in southern Shanxi, several local villagers allegedly explained: "After the Great Yuan Dynasty stabilized the country, people from different places lived together. They not only took their kin as kin, but also took the entire world as their kin. Why don't we establish incense-burning kin relations and glorify the Temple of the Three Efficacious Ones?"[133] When people with no kinship relations gathered in the same community, they found that worshipping the same deity gave them new bonds as "incense-burning kin relations" (*xianghuo qinyuan* 香火親緣). After the villagers completed the temple, they invited a Quanzhen Daoist surnamed Yang to be its abbot, and Yang worked with the villagers to make the temple a beautiful public place for local residents. Although we may choose not to take such a happy story

---

131. The term *changzhu* 常住 was originally a Buddhist word referring to the permanent assets of Buddhist monasteries. Quanzhen Daoists borrowed the concept from Buddhism.

132. "Chunyang wanshou gong tidian xiayuan tiandi changzhuhu ji" 純陽萬壽宮提點下院田地常住戶記, *JSL*, 792–95. The published text does not refer to the year in which the stele was erected. In June 2009 I found the list carved on the reverse of a stone stele on whose front are carved a 1222 inscription about repairing the temple to Lü Dongbin and an explanation for reinscribing the 1222 inscription on stone in 1324 by Quanzhen Daoists in the Palace of Eternal Joy. For the combined text, see Yuan Congyi 袁從義, "Youtang chunyang Lü zhenren citang ji" 有唐純陽呂眞人祠堂記, *JSL*, 447–48. The inscription on the reverse was presumably carved on the stone in the same year.

133. Li Zhijin 黎志謹, "Dachaoguo Xiezhou Wenxi xian Dongzhen Chengbeishang she chuangxiu Sanlinghou miao xiang ji" 大朝國解州聞喜縣東鎮城北上社創修三靈侯廟像記, *JSL*, 559.

at face value, especially when the author was a Quanzhen Daoist himself, the unmistakable fact is that many postwar villages in the thirteenth century chose to build Quanzhen establishments as a way to reconstruct community identity and solidarity.

Quanzhen clergy at the time also commonly gathered villagers to form a congregational-like community through Daoist rituals and ritual-based organizations. A 1261 inscription about the Hermitage of Realizing the Perfection (*Wuzhen an* 悟眞庵) from neighboring Henan provides a good example. A Quanzhen nun named Mu Shoumiao 穆守妙, who turned her house into the Quanzhen hermitage, led local villagers to build an "Efficacious Altar" (*lingtan* 靈壇).[134] The regular performance of rituals at the altar brought nuns and lay followers into a formal organization, in which they served diversified roles—including altar head (*zhutan* 主壇), altar manager (*zhangtan* 長壇), singing member (*gesheng* 歌生), and ordinary altar member (*tansheng* 壇生).[135] When Mu established her hermitage, she received help from a similar altar organization at another village in a neighboring county, indicating that organizations based on Quanzhen rituals connected different village communities, too.

In short, by 1262 Quanzhen Daoists had successfully transformed a small local temple to Lü Dongbin into a national pilgrimage center, a major Quanzhen institution with tremendous material wealth and a large number of clergy and affiliated lay followers in southern Shanxi. For local residents, the establishment of the Palace of Eternal Joy there brought valuable material and human resources and helped them reconstruct a normal everyday life after the war. While the peasants had no hope that the Mongols would provide tax relief or that local governors would help them rebuild their communities, they could depend on Quanzhen Daoists, the new social elite in north China. Some peasants entered the Quanzhen order to benefit from the legal privileges that Quanzhen clergy enjoyed. Others became affiliated with the Palace of Eternal Joy or its subordinate abbeys and convents in village communities through lay associations or other organizations based on Quanzhen ideas and rituals. Some villagers "donated" their land as Quanzhen monastic property

---

134. Su Zizhen 蘇子珍, "Weizhou Zuocheng xian Changle xiang dishi tuan chuangjian Wuzhen an ji" 衛州胙城縣長樂鄉第十疃創建悟眞庵記, *JSL*, 543–44.

135. Ibid., 544.

and became the tenants of Quanzhen establishments to escape the heavy tax burden imposed by the Mongol state or the local Mongol appanage holders. In addition to the Palace of Eternal Joy, approximately a dozen major Quanzhen institutions exerted great influence in postwar community rebuilding in similar ways throughout north China.[136] The powerful position of these top Quanzhen institutions, according to a contemporary observer, was really no different from that of a large and busy government office.[137]

As the Quanzhen Daoist order penetrated deep into the Shanxi region, local people who were not necessarily attached to a specific Quanzhen institution also commonly accepted Quanzhen norms and rituals. From officials to ordinary people, residents hired Quanzhen Daoist monks and nuns to build altars and perform rituals. They confessed their sins and prayed to Daoist immortals on behalf of their loved ones, including newborn babies and recently deceased spouses.[138] Li Junmin drafted a note for a man surnamed Qin in Zezhou subprefecture, thanking the Daoist immortals for bringing the man a son:

I did my utmost to punish myself and repent for my errors.
If that were not enough, I examined myself.
I thought to rely on the Daoist protective shadows to clean up my sins.
On this lucky day, I built a miraculous altar.
I gathered a group of elite Daoist priests, who knew the profound meanings of Daoist rituals.
I humbly hope that supreme immortals and various sages protect and bestow compassion on me as a response to my sincerity. Please grant great fortune to my son.
To fail to produce a male heir is the biggest sin. Please spare me from the criticism of not being filially pious.[139]

136. To name a few others, the Palace of Double Yang (*Chongyang gong* 重陽宮) in Shaanxi, the Great Palace of Everlasting Spring in Beijing, the Palace of Supreme Pureness (*Taiqing gong* 太清宮) and the Palace of Meeting the Primogenitor (*Chaoyuan gong* 朝元宮) in Henan, and the Palace of Eastern Flourishing (*Donghua gong* 東華宮) in Shandong. See Jing, *Daojiao quanzhenpai gongguan*, 178–211.

137. Wang Pan 王磐, "Chuangjian Zhenchang guan ji" 創建真常觀記, *JSL*, 616.

138. Li Junmin, "Guo Yanqing zhuijian furen qingci" 郭彥卿追薦夫人青詞, *QYW*, 4:84.

139. Li Junmin, "Qinshi dezi hou baoxie qingci" 秦氏得子後報謝青詞, *QYW*, 4:84.

Qin hired Daoists and performed Daoist rituals to gain spiritual protection for his baby son. Ordinary people genuinely believed in the miraculous power of Daoist immortals, which is also why they gave money to build Daoist monasteries in their communities.

Steles as a Medium of Social Power

Up to now, this chapter has presented a relatively positive picture of the Quanzhen Daoists in thirteenth-century northern Chinese society. We must remember, though, that most inscriptions were written by either Quanzhen Daoists themselves or scholars grateful to the Quanzhen Daoists for their social welfare projects in the wake of the Mongol conquest. In addition, we have a rich body of material on those projects because the thirteenth-century Quanzhen Daoists were particularly enthusiastic about creating, compiling, and preserving Quanzhen records, on both stone and paper.[140] Indeed, when numerous texts were lost in warfare, steles and printing served as important means by which Quanzhen Daoists strove for cultural authority and social power.

The Quanzhen Daoists brilliantly exploited the power of steles as a medium that allowed them to stress their privileged rights and consolidate their power. They invented the practice of carving tax-exemption edicts from Mongol rulers and placed them in many Quanzhen abbeys and convents.[141] These steles were commonly called imperial-edict steles (*shengzhi bei* 聖旨碑). In the Palace of Eternal Joy, Quanzhen Daoists erected at least eight different such steles carved with decrees that extended imperial protection to the temple and its lands—some in a colloquial Chinese that contained linguistic features of Mongolian languages, some in Mongolian, and some in both.[142] One stele included eight different edicts, and another clarified that it was a copy of a stele that recorded an earlier imperial edict.[143] One stele was carved with an edict issued by Khubilai

---

140. Boltz, *A Survey of Taoist Literature*, 68.

141. Feng Chengjun, *Yuandai baihua bei kao*, 28–46.

142. For the formats of imperial edicts in colloquial Chinese, see Zu and Funada, "Yuandai baihua beiwen."

143. *Sanjin shike zongmu*, 24–29.

Khan—probably in 1277, and the edict includes typical clauses of privileges the Mongol rulers gave to religious establishments at the time.[144] It says,

> By the power of Eternal Heaven, by the protection of the great and glorious fortune. Decree of the Khan. . . . This decree is given to Superintendent Wen Zhitong, Bai Zhichun, Zhu Zhiwan, and Daoist priests in the Palace of Pure Yang and Longevity (Palace of Eternal Joy), the Upper Palace at Nine-Peak Mountain, and the Palace of the River, the Efficacious Source built by the Perfect Man of Guangdao-chonghe. Messengers shall not stay in their monasteries and houses, nor shall they get post-horses or supplies, nor shall the commercial tax and land tax be paid. None, whoever they may be, shall take away any of their land or water, and gardens or mills.[145]

The most important clause here is the exemption from commercial and land taxes. In 1263 and 1264 Khubilai repeatedly issued edicts revoking the tax exemption granted to the Quanzhen Daoists by earlier Mongol khans and ordered all religious practitioners—including Quanzhen Daoists—to pay taxes if they farmed land and ran commercial enterprises.[146] But this religious policy was reversed in 1277.[147] It was reasonable that the Quanzhen Daoists at the Palace of Eternal Joy applied to the Mongol court in this year, asking Khubilai to issue a new imperial edict legitimizing their right to tax exemption.

Erecting an imperial-edict stele gave the Quanzhen clergy a crucial medium with which to control information about state policies. By acquiring decrees from Mongol khans and princes and inscribing them on stone steles in Quanzhen institutions across the country, Quanzhen monks and nuns consciously publicized the state's religious policy that served the clergy's interests. To emphasize their tax-exemption privilege, some Daoists even distorted the content of an imperial decree by purpose-

144. The edict was issued from Dadu in the year of the cow, which means either 1277 or 1289 during Khubilai's reign. Given the context, the year 1277 seems most likely. The stele—possibly a recarved one—was erected in 1327.

145. "Niu'er nian shengzhi beiji" 牛兒年聖旨碑記, *Yongle gong bihua*, 69.

146. *YS*, 5.95.

147. Chen Gaohua, "Yuandai fojiao siyuan fuyi," 7.

fully omitting critical words in the Chinese translation of the original edict in Mongolian.[148] By relentlessly producing a large number of similar imperial-edict steles, Quanzhen Daoists repeatedly sent the same message to society: they did not pay taxes, and their privileges and monastic property were protected by imperial decrees. Buddhists and Confucian students soon picked up this practice. Numerous imperial-edict steles installed in monasteries served as a powerful weapon that the clergy used to protect their property from their rivals, as well as from the state itself. As the 1277 stele from the Palace of Eternal Joy shows, imperial edicts always addressed their recipients with their full names and titles. Thus, these steles not only repeatedly claimed privileges granted by Mongol rulers but also distinguished those who had the right to inherit the privileges.

But for all their power, the Quanzhen Daoists remained vulnerable to political persecution.[149] Unlike their successful use of stone steles, the Quanzhen Daoists' use of printing to disseminate Quanzhen messages eventually brought disaster.[150] In 1281 Khubilai Khan ordered the burning of all Daoist texts and the woodblocks of the Daoist canon that Song Defang and Qin Zhi'an had spent more than seven years completing.[151] He spared only one text: *The Classic of Integrity and Virtue.*

Khubilai's order to burn the Daoist canon marked the culmination of a protracted contest between Buddhists and Quanzhen Daoists for Mongol patronage. The appropriation of Buddhist monasteries by Quanzhen Daoists was the key issue in many Buddho-Daoist disputes. In 1255 the Buddhist monk Fuyu 福裕 (1203–75), from the well-known Shaolin Monastery 少林寺 on Mount Song 嵩山 in Henan province, initiated the first Buddho-Daoist debate at the Mongol court. The Buddhists accused the Quanzhen Daoists of illegally occupying over five hundred Buddhist monasteries and their landholdings. Buddhists defeated Quanzhen

148. Irinchen, "Du 1276 nian Longmen," 120–21; Cai Meibiao, "Longmen Jianji gong bei" 龍門建極宮碑, in his *Basibazi beike*, 19–20.

149. Throughout the Yuan dynasty, the rise and fall of Quanzhen leaders was often tied to the fortunes of their major political patrons at the court. See Zheng, "Yuandai Quanzhen jiaozhu."

150. For Quanzhen Daoists' extensive use of print to spread their teachings, see Chia, "The Uses of Print," 201.

151. *YS*, 11.234.

Daoists in the debate, and Möngke Khan ordered the Daoists to return thirty-seven monasteries, but they did not carry out the order. As a result, in the following years, Buddhists from the Shaolin Monastery, together with Tibetan monks, appealed to the Mongol court—which organized two other debates, in 1256 and 1258.

Another key issue was the authenticity of the *Scripture on the Conversion of the Barbarians* (*Huahu jing* 化胡經), a sixth-century text claiming that the Daoist founder Laozi had gone west to convert the barbarians and that the Buddha was an avatar of Laozi. The text aimed to prove that Daoism was superior to Buddhism.[152] In the thirteenth century, proud of Qiu Chuji's western trip to meet Chinggis Khan and its parallels with Laozi's legendary journey, Quanzhen Daoists publicly preached the story of Laozi's journey. They distributed a new version illustrating the eighty-one incarnations of Laozi, carved scenes of these incarnations on stone steles, and painted them on the walls of many Daoist abbeys.[153] Most importantly, Quanzhen Daoists included the text in their new *Treasured Canon of Mysterious Capital*, which was the main cultural capital they used to propagate their teachings outside Quanzhen communities. Due to the shortage of texts throughout north China after the Mongol conquest, more than a hundred non-Daoist institutions, including local Confucian schools, borrowed the woodblocks of the canon from Song Defang to make extra copies for their own libraries.[154] Buddhists reacted strongly to the Quanzhen propagation of Daoist supremacy, resulting in fifty years of open controversy between Buddhists and Daoists.

The Mongol court accepted the Buddhist claim that the *Scripture on the Conversion of the Barbarians* was an apocryphal text written first in Chinese (and not in Sanskrit, as was the case with authentic Buddhist texts) and repeatedly ordered Quanzhen Daoists to burn all extant copies of the text. As viceroy of north China after 1253, Prince Khubilai presided over the third debate in his newly built town of Kaiping (later Shangdu 上都 [Upper Capital], now in Inner Mongolia, 275 kilometers north of Beijing) and clearly favored Buddhism. He decided that the Bud-

152. Buddho-Daoist debates about this text began in the Tang dynasty. See Kohn, *Laughing at the Tao*.

153. K. Ch'en, "Buddhist-Taoist Mixtures in the Pa-shih-i-hua T'u"; Jing, *Yuandai bihua*, 32–42.

154. Jinping Wang, "A Social History of the *Treasured Canon*," 23.

dhists had won the 1258 debate and forced the seventeen Daoists who had participated in the debate to be tonsured and undergo Buddhist ordination.[155]

After he ascended the throne in 1260, Khubilai continued to persecute the Quanzhen Daoists. In 1261 he ordered the destruction of all steles containing apocryphal texts. He also called on the Daoists to rearrange the statues of the founders of the three teachings on altars so that the Buddha was in the middle, flanked by Laozi on the left and Confucius on the right (the Daoists had placed Laozi in the center).[156] Because Khubilai wanted to consolidate his control over all of China, he could not tolerate the tremendous power of the Quanzhen Daoists, with their extensive landholdings, wealth, and followers. But in the 1260s and 1270s, the Mongols' main goal was the conquest of the Southern Song, and they had little time to check whether regional governors actually carried out their orders. The anti-Daoist campaign did little damage to the Quanzhen Daoist order, which continued to expand throughout north China.[157]

In 1276 the Mongols gained control of southern China, and they defeated the final remnants of the Song armies in 1279, when the infant who was the last emperor of the Southern Song dynasty died. Only then could Khubilai pay more attention to the Quanzhen Daoists. In 1280 he issued the following edict after deciding that two Quanzhen monks, in order to frame Buddhists, had set fire to a granary in the Palace of Everlasting Spring, the headquarters of the Quanzhen Daoists in Yanjing (which had become the capital of the Yuan): "Now, these Daoists from the Palace of Everlasting Spring have again committed outrages. They have confessed their crimes. Two of the principal criminals were executed, and others were sentenced to have their ears and noses sliced off, or to beatings, or to exile. This incident is now settled." Historians do not know whether Quanzhen Daoists actually set the granary on fire; it is equally possible that their Buddhist enemies staged the crime. In addition to condemning the crime, Khubilai was clearly concerned about the large

155. Nakamura, "Mongoru jidai no Dōbutsu ronsō"; Rossabi, *Khubilai Khan*, 37–43.

156. *Yuandai baihuabei jilu*, 104.

157. Buddhists continued to have a hard time achieving their goal of reclaiming monastic property from Quanzhen Daoists. See Bo Yongjian, "Yuandai de fodao chongtu."

numbers of people gathered in Quanzhen institutions. The edict continued: "Starting now, from the Huai region to the north, each Buddhist
and Daoist monastery is allowed to have a maximum of one hundred
monks. Whoever violates these words, whether Buddhists or Daoists, will
receive a double sentence."[158] This was the crucial point: Khubilai restricted the size of all religious communities to only one hundred clergy.
The implementation of this new policy would directly affect the strength
of the Quanzhen communities, as some Quanzhen establishments, even
at the village level, had several hundred monks and nuns.[159]

In the tenth month of 1281 Khubilai ordered the burning of all copies of the Daoist canon and its woodblocks, and he reissued his earlier
orders from the 1250s and 1260s to pull down all steles carved with illustrations of Laozi converting the Buddha. Khubilai's 1281 edict was
doubtless a severe blow to the Quanzhen communities, yet evidence of
the order's local implementation is surprisingly scarce. I have found only
one inscription, composed in 1284, that describes a prefect in Henan negotiating with canon-burning commissioners on behalf of Quanzhen
Daoists.[160] This piece of information indicates that the Mongol court
did send commissioners to supervise the canon burning at local levels, yet
the imperial order might not have been thoroughly implemented because
of the intervention of local officials who sympathized with Quanzhen
Daoists.

More remarkably, the Quanzhen Daoists skillfully used steles to control
the damage caused by the canon-burning catastrophe. Most Quanzhen
inscriptions written after 1281 do not mention the canon at all—neither
its glorious production history nor its tragic destruction. Instead, Quanzhen Daoists quietly shifted their self-presentation by deliberately ignoring
this politically sensitive event and producing new steles for foundational
figures in the canon project. Three major inscriptions dedicated to Song
Defang are most suggestive. Two steles, installed in 1262 and 1274, respectively, detailed Song's contribution to the canon project, while one
produced in or after 1289 (the stele was installed in 1320) did not devote

158.   *Tongzhi tiaoge jiaozhu*, 29.704–5.
159.   Li Zhiquan, "Qingxu zi Liu zunshi muzhiming" 清虛子劉尊師墓誌銘, *JSL*, 538.
160.   Ning Ji 寧楫, "Fengxun dafu Mengzhou zhizhou Ligong dezheng zhi bei" 奉
訓大夫孟州知州李公德政之碑, *QSXB*, 179.

a single word to the canon.[161] More interestingly, while both the 1274 inscription and the one on the 1320 stele were about Song's religious achievements, the 1320 stele repeated most of his accomplishments from the former inscription but omitted the printing of the 1244 canon. Clearly, to save themselves and their order, Quanzhen Daoists recast their history on stones, eliminating the production of the canon and rewriting the stories of their masters. Only when the political environment shifted again in favor of the Quanzhen order did Quanzhen Daoists choose to resurrect the history of the *Treasured Canon*'s publication by recarving old inscriptions destroyed during the catastrophe. That is the reason for the availability of the 1274 inscription, as it was reinscribed in or after 1335 on a new stone at the Palace of Eternal Joy at the order of Wanyan Deming 完顏德明, a Daoist from Song's religious lineage and the last Quanzhen patriarch under Mongol rule.[162]

Conclusion

Patronized by the new Mongol authorities and supported by numerous lay followers, Quanzhen Daoist monks and nuns extended their order to almost every corner of thirteenth-century north China and displayed their great confidence in proposing social innovations. Institutionally, thirteenth-century Quanzhen Daoists followed the new Quanzhen approach promoted by Qiu Chuji of building as many of their establishments as possible to help devotees survive the prevailing chaos. As a result, thousands of Quanzhen abbeys, convents, and hermitages in cities, towns, and villages across north China, tied together by a clear

---

161.   Li Ding, "Xuandu zhidao piyun zhenren," *JSL*, 547; Shang Ting, "Xuandu zhidao chongwen," *JSL*, 613; Wang Liyong 王利用, "Xuantong hongjiao piyun zhenren daoxing zhi bei" 玄通弘教披雲眞人道行之碑, *JSL*, 753–54. The 1262 stele bears Li Ding's inscription, and the 1274 stele Shang Ting's at the request of Song's disciple Qi Zhicheng 祈志誠, who was the Quanzhen patriarch from 1272 to 1285. The 1320 stele bears an inscription by scholar-official Wang Liyong written at the request of a second-generation disciple of Song at the Ancestral Hall on Mount Zhongnan.

162.   Since he served as patriarch after 1335, the stele must have been installed in that year or later. For more on him as the last Quanzhen Patriarch, see Zhang Guangbao, *Jin Yuan Quanzhenjiao shi*, 163–65.

structure of Quanzhen religious lineages, formed a nationwide Quanzhen monastic network. A dozen lineage-based regional centers formed the key nodes in this network, which was headquartered in Yanjing. All of these Quanzhen establishments enjoyed the privilege of tax exemption, and many of them had considerable landholdings and other wealth. While they marked the Quanzhen clergy's status as members of the social elite, as the Jin state schools had done for the Confucian literati, the Quanzhen institutions under Mongol rule were much larger and more numerous than the Jin Confucian schools.

Socially, the Quanzhen order was unprecedentedly inclusive. In addition to their strong connections to the Mongol khans, empresses, princes, and regional governors, Quanzhen leaders attracted a large number of men who had been Jin literati and who joined the Quanzhen order. Quanzhen masters also created new jobs for former Jin literati through the publication of the Daoist canon and the subsequent establishment of a new Daoist education system. The nationwide establishment of Daoist schools staffed by literati Daoists not only allowed many young northern men to receive a literary education but also helped Quanzhen Daoism become an important vector of intellectual and educational organization in north China. Meanwhile, the Quanzhen order accommodated many northern women who were either looking for protection or pursuing an alternative to family life. The Quanzhen order not only justified the mixing of men and women but also promoted women's roles in public life, both unthinkable in a pre-Mongol society that had firmly subscribed to Confucian teachings. In building large Quanzhen institutions like the Palace of Eternal Joy in southern Shanxi, Quanzhen monks and nuns cooperated with their common followers in almost every village, town, and city, providing them with material, ideological, and organizational support for the reestablishment of postwar local communities.

Khubilai's exhaustive efforts to suppress the Quanzhen Daoists shed light on how powerful they had become by the early Yuan. They turned religious authority into social prominence, and the connections among the clergy and between clergy and laity created new ties that supplanted the Confucian order to bind Chinese society together. The stele inscriptions discussed in this chapter accurately portray the profound transformation in northern Chinese society during and after the Mongol conquest, as the influence of the Quanzhen Daoist order grew in local society and encountered challenges from other social groups. The frenzy of stele production among Quanzhen monks and nuns in thirteenth-century north China, meanwhile, conveys both the Quanzhen Daoists' pride in their accomplishments and their anxiety about losing their privileges. After all, for most northern Chinese—religious and secular—Yuan China was a new world in which the success of individuals, families, and religious establishments hinged on the connections they had to the new Mongol authorities. As we will see in the next chapter, Buddhist monks from Mt. Wutai, capitalizing on their own distinctive order, were among those who exploited such connections to the fullest.

CHAPTER 3

The Buddhist Order, Political Clout, and Kinship Relations

In the summer of 1254, age sixty-five, Yuan Haowen visited the Mountain of Five Terraces (*Wutaishan* 五臺山, hereafter Mt. Wutai) in northern Shanxi. One of China's largest and most venerated pilgrimage sites, Mt. Wutai has been famous since the Tang dynasty (618–907) as the legendary abode of Bodhisattva Mañjuśrī (*Wenshu pusa* 文殊菩薩), the Buddhist bodhisattva of wisdom. During this trip, Yuan wrote sixteen poems depicting what he saw on the mountain. One poem observed: "In the turn of a hand, donations from lay people fill monasteries. Several thousand people from remote areas come to visit the Mountain of Terraces."[1] The revival of Buddhist communities on the mountain at that time was the work of Yuan's friend, Chan Buddhist Master Pu'an 普安 (1216–67), who restored traditional Buddhist festivals and repaired major monasteries on Mt. Wutai in the 1250s.[2] Pu'an was one of the few Chinese Buddhist monks who received support from the early Mongol khans to revive Buddhist communities that had been extensively damaged during the war in north China.

1. Yuan Haowen, "Taishan zayong shiliu shou, jiayin liuyue" 臺山雜詠十六首 (甲寅六月), *QJ*, 14.355.
2. In a poem he sent to Pu'an, Yuan described the master's arrival as bringing spring to the Buddhist world on Mt. Wutai. See Yuan Haowen, "Zengda Pu'an shi" 贈答普安師, *QJ*, 10.244. The poem is not dated but was most likely written when Yuan visited the mountain while Pu'an was still there.

Two other key Buddhist figures were a childhood friend of Pu'an, the monk Zicong 子聰 (1216–74; also known as Liu Bingzhong 劉秉忠, a name later granted by Khubilai) and the well-known Chan Buddhist Master Haiyun 海雲 (1203–57). Zicong accompanied Haiyun to meet Khubilai in 1239, when the twenty-three-year-old prince summoned Haiyun to his camp to ask him about state affairs. Zicong joined Khubilai's staff and eventually became one of his principal advisors.[3] He recommended Pu'an to Khubilai. Between 1247 and 1260 the Mongol rulers appointed Haiyun and Pu'an supervisors of Buddhist affairs in the Central Plain (*Zhongyuan* 中原)—in other words, north China.[4]

Like influential Quanzhen Daoist masters such as Qiu Chuji, eminent Buddhist monks like Pu'an, Zicong, and Haiyun played important roles in protecting the descendants of Confucian families and prominent scholars. They also persuaded the Mongol conquerors to lighten their grip on the vanquished.[5] Yet not only did Buddhist institutions receive the Mongols' imperial patronage more than a decade later than the Quanzhen Daoist order did, but they were also much less organized and influential before 1260. While Quanzhen leaders sent numerous disciples throughout north China to build monastic establishments and recruit followers, Haiyun and Pu'an had neither enough disciples nor enough funding to do the same. Before 1260, faced with the increasing power of Quanzhen Daoists, the central concern of Chinese Buddhist leaders was competing with them to obtain Mongol patronage and to protect the Buddhist community. Pu'an was reputed to have attended the first Buddho-Daoist debate at the Mongol court in 1255, and he fought Quanzhen Daoists' encroachment on Buddhist monastic land and other property.[6] While the intense rivalry between Buddhists and Daoists continued, the politi-

3. Chan, "Liu Ping-chung."

4. Yu Ji 虞集, "Foguo Pu'an dachanshi taming" 佛國普安大禪師塔銘, in his *Daoyuan xuegu lu*, 48.4b.

5. According to Buddhist sources, at the end of the Jin-Mongol war in the early 1230s, Haiyun convinced Šigi Qutuqu (ca. 1180–1260), the powerful grand judge (*jarquči*) appointed by the Great Khan for governing north China, to restore his honorific title to Duke of Overflowing Sageliness Kong Yuancuo 孔元措, a fifty-first-generation descendant of Confucius. Haiyun was also said to have helped the descendants of Yan Hui (521–490 BCE) and Mencius (372–289 BCE) to be exempted from labor service as students of the Confucian classics. See Jan, "Hai-Yün (1203–57)," 232–33.

6. Yu Ji, "Foguo Pu'an dachanshi taming," *Daoyuan xuegu lu*, 48.4b.

cal situation for the Buddhist order changed dramatically after Khubilai became great khan of the Mongol empire in 1260.

Buddhist Ascendance in the Yuan Regime

Khubilai's policies greatly helped promote Buddhism in north China. Like many earlier non-Chinese rulers, Khubilai adopted the Buddhist ideal of the *cakravartin* ruler (wheel-turning monarch; *zhuanlun wang* 轉 輪王 in Chinese) and was committed to supporting the Buddhist order.[7] For instance, he later sponsored Buddhist monks in editing and printing a new Buddhist canon based on a Jin version.[8] Yet unlike his predecessors, Khubilai specifically patronized Tibetan Lamaist Buddhism to legitimize his rule.[9]

As Tibetan lamas began to assume the leadership of the Buddhist order in the Mongol empire, eminent Chinese monks lost their prominent position in the Buddhist world in north China. In 1260 Pu'an resigned from his position as supervisor of Buddhist affairs in the Central Plain, probably because of the rise of Tibetan lamas. His funerary inscription, composed by a scholar-official, emphasizes that Pu'an's activities after resigning consisted solely of building Buddhist monasteries.[10] In 1261 Khubilai made the Tibetan lama 'Phags-pa (1235–80) the supreme head of the Buddhist clergy, awarding him the prestigious title of national preceptor (*guoshi* 國師). In return, 'Phags-pa identified Khubilai with Bodhisattva Mañjuśrī and portrayed him as a cakravartin monarch.[11] In 1270 Khubilai granted 'Phags-pa another prestigious title, imperial preceptor (*dishi* 帝師),

---

7. *The Prajñaparamita Sutra for Humane Kings Who Wish to Protect Their States* (*Renwang huguo banruoboluomiduo jing* 仁王護國般若波羅密多經) elaborates on the ideology of the *cakravartin* ruler. After Kumarajiva first translated the sutra into Chinese in 410–12, it became the centerpiece of imperial Buddhism and the Buddhist vision of the state in medieval China. See Kang Le, "Zhuanlunwang guannian."

8. The Jin canon was printed by a woman named Cui Fazhen 崔法珍 from southern Shanxi over the course of thirty years. See Chen Gaohua, "Yuandai chubanshi gaishu," 16–17.

9. Franke, *From Tribal Chieftain to Universal Emperor*, 58–63.

10. Yu Ji, "Foguo Pu'an dachanshi taming," *Daoyuan xuegu lu*, 48.4b.

11. Rossabi, "The Reign of Khubilai Khan," 6:461.

making the lama the personal religious master for the Mongol emperor.[12] Sh. Bira has used Tibetan sources to demonstrate that in his elaboration of "Two Orders" (the secular and the spiritual), 'Phags-pa introduced the political theology of the relationship between state and religion in the Tibeto-Mongolian Buddhist world. And by decreeing 'Phags-pa to be the imperial preceptor, Khubilai realized the theory of the Two Orders in the practice of his universal empire.[13] After Khubilai, all Mongol emperors had to receive Buddhist precepts from an imperial preceptor nine times before ascending the throne.[14] And Tibetan lamas, mostly close relatives of 'Phags-pa, successively occupied the position of imperial preceptor, thus serving officially as the supreme leader of Buddhism in the Mongol empire.

While granting Lamaist Buddhism the status of state religion, Khubilai established a distinctive system of Buddhist administration, which laid the institutional foundation for an emerging Buddhist order nationwide. The Bureau of Buddhist and Tibetan Affairs (*Xuanzheng yuan* 宣政院), founded in 1264, was the central agency that governed this order.[15] It had two functions: managing Buddhist clergy within the Mongol empire, including China, and having administrative jurisdiction over Tibet.[16] Although Tibetan lamas, especially those from 'Phags-pa's Sakya sect, often headed the Bureau of Buddhist and Tibetan Affairs, Tibetan Buddhism's rise to authority in Yuan China did not represent a doctrinal or even an ethnic remaking of the national Buddhist hierarchy. Chinese Buddhist communities largely maintained their existing monastic networks and structures of hierarchy.

In addition, the Yuan regime established regional Buddhist bureaus, differing from the local-level Buddhist offices that in earlier dynasties had functioned in counties and prefectures. Starting in 1277 the Yuan gov-

---

12. Petech, "'Phags-pa (1235–1280)."

13. Bira, "Qubilai Qa'an and 'Phags-pa La-ma," 240–49.

14. *Nancun chuogeng lu*, 2.20.

15. The bureau was originally established under the name of the Bureau of General Regulation (*Zongzhi yuan* 總制院). For an extended study of the bureau, see Nogami, "Gen no senseiin ni tsuite" 元 の宣政院について, in his *Genshi Shaku Rō den*, 221–39.

16. Franke, "Tibetans in Yuan China," 311–14; Petech, "Tibetan Relations with Sung China and with the Mongols."

ernment introduced at key provincial centers an intermediary level of administration that was charged with the macroregional management of Buddhist affairs in the provinces. Often called Buddhist supervisory offices (*shijiao zongshe suo* 釋教總攝所 or *shijiao zongtong suo* 釋教總統所), these bureaus operated with considerable administrative and judicial autonomy, just as the branch secretariats (*xingsheng* 行省) did at the top regional level of civil government.[17] Like the Bureau of Buddhist and Tibetan Affairs at the court, provincial Buddhist bureaus recruited both monks and laymen and gave them official ranks comparable to those in the ranking system for civil officials.[18]

To a degree that was quite unusual in Chinese history, the Yuan government treated Buddhist officials as comparable to civil officials, who had traditionally expected to impose a bureaucratic order over a vast and unruly empire. While the Song allowed the civilian bureaucracy to exercise much authority over the Buddhist administrations, including issuing ordination certificates and official monastic plaques and appointing Buddhist officials, the Yuan authorized the Buddhist administration to take charge of most affairs related to Buddhism.[19] Under this Mongol expansion of the Buddhist administrative structure, more Buddhist monks received official ranks, titles, seals, and accompanying privileges, all of which the Song and Jin dynasties had treated as the exclusive preserve of civil and military officials.[20] Consequently, as a Yuan civil official complained, when a monk received the position of Buddhist registrar (or when

17.   Of all the Buddhist supervisory offices that the Mongols established in China, the best known is the Chief Buddhist Supervisory Office of All Circuits in Jianghuai (*Jianghuai zhulu shijiao duzongshesuo* 江淮諸路釋教都總攝所), which was headed by the notorious Tangut monk Yang lian zhenjia 楊璉真伽. In 1292 this office was replaced by the Branch Bureau of Buddhist and Tibetan Affairs (*Xing xuanzhengyuan* 行宣政院), following the fashion of having branch secretariats as provincial offices of the central secretariat at the court. See Lai, "Guanyu Yuandai sheyu Jianghuai/Jiangzhe." According to Lai's research, existing historical records document the functioning of several Buddhist supervisory offices in the branch secretariats of Sichuan-Shaanxi, Ningxia-Gansu, Fujian, and Jiangxi.

18.   *YS*, 35.776.

19.   For the Buddhist administration's loss of authority in the Song, see You, *Song-dai siyuan jingji shigao*, 1–15.

20.   Nishio, *Chūgoku kinsei ni okeru kokka*, 239.

a Daoist priest received that of Daoist registrar), he would "exchange documents with civil officials of the third rank as equals."[21]

While in all imperial Chinese dynasties an individual's access to government office secured elite status for himself and his family, the Yuan distinguished itself from other dynasties by according Buddhist administrative positions a qualitatively and quantitatively significant role in officialdom. Indeed, the unusual privileges that Buddhist clergy enjoyed at the time led a large number of people to become monks and nuns. According to the official history of the Yuan dynasty, in 1291 the number of Buddhist monasteries registered with the Bureau of Buddhist and Tibetan Affairs rose to 42,318. In contrast, there were only about 21,300 Confucian schools in the country. In the same year, the number of registered Buddhist monks and nuns was 213,148 (the total population was 59,848,964).[22] But this official number was significantly smaller than the real number of Buddhist clergy. The scholar Yao Sui 姚燧 (1238–1313) estimated that the number of registered and unregistered monks was around one million.[23] This number was much higher than that in any dynasty before and after.[24]

The new Buddhist order also significantly differed from the Confucian and Quanzhen Daoist orders. The Confucian order, based on the educational and civil service examination systems in the Northern Song and the Jin, placed men from literati families in Confucian schools and government. The Quanzhen Daoist order from the 1220s to 1281 accommodated men and women from all social groups in Quanzhen establishments to help them survive the violence of the Mongol conquest and lead the postwar reconstruction of local society. While Buddhist monks and nuns also contributed to postwar social rebuilding, the new Buddhist order typically placed Buddhist monks in both the government and

21. Zheng Jiefu 鄭介夫, "Shangzou yigang ershi mu" 上奏一綱二十目, *Yuandai zouyi jilu*, 2:110.

22. *YS*, 16.354.

23. Yao Sui, "Chongjian Nanquanshan Dacihua chansi bei" 重建南泉山大慈化禪寺碑, *Mu'an ji*, 10.123.

24. According to Bai Wengu's demographic study on the clerical population in Chinese history, the numbers of Buddhist clergy ranged from 100,000 to 300,000 in the Tang and from 70,000 to 250,000 in the Northern Song, reaching around 400,000 in the Southern Song and Jin combined. Bai accepted Yao Sui's assessment and put the number in the Yuan at 1,000,000. See Bai, "Lidai sengdao renshu kaolun," 1–6.

monasteries. Moreover, while the Quanzhhen order was based on a single organized movement with a spreading infrastructure of sites, institutions, and agents, Buddhism had no such single religious movement or institutional infrastructure: instead, there were contending movements or agents under the umbrella of the Buddhist bureaucracy created by the state.

Many scholars have discussed the role of Buddhism in the Yuan state. One important question, however, remains unanswered: How did the powerful new Buddhist order established by and within the Yuan regime interact with local Chinese communities? This chapter offers an answer to this question by exploring how the new political and social roles of Buddhist monks formed novel ties between monastery and family in Yuan China. It demonstrates that the powerful Buddhist order during the Yuan provided many Chinese families with a unique approach to upward social mobility. The remarkably close ties between monastery and family seriously challenged traditional Chinese norms concerning family and kinship relations. As we will see, in Yuan China—where the chance to improve a family's fortune depended almost entirely on its members' ability to gain government appointments or their personal connections to powerful people, especially Mongol nobles—monk administrators in the Buddhist order often acquired both appointments and connections. More remarkably, to sustain the family benefit from the Buddhist bureaucracy, an elite monk's lay family often sent several men across generations to monasteries, and the kinship ties among those men improved junior members' chances to inherit the Buddhist administrative positions that their seniors once occupied. To benefit from what privileged and wealthy monks could offer, other families were willing to marry their daughters to monks.

The next section of the chapter focuses on the powerful Buddhist order based at Mt. Wutai, which accommodated both Chinese and lamaist Tibetan Buddhists. It looks at one specific location, Dingxiang county 定襄縣 near Mt. Wutai, and gives special consideration to the monastic careers of a Buddhist official named Zhang Zhiyu 張智裕 and the generations of his family in Anheng village 安橫村 in Dingxiang. After the 1280s, the Yuan regime established a distinctive official bureaucracy for Buddhist clergy and establishments on Mt. Wutai, as well as official and unofficial systems of patronage for Buddhist monks. Powerful Buddhist officials based at Mt. Wutai like Zhiyu were connected on the one hand to the Yuan rulers through the new Buddhist order, and on the other hand to local communities through the monks' kinship ties. Through contacts with powerful Mongols, Buddhist officials gained higher government appointments for themselves and their family members. These appointments were not limited to the Buddhist bureaucracy but stretched into other bureaucratic realms through recommendations rather than performance or success in examinations. Also, because official ranks and positions could often be inherited by elite monks with blood ties to their predecessors, the Buddhist order made it even more appealing for a family to send its sons to monasteries. Monks installed memorial steles and Buddhist chapels in their natal villages in honor of their fathers and other ancestors. Thus, Wutai monks were not only recognized as new social elites in local society but were also greatly appreciated as good filial sons for securing their descent line's secular prestige. Building on the discussion of Wutai monks' high likelihood of fathering sons even after joining the monastic order, the last section of the chapter examines the extraordinary connections between monastery and family through marriage ties, explaining how and why many Yuan Chinese perceived Buddhist monks as competitive candidates in the marriage market.

Monk Zhiyu and the Zhang Family in Dingxiang County

Dingxiang county is located in northern Shanxi, about 40 kilometers away from Mt. Wutai, about 100 kilometers northwest of present-day Taiyuan city, and about 550 kilometers southwest of the Yuan capital Dadu (modern Beijing). Local society in Dingxiang had been deeply influenced by Buddhist culture, particularly since the Tang certified the claim of the mountain to be the abode of Bodhisattva Mañjuśrī. Religious practitioners visited Mt. Wutai to experience the bodhisattva's divine presence.[25] In the Northern Song and Jin, despite the popularity of the civil service examinations and a revival of Confucian learning, the mountain retained

---

25. Stevenson, "Visions of Mañjuśrī on Mount Wutai."

its eminence in northern Chinese clerical and nonclerical circles as a place for serious Buddhist study and devout pilgrimage. The writings of residents and pilgrims continued to relate their visionary experiences with Bodhisattva Mañjuśrī on this mountain.[26]

Under Mongol rule, as the Confucian challenge receded and as the examination system gave way to a far more diverse array of routes into officialdom, Mt. Wutai rose to exceptional eminence. With hundreds of temples on its slopes, the Buddhist monks on the mountain were backed by the Mongol rulers in the capital and extended their power down into the surrounding villages. As indicated in inscriptions compiled in *On the Epigraphic Inscriptions of Dingxiang* by the Dingxiang scholar Niu Chengxiu 牛誠修 nearly a century ago, local families vied to have their sons become Wutai monks and gain official rank and privileges for themselves, their heirs, and their families.[27]

In 1300 and 1310 Zhiyu, a monk from the Cloister of True Countenance (*Zhenrong yuan* 眞容院), one of the most famous Buddhist monasteries on Mt. Wutai, had large steles set up to commemorate two fellow monks.[28] These two steles—the inscriptions on which are included in Niu's collection—at first sight appear to be a pair of conventional expressions of Buddhist piety. On closer inspection, however, their early history and inscriptions—both written by a monk named Fu (Fu jixiang 福吉祥)[29] at the request of Zhiyu—reveal much that is at odds with conventional preconceptions about Buddhist practice. Not only was the first of the monks commemorated by Zhiyu—Master Liang—actually his father, but also the Buddhist chapel where these steles were situated served as an

26. Gimello, "Chang Shang-ying on Wu-t'ai Shan."

27. *JSK*. This four-volume collection includes three inscriptions from the Northern Wei (386–534), one from the Northern Qi (550–65), three from the Tang, ten from the Northern Song, sixteen from the Jin, and fifty-two from the Mongol state and Yuan periods (1234–1368). Sources before and during the Tang period, including inscriptions engraved on cliff faces and Buddhist stone sculptures, demonstrate the long history of Buddhist culture in local society since the late fourth century.

28. The cloister was founded in the early eighth century and restored by Pu'an in the 1250s. In the Qing dynasty, the cloister became a Tibetan Buddhist institution, and today it is often called the Peak of the Bodhisattva (Mañjuśrī) (*Pusading* 菩薩頂).

29. During the Yuan dynasty Buddhist monks were often called "*jixiang* 吉祥," meaning "propitious."

ancestral shrine for Zhiyu's family, the Zhangs, in their home village.[30] Zhiyu's attachment to his father, family, and home village is also evident in the inscriptions. In addition to being biographies of the two deceased monks, these compositions include much information about Zhiyu and his family. Indeed, roughly half of the first inscription about his father, Master Liang, is devoted to Zhiyu's own life, and the second—despite its dedication to one of Zhiyu's religious masters, Abbot Miaoyan of Mt. Wutai's Diamond Monastery (*Jinjie si* 金昕寺)—tells much about Zhiyu, his family, and their village. Above all, these inscriptions portray Zhiyu as a filial son who was exceptionally dutiful in using his position in the Buddhist order at Mt. Wutai to secure wealth, honor, and status for his family, the very family that lived alongside the two steles he had erected. I have translated the 1300 and 1310 inscriptions in their entirety (appendix 2). In the following discussion, I quote only a few crucial passages.

THE NEW BUDDHIST ORDER, ON AND OFF MT. WUTAI

Over the first two generations of Yuan rule, the government's relationship with Mt. Wutai, as with many other religious centers in China, expanded and was formalized from indirect personal ties to direct institutional links and then to the installation of a regional administrative structure. While this trend can be seen as leading to greater government control of this large and powerful Buddhist center, the Yuan dynasty and Mt. Wutai's monasteries shared an interest in strengthening their ties. In the highly competitive world of Chinese and Mongol religious practice, close ties with the throne would have been considered highly beneficial for Mt. Wutai's monasteries, their teachings, and their monks. Likewise, the foreign dynasty's legitimacy would have increased in the eyes of many Chinese with its rulers' engagement with powerful Buddhist monks, especially if some of those monks were Chinese.

---

30. Fu jixiang, "Lianggong xiaoxing zhi bei" 亮公孝行之碑 (hereafter the Liang Stele; dated 1300) and "Xuanshou Wutai deng chu shijiao duzongshe Miaoyan dashi shanxing zhibei" 宣授五臺等處釋教都總攝妙嚴大師善行之碑 (hereafter the Miaoyan Stele; dated 1310), *JSK*, 3.6b–8b and 23b–28b.

Both Chinese and Tibetan monks influenced Khubilai's interest in and patronage of Mt. Wutai. According to an anecdote recorded in Buddhist sources, Khubilai once asked the Chinese Buddhist Master Jian 揀, "Where is the supreme field of merit?" Jian replied, "it is the Clear and Cool [Mountains] (*Qingliang* 清涼)" (another name for Mt. Wutai). As the result of this conversation, Khubilai was said to have begun patronizing monastic construction on the mountain.[31] 'Phags-pa, as Khubilai's most trusted Tibetan lama, likely played a vital role in promoting Mt. Wutai as well, since Mañjuśrī was the most important bodhisattva in Tibetan Buddhism. 'Phags-pa himself visited Mt. Wutai in 1258 and composed many poems and essays eulogizing Mañjuśrī.[32] Mt. Wutai became one of three centers for Tibetan Buddhism in China under Mongol rule, which gave it enormous imperial patronage (the other two centers were the Great Capital Dadu 大都 and the Upper Capital Shangdu 上都).[33]

Shortly after Khubilai Khan established the Yuan dynasty in 1271, he and his officials started to reshape the Buddhist order on Mt. Wutai through the assignment of monks to its major monastic positions. These monks, some of them senior Tibetan lamas, acted as government-appointed abbots and priests who performed Buddhist rituals on the mountain, especially offering incense and sacrifices to be represented as the emperor's own. This practice, unique to the Yuan dynasty, was termed substitute-sacrifices (*daisi* 代祀).[34] Previously, the Mongols had entrusted eminent Quanzhen Daoists with offering rituals to deities recognized in the traditional Chinese *Canon of Sacrifices* (*sidian* 祀典), while Chinese Buddhist monks performed Buddhist rituals at well-known Buddhist sites

31. *Fozu lidai tongzai*, 22.22b. The anecdote emphasizes that as a consequence of the conversation, Khubilai sponsored the building of five great Buddhist monasteries at Mt. Wutai as the merit fields (discussed in chapter 4) of the world. During his reign Khubilai did indeed patronize monastic construction on Mt. Wutai, but he simply repaired old monasteries instead of establishing new ones. See *Qingliangshan zhi*, 4.70.

32. Zhao Gaiping, *Yuan Ming shiqi zangchuan*, 128–31.

33. The Upper Capital Shangdu, also known as Xanadu, was the Mongol Empire's capital between 1260 and 1271, and the summer capital of the Yuan after 1271.

34. Morita Kenji, "Gencho ni okeru daishi."

such as Mt. Wutai.[35] The first Tibetan monk to hold such a government appointment, the lama Rin (1238–79; full name Rin-chen rgyal-mtshan, Yilianzhen 益憐眞 in Chinese sources), was selected by Khubilai's second son and heir apparent, Zhenjin 眞金 (1243–85) in line with his father's wishes.[36] The choice was far from accidental, since Rin was a half-brother of the favored Tibetan lama 'Phags-pa and inherited the post of imperial preceptor after 'Phags-pa returned to Tibet in 1274. As the Mongol emperor's representative at this Chinese mountain complex, Rin was associated through his natal family with a political and religious stance that identified the Chinese monastic center with the reigning Mongol ruler and Tibetan Buddhism.

Over the next two decades, Rin and lamas subsequently appointed to posts at Mt. Wutai as well as in Dadu, the capital, consolidated these close ties between Buddhist communities at Mt. Wutai and the Mongol imperial family. By performing Buddhist rituals on behalf of the Yuan dynasty with the aid of Chinese monks, and especially by supporting the appointment of Chinese monks to official positions at Mt. Wutai, these Tibetan lamas brought certain Chinese monks to the attention of the Mongol emperor and his family. They also had the emperor honor Chinese monks with official titles, thereby enabling these Chinese to communicate directly with other powerful Tibetan lamas at Mt. Wutai. For example, Rin had Zhiyu's mentor, Monk Zhi 志吉祥, join him in performing the incense offering ritual in 1272 and appointed him to the powerful Buddhist administrative position of chief sangha (meaning the monastic community of monks and nuns in Buddhism) registrar (*dusenglu* 都僧錄) on Mt. Wutai. Later Khubilai confirmed Rin's appointment and awarded Zhi an honorary title, Master Miaoyan 妙嚴大師, thereby easing his direct communication with the Mongol political elite.[37] Grand Buddhist ritual assemblies held in the capital also brought elite

35. For instance, the Great Empress Töregene was reported to have ordered Chan Buddhist Master Haiyun to hold a Buddhist ceremony on Mt. Wutai on behalf of the Mongol empire in 1245. See *Fozu lidai tongzai*, 21.14a.

36. Rin also offered incense at various temples dedicated to Chinese deities of major mountains, rivers, and the earth throughout 1272. See Sakurai and Yao, "Gen shigen kyunen kotaishi."

37. The Miaoyan Stele, 3.26a.

Wutai monks into direct contact with powerful Tibetan lamas. For instance, Monk Xiong 雄吉祥, after serving in one such assembly at Dadu in 1276, was promoted by the national preceptor—Rin himself—to the post of chief Buddhist judge (*dusengpan* 都僧判) on Mt. Wutai.[38] Similar privileges awaited other Chinese monks who were subsequently accorded elite titles and positions on Mt. Wutai. Nonetheless, these processes were not necessarily considered to have turned the Chinese Buddhist monks into Tibetan Buddhist monks.

Two decades spent nurturing the relationship between the Chinese mountain complex and the royal family culminated with the decision of Khubilai's successors to build imperial Buddhist monasteries on Mt. Wutai. From Khubilai's reign on, the Mongol emperors, empresses, and empress dowagers enthusiastically established imperial Buddhist monasteries to pray for divine blessings on the royal family. These imperial monasteries often received tremendous royal patronage and had a close affiliation with Tibetan Buddhism. Khubilai built three in the Great Capital and two in the Upper Capital, and his successors built more in both capitals and other places, including Mt. Wutai and localities like Huaizhou (now Qinyang city, Henan province) and Jiankang (now Nanjing), where Mongol emperors had resided before their enthronement. But after the mid-Yuan period Mt. Wutai was the most important center, after the two capitals, of imperial Buddhist monasteries.[39]

In 1294, Khubilai died. In the next year, his successor, Temür (Emperor Chengzong, r. 1294–1307, the third son of the deceased heir apparent Zhenjin), ordered the construction on Mt. Wutai of the first imperial monastery of an eventual five. Intended to commemorate his mother, the emperor's name for this monastery openly declared its active commitment to the dynasty: Great Monastery of Myriad Sacred Beings That Support the Kingdom (*Da wansheng youguo si* 大萬聖祐國寺). Very soon, this monastery became an important venue for Chinese monks' interaction with Tibetan lamas and members of the imperial family, specifically Emperor Temür's mother Kökejin (d. 1300) and her entourage. Upon the monas-

---

38.   Xing Yunxiu 邢允修, "Jixian an chuangjian Guanyin tang gongde zhi bei" 集賢庵創建觀音堂功德之碑, *JSK*, 3.10a.

39.   Chen Gaohua, "Yuandai xinjian fosi," 32–38; Gu Yinsen, "Shilun Yuandai huangjia fosi."

tery's completion in the summer of 1296, Kökejin made a pilgrimage to Mt. Wutai and granted ten thousand taels of silver to the monastery.[40] Fascinated by supernatural visions of light in the welcoming ceremony that Master Miaoyan presided over, she attributed these experiences to his powers. At various times thereafter, she made sure that Miaoyan benefited from her patronage, an archetypal example of how after 1295 the personal will of the emperor, crown prince, or empress dowager increasingly influenced the appointment of both civil and religious officials.[41]

Yuan imperial interest in Mt. Wutai did not stop at these personal ties. Starting in 1297 the government established new administrative links with Mt. Wutai that had a more far-reaching impact on its monastic complex as an institution than did the string of civil bureaucratic ranks, titles, and seals so far issued to its monks. A macroregional Buddhist supervisory office was set up on Mt. Wutai in 1297, just after the visit by the empress dowager. Appointed by Emperor Temür in 1297, Master Miaoyan became the first chief supervisor of the new Buddhist Supervisory Office of Five Circuits and Mt. Wutai. As the inscription of the Miaoyan Stele explains, "In the third month of the spring in the first year of Dade reign (1297–1307), the emperor appointed Master Miaoyan to establish a Buddhist Supervisory Office over Zhending, Ping [Pingyang, southern Shanxi], Shaan [Shaanxi], Taiyuan, Datong, and Mt. Wutai. Master Miaoyan became the head of the office and was granted a silver seal by the emperor. Master Fazhao (Monk Jiao), the supervisor of Buddhist monasteries on two of the five terraces and the Cloister of True Countenance, also joined the office."[42] Before this new arrangement, the Buddhist administration of the monastic complex at Mt. Wutai had enjoyed independence from the local prefectural Buddhist office since the late Tang dynasty but had never held authority beyond the mountain. The new Buddhist Supervisory Office of Five Circuits and Mt. Wutai now had considerable autonomy in handling Buddhist affairs in five circuits that covered a large portion of north China, most of which were under the direct administration of the central secretariat. In particular, the office had

40. *YS*, 18.392–93 and 19.410. For Kökejin's patronage of Buddhism, see Xu Zhenghong, "Lun Yuanchao Kuokuozhen taihou."

41. Sakurai, "Gendai shyukenyin no setsuritsu," 141.

42. The Miaoyan Stele, 3.26b.

the power to appoint local Buddhist officials, particularly within the Shanxi region.[43]

In accord with a common Mongol practice of assigning two people to the same post,[44] Emperor Temür's appointment of Master Miaoyan as the first chief supervisor of this new Mt. Wutai office was soon followed by his appointment of another senior Mt. Wutai cleric, Master Fazhao 法照 (Monk Jiao 教吉祥), to share this position. Their performance over the next two decades must have pleased the Mongol rulers, since the subsequent four-year reign of the Mongol ruler Khaishan (Emperor Wuzong [r. 1308–11]; Haishan 海山 in Chinese sources) began a period of intense imperial patronage of the Buddhist communities on Mt. Wutai. In all, from 1307 to 1326 the Mongol court deployed more than ten thousand soldiers and craftsmen to build four of the five imperial monasteries it established on Mt. Wutai over the course of the dynasty.[45]

43. For instance, in an unknown year of the Dade reign, a monk named Ju 聚 was first appointed as vice sangha chancellor of Yuzhou subprefecture 盂州 (present-day Yu county, Shanxi province) by the Bureau of Buddhist and Tibetan Affairs. After receiving a report about Ju's excellent performance in dealing with lawsuits, the Buddhist Supervisory Office of the Five Circuits and Mt. Wutai promoted him to sangha chancellor of Yuzhou subprefecture ("Chongjian Chongxing yuan ji" 重建崇興院記, *JSK*, 3.35b–36a). Some monks from village monasteries in Dingxiang county also served in the Buddhist Supervisory Office of Five Circuits and Mt. Wutai. For instance, in 1317 a monk named Yue 說 at the Puji Monastery in Dong village of Dingxiang served concurrently as a manager of the office ("Wenshu yuan bei ji" 文殊院碑記, *JSK*, 3.43b). Yet the lack of sources makes it difficult to assess the office's authority in jurisdictions beyond the Shanxi region. As Neil McGee's study of the Mysterious Teachings (*Xuanjiao* 玄教) during the Yuan shows, the Yuan formally delegated to different masters the authority to take charge of regional offices established for the Mysterious Teachings, but people often had overlapping authority—including the authority to appoint subordinate Daoist officers at sites within the delegated jurisdictions. See McGee, "Questioning Convergence." It is possible that the multicircuit authority granted to the Wutai office was similarly loose.

44. Endicott-West, *Mongolian Rule in China*, 45.

45. In addition to the Great Monastery of Myriad Sacred Beings That Support the Kingdom, the other four imperial Buddhist monasteries were one (name unknown) built by Khaishan in 1307; the Monastery of Universal Peace (*Puning si* 普寧寺), built by the empress dowager during the Zhida reign (1308–11); the Monastery of Universal Approach (*Pumen si* 普門寺), built by Emperor Yingzong in 1321; and the Monastery of Special Propitiousness (*Shuxiang si* 殊祥寺), built in 1326. See *Qingliangshan zhi*, 4.70; *YS*, 22.486, 489, 496, and 505, 23.516, and 30.668; *Fozu lidai tongzai*, 22.57b–59a.

The new Buddhist Supervisory Office of Five Circuits and Mt. Wutai integrated existing Buddhist lineages and monasteries on and off the mountain, contributing to the formation of a powerful macroregional Buddhist administrative network in Shanxi. Like many other major Buddhist establishments in Mongol China, Buddhist monasteries at Mt. Wutai—both imperial and nonimperial—became extremely wealthy thanks to the lavish patronage of the Mongol rulers. For instance, when Emperor Taiding (r. 1324–28) ordered the construction of the Monastery of Special Propitiousness at Mt. Wutai in 1326, he granted three hundred *qing* (roughly two thousand hectares) of land to the temple, all of which produced considerable tax-exempt income for the monastery.[46] Nonimperial monasteries at Mt. Wutai sometimes gained tax exemption for their landholdings via protective edicts issued by Mongol rulers. The Great Monastery of Longevity and Peace (*Dashouning si* 大壽寧寺) enjoyed such a tax break thanks to decrees from Emperor Temür, the empress dowager, and the imperial preceptor between 1297 and 1301.[47]

This substantial imperial support was followed by a rise in the Buddhist bureaucratic positions of some Chinese monks in Mt. Wutai's monasteries. Zhiyu's ascendance in the Buddhist bureaucracy was most probably made possible by the patronage of the empress dowager and by his discipleship to two leading monks on Mt. Wutai, Master Miaoyan, who received the official ranking of 2a, and Master Fazhao, who had served as Zhiyu's primary religious teacher at the Cloister of the True Countenance. When, in 1300, Zhiyu received the position of sangha chancellor (*sengzheng* 僧正) in Fenzhou subprefecture 汾州 in Shanxi, his appointment would have needed the support of these two teachers, as they then shared the power to appoint Buddhist officers in Shanxi. In fact, their support of Zhiyu is evident on the stele set up by Zhiyu for his deceased father in the following year: this stele's inscription was edited by Fazhao, and the seal-style characters at its head were written by Miaoyan.[48] The cases of Xiong's disciples provide the best example of this type of rise in position. When Xiong retired from his position of chief Buddhist judge on Mt. Wutai around 1301, his prestige and influence enabled him to have

---

46. *Fozu lidai tongzai*, 22.57b–59a; Chen Gaohua, "Yuandai fojiao siyuan fuyi," 9.
47. Chen Gaohua, "Yuandai fojiao siyuan fuyi," 10.
48. The Miaoyan Stele, 3.26b.

his senior disciple succeed directly to this position and to have his junior disciple serve as the chief superintendent of the Ten Monasteries at the Mountain Entrance (*Shanmen shisi dutidian* 山門十寺都提點).[49]

Off the mountain, imperial favor toward Mt. Wutai and its monks had extensive repercussions in local society. As already noted, the Mongol regime had shown more respect to Buddhist teachings and monks than to Confucian teachings and scholars and, after Khubilai's enthronement, more than to Daoist teachings and priests as well. In Khubilai's early reign, local Chinese Hereditary Vassals recognized the Buddhist role in local community building.[50] For instance, in 1260 a military strongman, Zhao Yi, who had just inherited his father's position as magistrate of Dingxiang county, decided to build a Buddhist monastery at Fanglan town. Zhao Yi's father had moved his fellow villagers from Hutaoyuan town in 1235 and had difficulty in consolidating his family's power at Fanglan due to the fragmentation of village communities in the area. Zhao Yi believed that a Buddhist monastery could function as "a place for burning incense, making prayers, and assembling and governing [local villagers]."[51] Later, he appealed to the Office of Chief Buddhist Registrar at Mt. Wutai to invite Monk Ju (*Ju juxiang* 炬吉祥) to Fanglan to preside over the newly built monastery. After mobilizing local residents to complete the monastic construction, Ju erected a stele to commemorate the efforts of Zhao Yi and his family to prevent local disorder by creating and sponsoring the Buddhist monastery. This episode suggests that even members of the local military elite saw the Wutai monks' potential in binding a fragmented rural community together and tried to cooperate with them.

While both Quanzhen Daoist and Buddhist establishments, supported by different local strongmen, had played similar roles in Dingxiang villages during the Jin-Yuan transition, Mt. Wutai Buddhism increasingly became the ambitious locals' religion of choice from Khubilai's reign onward, and Wutai monks gained overwhelming advantages in their

---

49.   Xing Yunxiu, "Jixian an chuangjian Guanyin tang," *JSK*, 3.10b.

50.   Dingxiang county during the Jin-Yuan transition was controlled by several families of Hereditary Vassals. See Iiyama, *Kingen jidai*, 185–94.

51.   "Chuangjian Yongsheng yuan gongde ji" 創建永聖院功德記, *JSK*, 2.38a.

competition with their Daoist rivals.[52] In 1296, just after the empress dowager's visit to Mt. Wutai, a local Daoist priest surnamed Zhou commented on Buddhist hegemony. The authority of Buddhist monks on Mt. Wutai had become so great, he protested, that no one dared to oppose them. He told of a fellow Daoist priest who, seeing the way the Mt. Wutai winds were blowing, had not only changed his vocation to that of a Buddhist monk but had also presented to some Wutai monks the Daoist Abbey of the Prospering Kingdom (*Xingguo guan* 興國觀), where he and other Daoist priests had been residing. The Wutai monks who took his donation then ordered that the Daoist abbey be turned into a Buddhist monastery and that all its resident Daoist priests convert to Buddhism. Only two of the priests resisted, both at great personal cost: one committed suicide, and the other (Zhou himself) was locked up, tortured, and forced to shave his hair and beard to look and act like a Buddhist monk. For nearly two decades he lived under the Mt. Wutai Buddhists' monastic control until he escaped to the capital, where he felt safe enough to press charges against these monks back in Shanxi. Only after winning the lawsuit did Zhou regain the abbey for the Daoists.[53] This case also suggests that local Buddhists (and Quanzhen Daoists, too, in their period of dominance) tended to interpret state support for their order as a grant of some government powers, including the power to coerce. While the state had not necessarily intended any such general grant, it did allow the Buddhist and Daoist administrations to take charge of their own religious affairs, thus leaving enough room for the two orders to interpret and exercise their authority in local contexts.

Local Confucian scholars likewise recognized the change in circumstances. They may have continued to resort to clichés in speaking of Mt. Wutai as "a numinous mountain that breeds outstanding things and manifests extraordinary visions that surprise the world."[54] But they, too, were aware of its political ascendance, especially the power of the Buddhist officials appointed to its new Buddhist Supervisory Office. In 1301 a county school teacher named Xing Yunxiu 邢允修 concluded that

---

52. For the similar roles played by Quanzhen Daoist abbeys in Dingxiang villages, see "Xuanyuan guan ji" 玄元觀記 and "Chuangjian Chongyang guan ji" 創建重陽觀記, *JSK*, 2.13a–15a and 15b–18b.

53. Li Kui 李揆, "Chongjian Xingguo si bei" 重建興國寺碑, *JSK*, 4.31b–33b.

54. Xing Yunxiu, "Jixian an chuangjian Guanyin tang," *JSK*, 3.9b.

the Cloister of the True Countenance—Zhiyu's principal base on Mt. Wutai—had become the home of a remarkably talented group of people: "Many monks from there have received honorific titles and occupied official positions (*shoujue juguan* 授爵居官), such as sangha commander (*sengtong* 僧統), sangha registrar (*senglu* 僧錄), and sangha chancellor (*sengzheng* 僧正). Yet only the position held by Master Fazhao, Supervisor of Buddhist Affairs of the Five Circuits (*wulu zongshe* 五路總攝), is most magnificent (*jisheng* 極盛)."[55] Xing spoke highly of these monks and especially of their success in an official world previously off-limits to tonsured males. His comment suggests some local scholars' acceptance of the Mongol rulers' initiative in appointing Buddhist monk administrators to some government posts and treating them as government officials.

Such acceptance was more a general empirewide stance than an exceptional local attitude, as is clear from Mark Halperin's observation about Yuan literati in southern China: they too "stressed the special ties that these monks had with their government in both the forms of prestigious position and court favor."[56] The "prestigious position and court favor" was not the same thing as formal authority, but rather informal kinds of power that attracted others to use connections to persons with prestige and favor to achieve their ends. In other words, Buddhist officials in the Yuan enjoyed both greater formal authority over Buddhist affairs and considerable informal power in the secular world due to their capacity to form and mediate connections to the Mongol rulers.

In sum, the Mongol ruling family's lavish patronage of Mt. Wutai's Buddhist establishments consolidated the power of Buddhist administrators there and elsewhere. Wutai monks had more opportunities to be officially appointed as local Buddhist officials, and they had an advantage over local Daoists in competition for monastic buildings and lands in and beyond Shanxi.[57] Moreover, the Wutai monks who received these official titles came to be more respected or feared by non-Buddhist

55. Xing Yunxiu, "Jixian an chuangjian Guanyin tang," *JSK*, 3.9b.
56. Halperin, "Buddhists and Southern Literati," 1453.
57. Powerful Mt. Wutai monks also gained control of lower temples in Zhending circuit in the Hebei region. See Zhang Guowang, "Yuandai Wutaishan fojiao zaitan."

figures and institutions. Leading monks like Master Miaoyan and Master Fazhao were viewed as members of a powerful local elite; they had the power to ensure that a disciple of theirs like Monk Zhiyu could rise to become a prefectural official in the new macroregional Buddhist administrative network centered on Mt. Wutai. These Buddhist officials might not have had the formal political power to govern a jurisdiction beyond the Buddhist order, but they certainly had the informal power—similar to that of a Chinese officeholder in preceding dynasties—to influence local society. It was only to be expected that within a few years the aspiring monk Zhiyu would form his own personal connections and gain the special status of "*huja'ur* monk" on Mt. Wutai.

"*HUJA'UR* MONKS" ON MT. WUTAI

Starting in the last decade of the thirteenth century, increasing numbers of Mongol rulers and nobles made visits to Mt. Wutai, either as pilgrims or to escape from the sweltering summers of the north China plain to the mountain's refreshing coolness. Their increased presence on Mt. Wutai smoothed the way for its monks' establishment of personal connections to the Mongol elite and thereby for their acquisition of the status of a "*huja'ur* monk." The *huja'ur* connection, as discussed in the introduction, served as a special recognition of loyalty that bound Mongol rulers and their subjects. It was the most effective way to gain official rank, privilege, and elite status in Yuan China. Some Chinese records from the Yuan period refer to those who had such connections as *genjiao ren* 根脚人, which literally means "men with *huja'ur*."[58] I use the term *huja'ur monk* to refer to the group of Buddhist monks who had personal connections to Mongol rulers, thereby gained official positions in the Buddhist administration, and later transmitted their advantages and even their positions to their disciples or kinsmen. It should be noted that no precise term for *huja'ur* monk such as *genjiao seng* 根脚僧 appears in Yuan sources. Nonetheless, I adopt this term for two reasons: First, the *huja'ur* concept profoundly affected all levels of recruitment of government officials in the Yuan dynasty. However, scholars have not paid enough attention to the

58. Funada, "Semuren yu Yuandai zhidu," 166.

use of the *huja'ur* connection in the Yuan's religious administration. Second, while there are alternative terms like *elite* or *powerful monks* or *Buddhist officials*, these terms fail to capture the nuances of this distinctive Mongolian recruitment practice.

Huja'ur monks on Mt. Wutai consisted of two groups of clergy, distinguished by their proximity to the Mongol imperial family, their monastic position on Mt. Wutai, and their consequent powers of appointment. The first group included the abbots of Mt. Wutai's newly constructed imperial Buddhist monasteries, who often hosted Mongol nobles during their visits to Mt. Wutai. The first of these abbots were appointed directly by Tibetan imperial preceptors and Mongol emperors, and they had the privilege of transmitting their abbotship to others in their religious lineage, just as those with a *huja'ur* connection elsewhere in government could have their sons or others inherit their post from generation to generation.

Thus, the abbotship of the Great Monastery of Myriad Sacred Beings That Support the Kingdom came under the control of the monastic lineage of the famous teacher Master Wencai 文才 (1241–1302; religious name Haiyin 海印). A leader of the Huayan 華嚴 school of Chinese Buddhism in the late thirteenth century, Wencai had—at the recommendation of the imperial preceptor—been appointed this monastery's first abbot by Emperor Temür when construction of the monastery was completed in 1297. After Wencai died in 1302, his direct disciple Yan Jixiang 嚴吉祥 (1272–1322), and later Yan's younger brother Jin Jixiang 金吉祥, inherited the abbotship.[59] It is not clear whether this arrangement was at Wencai's command, but it certainly corresponded to the Mongols' recruitment tradition of appointing men from a family—though in this case it was a Buddhist lineage—that had already demonstrated its loyalty to their regime.[60]

---

59. *Fozu lidai tongzai*, 22.25a–26b. For a biographical study of Wencai, see Chikusa, *Chūgoku bukkyō shakaishi kenkyū*, 194–95.

60. Yan was summoned by Empress Dowager Taji (ca. 1266–1322) around 1313 to be the abbot of the Monastery of Universal Peace (*Puan si* 普安寺), a prestigious imperial monastery in Dadu, the capital. Jin inherited the abbotship of the Great Monastery of Myriad Sacred Beings That Support the Kingdom. After Yan died in 1322, Jin moved from Mt. Wutai under an imperial order to inherit his brother's position, demonstrating again the importance of the *huja'ur* tie in the Mongols' religious administration.

Hereditary privilege among elite Buddhist monks was common at the time.[61] The imperial family and their trusted Tibetan lamas favored Wencai's lineage partly because during the Yuan, Huayan Buddhism had the closest relation with the Sakya sect of Tibetan Buddhism that produced imperial preceptors, due to the two schools' doctrinal connection.[62] Another Wencai disciple, Master Yin 印公, also an influential *hua'jur* monk from Mt. Wutai, studied with Tibetan lamas. In 1312 the Mongol emperor and empress dowager sent Yin to Mt. Wutai to lecture at the Great Monastery of Myriad Sacred Beings That Support the Kingdom and made him its abbot in 1314 (he probably coheaded the monastery with Jin after Yan moved to Dadu). Yin not only studied Tantric Buddhism with an imperial preceptor and two other Tibetan lamas from 1319 to 1321, but he also received gifts of clothing and fifty taels of silver from the imperial preceptor when the latter visited Mt. Wutai in 1320. Yin left Mt. Wutai only in 1322, when the emperor summoned him to be abbot of an equally, if not more, prestigious imperial monastery in the capital.[63] We do not know who inherited the abbotship of the Monastery of Myriad Sacred Beings That Support the Kingdom after Jin and Yin both left Mt. Wutai to go to Dadu in 1322. Yet Wencai's lineage clearly monopolized

---

See Monk Yan's biography in *Fozu lidai tongzai*, 22.59a–60a; Chikusa, *Sō Gen bukkyō bunka shi kenkyū*, 206.

61. For other examples, see "Xijing Dahuayan si Fori yuanzhao Minggong heshang beiming bing xu" 西京大華嚴寺佛日圓照明公和尚碑銘並序, *Liao Jin Yuan shike wenxian quanbian*, 1:280–83.

62. Chen Gaohua, Zhang, and Liu, *Yuandai wenhuashi*, 65–67.

63. Fahong 法洪, "Gu ronglu dafu dasitu Dachengtian husheng si zhuchi qian Wutai Dawansheng youguo si zhuchi Baoyun pumen zongzhu Guanghui miaobian shuzong hongjiao dashi Yingong beiming" 故榮祿大夫大司徒大承天護聖寺住持前五臺大萬聖佑國寺住持寶雲普門宗主廣慧妙辯樹宗弘教大師印公碑銘 (dated 1339), transcribed by Yamamoto Meishi 山本明志 from an extant stele at the Monastery of Southern Mountain 南山寺, the former Great Monastery of Myriad Sacred Beings That Support the Kingdom. Yamamoto kindly shared his transcription with me on December 24, 2011. According to the inscription, Yin learned the *Huayan Sutra* with Wencai. He was first summoned by Empress Dowager Taji's decree to lecture on the sutra in Dadu in 1312 and then in the Upper Capital in 1313. From then on, favored by the emperess dowager, Yin received a great deal of imperial patronage. During his time on Mt. Wutai, Yin—supported by Emperor Yingzong (r. 1320–23)—used wealth he received from the imperial family to build a new imperial Monastery of Universal Approach and became its first abbot, which again indicated the strong influence of Wencai's lineage on Mt. Wutai.

the abbotship of the imperial monastery for at least three decades after its establishment in 1295.

The second group of *huja'ur* monks on Mt. Wutai included monks like Master Miaoyan and Monk Zhiyu, who did not belong to imperial monasteries but had personal connections to the Mongol ruling family, often through the abbots of Mt. Wutai's increasing number of imperial monasteries. For instance, in the fifth month of 1309, Crown Prince Ayurbarwada (Emperor Renzong [r. 1311–20], Aiyulibalibada 愛育黎拔力 八達 in Chinese sources) sent a high-ranking official to promote Zhiyu to be the deputy sangha registrar of Mt. Wutai. The official summoned Zhiyu to the Great Monastery of Myriad Sacred Beings That Support the Kingdom, where Abbot Yan presented Zhiyu with the formal letter of appointment as well as Buddhist robes as the prince's gift.[64] Moreover, in the seventh month of 1309, after receiving a report from Empress Dowager Taji (ca. 1266–1322, Daji 答己 in Chinese sources; the mother of Khaishan and Ayurbarwada) about Zhiyu, Emperor Khaishan issued an edict to Zhiyu, ordering that "Zhiyu is to be supervised under Monk Hai's name on Mt. Wutai, and be made the sangha registrar."[65] "Under Monk Hai's name" here refers to the teacher-disciple lineage of Wencai in general and to Yan specifically, and thus it places Zhiyu under them and not under his primary religious teacher, Master Fazhao at the Cloister of True Countenance. This arrangement emphasized the importance that the Mongols placed on the maintenance of close personal ties of loyalty between them and those they appointed to powerful official positions, religious as well as secular. Yan would go on to serve them as the Chief Supervisor of the Buddhist Supervisory Office of the Five Circuits and Mt. Wutai, starting in 1310 (along with Master Fazhao).[66]

Zhiyu's personal connections with the Mongol rulers—and thus his ability to directly manipulate these ties to advance his official monastic career—date from 1309, which was a peak of imperial patronage of Mt. Wutai. In the fifth month of 1309, Crown Prince Ayurbarwada visited

64. The Miaoyan Stele, 3.25a–25b.
65. Ibid., 3.25b.
66. Ibid., 3.24a, 27b. For the full religious and official titles of Monk Yan and Master Fazhao that appear on the Miaoyan Stele, see appendix 2.

Mt. Wutai, followed in the next month by the empress dowager on a pilgrimage to the mountain. By this time Zhiyu had been promoted to be sangha registrar of the Cloister of the True Countenance, but over the next three months he received a series of imperial decrees and edicts—from the crown prince, the empress dowager, and eventually Emperor Khaishan himself—that conferred on him gifts including Buddhist robes and the official title of chief sangha registrar at Mt. Wutai.

Precisely what persuaded the Mongol imperial family, and especially the empress dowager, to favor Zhiyu with this appointment is not clear. But Zhiyu's close personal connections with *huja'ur* monks at Mt Wutai, and especially with his teacher Master Miaoyan, must have mattered. Miaoyan was the previous chief sangha registrar of Mt. Wutai and had greatly impressed an earlier empress dowager with his magic. And if any doubt remains about the importance of this tie, recall that the second of the steles Zhiyu erected at his family's Buddhist chapel in Anheng village was for Master Miaoyan and dates from 1310, the year after Zhiyu had replaced him as the chief sangha registrar of Mt. Wutai and had become one of the highly placed *huja'ur* monks. Although it is hard to determine the precise size of the circle of *huja'ur* monks on Mt. Wutai, the number of its members was probably restricted. Consisting of those monks privileged to enjoy a personal tie to the Mongol imperial family, it would have been an exclusive club with membership closed to the great majority of monks.

In short, as a center for both Chinese and Tibetan Buddhism in Yuan China, Mt. Wutai was a vital meeting place for the Mongol imperial family, powerful Tibetan lamas, and Chinese Buddhist monks. The relatively easy access it afforded them to Mongol rulers and Tibetan lamas helped Chinese monks like Miaoyan, Yan Jixiang, and Zhiyu not only to succeed in their Buddhist administrative careers but also to join the exclusive club of *huja'ur* monks on Mt. Wutai. In this respect, Tibetan Buddhism had a significant impact on the status of Chinese Buddhist monks in the new Buddhist order established by and within the Mongol regime. Yet Tibetan Buddhism apparently mostly influenced the monks who associated with lamas and did not penetrate Chinese village communities away from Mt. Wutai. Tibetan Buddhism's impact on the lower ranks of Chinese society was indirectly filtered through eminent Chinese monks like Zhiyu to their own families and kinsmen.

MONK ZHIYU'S KINSHIP TIES

These monks' formal and informal ties with Buddhist monasteries and the Mongol government were crucial for more than their personal success within the Buddhist world. They could also, as the case of Monk Zhiyu shows, prove highly beneficial to the monk's natal family and kinsmen, in this case the Zhangs of Anheng village. The Anheng Zhangs were, according to one of the late thirteenth-century inscriptions in Niu Chengxiu's collection, "a large and old descent group in Anheng village."[67] But most male Zhangs were then working in humble positions as farmers, craftsmen, and village teachers, and a few of them were county government clerks. Their main claim to social and political distinction at this time would have been the position of some of their members in the Buddhist order on Mt. Wutai.

In all, at least five close family members were associated with monasteries on Mt. Wutai or in its immediate vicinity during the three generations beginning with Master Liang in the last quarter of the thirteenth century: Liang, his sons Zhiyu and Zhize, and Zhiyu's sons Zhiyin and Zhiqi (their names are in bold in fig. 3.1).[68] Here we have a concrete example of the striking phenomenon of Buddhist monks with sons, the implications of which will be discussed below. It seems likely that these Zhangs spent only a part of their adult life under monastic vows, and it

---

67.　"Leshan Laoren muchuang" 樂善老人墓幢, *JSK*, 3.4b.

68.　For men in Zhiyu's generation, the character *zhong* (仲, meaning "intermediate") generally served as the first character in their given name, but in accord with a popular local custom for the first character in monks' dharma names (*faming* 法名 or *jieming* 戒名, the name given to the recipient of the Buddhist precepts, replacing one's secular name), both Zhiyu and Zhize had *zhi* (智, meaning "wisdom") as the first character instead. The 1300 stele mentions four of Master Liang's grandsons, each of whose names had *dao* (道, meaning "the way") as the first character. Yet judging from other steles, especially the 1349 inscription that lists the names of Zhiyu's and Zhize's sons and grandsons, the first character in the given names of males in the generation of Zhiyu's sons was *zhi* 智, and that of the next generation's males (that is, Zhiyu's grandsons) was *ju* (居, meaning "reside"). Three of Master Liang's grandsons, as listed in the Liang Stele, had names that began with the character *dao*—Daoyin 道印, Daoqi 道玘, Daojie 道傑; these names clearly referred to Zhiyu's three sons (listed on the 1349 stele as Zhiyin 智印, Zhiqi 智玘, and Zhijie 智傑). It is also possible that when Niu Chengxiu transcribed the inscription of the 1300 Liang Stele, he mistook *zhi* for *dao* and *jun* for *fa*, as some parts of the stele had become indecipherable.

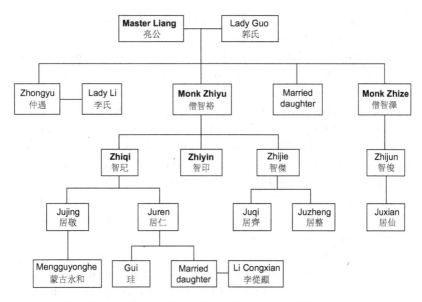

FIGURE 3.1 Family tree of Monk Zhang Zhiyu. Many monks did not keep their vows of celibacy under Mongol rule. Master Liang, a fully ordained Buddhist monk, fathered four children who lived to adulthood, and his son Zhiyu, also a fully ordained Buddhist monk, had three sons. For the convenience of graphic making, these names are not listed following their birth order. The names in bold are all monks, showing the Zhang family's dedication to Buddhism.

is far from certain how long and at what stage in their life they stayed in a monastery. Master Liang was arguably the founding figure for the monastic Zhangs, but the surviving sources suggest that his son Zhiyu had more direct influence on most of the Zhangs we know to have entered the Buddhist world. He was their senior, and they appear to have been major beneficiaries of his eventual eminence on Mt. Wutai and his *huja'ur* connections.

A review of these Anheng Zhangs' rise in Buddhist officialdom shows the range of their immersion in the local Buddhist administration in the wake of Zhiyu's own ascendance. His younger brother, Zhize, and his oldest son, Zhiyin, not only were local Buddhist officials, but they also in turn occupied the position of sangha chancellor of their home prefecture of Xinzhou, suggesting that they might have had privileged access to this post. Indeed, the sons may well have inherited it, just as descendants of men with *huja'ur* connections to the Mongols often inherited posts in the local civil government.

In addition, Zhiyu's second son, Zhiqi, enjoyed a position on Mt. Wutai of considerable responsibility and potentially rich rewards. He was a courier (*xuanshi* 宣使) of the Office of Special Propitiousness (*Shuxiang yuan* 殊祥院) and thus a member of a special state agency set up to administer the property of imperial Buddhist monasteries, such as those on Mt. Wutai.[69] The Zhang men's positions in the Buddhist administration might even have helped their descendants gain clerkships in local government; Zhiqi's son Juren was a tax collector at a local river port.[70] In addition to Zhiyu's direct family, other members of Zhiyu's Zhang lineage in Anheng village also entered the Buddhist order on Mt. Wutai, especially the Cloister of True Countenance.[71]

For this number of Chinese males in a single family to take Buddhist vows over three consecutive generations was not exceptional, especially in medieval times.[72] Nonetheless, these Anheng Zhangs' involvement—it is tempting to see it as strategic—shows how a family's fate and fortune might become linked to monastic institutions. The Zhang family maintained close ties to not one but three Buddhist establishments at

69.   A 1317 government regulation on the promotion of clerks in offices overseeing Buddhist monastic property stated that these rules also applied to staff members in the Office of Special Propitiousness on Mt. Wutai (*YS*, 84.2099). As mentioned above, the Yuan court built the Monastery of Special Propitiousness on Mt. Wutai and granted around two thousand hectares of land to the monastery in 1326 (*YS*, 30.668). The Office of Special Propitiousness, in which Zhiqi served as a courier, very likely had charge of that monastic property. For a discussion of the unique offices in charge of monastic property in the Yuan dynasty, see Xie and Bai, *Zhongguo sengguan zhidushi*, 225–30.

70.   Monk Ai 靉吉祥, "Da Yong'an si ji" 大永安寺記 (the 1349 stele), *JSK*, 4.39b.

71.   The number is unclear, but so far I have identified two members. See "Leshan Laoren muchuang" (dated 1300) and "Zhang Jingzong gongde chuang" 張敬宗功德幢 (dated 1333), *JSK*, 3.4a–6a and 4.16a. The 1300 tomb pillar was dedicated to Zhang Wenzhan 張文展, whose fifth son was a Buddhist monk named Miao from the Cloister of the True Countenance and who had erected the pillar for his father. All of Miao's lay brothers had the same character in their names: *zi* (子, meaning "son" or "seed"), which was the first character in the given name of males in the generation of Master Liang. Zhiyu's grandfather, Zhang Wenhai 張文海, also had the character *wen* (文, meaning "civil") in his name. Zhang Wenzhan and Zhang Wenhai were undoubtedly relatives in the same generation.

72.   For examples, see Zürcher, *The Buddhist Conquest of China*, 206–10; Jinhua Chen, "The Birth of a Polymath."

three rather different levels in the hierarchy of monastic institutions: the Buddhist communities on Mt. Wutai and two far less grand Buddhist establishments in Anheng village, the Great Monastery of Eternal Peace (*Da yong'an si* 大永安寺) and the Merit-Worship Chapel (*Chongfu an* 崇福庵).

At the first of these levels, the Zhangs acquired connections far beyond their village community through their ties to Buddhist communities at Mt. Wutai. The breadth of the religious (and political) network that Zhiyu created for himself and the Zhangs through his Mt. Wutai connections is evident in the stele he installed in 1310. Although he ostensibly set up this stele for Master Miaoyan, its inscription actually celebrates the eminence of his and his lay family's connections. Alongside Zhiyu's family members are listed the great and the good who helped with the making and installation of this stele: Master Fazhao, in his position as Chief Supervisor of the Buddhist Supervisory Office at Mt. Wutai; a sangha judge of ten Buddhist monasteries who belonged to the Cloister of the True Countenance; a former Dingxiang county magistrate; and several high-ranking court officials who were involved in promoting Zhiyu in the summer of 1309, including a manager of governmental affairs (*pingzhang zhengshi* 平章政事), rank 1b.[73] In addition, the local Confucian scholar Xing Yunxiu provided the calligraphy for the inscription carved into the stele, and Monk Yan, the abbot of the Great Monastery of Myriad Sacred Beings That Support the Kingdom and the Chief Supervisor of the Buddhist Supervisory Office at Mt. Wutai, wrote the characters that were carved into the heading of the inscription. Here we see Zhiyu's—and by extension, the Zhangs'—clerical and political connections writ large.

At the second level, the Zhang family sought to elevate their status in the community by cultivating, for at least a few generations, patronage ties to the Great Monastery of Eternal Peace, a local Buddhist monastery that may date back to the Tang dynasty and that still functions in the village today. In 1297 Zhiyu donated a gold-plated Buddha image to the monastery and hired workers to repair an ancestral tablet that the Zhangs had previously installed there, presumably with the expectation

---

73. The Miaoyan Stele, 3.27b.

that the monks would provide ancestral prayers, offerings, and rituals.[74] Zhiyu's offspring continued to sponsor this local monastery: for example his grandson, the local clerk Juren, gave it a stone to be used as a stele to commemorate its renovation.[75] The back of the 1349 stele lists the names of those Zhangs—Zhiyu, his younger brother Zhize, and their sons and grandsons—who served as chief sponsors of this monastery's reconstruction project. Most other chief donors also had family members who held titles and positions associated with the Yuan government or monasteries and state agencies at Mt. Wutai.[76] The Zhangs, like other chief donor families, were clearly asserting the status of village elite, a status that had two sources: their continuous financial and material support for the village monastery and their men's success in the political and clerical worlds.

At the third level, the Zhang family used the Merit-Worship Chapel to memorialize its members' powerful connections and their secular success, thanks to the monk Zhiyu. Zhiyu took charge of building the chapel, most likely on land owned by the Zhang family. It was at this chapel that the 1300 and 1310 steles were installed, the latter's inscription reporting that this family had achieved extraordinary prestige: Zhiyu, one of its members, had been favored with imperial decrees of appointment from Emperor Khaishan and Crown Prince Ayurbarwada. Traditionally, Buddhist disciples in Dingxiang county and elsewhere in China tended to erect commemorative steles for their masters in a Buddhist monastic space. This particular stele's installation—not in the Diamond Monastery where Master Miaoyan resided on Mt. Wutai, but in the Merit-Worship Chapel that Zhiyu had built for his family in Anheng—underlines how he had succeeded in using Buddhist monuments for the benefit of his kinsmen. Whereas in earlier times a Buddhist clergyman's family background often affected the rise or fall of his or her sect (especially when that family's gain or loss was tied up with court politics),[77] in the Yuan, it was far easier for influence to flow in the opposite direction: a monk's

---

74. The Liang Stele, 3.7b, and the Miaoyan Stele, 3.26b.

75. "Da Yong'an si ji" 大永安寺記 (the 1349 stele), *JSK*, 4.39b.

76. Niu Chengxiu did not include the full information on donors on both the front and back of the 1349 stele in *JSK*. I transcribed this part of the inscription from photos taken from the site.

77. Jinhua Chen, "Family Ties and Buddhist Nuns."

fortune in the Buddhist world was likely to affect his natal family's fortune in the secular world.

The Merit-Worship Chapel's existence as a family shrine indicated the Zhang family's elite status in the village world. In the Jin-Yuan period, great families in Dingxiang built private Buddhist chapels as family shrines to worship both Buddhist deities and ancestors. Thanks to Zhiyu's official title in the Buddhist bureaucracy, his natal family seems to have enjoyed official status, however unconventional, and was thus entitled to build the Merit-Worship Chapel as its family shrine. The 1300 and 1310 steles installed in the chapel contain the genealogical and biographical information of five generations of Zhang family members. In contrast, other members of the Zhang extended family, who as commoners did not enjoy the official status that came to Zhiyu's direct family, used Zunsheng Dhāraṇī pillars to record their ancestors' epitaphs. Zunsheng pillars were normally eight-sided stones, carved with Buddha images and with the Dhāraṇī text, in full or in excerpts, of the *Buddhosnīsavijayadhāraṇī Sūtra* (*Foding Zunsheng tuoluoni jing* 佛頂尊勝陀羅尼經). As I have demonstrated elsewhere, while people across classes in northern Shanxi widely used Buddhist monuments—including Zunsheng Dhāraṇī pillars, stone steles, and private Buddhist chapels—to consolidate kinship ties in the Jin-Yuan period, Zunsheng Dhāraṇī pillars were mostly used by commoners and the other two were chiefly used by local elite families who had wealth or official status.[78]

Indeed, many other local kinship groups in Dingxiang also capitalized on their relatives' status as elite Wutai monks. In that the Zhang family was not alone. Consider the case of the Wang clan at Jizhuang village. In 1297 the Wangs erected a longevity pagoda for Master An 安公, their kinsman who at the age of nine became a disciple of Master Wenjun 文俊, an elite monk from the Cloister of True Countenance. When the longevity pagoda was erected, An was the abbot of the Cloister of Abundant Merit (*Hongfu yuan* 洪福院), located in Jizhuang village and a subordinate temple of the Cloister of True Countenance on Mt. Wutai.[79] According

78. Jinping Wang, "Clergy, Kinship, and Clout," 216–24.

79. Master Yuanrong 圓融大師, "Wutaishan Hongfu yuan Angong jiangzhu shouta ji" 五臺山洪福院安公講主壽塔記, *JSK*, 3.2a. At least from the Tang dynasty on-

to the inscription on the pagoda, Master An's younger brother and nephew also became Buddhist monks, and this nephew followed him into the Cloister of Abundant Merit. Echoing in the prominence of Zhiyu's and his ancestors' biographies on the steles he erected, Master An's longevity pagoda confirms the practice of turning Buddhist monuments into media for writing someone's genealogy. The inscription includes a brief genealogy of the Wangs, listing all the names in Master An's elder brother's family for three generations. In addition to affirming ties among themselves, these kinsmen erected the monument in honor of Master An because he alone among the Wangs had formed connections with powerful secular and religious figures: he had received a decree and an honorary religious title from a Mongol prince and had been associated with Master Wenjun (a former sangha judge at Mt. Wutai) and Master Fazhao (head of the Buddhist Supervisory Office there).

Master An's case was far from unusual, as dense temple networks in northern Shanxi villages strengthened bonds between local kinship groups and Buddhist monasteries. Thus, while many of these villages had one of their own (like Master An) stay on and serve as a monk in their village temple, other villages invited a neighboring village's monk to head their temple. These network ties could also operate hierarchically, either when a monk would dispatch his disciples to temples in other villages or when village temples were integrated as subordinate temples into a larger Buddhist establishment, like the Cloister of the True Countenance, based at Mt. Wutai.[80]

In another case, when Zhao Deren, the community head (*shezhang* 社長) of an unknown village in Dingxiang, died, his children installed a Zunsheng Dhāranī tomb pillar in 1317 to inscribe an epitaph for their father as well as a chart of the Zhao descent group. Interestingly, the epitaph

---

ward, pious Buddhist followers in China started to install Zunsheng Dhāranī pillars near their ancestors' tombs or within ancestral graveyards and to inscribe epitaphs on them. Such Zunsheng Dhāranī pillars were naturally called tomb pillars (*fenchuang* 墳幢 or *muchuang* 墓幢). In the Liao, Jin, and Yuan periods tomb pillars erected for Buddhist monks were often called "pagodas" (*ta* 塔) instead of "pillars" (*chuang* 幢); when a tomb pagoda was intended for a still-living monk, it was called a "longevity pagoda" (*shouta* 壽塔). See Ye, *Yu shi*, 138.

80. "Puxian heshang jingchuang" 普顯和尚經幢 and "Chongxiu zhengdian dong-lang zhi ji" 重修正殿東廊之記, *JSK*, 2.20a–21b and 51a–53b.

began by identifying Deren as a cousin of a Wutai monk, Zhizu 智足, who had received three decrees respectively from an imperial prince, an imperial princess, and an imperial-son-in-law that appointed him to supervise the construction of Buddhist monasteries on Mt. Wutai. Before that appointment, Zhizu also served as a vice sangha chancellor of Pingding subprefecture 平定州 in northern Shanxi.[81] Clearly, the Zhao men tried to use their clerical relative's imperial connections and government position to elevate their own status in their village.

If Zhiyu's case tells us of the ways in which high-ranking Buddhist officials at Mt. Wutai actively benefited their lay families, cases like Master An's and Zhizu's demonstrate how more humble kinship groups tried to associate themselves with their clerical relatives at the middle and bottom of the Mt. Wutai Buddhist order. Either way, elite Wutai monks became extremely important for their lay kin in the Yuan. They provided routes by which lay relatives could attempt to raise or maintain their status, and people of the time like the Zhang family saw these routes as ones likely to lead to success. We may interpret this phenomenon as a new kind of "laicization" of Buddhism, borrowing from Robert Hymes's term discussed in the introduction. The "laicization" of Buddhism in the Song, as Hymes argues, included clerical eagerness for powerful lay ties, which consequently yielded some religious authority to the laity.[82] In contrast, the "laicization" of Buddhism in the Yuan worked in the opposite direction: the clergy had access to political authority, which resulted in the laity's eagerness to form powerful religious ties. With the dramatic change in political and social dynamics also came a sharp departure in the way Mt. Wutai's monks were presented as highly filial sons in local stone steles installed by monks.

THE NEW INTERPRETATION OF BUDDHIST MONKS AS FILIAL SONS

Over many centuries Chinese apologists for Buddhism had devised a powerful set of arguments and practices that emphasized the compatibility of Buddhist teachings with the Confucian requirements for a son

---

81. "Gu Zhaogong muzhiming" 故趙公墓誌銘, *JSK*, 3.41b–42b.
82. Hymes, "Sung Society and Social Change," 598–99.

to display filial piety.[83] Some even argued that Buddhism rather than Confucianism offered a son the best way to perform his filial duties.[84] Just as he should enter the Buddhist sangha to repay his parents' favors and win them entrance to the Buddhist paradise, so should he perform Buddhist practices like the annual Ghost Festival rite and make donations to the sangha to redeem their sins.[85] Some Song dynasty Confucian literati approved the expression of filial piety in Buddhist ways, writing favorably of the use of Buddhist monks to tend to ancestral halls and grave sites.[86] In the Yuan dynasty southern Chinese literati also highlighted instances of Buddhist monks' filial devotion to their deceased parents.[87] In brief, the traditional Buddhist discourse on the practice of filial piety overwhelmingly stressed the son's potential to improve the afterlife of his parents and other ancestors.

In both the 1300 Liang Stele and the 1310 Miaoyan Stele, however, the filial focus has been expanded to encompass the worldly benefits that a monk's filial behavior can win his parents during their lifetime. This worldly understanding of a monk's filial rewards is evident in the two steles in a variety of ways, not least in their size. They are huge: the stele of 1300 stands about 3.2 meters high and is slightly less than a meter wide, while the stele of 1310 is the largest of all the inscribed steles in Niu Chengxiu's collection, some 4.0 meters high and 1.2 meters wide. Even an illiterate onlooker would walk away impressed by this son's exceptional effort to win permanent fame and glory for his family and to assert its preeminence in the village and prominence in the greater world.

To the literate, the steles' inscriptions, both written by Monk Fu, who was Zhiyu's colleague at Mt. Wutai, impart the same impression, but in more detail and with more use of rhetorical strategies. They tell of this monk's ties to the good of both the sangha and the secular world (including a Mongol emperor). Fu portrays Zhiyu as being as filial as Zeng-

83. Scholars have pointed out that the concept of filial piety is not unique to Chinese Buddhism. For the examples of filial love that Buddhist priests feel toward their parents in early Indian Buddhism, see Schopen, "Filial Piety and the Monk" and a revised version in his *Bones, Stones and Buddhist Monks*, 56–71.

84. Gregory, *Tsung-mi and the Sinification of Buddhism*, 31–32.

85. Teiser, *The Ghost Festival in Medieval China*, 65 and 201.

86. Halperin, *Out of the Cloister*, 205–15.

87. Halperin, "Buddhists and Southern Literati," 1472–76.

can 曾参 (505–435 BCE), one of Confucius's students who was famous for his filial piety. Zengcan was one of the main characters in the twenty-four tales of filial piety, which were extremely popular in tomb decorations in Shanxi during the Yuan—even for tombs of the clergy, as demonstrated in the previous chapter.[88] In Fu's account, Zhiyu had two parallel identities, as a Buddhist monk and as a filial son. Similar language had already appeared in earlier Buddhist inscriptions from Dingxiang county. During the Jin-Yuan transition many local pagoda or stele inscriptions praised Buddhist monks for their dual demeanor of "serving the master" (*shishi* 侍师) while "practicing filial piety" (*xingxiao* 行孝).[89] But the 1300 and 1310 steles push the idea of a Buddhist monk as a filial son to an unprecedented level.

First, the two steles praised Zhiyu for making filial piety steles to eulogize his parents, something every good son was expected to do (Master Liang was acclaimed for erecting a filial piety stele for his own parents). Fu also framed Zhiyu's installation of the memorial stele for Liang in a miracle story, illustrating the new discourse on filial piety:

> In the same year [1300], Zhiyu hired people to cut a stone and inscribe the stele. Auspicious signs appeared. There were more than ten thousand contributors, and the stele cost more than fifty ingots. People tried to carry the stone stele yet failed to move it. Zhiyu then stepped forward. He burned incense and prayed, "I pray for a blessing from the saint and the eight groups of spiritual beings [Buddhist tutelary deities]." Suddenly, a sound like thunder came from the sky. Clouds and fog emerged from nowhere. The stele was lifted up in the air and moved to the Merit-Worship Chapel by the working of supernormal powers. People called it "the miraculous stele."[90]

In Fu's narrative, Zhiyu's filial behavior far exceeds that of the ordinary lay mortal, as evidenced by his supernatural ability to invoke and receive a god's aid in moving "the miraculous stele." In addition, typical

88. Scholars have shown that the twenty-four tales popular in north China differed from those popular in the south. The tale of Zengcan appeared in both northern and southern versions. See Dong Xinlin, "Beisong Jin Yuan muzang."

89. "Puqi heshang tachuang" 普圮和尚塔幢 and "Yingbian dashi Chenggong beiming" 英辩大師澄公碑銘, *JSK*, 2.6a–6b and 50a.

90. The Liang Stele, 3.7a–7b.

Buddhist rhetoric about miraculous Buddha images appears to have been transposed onto a filial piety stele.[91] In this way, the Buddhist miracle-story tradition and the cult of filial piety are skillfully fused together.

Most strikingly, both stele inscriptions laud the son for burnishing his family's social standing and increasing its fortune through official appointments. As the 1300 inscription explains: "Then, in the fourth year of the Dade era [1300], Master Zhiyu was specially appointed the sangha chancellor of Fenzhou subprefecture and occupied an official position of rank 5a. His family's reputation is celebrated. [It is] rich and titled, [it merits] songs of splendor, and ballads tell of its pleasure upon pleasures. His fame extends across the whole country."[92] Such flowery language can usually be dismissed as a potpourri of clichés. But here it needs to be read with an awareness of its context: phrases normally showered on successful graduates of the civil service examinations are being used for a Buddhist monk to honor his official success and his contribution to his family's fame and well-being.

Like his Mongol rulers, in both stele inscriptions Fu treats religious officials little differently from civil officials. He sees Zhiyu not just as a Buddhist monk but also as a middle-rank government official, whose office and title exalted his family. Thus, for Zhiyu's installation of the memorial stele for his father in 1300, Fu details the number of its donors (over ten thousand) and the size of their donation (over 50 ingots [*ding*], the equivalent of 250 ounces [*liang*] of silver in the Yuan monetary system). While these figures are hyperbolic, their use buttresses Fu's assertion that as a monk Zhiyu brought exceptional fame and wealth to his family. Fu's portrayal of Zhiyu's younger brother, Zhize, likewise appropriates

91. The miraculous story recorded in the 1300 Liang Stele bears some similarity to early stories about Asoka images recorded in the biographies of earlier Buddhist masters. In earlier Buddhist writings, Buddha images miraculously indicated their wish to be moved to new locations. For instance, in one story of the early Buddhist master Huiyuan, it is said that Tao Kan 陶侃, a military governor, tried to move the image, but the image would not budge. But at the request of Huiyuan 慧遠, the image suddenly became light. For studies of Asoka image stories, see Shinohara, "Stories about Asoka Images."

92. The Liang Stele, 3.7a.

familiar Confucian phrases to celebrate his worldly accomplishments. Zhize is praised for being "benevolent and virtuous. He respects his parents and maintains harmony with others. He is capable of setting up family property and being lavish in his [patronage of] ritual and music."[93]

These acts of filial piety and their celebration by Fu came only after Zhiyu had succeeded in his Buddhist career and consequently raised his family's standing in the secular world. All three of Zhiyu's filial bequests occurred after he received imperial decrees from Mongol nobles and promotions in the Buddhist world. His first filial act, the remaking of the ancestral tablet and its placement in the Monastery of Great Peace in 1297, is mentioned in the 1300 inscription after he had received two decrees from a Mongol prince. The installation of the stele of 1300 at the Merit-Worship Chapel followed immediately after his appointment as sangha chancellor of Fenzhou, and the making and installation of the stele of 1310 occurred shortly after his promotion to chief sangha registrar by Emperor Khaishan. These actions were a meaningful display of status, aimed not at the monastic community on Mt. Wutai but at Zhiyu's family's home in Dingxiang. Each instance of filial generosity is thus presented as the outcome of a prior ascent up the rungs of the Buddhist ladder of secular success. Zhiyu's contemporaries, clergy and laity alike, would have understood this linkage.

The more worldly appreciation of filial piety therefore embraced the two identities of Zhiyu (that of a Buddhist monk and that of a government official) and two worlds (this one and the afterlife) in which his parents would benefit from his filial piety. It also promoted the notion that such a monk made a better filial son than did an ordinary layman. Not only did a monk's religious identity impart sacredness to common acts of filial piety like the raising of a parent's memorial stele, but his official identity also contributed to his lay family's rise in the world and its eminence in the surrounding countryside. Accordingly, a Buddhist monk's career rose in prestige among those able to see the concrete benefits that a family could accrue in this world from having one of its member succeed in the sangha. This concept of the Buddhist monk as a filial son thus differed considerably from traditional Buddhist discourses of filial piety. Instead

93. The Liang Stele, 3.7b.

of an emphasis on the monk's salvation of his ancestors in the afterlife, the focus was on the filial monk's ability to improve their material and physical well-being in their lifetime. The conflicts that could arise from a monk's being obliged to serve both parents and religious masters, and both the family and the monastery, were here muted if not overcome by his success in a clerical career that to some extent had become secular.

Thus, we know that Zhiyu was celebrated as having successfully served both his family and Buddhist institutions on Mt. Wutai. Yet given that he had three sons and his younger brother, Zhize, also had a son, how do we assess their marital status and observance of celibacy? Neither the 1300 Liang Stele nor the 1310 Miaoyan Stele specifies at exactly what age Zhiyu and Zhize became monks.[94] Did the two monks enter the Buddhist order after they had already been married and fathered sons? Fu does not say. But why? If they indeed had sons before joining the Buddhist order, why would Fu not say so to avoid any potential suspicion that they violated the Buddhist precept of celibacy? Could Zhiyu and Zhize have had sons after becoming monks?

This puzzle may reveal the hidden tension between Buddhist practice and Confucian virtues in the new interpretation of Buddhist filial piety. Zhiyu's older brother Zhongyu had died and left no male offspring to continue the Zhang family line. With Zhongyu's death, Zhiyu and his younger brother Zhize would have assumed this family obligation. Fu probably remained silent on when Zhiyu and Zhize became Buddhist monks because it was too embarrassing to admit that Wutai monks had wives and fathered children, although as we will see below, this was not uncommon in Yuan China.

As Zhiyu's case shows, in their own writings Wutai monks openly promoted Buddhist monks as better filial sons and publicized the same view on stone steles. But they did not—and would not—similarly brag about their marital role, which (unlike their filial role) was not justified by state and society. This means that almost no local inscriptions reported on Yuan monks' marriages. Instead, we have to rely on the biased records

94. The account of Zhiyu in the 1300 Liang Stele mentioned that in 1284 he built a tall pagoda, so the only thing we can infer is that Zhiyu should have entered the Buddhist order earlier than 1284. See the Liang Stele, 3.7a.

of their opponents—in the government, among Confucian scholars, and among Buddhist monks who held to traditional Buddhist monastic rules—to examine the unconventional familial roles that many Yuan monks played as husbands and sons-in-law in both the north and the south.

Buddhist Monks as Husbands and Sons-in-Law

A recent study of family matters in early Indian Buddhist *vinayas* by Shayne Clarke finds that in Indian Buddhist law codes, marital dissolution was not a prerequisite for the monastic life, and Indian monks could continue to visit and interact with their wives and children.[95] Yet in Chinese society by the Yuan dynasty, it had long been both a Buddhist monastic rule and a social norm that anyone who entered a Buddhist order had to take a vow of celibacy and sever all ties to his or her natal family. Most Chinese imperial statutes also forbade monks and nuns to marry. In the Yuan dynasty, except for Buddhist monks within the former Xixia territory who were legally allowed to have wives, the government in general forbade monks—both Buddhist and Daoist—to have wives and children.[96] Yet many Chinese monks in the Yuan period did not honor their vows of celibacy, and some even married openly.

During Khubilai's reign, the scandal that Buddhist monks had wives and fathered children had already drawn the imperial government's attention. For instance, Khubilai once ordered Buddhist monks to repair monasteries as a way to repent for violating their vows of celibacy.[97] In 1292 Khubilai issued an edict about recruiting Buddhist officials and emphasized the criterion of their having no wives.[98] In the next year Khubilai ordered the defrocking of Buddhist officials who had wives, but those whose rank was above or equivalent to sangha head (*zongtong*

---

95. Clarke, *Family Matters.*

96. Ōyabu, *Gendai no hosei to shūkyo,* 158–61.

97. *Fozu lidai tongzai,* 22.24a.

98. Hu Juyou 胡居祐, "Xuanshou zhulu shijiao duzongtong fohui putong ciji dachanshi fenxi Mangong daoxing bei" 宣授諸路釋教都總統佛慧普通慈濟大禪師汾溪滿公道行碑, *Jinshi cuibian buzheng,* 3.14b–19b (*SSXB,* ser. 1, 5:3522–25).

總統)—such as heads of Buddhist Supervisory Offices—were not included.[99] The Yuan regime did not necessarily allow high-ranking Buddhist officials to marry, but it surely was more lenient toward them if they violated their vows of celibacy. Given the frequent imperial orders forbidding Buddhist and Daoist officials to have wives or children, the practice must have been common at the time.[100]

The Yuan government was aware that the fundamental reason for the popularity of clerical marriage was the clergy's exemption from the duty of labor service and taxation, which led many civilians to take monastic vows but actually live outside monasteries with their families. To deal with this problem, Khubilai issued an edict in 1293 ordering that monastic land belonging to Buddhist and Daoist monks without wives would enjoy the tax break, but land belonging to monks with wives would be taxed.[101] Interestingly, and rather strangely, this edict did not order monks with wives to either return to their secular lives or permanently divorce their wives. It seemed that as long as monks paid taxes, they could stay in monasteries while living with their wives.[102] The government regulations on these issues became more specific only after legal cases of clerical marriage were sent to the central court for review. According to an edict issued in 1311, when a southern Daoist official was found guilty not only of having a wife and fathering children but also of hiring three more women as his temporary concubines, the court originally used the law against Buddhist officials having wives to sentence the Daoist official to be beaten sixty-seven times with sticks and then to resume secular life. Eventually the Daoist official was exempted from the beating and received only the

---

99. *YS*, 17.374.

100. On the popularity of taking wives among Yuan Buddhists and Daoists, see Tan, *Chongtu yu qixu*, 24–30.

101. *YDZ*, 2:957.

102. The Yuan court seemed not to realize the bold implication of this edict. Hymes shared with me his brilliant reading of this edict: If the court's major concern was that people who became monks simply to seek the tax exemption were insincere Buddhists, allowing married monks to remain married so long as they paid taxes would look like a test of their sincerity in faith. That is, if married monks did not just join the Buddhist order for the tax exemption, they would stay in the monastic order even if they had to pay taxes. And Buddhists whose faith had been tested and proved would be Buddhists who were married. It thus seems that someone can be a perfectly sincere and believing monk and yet marry, which is surprising.

punishment of resuming secular life and fulfilling the duty of labor services.[103] This case shows that by 1311, the Yuan court had established a specific way to deal with Buddhist officials who had wives and extended that approach to Daoist officials after 1311. Yet the legal punishment for clerical marriages was relatively lenient; thus the stakes were not too high for monks who violated the rule.

Stories of monks living with their wives were not rare in Yuan China, and such behavior was constantly criticized by both Buddhist monks and Confucian literati. Some elite monks, both Tibetan and Chinese, put Yuan monks into two simple categories—"good monks" (*haoheshang* 好和尚) and "bad monks" (*daiheshang* 歹和尚)—and referred "bad monks" to Buddhist officials (*sengguan* 僧官). Having a wife (and possibly a concubine) was one of the characteristics of a "bad monk." The Tibetan lama Tanba (1230–1303; Danba 膽八 in Chinese sources) was one of the elite monks who criticized Buddhist officials. As a disciple of 'Phags-pa, Tanba played significant roles in many important religious matters in Yuan China.[104] When Ayurbarwada—the Mongol ruler who was most prone to Confucian teachings—came to the throne in 1311, he tried to abolish the Buddhist and Daoist bureaucracies, and he quoted Tanba's words to justify his decision: "Good monks do not want to become Buddhist officials."[105] The Chinese monk Nianchang 念常 (1282–1341), who wrote a Buddhist history from its beginning up to his time, echoed Tanba's and Ayurbarwada's statements, lamenting that when the imperial court granted honorific titles and ranks to the clergy, Buddhist monks competed with each other to gain official positions, have wives and children, and serve both their rulers and their parents. Nianchang claimed that good monks did not approve of these corrupt practices.[106] From that perspective, Nianchang spoke highly of Weicai's disciple Master Xing 性公 (d. 1321) as a role model for good monks: although appointed by Empress

---

103. *YDZ*, 2:1137.

104. Tanba was stationed at a Buddhist monastery on Mt. Wutai in 1260s, participated in burning the Quanzhen Daoist canon in 1281, convinced Temür to revive the policy of granting Buddhists and Daoists tax exemption, and later was in charge of the largest imperial monastery in Dadu, until his death in 1303. See *Fozu lidai tongzai*, 22.26b–29b; *YS*, 202.4519.

105. *Tongzhi tiaoge jiaozhu*, 29.709.

106. *Fozu lidai tongzai*, 22.42b–44a.

Dowager Taji to serve as the abbot of the imperial Monastery of Universal Peace on Mt. Wutai, Master Xing never had any interest in associating with political nobles or flattering powerful Tibetan lamas.[107]

Scholar-officials described one serious problem of their time as "the tyranny of heterodoxies" (*yiduan taiheng* 異端太横), which included the fact that "monks of Buddhism and Daoism today have wives and father children."[108] Some southern scholars, deeply contemptuous of this social phenomenon, tried to blame foreign influence and suggested that northerners were particularly subject to it. A late Yuan scholar named Ye Ziqi 葉子奇 reported that many Buddhist monks in north China openly had wives and even housed women in their monasteries, and that these monks had simply adopted the practices of Tibetan lamas.[109] Ye might have been telling the truth. Both Nianchang's Buddhist history and government legal documents record that a non-Chinese Buddhist registrar of Luzhou subprefecture in southeastern Shanxi had gathered women in an imperial monastery. This scandal made Ayurbarwadà particularly angry and drove him to try to abolish the Buddhist bureaucracy—an effort that eventually failed, because the imperial monastery where the scandal had happened belonged to him.[110]

Sensitive Yuan critics documented another aspect of the strikingly new role of Buddhist monks as husbands and sons-in-law to criticize that social practice. The best example is a satirical poem titled "The Lady Living in the Separate Residence" ("Waizhai fu" 外宅婦), written by the late Yuan scholar Zhu Derun 朱德潤 (1294–1365). The poem describes the prosperous life of a woman married to a Buddhist monk, although without specifying the locality of the monk in question. It pinpoints the edge that Buddhist monks had over other social groups—including poor Confucian scholars—on the marriage market and shows why some underprivileged families perceived monks as good husbands and sons-in-law.

The term "Separate Residence" (*waizhai* 外宅) has two meanings in classical Chinese. It can refer to a person's villa outside the city or another residence separate from that person's main house, or it can denote

---

107. Ibid., 22.57b–59a.
108. Zhang Yanghao 張養浩, "Shizheng shu 時政書," *Yuandai zouyi jilu*, 2:198–99.
109. *Caomu zi*, 4.84.
110. *Tongzhi tiaoge jiaozhu*, 29.708–10; *Fozu lidai tongzai*, 22.43b.

a woman who is living with a man in a house separate from the man's home with his legally married wife. Judging from the context, the term "*waizhai*" in the poem basically means a residence that is separate from the monk's daily dwelling, which is the Buddhist monastery. But it also hints at the second meaning with the intent of ridiculing the monk's marriage, which was illegal and a violation of monastic vows, however common such unions may have been at the time.

The poem captures many privileges of the Buddhist clergy that prompted Chinese parents in the thirteenth and fourteenth centuries to marry their daughters to monks and send their sons into monasteries. It reads:

外宅婦	The lady living in the separate residence;
十人見者九人慕	Nine out of ten people envy her.
綠鬢輕盈珠翠妝	Her black lustrous hair is decorated with pearls and jade.
金釧紅裳肌體素	Her white body is covered by gold jewelry and red clothes.
貧人偷眼不敢看	Poor people do not dare to steal a glance at her.
問是誰家好宅眷	They ask from which good household this lady comes.
聘來不識拜姑嫜	After being married, the lady need not serve her parents-in-law.
逐日綺筵歌婉轉	Instead, she enjoys gorgeous feasts and concerts every day.
人云本是小家兒	A man said that this lady was his daughter.
前年嫁作僧人妻	The year before last, she married a Buddhist monk.
僧人田多差役少	The monk has many lands and performs minimal labor service.
十年積蓄多財資	He has saved a fortune in ten years.
寺旁買地作外宅	He bought some land next to his monastery and built a separate house.
別有旁門通巷陌	The house has a side gate connecting to the lanes outside.
朱樓四面管弦聲	The magnificent multistory building was surrounded by music.
黃金剩買嬌姝色	With the remaining gold, the monk bought the young beautiful lady.
鄰人借問小家主	A neighbor asked the father of the lady:
緣何嫁女爲僧婦	"Why did you marry your daughter to a monk?"
小家主云聽我語	The father said, "Please listen to what I have to say.
老子平生有三女	I have three daughters.
一女嫁與張家郎	One is married to a son of the Zhang family.

自從嫁去減榮光	She has lost her bloom since she married to him.
產業既微差役重	The Zhang man has little property yet performs heavy labor service.
官差日日守空床	He does tasks for local officials every day, leaving my daughter an empty bed.
一女嫁與縣小吏	My second daughter is married to a humble county clerk.
小吏得錢供日費	The clerk has enough money for their daily expenses.
上司前日有公差	In the old days his boss sent him away on official business.
事力單微無所恃	My daughter had hardly any servants to rely on.
小女嫁僧今兩秋	My youngest daughter has been married to the monk for two years.
金珠翠玉堆滿頭	Her hair is covered with gold, pearls, and fine jade.
又有肥膻充口腹	She has delicious meat to eat.
我家破屋改作樓	And my shabby house was rebuilt to become a multistory building."
外宅婦，莫嗔妒	The lady living in the separate residence—you should not be angry or jealous.
廉官兒女冬衣布	Children of a virtuous official only wear cotton winter clothes.[111]

The poem vividly depicts a society in which wealth and privilege, such as the exemption from labor service and taxation, shaped the strategies of ordinary Chinese families as they tried to find spouses for their daughters. In this society, a Buddhist monk offered much more as a potential husband and son-in-law than a clerk or an ordinary farmer did. The monk not only provided his wife with a comfortable life but also enriched the family of his father-in-law.[112] Given its satirical nature, the poem could have exaggerated the situation to strengthen its effect, so we may not treat it as a direct window into social reality. But the poem undoubtedly re-

---

111. Zhu Derun, "Waizhai fu" 外宅婦, *Cunfuzhai ji*, 10.313–14.

112. Many Yuan inscriptions mentioned the personal property of Buddhist monks. Even a not particularly famous monk could accumulate a large amount of money. For instance, the monk Puxuan, an abbot of a local Buddhist cloister in Henan, left 7,500 strings of cash when he died in 1346. See "Yuanji lingyin daheshang changgong zhi ji" 圓寂靈隱大和尚供之記, *Jinshi cuibian buzheng*, 4.24b–25b (*SSXB*, ser. 1, 5:3547–48).

flects a degree of truth, particularly with respect to a Buddhist monk's advantage as a marriage partner.

The more striking message in this poem is that a Buddhist monk had an even better future than a Confucian student studying in schools. A Confucian education guaranteed students who officially registered as "Confucian households" exemption from labor service yet offered little chance of wealth. Zhu Derun makes this point in his last comment, suggesting that children of a virtuous official—most likely referring to a scholar-official—did not have as prosperous a life as the monk's wife did. In another poem, Zhu reports that students who had a small school stipend were so poor that they were happy to write inscriptions eulogizing the virtuous governance of high-ranking officials, regardless of the truth, provided that they were paid for their writing.[113]

The poem offers a sharp contrast to the advice on occupations for young relatives in literati families in the famous twelfth-century manual *Precepts for Social Life* (*Shifan* 世範), written by the Southern Song scholar-official Yuan Cai 袁采 in 1178:

> Assuming they have no hereditary stipend or real estate to depend on, the sons and younger brothers of gentlemen-officials (*shidafu* 士大夫) will need to plan for a way to support their parents and children. In such cases, nothing is better than becoming scholars. Those with superb natural abilities can study for the *jinshi*: the best of them can take the degree and gain wealth and official rank; the next best can set themselves up as teachers, thus receiving tuition income. Of those without the ability to pursue the *jinshi*, the best can become clerks and work with documents; the next best can practice punctuating reading for children and become their tutors. If the profession of scholar is not possible, then the arts and skills of medicine, Buddhism and Daoism, farming, gardening, commerce, and crafts can all provide support for your family without bringing shame to your ancestors.[114]

---

113. Zhu Derun, "Dezheng bei" 德政碑, *Cunfuzhai ji*, 10.312.

114. *Yuanshi shifan*, 2.18. For an English translation of this passage, see Yuan, *Family and Property in Sung China*, 267–68. My translation restores the term *jishu* 伎術 (people who master specific crafts)—omitted in the published translation by Patricia Ebrey—which is one potential occupation that Yuan suggests for those who cannot be scholars. Also, the term *nongpu* 農圃 means both farming and gardening (Ebrey translates it as gardening alone).

Becoming examination students or literati was the best choice for young men in the south during the twelfth and thirteenth centuries. Yet after the Mongols conquered both the north and the south and overturned the traditional social order, for many Chinese men it was better to be a monk than a scholar in terms of having the means to support one's family.

Another Confucian scholar, Wang Yuanliang 汪元量, made this point explicitly in a poem titled "Laughing at Myself" ("Zixiao" 自笑), composed in 1281:

釋氏掀天官府	Buddhists have a government that could overturn the heaven.
道家隨世功名	Daoists enjoy honor and fame of the world.
俗子執鞭亦貴	Ordinary people could become eminent as well once taking up the whip [joining the military].
書生無用分明	Clearly, scholars are utterly useless.[115]

This poem attests to the belief of the literati that the religious life and the military became the two most popular careers for Chinese under Mongol rule. As with Zhu's poem, we need not take Wang's description at face value, particularly as we know from sources that in south China, literati continued to hold considerable social power on the local level. Rather, we should read the poem as the complaint of a Confucian gentleman who resents the bestowal of any wealth or honor on clergy or military men and who feels he has been bested by men who are less morally worthy.

Scholars like Zhu and Wang complained about the literati being down and out while Buddhist and Daoist monks had power, honor, wealth, and even women in Yuan China. On the surface, the complaint in these protest poems was oriented toward the clergy. Yet essentially the criticism was of the Yuan political system. Not surprisingly, extreme anticlerical scholars such as Kong Qi 孔齊 (ca. 1310–after 1365), a descendent of Confucius, not only singled out monks and women as usurpers of traditional institutions of public authority (that is, the government and family) but even claimed that these people and the power they exercised

---

115. *Zengding Hushan leigao*, 73.

were at the core of the Yuan dynasty's malaise.[116] Kong attributed the breakdown of proper moral order in the monastery and the family to poor political leadership under the Mongols. Many of his fellows likely shared his view. Writings of these literati hinted at the subversive effect of the contradiction between the normative values and actual life experience of the traditionally privileged social groups such as the Confucian literati and those of previously marginalized social groups such as the clergy. This contradiction formed a critical part of late Yuan social tensions that eventually led to massive local rebellions.

Conclusion

Mongol-Yuan rule caused significant changes in the making and composition of the political elite of north China. While titles and positions in the civil bureaucracy continued to signify elite political status, the routes to this status and power changed greatly from Song and even Jin times. Examination degrees no longer functioned as the key marker of elite legal and social status. Instead, the new regime had multiple power centers, one of which—especially after Khubilai's ascendance to the throne—was the Buddhist bureaucracy. Virtually any position in the government or government-related agencies could conceivably qualify its holder for admission to the national, regional, county, or village elite. Even a village monk, as long as he received an official appointment or a decree from a Mongol noble, could see his social position and status transformed overnight from ordinary to distinguished. True, Buddhist monks did not supplant civil officials in running the empire. But the Mongol rulers favored Buddhism, gave Buddhist monk-administrators considerable power, and conferred on Buddhist officials a legal and social status akin to that enjoyed exclusively by civil or military officials in other dynasties. In this respect, the Buddhist ascendance under Mongol rule seriously challenged the Confucian official's traditional dominance in the Chinese bureaucracy, as well as the social and legal order that had supported his privileged position in Chinese society.

116. Smith, "Fear of Gynarchy in an Age of Chaos"; Halperin, "Buddhists and Southern Literati," 1491.

Significant change also came to the social role of Buddhist monks under Mongol rule. Prominent monks in the influential Buddhist order based at Mt. Wutai were able to pursue family agendas in not just monastic but also governmental institutions. In a society where the educated and uneducated openly vied for official status and appointment, *huja'ur* monks like Zhiyu used their prestigious positions to open doors for family members who wanted a career as a Buddhist official or clerk in government agencies charged with handling Buddhist matters. Consequently, ties to the Mt. Wutai Buddhist order improved a monk's chance of achieving an official rank and office that his relatives could inherit. As monastic lineages and lay kinship groups overlapped in the thirteenth and fourteenth centuries, Buddhism was enveloped by the kinship system and practices of northern Shanxi. Local people there also established memorial steles and private Buddhist chapels to consolidate kinship ties as well as ties between monasteries and families.

Understandably, many people in Yuan China came to regard a position and rank in the Buddhist order as a way to attain power, wealth, and prestige for themselves and their families. On the one hand, some Buddhist monks justified their improved status on secular grounds. They saw themselves, quite likely as their natal families would have wished, as filial sons who raised their families in the world by gaining powerful positions in the Buddhist administration established and authorized by the Yuan government. This concept of the Buddhist monk as a filial son differed considerably from the traditional Buddhist understanding of filial piety. Emphasis shifted from the monk's salvation of his ancestors in the afterlife to his ability to improve their material and physical well-being in their lifetime. Buddhist officials like Monk Zhiyu at Mt. Wutai thus linked the Yuan state and the family just as Confucian officials had linked state and family in earlier Chinese dynasties. On the other hand, some humble families saw a wealthy Buddhist monk as a desirable husband for their daughter and a helpful son-in-law. The clergy's encroachment on the marriage market, though forbidden by the Yuan government and severely criticized by disciplined clergy and literati, was persistent at the time because it was supported by the clergy's remarkable wealth and their privilege of exemption from labor service and taxation. As a powerful political agency and social institution, the Buddhist order thus interacted with the institution of family and played a critical role in reshaping kinship relations in Yuan China.

Their profound impact on other social institutions was a salient feature of the Buddhist and Daoist orders in the Mongol-Yuan era. Equally striking was the two religions' deep penetration into distinctive village organizations in north China, which—as we will see in the next chapter—subsequently affected the restructuring of the rural socioeconomic order in local societies responding to wars or disasters.

CHAPTER 4

Clergy, Irrigation Associations, and the Rural Socioeconomic Order

Between 7:00 and 9:00 p.m. on September 25, 1303, a catastrophic earthquake that was probably at least an 8 on the Richter scale struck many regions of north China, especially Shanxi. Zhaocheng county 趙城縣 in Pingyang circuit (southern Shanxi) was at the epicenter. The earthquake wiped out entire villages and killed roughly 200,000 people in Pingyang alone—about 30 percent of the circuit's population. Across the entire circuit, 70 percent of the buildings were destroyed.[1] The devastating earthquake led to a new wave of infrastructure and community rebuilding in southern Shanxi in the next two decades, in which there were several aftershocks.[2]

Three months after the 1303 earthquake, the surviving leaders of the North Huo Canal Association in Zhaocheng county initiated a project to repair damaged irrigation works. Two years later, under the supervision of local officials and with the assistance of Buddhist monks from the

---

1. Recently published inscriptions about earthquakes in Shanxi provide the statistical information, which proves reliable when we compare the different records. A cliff inscription in Yonghe county gives precise data on the circuit's casualties: 176,365 individuals from 54,650 households died, and individuals from more than 54,000 households were injured. An inscription from Daning county describes a similar toll: 175,800 people in Pingyang circuit died. An inscription from Pingyao county documents a slightly higher number: there were more than 200,000 dead and hundreds of thousands injured. See *Shanxi dizhen beiwen ji*, 48, 55–56, and 66.

2. *YS*, 21.459; *Shanxi dizhen beiwen ji*, 65.

PLATE 1 Lay Buddhist women chanting texts in a morning ritual at Cuizhuang village, Zezhou county, Shanxi province, 2006. These village women wear brown Buddhist robes only when they are performing religious rites. The red banner on the left wall above the head of the second woman on the left is an award from the local government. Its presence continues a thousand-year-old tradition of displaying proof of government support near religious sites. Author photo.

PLATE 2   The tombs of the Yuan family, Xinzhou, Shanxi province. As a famous historical site in Shanxi, this courtyard attracts visitors who come to pay their respects to Yuan Haowen, the great northern Chinese poet, scholar, and historian in the Jin and Mongol period, who is an important figure in this book. It includes the tombs of six generations of Yuan men from Yuan Haowen's great-grandfather to his grandson. The courtyard was restored in 1794 by a local official who admired Yuan Haowen's literary achievements. Building a wall around the court-yard, he restored fallen tomb stelae and animal-shaped tomb guardians, which are shown here. Author photo.

PLATE 3   The grotto of Lü Dongbin at Nine-Peak Mountain, about eighteen kilometers north of the Palace of Eternal Joy, Ruicheng county, Shanxi province. This grotto, carved into a massive rock at the top of a steep peak behind the ruined Upper Palace, is the Quanzhen pilgrimage site at Nine-Peak Mountain. Today pilgrims continue to visit the grotto and offer sacrifices. The offerings of beer bottles on the altar table speak to the profound connection in Chinese popular culture between Lü and the alcohol trade. Author photo.

PLATE 4 The site of the Upper Palace of Purified Yang at Nine-Peak Mountain. The monastic complex of the Upper Palace was completely destroyed by the Japanese army during World War II. Only four large imperial-edict steles from the Yuan dynasty still stand at the site, testifying to the monastery's glorious past. The stele shown here contains eight edicts extending imperial protection to the palace and its lands. The red characters in the last two lines on the left are graffiti added by modern visitors. Author photo.

PLATE 5 A stele dated 1262 at the Palace of Eternal Joy. In that year, Khubilai Khan ordered Wang E, a court official, to commemorate the building of the new Palace of Eternal Joy. Quanzhen Daoists from the palace then hired a local stonemason to inscribe Wang's commemorative text on the front of this large stele. Like almost all steles carved at the time, this one has a name plaque at the top with dragons carved in relief and stands on the back of a turtle, a symbol of longevity. The inscription on the back of the stele provides a list of the names, localities, and occupations of donors in the building project, testifying to the close ties between local communities and the Daoist temple complex. Author photo.

PLATE 6 The Pavilion of Water Distribution at the Huo Spring, Hongtong county, Shanxi province. This centuries-old building, renovated many times, has been distributing water for the large Huo Spring irrigation system since the Jin dynasty. Under the pavilion, nine iron pillars divide the water into ten equal parts. Behind the pavilion, a stone weir divides the flow of spring water using a 7:3 ratio. Three parts of the water flow into the South Huo Canal at the left side of weir, and seven parts flow into the North Huo Canal at the right side. The use of iron pillars and the stone weir to divide water began in 1726. Today, in addition to irrigating more than six thousand hectares of farmland, the Huo Spring canals supply water to modern industry and city dwellers. Author photo.

PLATE 7 The main hall of the King of Brilliant Response at the Water God Temple, rebuilt 1305–19, Hongtong county, Shanxi province. The hall has been famous around the world since 1934 when two couples—the Chinese architects Liang Sicheng and Lin Huiyin and the American sinologists John K. Fairbank and Wilma Denio Fairbank—visited the Grand Monastery of Victory while investigating ancient Chinese architecture in Shanxi province. In 1935 Liang and Lin published their report of their investigations, in which they highlighted the Hall of the King of Brilliant Response for its stunning Yuan-dynasty murals, which are the only surviving example of temple murals that do not focus on Buddhist or Daoist themes. The most famous mural depicts a drama performance (see plate 8). Author photo.

PLATE 8 Mural of a theatrical scene on the southeastern wall of the Hall of the King of Brilliant Response, Hongtong county, Shanxi province. This mural captures two key features of popular culture in Shanxi during the Mongol-Yuan era: the efflorescence of religion and the popularity of drama. It shows a real play that was staged during a temple festival in 1324 by the theatrical troupe of Zhong Duxiu, a celebrated actress active in the Pingyang area of Shanxi province. Among the five main actors in the front row, the central character, wearing red, is a female dressed as an official. She is the actress Zhong Duxiu. The second figure from the left is a Buddhist or Daoist monk. Courtesy of Cultural Relics Press.

Monastery of Grand Victory (*Guangsheng si* 廣勝寺), those leaders organized local villagers to rebuild the Water God Temple (*Shuishen miao* 水神廟) next to the monastery. This temple was dedicated to the deity of Huo Spring 霍泉, the main body of water used by local residents for drinking and irrigating their fields of millet, rice, and wheat, the three most common crops planted in local irrigated farmland.

The North Huo Canal Association was an autonomous irrigation association established by local residents to allocate water from Huo Spring. Irrigation associations played leading roles in reestablishing local society in Zhaocheng and neighboring Hongtong county after the devastating earthquake. These associations also frequently financed temple repairs and met in temples, like the Water God Temple, to conduct business or hold temple festivals. The North Huo Canal Association in Zhaocheng and the South Huo Canal Association that extended to Hongtong had been the two major irrigation organizations in the two counties since the late eighth century.

As one of the few types of local organizations sanctioned by imperial rulers, irrigation associations allowed villagers to form their own institutions that integrated different rural communities and thus created a distinctive space for villagers to obtain prestige, power, and wealth. Since ancient times, Shanxi peasants had dealt with water shortages by developing either large or small canal networks to collect water from all available sources—including rivers, springs, floods, rain, and wells. Gaining access to canal water was a matter of life and death for local peasants.[3] Water management thus became a focal point in local struggles as well as a major site of power relations and negotiations among local, and even regional and interregional, forces. As independent village organizations for distributing water—the crucial agricultural resource—irrigation associations wielded considerable power in local society, and they offered a mechanism for structuring rural socioeconomic relations.

3. In some regions where water was extremely scarce and there was not enough for drinking and other daily uses, local peasants established regulations strictly forbidding the use of canal water to irrigate farmland. For a study of a system that implemented such regulations, known as the Four Communities and Five Villages (*sishe wucun* 四社五村) in the border areas of Hongtong and Huoxian counties in southern Shanxi, see Dong Xiaoping and Lamouroux, *Bu guan er zhi.*

For this reason, and also due to the availability of sources, this chapter explores the new leading role of religious institutions and their clergy in the rural socioeconomic order under Mongol rule by examining their positions in irrigation associations. Unlike the previously discussed nationwide Confucian and religious orders, irrigation associations were predominantly regional or local in scale. Large irrigation associations covered dozens of villages across counties and even prefectures, while small ones included only one or a few village communities. Even in large irrigation systems, water users often split the system into several subunits, which managed water distribution and management in different localities. Regardless of their size, most local irrigation associations in the Mongol-Yuan period involved Buddhist and Daoist institutions, which became a significant part of the rural economy due to their ownership of massive areas of farm land and numerous mills. Meanwhile, the clergy's privilege of tax exemption placed the religious institutions in an advantageous position in the power structure of local rural society.

Irrigation associations thus provide us with a distinctive lens through which to examine how Buddhist and Daoist establishments, under Mongol rule, characteristically extended their influence in socioeconomic institutions outside the monasteries. In the previous two chapters, we have seen how Quanzhen Daoist monks and nuns helped villagers rebuild their communities by providing material, ideological, and organizational support, and how powerful Mt. Wutai Buddhist monks used their political connections and official status to help their kinsmen achieve elite status in northern Shanxi villages. In both instances, villagers relied on the Quanzhen Daoist or Buddhist order to a great extent. The interactions between clergy and villagers in the irrigation associations were different, however. Buddhist and Daoist clergy might seem to be a less potent force in this chapter than in the previous two, and it is true that sometimes they were not even the most critical figures in irrigation associations. We can understand the extraordinary significance of the clergy's strong presence in irrigation associations in the Mongol-Yuan period only by understanding how the irrigation societies worked.

This chapter first describes the unique nature of irrigation associations as a type of village organization and the Mongols' distinctive impact on Shanxi's irrigation associations, a topic that has not received enough scholarly attention. Then, after briefly explaining how a typical

irrigation system worked in Shanxi, the chapter explores various irrigation systems to demonstrate how Buddhist and Daoist clergy interacted
with different institutions and their personnel—especially village leaders
and local government officials—to create remarkably new socioeconomic
dynamics surrounding the allocation of water resources in Shanxi under
Mongol rule. I argue that these new dynamics were characterized by the
broad and consistent overlap between Buddhist and Daoist institutions
and local irrigation associations. The clergy's deep penetration into local
irrigation associations that enjoyed a high degree of local autonomy
happened only during the Mongol-Yuan period, which attests to the
astonishing power of religious institutions in organizing local society
and economy at the time.

Distinctiveness of Irrigation Associations and the Mongols' Impact

Irrigation associations were distinctive for their exclusive membership,
customary laws, and unique value systems. Members of an irrigation association were often called water households (*shuihu* 水户) in Shanxi. For
an association that had water households from several villages, village often
became a higher level of membership. Water households formed a cohe-
sive socioeconomic community, bound together not by rural administrative
systems, kinship, class identity, or religious piety but by the canals, as
the collective property of member villages. In irrigation associations, the
primary identity of Buddhist and Daoist establishments was not as religious institutions but as water households, although they were very large
"households" indeed.

Within irrigation associations, long-standing irrigation regulations
(*shuili* 水例 or *shuifa* 水法) functioned as authoritative customary laws.
These regulations structured the connections among water households and
the villages they lived in, which held rights to canal water. Meanwhile,
by treating local regulations as ancient precedents (*guli* 古例), villagers
had a unique organizational form and a powerful platform for seeking
state support for local interests. Ordinary Chinese villagers normally
had no access to the broader political world. Yet irrigation regulations

became important cultural resources that Shanxi peasants applied systematically to redistribute water rights in their favor and to negotiate water disputes with officials. Most imperial states authorized irrigation associations to levy water fees and summon laborers, two rights normally reserved for the government.

Irrigation associations also had unique belief and moral systems that differed from the orthodox teachings of Confucianism, Buddhism, and Daoism. Most irrigation associations had temples dedicated to specific water-providing deities, such as dragons and historical figures famous for developing irrigation projects. Water households generally considered water a gift provided by a higher power, usually a local deity and occasionally a political authority in this world. The profits drawn from a gift are understandably difficult to share, just like those provided by any gods. This gift to be shared within the circle of irrigation beneficiaries is a collective advantage, and then a social resource, since the distinction it engenders divides people who have the right to share profits from people who do not. Thus, the water households in the irrigation associations could benefit from the gods' profitable gift, but those outside could not.

Worship of water-providing deities through ritual offerings and temple construction was therefore crucial in any irrigation system, as such worship emphasized and reinforced the exclusive rights of the members of the irrigation association. In Shanxi's irrigation systems, water users often approved of the use of violence in conflicts over water, worshipped brave men who sacrificed their own lives to gain water for their villages, and created a hierarchal order of water deities to consolidate the hierarchical order of water allocation and water control in real life.[4]

The distinctive nature of irrigation associations makes them a unique window into the changing power dynamics between organized religious institutions and territorial village organizations in Shanxi during the Mongol-Yuan era. On the one hand, the fact that the clergy maintained leadership roles in irrigation associations demonstrates how they held advantages, if not were dominant, in their relationships with villagers, even though villagers were organized and had both official and customary laws on their side. On the other hand, relationships between

---

4.   Harrison, "Daode, quanli yu jinshui"; Zhang Junfeng, *Shuili shehui de leixing,* 78–93.

water god temples—the ritual centers of irrigation associations—and monasteries reveal how the Buddhist and Daoist clergy reconciled their religious teachings with the distinctive moral and cultural values pervading irrigation societies. Moreover, clergy-villager relationships were affected by the Mongol regime's active presence in Shanxi's irrigation societies.

Contrary to Karl Wittfogel's famous hypothesis that the Mongols remained unfamiliar with the traditions and mores of the hydraulic Chinese civilization they conquered, the Mongols were already deeply involved in restoring, developing, and administering local irrigation communities in the Great Mongol State period.[5] As the Mongol regime created multiple centers of legitimate political power, many of them exercised influence in local society and the increasingly complicated power relations in Chinese irrigation communities.

From the beginning of their reign, the Mongol rulers and local governors both imposed their influence on local irrigation communities in Shanxi. In one instance, Möngke Khan (r. 1251–59) issued an edict ordering all irrigation systems in southern Shanxi to adopt the irrigation regulations created by users of the Huo Spring in Zhaocheng and Hongtong counties.[6] Some hereditary local governors also organized the building of new irrigation systems to develop the local agrarian economy. Yuan Haowen wrote an inscription to report that a local official successfully organized people in Dingxiang county to build new canals at the Huo River in 1242 and 1243.[7] Local Buddhist monks such as Master An from Jizhuang village—discussed in the previous chapter— contributed to building those new canals.[8]

The involvement of appanage holders was one of the Mongol state's most unusual impacts on Shanxi's irrigation society. Appange holders set

5. Wittfogel, *Oriental Despotism*, 127.

6. According to a gazetteer of Quwo county in southern Shanxi, the edict stated: "Regarding commoners irrigating farmland in Pingyang circuit, assign two officials to take charge. Follow the water law of the Huo Canals to use water by turn in a cycle." Precisely because a Warm Spring (*wenquan* 溫泉) irrigation community in Quwo abided by the order to observe the Huo Spring irrigation principles—which was reiterated by the government in 1306—we know of the existence of this edict and its effects. See *Xinxiu Quwo xianzhi* [1758], 19.4.

7. Yuan Haowen, "Chuangkai hushui quyan ji" 創開滹水渠堰記, *QJ*, 33.687–89.

8. Master Yuanrong, "Wutaishan Hongfu yuan Angong jiangzhu shouta ji," *JSK*, 3.2a.

up subordinate agencies to specifically deal with irrigation affairs, impos-
ing an extra layer of external authority in addition to the central and
local governments on the already complex power structure of Shanxi's
irrigation communities. For instance, Prince Batu (d. 1255; known as Badu
dawang 拔都大王 in Chinese sources)—Jochi's son and successor and the
founder of the Golden Horde—received Pingyang circuit as his appanage
in 1236. He set up the Chief Office of River Supervision of Pingyang
Circuit (*Pingyanglu dutihesuo* 平陽路都提河所) and sent many of his retainers to run the office. In 1251 Batu issued a decree to settle a water
dispute in Yicheng county; his retainers stationed in Pingyang carried out
his order. Local irrigation leaders needed to gain and annually renew
permits from this office to operate their irrigation systems.[9]

After Khubilai Khan established the Yuan dynasty, in addition to restraining the autonomous power of Hereditary Vassal families and appanage holders, the state began to play a more vigorous role in developing
and administering large-scale water control and irrigation projects in
China. The central government created irrigation bureaucracies, appointed
hydrologists and clerks to operate some large-scale irrigation systems, and
promulgated official regulations for water control—including those for
farmland irrigation and mill operation. For instance, one regulation ordered mill owners to use canal water only after landowners had finished
irrigating farmland.[10] The state encouraged the construction of watermills,
and it ordered government officials to help local water users build waterwheels if they did not know how to do so.[11] By the time the famous
agronomist Wang Zhen 王禎 (fl. 1333) had finished his illustrated *Treatise
on Agronomy* (*Nongshu* 農書) in 1313, he had already taught peasants in
many regions where he had served as a local official to apply advanced
agricultural technology, including irrigation works and various types of
watermills. The Yuan central government also ordered woodblocks
carved for the book and printed many copies to distribute to local
governments.[12]

9.   Iguro, *Bunsui to shihai*, 89–103 and 109.

10.   For a general survey of irrigation development and management under the
Mongol state, see Nagase, *Sō-Gen suirishi kenkyū*, 281–320.

11.   *Tongzhi tiaoge jiaozhu*, 16.459.

12.   *Donglu Wangshi nongshu*, 4–7.

At the regional level, court-appointed officials began to play a major role in governing local society, including supervising the development of large-scale irrigation projects. For instance, in 1271, an official named Zheng Ding 鄭鼎 led local people in Pingyang circuit to divert water from the Fen River—the biggest river in Shanxi—to develop a canal, which irrigated a large swath of farmland in three counties: Hongtong, Zhaocheng, and Linfen (the seat of Pingyang circuit). After they completed such irrigation projects, officials often followed local custom and entrusted local irrigation associations with managing the resulting systems' daily operations.[13]

In the Yuan period, the major players in the power relations of local irrigation societies thus included officials of governmental or government-related agencies; members of irrigation associations; and representatives of other powerful social institutions, especially Buddhist and Daoist monasteries. In explaining the interactions among these players, this chapter underlines the leading roles of Buddhist and Daoist orders in irrigation works, one of the socioeconomic features that distinguished the Mongol era in the history of not just Shanxi but also other northern Chinese regions.[14]

Given the importance of irrigation in local society around modern Hongtong—which included old Zhaocheng and Hongtong counties[15]—and the unusual availability of primary sources from there, this chapter concentrates on this area. Flanked by Huo Mountain on the east and the Lüliang Mountains on the west, the Hongtong region is one of the most developed irrigation zones in Shanxi because its mountainous topography creates plentiful springs. According to a modern survey, about 126 springs of different sizes exist in 105 villages in Hongtong, and most of the springs are used for irrigation. The Song, Jin, and Yuan periods marked

---

13. *Pingyang fuzhi* [1615], 4.82. In some regions, like Shaanxi, officials and clerks directly administered the daily operations of some large-scale irrigation systems, such as the Jing Canal 涇渠. See Chen Guang'en, "*Chang'an zhitu* yu Yuandai."

14. For instance, in the neighboring Shaanxi region, a famous Quanzhen master, Wang Zhijin 王志謹 (1177–1263), mobilized more than a thousand Quanzhen Daoists in 1247 to dig canals that extended more than ten kilometers and conducted water from the Lao River to irrigate massive areas of farmland and power tens of watermills, which contributed to an immediate increase of productivity in local agriculture. See Xue Youliang 薛友諒, "Qiyun Wang zhenren kai laoshui ji" 棲云王真人開澇水記, *JSL*, 620–21.

15. The two counties merged to become present-day Hongtong county in 1954.

the peak of irrigation systems there: seven canals were established in the Northern Song to irrigate 16,000 *mu* of paddy fields (approximately 1,066 hectares), another four were developed in the Jin to irrigate 23,000 *mu* of paddy fields (1,533 hectares), and four more in the Yuan irrigated 44,600 *mu* of land (2,973 hectares).[16]

Published irrigation documents from the Hongtong region are particularly rich in information.[17] These irrigation documents, together with new materials collected through fieldwork, show how local villagers allied with Buddhist and Daoist clergy to solve water disputes; operate water distribution and water management; and rebuild the local irrigation system, including temples dedicated to water-providing deities, after the social disorder caused by war and natural disaster. We will return to these issues after describing a more or less typical irrigation system in Shanxi.

Sketch of a Typical Irrigation System

In Shanxi before the eleventh century, local people had invented an ingenious method for calculating water use. Dividing the water among villages was straightforward: they surveyed the land in each village, calculated the total number of *mu*, and then assigned each village a propor-

---

16. *Hongtong xian shuili zhi*, 2–3.

17. In addition to local gazetteers and inscriptions in different collections, I used three major publications in this study. One is *Hongtong xian shuili zhi bu* (*ZB*), edited by Sun Huanlun. This text is based on a detailed survey of the forty-one canals in Hongtong when Sun served as magistrate there in 1915. In his book, Sun drew detailed iconographies of those canals and transcribed many local irrigation documents from both stone and paper (most of the paper documents about irrigation rules date to after the sixteenth century, but many claim to date from the twelfth century). The second publication is the *Hongtong xian shuili zhi*, which was compiled by technicians from the Bureau of Irrigation in Hongtong and local scholars between 1986 and 1990. This book is mostly about modern irrigation projects and administration, but it provides a helpful introduction to the geographical, topographical, and historical conditions of local irrigation works and also transcribes some local irrigation documents. The third publication resulted from a comprehensive survey of water management in Shanxi and Shaanxi conducted by Chinese and French scholars during the late 1990s. That project published four volumes of irrigation documents collected during their field research, one of which covers Hongtong: *Hongtong Jiexiu shuili beike jilu* (*JL*).

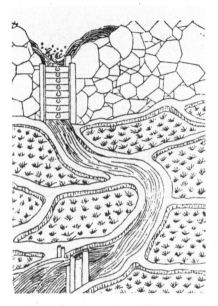

FIGURE 4.1 An image of a sluice gate from Wang Zhen's fourteenth-century *Treatise on Agronomy*. Because water rights were so valuable, fierce conflicts often arose among member villages and water households of an irrigation association when villagers secretly changed the width and depth of sluice gates. On the upper left, the current of a main canal is flowing rapidly behind a wall-shaped weir. A sluice gate is in the middle of the weir. Once the gate is open, water from the canal flows into the recipient village's branch canal, which occupies the center of the illustration. From Wang Zhen, *Donglu Wangshi nongshu*, 567.

tional share of water, delivered by opening a sluice gate, based on how much land in each village was irrigated (fig. 4.1).

Originally, the sluice gate controlled the water flow from the main canal, locally called the "mother canal" (*muqu* 母渠), to a branch canal for each village. The size and location of the sluice gate determined the amount of water that flowed in a given period of time. When it was one village's turn to receive water, the other villages were all supposed to close their sluice gates so that the water flowing through the main canal was directed to the recipient village's branch canal.

Late in the eleventh century, Shanxi villagers began to use water to power mills (fig. 4.2). From then on, the considerable profits to be made

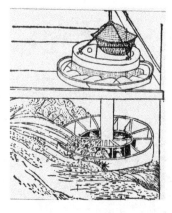

FIGURE 4.2 A water-powered mill shown in Wang Zhen's *Treatise on Agronomy*. The water-powered millstone existed in China from at least the fifth century onward, and Buddhist monasteries had a long history of earning additional revenues by running watermills. This fourteenth-century image of a water-powered mill for grinding grain with a horizontal waterwheel shows a moving millstone at the top and a fixed bed stone at the bottom that are connected by a long vertical shaft. The waterwheel is fixed horizontally by the bed stone. The force of water, when it strikes the wheel, produces the rotating motion of the vertical shaft, which moves the millstone. From Wang Zhen, *Donglu Wangshi nongshu*, 607.

by running a mill continuously attracted local people to invest in mills, particularly wealthy families or monastic communities. Mill owners often competed with peasants for water. Some irrigation associations had to place restrictions on the establishment of mills to protect landowners, and others gave landowners priority in using canal water to irrigate cultivated fields.[18]

18.   A register of the Canal of the Beneficial Source (*Runyuan qu* 潤源渠), dating to 1700 but originating in 1026, states that if someone wanted to build a watermill along the canal, the person needed to submit a written application to the Eight-Village Canal Association. If some powerful local families built mills without the permission of the association, villagers could remove those mills by force and levy fines on the mill owners (*ZB*, 79). In the Subsidiary Huo Canal Association (*Fuhuo qu* 副霍渠) that was established in the 1400s, mill households were forbidden to run their watermills when landowners were using the canal water to irrigate land. If some "evil" mill households operated their mills in spite of this rule, the canal supervisor was to report this to the county government and punish those households. But the regulations also gave mill

As a result of the mills, the amount of land in each village no longer represented its need for water. Local people then calculated each village's need in terms of man-days of work (called *fu* 夫, literally "laborer"), which tied each village's water allotment to its labor obligation for public works projects such as the repair of irrigation infrastructure and water god temples. Villages needed one *fu* for a certain number of *mu* under cultivation (the number varied in different irrigation systems) and a certain number of *fu* for each mill. The final calculation was to convert *fu* into water, in units of *cheng* 程, which determined how long the sluice gates for each village would remain open in a given cycle of water distribution.

Here is a hypothetical example of how such a calculation would have worked. Assume that in an irrigation association, each village provided one *fu* for every fifty *mu* of irrigated land it owned and two *fu* for every one of its mills. An entire cycle of water distribution was ten days, and the number of *fu* in all of the villages in the the irrigation association was forty. If a given village contributed four *fu* (two *fu* for one hundred *mu* of land and two for a single mill), it would then be entitled to one tenth (4/40) of the water in each ten-day cycle, or one full day of water. In this example, the villagers would have called a day of water four *fu*. Of course, this is a simplistic rendering of an intricate and complex system. In practice, the fixed time cycle of water distribution was calculated not only in days but also in hours, kept track of by burning incense sticks.[19] Normally, each village had a fixed number of *fu* that it needed to provide. In some cases, two or more villages provided *fu* cooperatively when their irrigated fields were calculated together for some reason (most likely because the fields were next to each other).[20] In principle, the number of *fu* from a unit (either one village or one village alliance) determined the

households the right to apply to canal supervisors to use canal water when, on rainy days, it was not needed for farmland (*ZB*, 99).

19. For example, in the South Huo Canal Association, a cycle of water allocation changed from one month and six days to one month and four days and then to thirty-five days and sixteen hours over time. Proportionally, one *fu* equaled two days' share of water in the last fixed cycle. See *ZB*, 71; Amano, "Chūgoku ni okeru suiri," 136.

20. In one instance, an irrigation document about the South Huo Canal dated 1139 stated that Daojue and Caosheng villages at Zhaocheng county had 15.2 *qing* 頃 (101 hectares) of irrigated land in all and provided 30.4 *fu* together. Meanwhile, Daojue village alone offered twelve *fu* for six mills and two *fu* for the two waterwheels it owned (*ZB*, 66).

water fees needed annually to pay for regular public works and occasional emergencies.

Most irrigation associations in Shanxi followed one of two basic models for rotating water distribution: distributing water by starting from upstream locations and moving downstream (*zishang erxia* 自上而下), or beginning with downstream locations and progressing upstream (*zixia er shang* 自下而上).[21] The majority of Shanxi's irrigation systems adopted the latter model for the sake of safeguarding the water supply of downstream villagers. Yet as revealed by the local slogan "using upstream to control downstream" (*yishang baxia* 以上把下), in either case upstream users had a natural advantage, and inevitable conflicts followed when downstream users demanded their fair share of water. As a solution to this problem, irrigation associations often established administrative systems that favored downstream communities—such as selecting association heads only from downstream villages—to use social power to counterbalance the natural advantage enjoyed by upstream communities.

The daily operation of water allocation and management relied on a group of irrigation leaders, often called canal supervisors (*quzhang* 渠長 or *qushou* 渠首), canal managers (*qusi* 渠司), water inspectors (*shuixun* 水巡), and ditch heads (*goutou* 溝頭). The range of these irrigation leaders' responsibilities reveals the centralized structure of irrigation administration. As heads of irrigation associations, in addition to presiding over annual sacrifices to water gods, canal supervisors made the major decisions about the daily operations of water management, including collecting water fees, modifying irrigation regulations, and assembling laborers for public works. Canal managers assisted them, specifically by dealing with disputes. As canal supervisors' direct assistants, water inspectors traveled constantly from village to village, supervising the work of water allocation and system maintenance performed by ordinary water users. Ditch heads were at the lowest level of irrigation administration. They kept track of opening and closing sluice gates that connected their village's branch canals to the main canal. They also led their fellow

21. A few irrigation associations in Hongtong applied both principles in combination. In one year, they would allocate water in a downstream direction, and in the next year, they would reverse the process. Alternatively, they could use the downstream-toward-upstream model at the main canal and the upstream-toward-downstream model at the branch canals (*ZB*, 81, 137, and 141).

villagers in clearing and repairing branch canals, overseeing villagers' conduct to prevent the theft of water, and—under the leadership of canal supervisors—organizing villagers to participate in public works and to pay water fees.[22]

An effective communication system among an irrigation association's member villages was the key to the daily operation of water distribution. By at least the early Mongol era, Shanxi peasants had already invented a local system for delivering messages beyond oral communication: special wooden plates, called ditch sticks (*gougun* 溝棍) or water plates (*shuipai* 水牌).[23] Villagers used these plates to transfer the water rights among users and between member villages.[24] An individual water household installed a water plate in its field during its turn to use the water. When a village had finished draining the water from the mother canal to its fields, water users in this village sent the plate on to the next village. Effective communication between villages also relied on the daily movements of all irrigation leaders. Ditch heads had to walk to nearby villages to deliver ditch sticks even late at night or in heavy rain. Water inspectors went on routine tours to examine water use in every village in each water-distribution cycle. Canal supervisors and canal managers sometimes conducted inspections as well. They often had to travel on foot day after day.

Even though most peasants—the principal members of any irrigation community—were unable to read and write, many of peasants in Shanxi managed to create written irrigation documents. These documents existed in two physical forms and played a significant role in the operation of an irrigation system. One form was inscriptions carved on stones, often called canal steles (*qubei* 渠碑), water steles (*shuibei* 水碑), or irrigation steles (*shuili bei* 水利碑). A common practice was to erect steles to record various irrigation events, including the initiation of an irrigation project, the establishment or repair of temples to water deities, the full story of

22. Li Xiaocong 李孝聰, Deng Xiaonan 鄧小南, and Xiao Jun 筱君, "Introduction," in *JL*, 31–34.

23. Iguro, *Bunsui to shihai*, 106–7.

24. In some communities, a paper note given by association heads would be attached to the ditch stick to reinforce its authority. In others, when a new canal supervisor assumed his post, he needed to turn in the old water plate to the local government in exchange for a new one. *ZB*, 43–44 and 110–11.

water disputes, and the creation or modification of irrigation regulations. For instance, a Jurchen official installed a stele at the Huo Spring irrigation system in 1139, recording major water disputes between Hongtong and Zhaocheng counties since the 1040s and the solution he reached after thorough site investigations. The stele is still standing in the Water God Temple mentioned at the beginning of the chapter.[25]

The other form was handwritten or printed copies of items called canal registers (*quce* 渠冊), itemized canal lists (*qutiao* 渠條), or irrigation registers (*shuili bu* 水利簿). These documents recorded regulations for membership, leadership, distribution of water, labor obligations, water fees, fines, and ritual procedures for sacrifices to water deities. In Shanxi from the Northern Song dynasty on, local officials traditionally stamped their seals on canal registers to confer legal authority on the irrigation regulations recorded in these documents. For instance, after establishing the *Canal Items of the Small Huo Canal* in 1046, association members (most likely their canal supervisors) applied to the Zhaocheng county government twice for official seals on their newly recopied texts, in 1136 and 1189.[26]

While steles often appeared in public places like local water god temples or local government offices, canal registers were less accessible to the public: they were often held by irrigation leaders at their posts and carefully preserved. Members of irrigation associations took great care of canal registers, many of which record punishments for those who neglected them. For instance, an undated South Huo canal register dictates that such registers should be wrapped in a particular way to prevent damage. If someone needed to take a register to a different location, he could not insert it into his boot or sleeve. When it was time for one leader to hand the texts over to another leader, they both needed to check carefully that every page was complete and neatly written. If any pages were damaged or missing, the person responsible for taking care of the texts would be fined a fixed amount of white rice as punishment.[27]

25.   Yang Qiuxing 楊丘行, "Duzongguan zhenguo ding liangxian shuibei" 都總管鎮國定兩縣水碑, *JL*, 4–5. For a detailed study of this stele, see Iguro, *Bunsui to shihai*, 38–56.

26.   "Chuangxiu Fuhuo miao ji" 創修副霍廟記, *ZB*, 93.

27.   *ZB*, 72.

The authority of words on stones raises the question of village literacy rates, which is always difficult to determine in traditional China. Villagers presumably installed these steles not for themselves to read but for educated men, literate clergy, and local officials to explain to them. The illiterate villagers tended to trust the power of the written word to resolve future disputes.

Irrigation steles and canal registers were the two most important records of irrigation regulations, which functioned as customary laws in local society. The regulations were important cultural resources by which Shanxi water users created and reinforced water-use practices to favor their own interests. Now that we have seen how a typical irrigation system worked in the abstract, let us examine how different irrigation systems in Shanxi worked in practice and how they illuminate the various roles that Buddhists and Daoists played in these systems.

The Clergy and Small-Scale Irrigation Systems

The formation and operation of an irrigation association, even in small-scale systems, often reflected an inherent tension between coordination within the system and competition among member villages and institutions. This tension could destabilize the defined hierarchical order so that it was continuously redefined in local conflicts, especially in times of water shortage and water disputes. The changing power dynamics between the clergy and villagers in this highly competitive village organization therefore best suggests the role of religious institutions in socioeconomic organization in Shanxi. The following two case studies demonstrate the clergy's relationships—cooperative in the first case and relatively coercive in the second—with their fellow villagers in maintaining an old irrigation system or creating a new one.

The first case involves a water dispute in the early Yuan period surrounding the downstream Duzhuang village, located in Huoyi county, near Hongtong. In the dispute Duzhuang villagers used a historical legend to legitimate their monopoly over a local canal and prevent upstream villagers from using the water. The Duzhuang villagers also reinforced the new order after the dispute by putting up two stone steles. Published inscriptions from these two steles allow us to glimpse interactions among thirteenth-century rural communities that are not visible in any other available source. This case exemplifies how Shanxi villagers creatively used resources available to them to define what gave them a fundamental and exclusive right to water. In this case, Buddhist and Daoist clergy acted as members of Duzhuang village and cooperated with other villagers to fight for shared interests.

The legend concerned the Tang emperor Li Shimin 李世民 (Emperor Taizong, r. 627–49), who led his army through the county during a campaign against the last ruler of the Sui Dynasty (581–618). According to the Duzhuang villagers' oral accounts, recorded in 1273, the Tang army lacked food and water, and a wealthy Duzhuang villager, Du Shiwan 杜十萬, donated a huge amount of food to supply Li Shimin's soldiers. Li's horse, making strange sounds, continuously circled a particular piece of ground. Li used his sword to dig into the earth, and soon a stream of spring water gushed out. Amazed, Li named the water source the Divine Spring of the Running Horse (*Mapao shenquan* 馬跑神泉). After Li became emperor in 627, he granted the title great general (*dajiangjun* 大將軍) to Du and offered to reward him with gold and silk. Du allegedly rejected the wealth and suggested that all he wanted was water, due to the difficulty of digging a well in his native village. The emperor then granted the permanent and exclusive ownership of the spring to him and forbade all neighboring villages to use the spring water. Duzhuang villagers later inherited the ownership of the spring. Since the spring was located in a distant village, Duzhuang villagers built a canal to bring the water to their village. They also created a water regulation inscribed on a stele to stress that other villages along the canal did not have the right to use it.[28]

The Duzhuang villagers' testimony sheds light on a distinctive system for defining the ownership of water in a local village. Regardless of the accuracy of the Divine Spring legend, this narrative empowered the Duzhuang villagers to monopolize limited water and to force other villages to accept their control. It was a vivid expression of the "gift" economy in irrigation communities. In addition to using the common discourse

---

28. Gao Hong 高鴻, "Tangtaizong yuci Dujiangjun shenquan ji" 唐太宗御賜杜將軍神泉記, *Shanyou shike congbian*, 25.45a–46a (*SSXB*, ser. 1, 20:15535).

linking water to a divine power (in this case, the deity of the Divine Spring) the legend also reinforced the message that water was a gift provided by imperial authority (here, the mighty Emperor Taizong). To challenge the existing water use order meant that one first had to impugn the credibility of the legend. No historical document verifies the tale, which has all the earmarks of something made up.

In their thirteenth-century retelling of the tale in the "Record of Tang Emperor Taizong Granting the Divine Spring to General Du," the Duzhuang villagers skillfully interwove their legend with another widely accepted account that allegedly referred to the same historical moment: the god of Huo Mountain, in the form of an old man with a white beard, appeared before Li Shimin and guided him on a march through local mountainous areas. Li, after becoming emperor, granted high honors to the mountain god by renovating its temple, upgrading its divine rank, recording its biography, and constantly sending imperial envoys to pay homage and make sacrifices to it.[29] When the villagers connected their own story with this well-documented legend about the mountain god, they strengthened their claim.

Over time, the Duzhuang villagers allied with another village and gave up their exclusive right to the canal water to solve an urgent problem that resulted in less water flowing to Duzhuang. They received permission from Songbi village, along the middle reaches of the canal, to use its abandoned pond to store canal water so that it would flow freely when a sluice gate at the pond was opened. In return, Songbi villagers, who assumed the obligation of opening and closing the sluice gate, obtained the right to use the canal water, which was still off limits to all other villages.[30] This development shows that coordination between villages often resulted not from the necessity of managing water but directly from an agreement among villages.

Interestingly, villagers in neighboring communities seemed to accept the principle that they had no right to the canal water, but they constantly

29. *Jiu Tangshu*, 21.819; *Tang huiyao*, 22.427. This state-sanctioned legend was very popular locally. Some scholars argue that one mural on the southeast wall of the Hall of the King of Brilliant Response (*Mingying wang dian* 明應王殿) represented this legend (Jing, *Water God's Temple*, 73).

30. "Huoyi xian Duzhuang bei" 霍邑縣杜莊碑, *Shanyou shike congbian*, 25.43a–44b (*SSXB*, ser. 1, 20:15534).

broke the rules and challenged the established order in small ways, using what James Scott has described as "weapons of the weak."[31] In 1273, in a rare mention of female protagonists, records indicate that two villagers' wives at Songsheng village broke canal weirs, and two other villagers allowed cattle to drink water from the canal. Four Duzhuang villagers immediately went to the county government to sue these men and women. They filed a cosignatory complaint (*lianming zhuanggao* 連名狀告)—a lawsuit filed by a group of people whose names all appeared on the petition. Cosignatory complaints were a common strategy that many water users in Shanxi employed to attract the attention of local officials in disputes.

However, instead of litigating with the Duzhuang accusers at the county seat to contend for a fairer distribution of the spring water, six Songsheng villagers entrusted several communal village leaders (*shezhang* 社長) and one additional village elder (*xianglao* 鄉老) from four neighboring villages to negotiate directly with the Duzhuang villagers. In the end, a private agreement (*siyue* 私約) was reached that restored the Duzhuang villagers' monopoly, ordered the two women to repair the damaged weir, and stipulated punishments for those who dared violate the water use rules in the future.[32]

The involvement of neighboring village leaders in the private settlement of the case demonstrates that villagers had local networks whose members could reach out to each other and were capable of resolving small-scale disputes without involving officials. In the Yuan dynasty, these rural networks often overlapped with the new rural administration system of communal villages (*she* 社) established by Khubilai in 1270. In this system, every fifty households were organized into a *she*, which was led by a communal village head (*shezhang* 社長) selected by members of the community. His main duties included advising farmers, supervising water control, and settling disputes. To reward him for his work, the communal village head would be exempted from the duty of labor service.[33]

31. Scott, *Weapons of the Weak*.

32. "Huoyi xian Duzhuang bei," *Shanyou shike congbian*, 25.43b–44a (*SSXB*, ser. 1, 20:15534).

33. *YDZ*, 2:916–21; Yang Ne, "Yuandai nongcun shezhi yanjiu."

Yet in this instance, Duzhuang villagers persisted in bringing a suit before local government officials, seeking an official document to legalize their private agreement. In their own words in the cosignatory complaint, "We are afraid that even if we have the private agreement, if we do not have evidence of official investigation and approval, things will become ambiguous over time."[34] For Duzhuang villagers, official approval of their new water agreement strengthened its authority and their position in future disputes. In other words, for local irrigation societies, the government played an important role as the ultimate authority for recognizing the new balance of hierarchical relations that villages had agreed to after conflicts. One important way to consolidate this new balance was to produce new irrigation documents. After receiving the official document (*gongju* 公據) verifying the final settlement of the case, the Duzhuang villagers asked Magistrate Gao Hong to compose a record of the Divine Spring of the Running Horse since, as they claimed, they had an old stele about the spring and their rights to it, but it had been damaged by fire during the Jin-Mongol war. Gao agreed and wrote the "Record of Tang Emperor Taizong Granting the Divine Spring to General Du" based on what local elders told him. Later, in the third month of 1275, thirty-one Duzhuang households installed a stone stele recording the original complaint, the private agreement, and the official decision. About four months later, villagers installed another stele for the record composed by Gao; the record is the main source for the Divine Spring legend described above.[35] Duzhuang villagers secured their victory and reinforced their tradition of water use by giving it material form.

In the dispute, the clergy acted not just as members of the Duzhuang village group that initiated the lawsuit but also as providers of broader social and political ties to outside help. A lack of linguistic sophistication in the complaint and the private agreement suggests that the authors had a relatively low level of education. Perhaps the authors were residents of the village who had not received much education but were capable of reading and writing. But more likely they were Buddhist and Daoist monks

34. "Huoyi xian Duzhuang bei," *Shanyou shike congbian*, 25.44a (*SSXB*, ser. 1, 20:15534).

35. Gao Hong, "Tangtaizong yuci Dujiangjun," *Shanyou shike congbian*, 25.46a (*SSXB*, ser. 1, 20:15535).

in village monasteries who had studied religious texts. Among the four villagers who signed the complaint to the county government, one was a Buddhist monk. And among the list of thirty-one Duzhuang village households that installed the stele, three were either Buddhist or Daoist monasteries. Notably, a Daoist official surnamed Zhou 周, the chief Daoist judge of Pingyang circuit at the time, wrote the calligraphy for Gao's text. Duzhuang villagers might have reached Zhou through the Daoist establishment in their village. Religious lineages were clearly helpful social resources through which illiterate villagers could reach out to educated outsiders to produce written irrigation documents.

In the second case, involving the Dayin Buddhist Monastery at Zhangshang village in Jiang county 絳縣 of Pingyang circuit, Buddhist monks organized local peasants to develop irrigation projects and established systems of water use that gave priority to Buddhist communities. Buddhist monks from the monastery took advantage of an existing hierarchical relationship between seven subordinate neighboring villages and a mysterious Dayin General (*Dayin jiangjun* 大陰將軍) connected to the monastery. The identity of this Dayin General is unclear; he might have been a deity worshipped by local people, but more likely he was a living or deceased military leader who had been the lord of the seven villages. According to an original irrigation regulation created by the seven villages in 1255, a village that violated the regulation would be punished by providing ten *shuo* 碩 (the same as the *shi* 石, a Chinese unit of dry measure) of white rice for an army affiliated with the seven villages and two sheep for the local county government. Clearly, the seven villages had certain institutional ties to the military.

Invoking the relationship between the Dayin General and the seven villages, in 1300 the Buddhist lecturer Wei (*Wei jiangzhu* 威講主) from the Dayin Monastery renewed the 1255 irrigation regulation to give the monastery not only preferential rights to, but also the longest time of, water use in each water-distribution cycle. The Buddhist clergy's position in this relatively small-scale irrigation system continued after 1300, as shown by the fact that another Buddhist monk, a former sangha judge of Xie subprefecture, inscribed the 1300 regulation on a stone stele in 1337.[36]

36. *Hedong shuili shike*, 187–88.

Despite the use of different tactics, the clergy's purpose—justifying their privileged water rights—resembled that of the Duzhuang villagers.

In sum, the cases of Duzhuang village and the Dayin Monastery illustrate two roles—water users and water-regulation makers—that clergy and religious establishments played in local irrigation systems in the Mongol-Yuan era. The clergy at the time had both the ability to help their fellow villagers monopolize water use in an irrigation system and the authority to obtain the desired amount of water for monastic interests. These two examples involved simple irrigation systems in a single irrigation association and a few villages.

The Clergy and The Large-Scale Huo Spring Irrigation System

Larger irrigation systems involved more interested parties with much more intricate relations. For instance, in the Huo Spring irrigation system mentioned in the beginning of the chapter, multiple irrigation associations, religious communities, and different levels of government all interacted in rebuilding the irrigation system after the Mongol conquest and after the devastating earthquake in 1303. Locally derived ideas, principles, and institutions of large-scale irrigation systems bound the clergy and villagers together for community rebuilding in ways quite different from what we have seen in previous chapters. On the one hand, Buddhist monks from the Monastery of Grand Victory built ideological and institutional ties between their monastery and the Water God Temple, the ritual center of the Huo Spring irrigation system. On the other hand, Buddhist and Daoist establishments as water households in irrigation systems used their religious lineages and networks to help their affiliated villages and irrigation associations rebuild irrigation infrastructure after wars and disasters as well as engage officials of the local government.

The Huo Spring originates as a subterranean stream beneath Huo Mountain 霍山 and produces a large pond at the southwest foot of the mountain, seventeen kilometers northeast of present-day Hongtong county. After the seventh century, local people built two canals—the North Huo Canal and the South Huo Canal—to conduct water from the Huo Spring to irrigate farmland in both Zhaocheng and Hongtong counties. The Northern Song government established a 7:3 water distribution ratio between the North Huo Canal and the South Huo Canal in 1045, and the proportion did not change in later periods (see plate 6).[37]

Over time local people extended the two canals to create a complex Huo Spring irrigation system consisting of two major canals and three affiliated canals. In the late eleventh century local people used extra water from the two major canals to develop the Small Huo Canal (*Xiaohuo qu* 小霍渠) and the Pure Water Canal (*Qingshui qu* 清水渠). These two affiliated canals irrigated the paddy fields of nine more Zhaocheng and Hongtong villages. One more affiliated canal was developed in the early fifteenth century (fig. 4.3).[38]

The Huo Spring irrigation system contributed to a favorable environment for both agriculture and living. As a 1283 inscription explains, "Four canals cover the borderland between Zhaocheng and Hongtong counties, and they extend west to the Fen River. Within the area about one hundred square *li* [equivalent to 2,500 square kilometers], big trees are seen in villages, and cultivated fields are connected by footpaths. The forest is beautiful, and crops of millet and rice are luxuriant. These are all the benefits of the Huo Spring. The temple dedicated to the deity of the Huo Spring has stood near the spring for a long time."[39] For local residents, the abundant water from Huo Spring made the cultivation of rice possible.[40]

37. The Northern Song government decided on this proportion in 1045 after resolving a series of water disputes. According to the official data used by the government, together the two canals at that time irrigated 964.178 *qing* (6,425.85 hectares) of paddy fields and drove forty-five watermills belonging to 1,747 households in 130 villages of two counties. See Yang Qiuxing, "Duzongguan zhenguo ding liangxian," *JL*, 4.

38. Judging from a 1088 poem about Huo Mountain, which states "the spring water contributes to the fertility of a thousand *qing* of land; the source extends to four canals," the four-canal structure of the Huo Spring irrigation system had fully taken shape at that time. See Zhang Shangying 張商英, "Ti Huoyue" 題霍岳, in *Huoshan zhi*, 123.

39. Liu Maobao 劉茂寶, "Chongxiu Mingyingwang miao bei" 重修明應王廟碑, *JL*, 9.

40. In some communities, water scarcity prevented the cultivation of rice and other hydrophytes. For instance, a 1571 canal register of the Pure Spring Canal records that since local villagers had developed the canal in 1024, villagers cultivated only hemp, vegetables, wheat, and millet in the farmland irrigated by the canal and were forbidden to plant lotus, cattails, or rice. See *ZB*, 110.

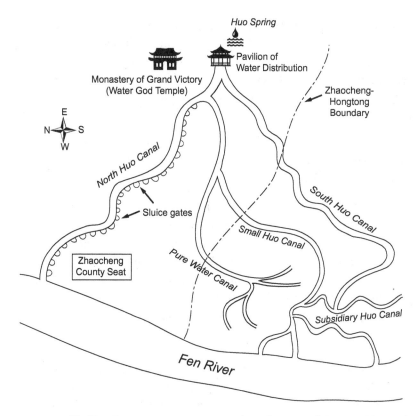

FIGURE 4.3 The Huo Spring irrigation system in the early twentieth century. The Pavilion of Water Distribution (plate 6) is at the top of this diagram, dividing the water in the irrigation system into two channels at a ratio of 7:3. On the left, the water flowed into Zhaocheng county; on the right, it flowed into Hongtong county. The formation of the system of five canals (the North Huo, South Huo, Small Huo, Pure Water, and Subsidiary Huo) took about eight centuries and spanned the Northern Song, Jin, Yuan, and Ming dynasties. In addition to the Huo Spring, the Fen River, the biggest river in Shanxi province, is another major source for irrigation in the Hongtong area. Drawing by Zhao Jiemin based on an illustration courtesy of Zhang Junfeng.

To express their gratitude, they built the Water God Temple to offer sacrifices to the deity of Huo Spring. Both historical records and local legends portrayed the water god, a dragon deity, as the oldest son of the god of Huo Mountain and addressed him by the nickname *dalang* 大郎 (literally, the oldest son). Due to his great power as a rainmaking god, the Northern Song government granted the temple a plaque titled "Brilliant

Response" (*mingying* 明應). Local people later added to this plaque and gave the god the honorific title "King of Brilliant Response" (*Mingying wang* 明應王).[41] With the development of the Huo Spring irrigation system, the Water God Temple became the ritual center for the local irrigation communities, particularly for the North and South Huo Canal Associations.

THE BUDDHIST MONASTERY OF GRAND VICTORY
AND THE WATER GOD TEMPLE

In the early thirteenth century, monks from the nearby Buddhist Monastery of Grand Victory became actively involved in the Water God Temple and began to play a distinctive part in the Huo Spring irrigation communities. On the first day of the eleventh month of 1283, a group of monks from the monastery financed the erection of a stele recording the culmination of a forty-nine-year project begun in 1234 to rebuild the Water God Temple. The inscription reads:

> Each year, on the eighteenth day of the third month, which is the god's birthday, people offer a musical performance of flutes and drums and burn incense and paper money. Many people flock to it and enjoy the celebration. At the end of the Jin dynasty, the temple burned down during the endless warfare. The lives of local residents were disrupted. Those who survived could not support themselves, let alone pay for sacrificial offerings to the water god! . . . Then the monk Daokai, a *vinaya* master in the Monastery of Grand Victory and a former sangha registrar of Pingyang circuit, became concerned about the temple's dilapidation and attempted to repair it. He sighed and said, "This temple benefited people, and the official canon of sacrifices recorded its name. Even though it is the officials' responsibility to maintain it, the temple is also a merit field of our monastery. How can we endure its continued disrepair?" Daokai then bought materials and employed craftsmen to build the temple in a new site and abandoned the old one. The North Huo Canal Supervisor Chen Zhong and others

---

41. *Song huiyao jigao*, 20.101. Anning Jing argues that the water god is the Huo Mountain god himself, the spirit of Huo Spring and the Huo Mountain god having been intentionally combined (*The Water God's Temple*, 104–15). This is clearly a misunderstanding; they were separate deities.

supported Daokai and paid for a main hall with eighteen tiled columns. Buddhist monks built a house nearby so that they could sweep the temple [it means taking care of the temple in general].[42]

Clearly, the monastic community did not belong to any canal association but had maintained a significant role as the caretaker of the Water God Temple since 1234. The monastery, which still stands today, has two compounds: the Lower Monastery (*xiasi* 下寺), standing northeast of the temple, and the Upper Monastery (*shangsi* 上寺), about a mile away on a hillside of Huo Mountain.[43] Inscriptions at the Upper Monastery reveal that the monastery was established in the late eighth century.[44]

As the story of the *vinaya* master Daokai 道開 illustrates, during the Jin-Yuan transition Buddhist monks from the Monastery of Grand Victory cooperated with the North Huo Canal Association (and later the South Huo Canal Association as well) to rebuild the Water God Temple. And the monks took the lead in the first few decades following the end of the Jin-Mongol war, at a time when local officials and residents did little. For four decades after Daokai died, monks from the Monastery of Grand Victory continued to take principal responsibility for building the halls of the temple, while North Huo canal supervisors only assisted monks in preparing construction materials such as ceramic tiles, stone slabs for the floor, statues, paint, and glue.[45] Not surprisingly, the monks were able to take the lead because their monastery received imperial patronage from the Mongol rulers. In addition to the Buddhist canon given by Khubilai Khan, the monastery also housed a portrait of Khubilai, which was a special privilege for Buddhist monasteries in the Yuan.[46]

42. Liu Maobao, "Chongxiu Mingyingwang miao bei," *JL*, 9.

43. For the architecture of the monastery and the murals in the Lower Monastery, see Jing, *The Water God's Temple*, 200–25.

44. "Tang Dali sinian zhuangqing zhisi wen bei" 唐大曆四年狀請置寺文碑, in *Guangshengsi zhi*, 37–39.

45. Liu Maobao, "Chongxiu Mingyingwang miao bei," *JL*, 9.

46. Wanglahala 王剌哈剌, "Chongxiu Mingyingwang dian zhi bei" 重修明應王殿之碑, *JL*, 15. According to Hong Jinfu, Buddhist monasteries that held Khubilai's portrait—such as the White Pagoda Monastery (*Baita si* 白塔寺) and the Great Monastery of Sagely Longevity and Perfect Soundness (*Da Shengshou Wan'an si* 大聖壽萬安寺) in Beijing—often built a special portrait hall (*yingdian* 影殿). Most portrait halls for emperors and empresses in the Yuan dynasty were established in Buddhist monasteries

Notably, Daokai justified his initiation of the temple project by using the Buddhist concept of "field of merit" (*futian* 福田), which had significant implications for the relationship between the Buddhist monastery and the Water God Temple. The Buddhist concept of the merit field concerns donations made by the laity to a Buddhist order. As Michael Walsh explains, the phrase "field of merit" implies that "any donation to the Buddhist sangha is like planting a seed in the 'great field of merit'—it will grow and provide the donor with more than they originally donated."[47] Even though monks and nuns could also gain merit by making donations for the embellishment of sacred objects and sites, these were usually Buddhist items, such as stupas, monasteries, and icons.[48] In other words, for monks and nuns, only Buddhist institutions would normally be seen as merit fields. Daokai's testimony seems to suggest that the Water God Temple had become an inseparable part of his monastery and thus an actual Buddhist space. As far as Buddhist attitudes toward local cults were concerned, early Chinese monks either felt compelled to convert and subdue local deities or tried to peacefully coexist with local cults in exchange for recognition of the legitimacy of their own activities.[49] Daoikai seems to have taken the former approach and claimed the dominance of Buddhist power over the water god.

However, the water god was not an ordinary local deity; he was a critical part of the local Huo Spring irrigation system. A text in the Chinese Buddhist canon explicitly categorizes the building of irrigation canals as one way for lay people to gain merit.[50] Rebuilding the Water God Temple would indirectly help maintain irrigation canals, since the Huo Spring water was the gift of the water god, and the lack of a temple dedicated to the god would lead to the diminution or even disappearance of the water. Therefore, by rebuilding the temple, Buddhist monks helped sustain an important field of merit for their lay neighbors. Only

---

in the Beijing area; there were only a few elsewhere. See Hong, "Yuan 'Xijinzhi yuan-miao xingxiang,'" 23 and 30.

47. Walsh, "The Economics of Salvation," 361.

48. For the concept of "field of merit" and merit making in Indian and Chinese Buddhism, see Kieschnick, *The Impact of Buddhism on Chinese Material Culture*, 157–64; ter Haar, *The White Lotus Teachings*, 24–28.

49. B. Faure, *Chan Insights and Oversights*, 156–59.

50. Walsh, "The Buddhist Monastic Economy," 1293.

in this implicit conceptual context that blended Buddhist doctrines and locally derived ideas was it theoretically legitimate for Buddhist monks to act as sponsors for the water god. And once the Buddhist monastery established itself as the sponsor of the water god, it became, by extension, the guardian of the crucial "gift" economy that spread from the Huo Spring to all villagers in the Huo Spring irrigation system, and thus an irreplaceable player in that system.

In addition to theoretically justifying their intimate relation with the Water God Temple, Buddhist monks of the Monastery of Grand Victory also tied the two establishments together institutionally by establishing the Lower Monastery right next to the temple. When Daokai led his disciples to rebuild the temple, the monks built a house near the temple so that they could take care of it. Most likely, this house was the origin of the Lower Monastery. Art historians' studies of the murals in the main hall of the Lower Monastery, which are now in New York's Metropolitan Museum and the Nelson-Atkins Museum of Art in Kansas City, provide indirect evidence. These studies show that the murals date to the late thirteenth or the early fourteenth century, the period when Buddhist monks were rebuilding the temple.[51] By taking the initiative in rebuilding and caring for the temple, monks from the Monastery of Grand Victory institutionalized the relation between the temple and the monastery and over time guaranteed the monastery's share of the water fees collected from local water users by the irrigation associations. These obligations and rights of the monastery were specified in later irrigation documents.[52]

Despite the monks' continued efforts, the temple project progressed painfully slowly. The problem was that the North and South Huo Canal Associations had a long history of conflicts over water. Both earlier and later sources document violent water disputes between the South Huo Canal Association members in Hongtong county and water users in Zhaocheng county. In the late twelfth century, their enmity was so strong that one gazetteer claims people in the two counties even stopped marrying each other.[53] This long-term problem within the Huo Spring

51. Baldwin, "Wall Paintings of the Assembly of the Buddha."

52. Wang Yingyu 王應豫, "Shuishen miao jidian wenbei" 水神廟祭奠文碑, *JL*, 49–55.

53. *Zhaocheng xianzhi* [1827], 36.1.

irrigation system meant that higher authorities than irrigation associations were required to coordinate different interests. Monks from the Buddhist Monastery of Grand Victory, though influential, did not have sufficient authority to bring the North and South Huo Canal Associations together. Only government officials could do so.

THE GOVERNMENT'S ROLE

The turning point in the rebuilding of the Water God Temple came when Zhang You 張祐, who had just been appointed magistrate of Zhaocheng county in the rainless summer of 1278, visited the still-unfinished temple to pray for rain. While praying to the water god, Zhang silently pledged that he would complete the temple's reconstruction. Rain came even before Zhang had time to return to his office. Pleased by the water god's immediate response, Zhang supervised the temple project personally.[54] This narrative is familiar. We can find example after example of grateful local officials who committed themselves to building new temples after local deities brought rain.

What is new in this story is Zhang's significant role in bringing water users in different irrigation associations together. The inscription on the 1283 stele records that, after North Huo Canal Association members completed their task of building the main hall, Zhang sent an official request to the acting magistrate of Hongtong county, asking for his cooperation in summoning the members of the South Huo Canal Association to work on their assigned task: building the temple's main gate. At the urging of both counties' local officials, two South Huo canal supervisors organized their fellow association members to obtain lumber, transport it to the temple site, and build the gate.[55] Similarly, when another drought occurred in the summer of 1279, a senior official came to the temple to pray for rain. He ordered that, in addition to the North and South Huo Canal

54. Liu Maobao, "Chongxiu Mingyingwang miao bei," *JL*, 9–10.
55. Another 1283 stele reports that the South Huo Canal Association eventually built the main gate and made statues of two gods guarding the gate. The stele also indicates that the association at the time already had a complete managerial group, including two canal supervisors, one canal manager, and thirteen ditch heads. See Xu Siwen 許思溫, "Nanhuoqu chengzao sanmenxia ershen beiji" 南霍渠成造三門下二神碑記, *DQ: Hongtong*, 65.

Associations, the Small Huo Canal and the Pure Water Canal Associations also participate in completing the temple's remaining unfinished buildings.[56]

Although the government played an important part in coordinating different interests in the Huo Spring irrigation systems, it had a limited role in the daily work of the irrigation associations. The local government in Shanxi generally did not send officials or clerks to directly administer temple building or water management for an irrigation community. Instead, officials accepted irrigation associations' ranking of local people and entrusted the leaders of these associations to perform these tasks.

The government's role was also limited in helping local society rebuild itself after disasters. Following the 1303 earthquake, both the central and local governments responded to the calamity inadequately. The court originally just sent special envoys three times to make sacrifices to the god of Huo Mountain, begging the god to be merciful and end the earthquakes.[57] Because of the continuous aftershocks, in 1305 the court changed the circuit names of Pingyang to Jinning (晉寧, "the peace of southern Shanxi") and of Taiyuan to Ji'ning (冀寧, "the peace of northern Shanxi"). Although the central government later made some top-down relief arrangements, it gave priority to aiding officials, military and postal households, and Buddhist and Daoist clergy.[58] Moreover, local officials' ruthlessness and corruption worsened the situation.[59] Officials in Huozhou subprefecture forced its three subordinate counties (including Zhaocheng county) to pay for the building of a new government office in 1305 to host visiting members of the imperial family.[60] Remember that Zhaocheng was the epicenter of the earthquake: many villages there were destroyed completely, and surviving local residents desperately needed relief from the government. Yet a local market official, in a report to his superior, even minimized the extent of damage in his county so

56.   Liu Maobao, "Chongxiu Mingyingwang miao bei," *JL*, 10.

57.   *Shanxi dizhen beiwen ji*, 8–9, 11, and 65.

58.   *YS*, 21.459 and 462. Oda Yaichirō even argues that the Mongol government's weak response to this devastating earthquake marked the beginning of the dynasty's decline ("Gen Daitoku shichinen Sansei," 273).

59.   *YS*, 21.454.

60.   "Huozhou chuangjian gongyu ji" 霍州創建公宇記, *Shanxi dizhen beiwen ji*, 13–14.

that he could continue to levy commercial taxes.[61] Few local officials organized the burying of the many exposed corpses, provided medical assistance for the injured, or resettled the homeless.[62] In general, the government left rebuilding the local socioeconomic order to local residents. Ultimately, it was the village organizations and other social institutions—particularly religious institutions—that led the surviving local society in accomplishing this task.

IRRIGATION ASSOCIATIONS IN
POSTEARTHQUAKE RECONSTRUCTION

In spite of the government's inadequate response, the North and South Huo Canal Associations had fully recovered within two decades and proved themselves to be strong local organizations capable of quickly integrating different groups of people and institutions to rebuild the local economy and society after the emergency. Above all, they successfully brought local officials, clergy, and ordinary peasants together to restore the irrigation system, which allowed the agrarian economy to revive. Three months after the 1303 earthquake, North Huo Canal Supervisor Guo Mao 郭髦 took the initiative in repairing damaged canals and first reported on the condition of local canals to the circuit government. The circuit government then designated two local officials—the Zhaocheng magistrate and his direct superior, the vice prefect of Huozhou subprefecture—to help restore the irrigation canals. These officials entrusted Guo with organizing water users to clear blocked canals. At this stage, neither officials nor canal supervisors from Hongtong were involved, and the water users who participated in these repairs came from the North Huo Canal Association alone.

Next, in spite of the impoverished local economy, the North and South Huo Canal Associations participated in rebuilding the destroyed Water God Temple, through which the god's precious gift could be secured and the irrigation community's extensive web of social relations reconstructed. Irrigation association leaders, the major players in this web, connected water users from different villages and subunits in their own

61. "Zheng Zhiyi xingzhuang" 鄭制宜行狀, *Shanxi dizhen beiwen ji*, 62.
62. *Shanxi dizhen beiwen ji*, 51.

organizations with "outsiders," including neighboring irrigation associations, government authorities, and influential local individuals, families, and institutions. The reestablishment of this extensive web of connections made it possible to reconstruct the local irrigation community in the two decades after the earthquake.

The Water God Temple was completely destroyed during the earthquake and remained that way for two years. In the fall of 1305, an inspector from Jinning circuit came to the temple to offer incense. After seeing its ruined state, the inspector met with county officials and Shi Gui 史珪, acting North Huo Canal supervisor, ordering them to rebuild the temple under the direction of a vice county magistrate. Over the next fourteen years, the North and South Huo Canal Associations cooperated to rebuild the main hall of the temple—but not the complete temple compound, which would have included at least a main gate and front and rear halls. That main hall is the Hall of the King of Brilliant Response (*Mingying wang dian* 明應王殿) that visitors can see today (see plate 7).

After the main hall was completed in 1319, seven leaders of irrigation associations, including the abbot of the Daoist Palace of Heavenly Peace (*Tianning gong* 天寧宮), visited the acting Zhaocheng county magistrate. The irrigation leaders asked the magistrate to compose a record to commemorate the temple's reconstruction and to thank those who had contributed to the project. The magistrate, a Mongol official named Wanglahala 王剌哈剌 who had studied Chinese, eventually wrote the "Record of Rebuilding the Hall of the King of Brilliant Response" in fairly elegant classical Chinese, the source for the account in the preceding paragraph. Later in 1319, several leaders of the North and South Huo Canal Associations inscribed his account on the front side of a large stone stele and installed it in the temple.[63] The stele still stands today, at the eastern corner of the Hall of the King of Brilliant Response.

Wanglahala's record also explains how the North and South Huo Canal Associations successfully rebuilt the irrigation system after the earthquake. The established procedure for creating an irrigation association, as well as previous experiences of managing emergencies allowed irrigation communities to start the recovery process soon after the earthquake. The

---

63.   Wanglahala, "Chongxiu Mingyingwang dian," *JL*, 15–16.

Mongol official describes the principal obligations and rules of the North and South Huo Canal Associations:

> Build sluice gates, water dividers, dikes, and weirs; establish positions of canal supervisor, ditch head, and water inspector; prevent the local wealthy strongmen from behaving recklessly; divide upper, middle, and lower portions of canals for the convenience of controlling water. During the year, when canal weirs are breached or damaged by heavy rain and flood, summon male laborers to fix them, more from the rich and fewer from the poor. If more than a few persons are delayed or absent from their duties, punish them by levying fines and make sure that penalties are enforced. Items in the irrigation regulations that were established in the old days are as bright as the sun and the stars. Who dares to add or delete even one word![64]

These obligations and rules, as part of irrigation regulations, provided a crucial guide for restoring a functioning irrigation system. Indeed, the postearthquake recovery began with repairing the irrigation infrastructure under the leadership of North Huo Canal Supervisor Guo. Equally important, irrigation associations were able to use their organizational abilities to acquire the requisite material resources and manpower for post-disaster reconstruction.[65] The practice of making levies of male laborers based on water users' wealth, instead of the usual calculation system of *fu* labor, reveals great flexibility. This was particularly meaningful for postdisaster adaptation, given that many water users were dead or had been impoverished by the earthquake.

This flexibility applied to the cooperative project of rebuilding the Water God Temple as well. According to Wanglahala's record, in 1305, "North Huo Canal Supervisor Shi Gui and two South Huo Canal

64. Ibid., 15.

65. We do not know the precise number of laborers that the North and South Huo Canal Associations' leaders summoned for public works. However, in one case, an ordinary villager was able to assemble hundreds of laborers for irrigation work. According to a 1337 inscription at a village in Qinshui county in southern Shanxi, a villager surnamed Quan successfully mobilized more than 750 and 1,100 laborers, respectively, in 1327–29 and in 1332 to excavate canals for conducting river water and for drainage. See "Zhiyuan sannian xiuqu guangai guitiao bei" 至元三年修渠灌溉規條碑, *Qinshui beike soubian*, 387–88.

Supervisors—Du Yu 杜玉 and Hu Fu 胡福—assembled laborers. They calculated the water use for each village and then made plans for the construction project. The rich donated money, and the poor contributed their labor."[66] Canal supervisors clearly led water users in carrying out collective undertakings, creating detailed plans and well-calculated assignments. The strategy of general cooperation with separate assignments minimized conflicts between the associations. In addition to building the main hall, the associations also sponsored the painting of murals on the eastern and western walls of the Hall of the King of Brilliant Response, and they installed two stone steles in 1324.[67]

The North and South Huo Canal Associations also cooperated in holding a temple festival to jointly celebrate the water god's birthday on the eighteenth day of the third month. Wanglahala reports: "The two canal [associations] sponsor musical and theatrical performances, material offerings, and sacrificial rituals. People enjoy the entertainment for several days and indulge their appetites for food without stop."[68] Money and materials used in the festival, especially those for making sacrifices to the water god, often came from regular water fees collected from water households by the two canal associations. Entertaining performances were usual in temple festivals. Like material and ritual sacrifices, musical and theatrical performances were regarded as sacrificial offerings to the water god to repay the favor of his precious gift (the Huo Spring water); water users were required to contribute funds to hire musicians and performers. Sponsoring theatrical performances became the fixed responsibility of the two canal associations, which likely held such a temple festival in 1324 and hired a locally popular troupe from Linfen to perform at it. Among the murals in the Hall of the King of Brilliant Response, the most famous is a scene of a theatrical performance by a group of actors and actresses (see plate 8). In the mural, the valance on the top reads "Zhongduxiu, beloved in the capital of Yao [Linfen] and actress of the Grand Guild, performed here in the fourth month of the

66. Wanglahala, "Chongxiu Mingyingwang dian," *JL*, 16.
67. "Beihuo qu caihui dongbi ji" 北霍渠彩繪東壁記 and "Nanhuo qu caihui xibi ji" 南霍渠彩繪西壁記, *JL*, 25–30. For scholarly studies of these murals, see Jing, *The Water God's Temple*, 70–199.
68. Wanglahala, "Chongxiu Mingyingwang dian," *JL*, 15–16.

first year of Taiding era [1324]" (堯都見愛　大行散樂忠都秀在此作場　泰定元年四月).

Existing irrigation regulations allowed canal supervisors to exercise their authority over other water users, for example to "prevent the local wealthy strongmen from behaving recklessly." Irrigation regulations inscribed on steles or recorded in canal registers reinforced the leaders' authority to enforce penalties. The complex nature of the power relations—including those between villages, between monastic communities and village communities, and between the two associations—illuminates social connections surrounding irrigation associations at that time. An inscription on the back of the 1319 stele titled "Record of Contributors' Names" is particularly informative about these power relations.

The stele lists more than 230 individuals who contributed money and labor to repair the main hall. A scholar named Xue Guorui 薛國瑞, who was the head of Huozhou subprefecture's medical school at that time, edited the list.[69] For each donor, he listed the county, canal, village, any position of irrigation leadership, and name. Of these contributors, 209 individuals held ranks in the irrigation associations in twenty-eight North Huo Canal villages and thirteen South Huo Canal villages.[70] Judging from this list, by 1319 both the North and South Huo Canal Associations had completely recovered from the damage of 1303 earthquake.

More importantly, the list indicates a hierarchy of power relations among villages, in which some monopolized the canal supervisor positions. In the North Huo Canal Association, canal supervisors came only from Guoxia (sometimes spelled Kuoxia) village 郭下村, located near the top of the North Huo Canal and close to the Water God Temple. Because of its location, Guoxia naturally had an advantageous position for gaining access to water. But that alone was not a sufficient reason for all canal supervisors to come from that particular village.

Later sources show that the North Huo Canal supervisors had the important task of guarding weirs at the Mouth of Water Distribution

---

69. The Mongol rulers created a new medical school system, modeled on the Confucian temple schools, in each administrative unit to train doctors. See Shinno, "Medical Schools and the Temples of the Three Progenitors in Yuan China."

70. Xue Guorui 薛國瑞, "Zhuyuan timing zhi ji" 助緣題名之記, *JL*, 20–22.

(*Fenshuikou* 分水口) at the Huo Spring.[71] The mouth, shown in plate 6, was important in maintaining the 7:3 proportion of water distribution between the North and South Huo Canals and was also the focus of many water disputes between the two irrigation associations. The 1319 record by Wanglahala explains that irrigation associations were in charge of deciding the sizes and locations of "sluice gates, water dividers, and weirs." Yet in practice, individual water users and allied villages often openly or secretly changed or damaged gates and weirs to obtain more water for themselves. Other North Huo Canal villages relied on Guoxia villagers to keep a close eye on the Mouth of Water Distribution at the Huo Spring and prevent users of the South Huo Canal from stealing water. In return, they were willing to give Guoxia villagers a monopoly over the position of canal supervisor. This arrangement once again demonstrates that water-management coordination often depended on a social agreement among villages.

The method of selecting canal supervisors in the South Huo Canal Association was quite different from that in the North Huo Canal Association and illustrates a different type of power relation among member villages. In the 1319 list, among thirteen South Huo Canal villages (four in Zhaocheng and nine in Hongtong), five provided canal supervisors: two downstream villages in Zhaocheng (Xi'an and Dong'an) and three downstream villages in Hongtong (Fengbao, Zhou, and Feng). This arrangement was clearly designed to counterbalance the general disadvantage of downstream villages. It also highlighted the separation of the four Zhaocheng villages from the nine Hongtong villages. In the list, Xue explicitly distinguished the villages in Zhaocheng from those in Hongtong. This arrangement was the outcome of a centuries-long power struggle between water users in the two counties. Every water dispute in the continuous power struggle was a chance to define a new hierarchical order among those water users. The villages often approved that hierarchical order for a time and then challenged it again later, to create a new set of traditional practices.[72]

71. Wang Yingyu 王應豫, "Yihou Liugong jiaozheng Beihuo qu jisi ji" 邑侯劉公校正北霍渠祭祀記, *JL*, 45.

72. According to a South Huo Canal register dated 1139, the South Huo Canal originally irrigated the paddy fields of four villages in the southernmost part of Zhaocheng. In the late eighth century, Hongtong villagers in the area adjoining Zhaocheng

The 1319 list also documents the participation of non-Chinese households in irrigation associations. A man named Budawu 布達兀 (obviously a foreign name) was one of nine ditch heads from Guoxia village. The name by itself does not indicate whether he was a Mongol or a Chinese who took a Mongolian name. Yet irrigation documents from Hongtong report that some Mongols forcefully encroached on local peasants' paddy fields from the early years of their conquest. For instance, according to a local canal register, in the 1250s two Mongol households settled in two villages belonging to the Lianzi Canal Association (連子渠). The Mongols seized local paddy fields by force and rented them to local farmers for several years. Later, when these Mongols were ordered to move to another prefecture, several water households in the Lianzi Canal Association, probably tenant farmers of the Mongols, paid them money to redeem the land.[73] This story testifies to the presence of Mongol households in the local irrigation communities of southern Shanxi. This presence was particularly apparent after Pingyang circuit became the appanage of Prince Batu. The Mongol regime ordered that a Mongol household must reside in a village within the fief of a Mongol prince—which was why the two Mongol households had settled in the two member villages of the Lianzi Canal Association in the first place.

Clearly the village was the most important socioeconomic unit in the Huo Spring irrigation system. And irrigation associations had a strong structure that allowed them to sufficiently mobilize member villages to rebuild the irrigation infrastructure and re-create the structure of power

---

gained permission to use spare water from the South Huo Canal. In 1045, after resolving a series of water disputes, the Northern Song government decided on the 7:3 proportion of water distribution between the north and south canals. The proportional distribution model recognized the equally legitimate rights of Hongtong and Zhaocheng water users. By 1139 it had become an irrigation regulation that South Huo Canal supervisors would be selected from the three farthest downstream villages (Fengbao, Zhou, and Feng) only. Yet water disputes between the two counties did not stop: conflicts between the upper four villages and the lower nine villages continued and sometimes turned violent. In 1218 the Pingyang prefectural government ordered the four villages in Zhaocheng and the nine villages in Hongtong to separately select their canal supervisors. From then on, the order of separated irrigation administration between the two counties within the South Huo Canal Association took shape and grew into a fixed tradition. See *ZB*, 65–66 and 70.

73. *ZB*, 166.

relations among themselves. In this society, other social institutions such as religious establishments and local schools were not inherently needed. They had a position in irrigation associations essentially because of their water-household identity. Their strong presence and leadership roles in irrigation associations, then, indicated their superior socioeconomic power compared to peasant water households in local society.

RELIGIOUS ESTABLISHMENTS AND SCHOOLS
AS WATER HOUSEHOLDS

Most remarkably, the 1319 list illuminates the unusual prominence of both Daoist and Buddhist clergy as irrigation association leaders. In addition to the Buddhist Monastery of Grand Victory, eleven Buddhist monasteries and twelve Daoist abbeys contributed to temple construction. More importantly, the abbots of twenty-one Buddhist and Daoist monasteries acted as canal supervisors, canal managers, water inspectors, and ditch heads in the North and South Huo Canal Associations. Most of these monasteries were located in member villages (thirteen were in twelve North Huo Canal villages, and five were in four South Huo Canal villages).

Many of these monasteries were products of the vigorous, expanding religious orders of the thirteenth century. The Everlasting-Spring Abbey (*Changchun guan* 長春觀) in Shangjiluo village 上紀落村, a member village of the North Huo Canal Association, provides the best example. Two Yuan-dynasty steles still stand at the remains of the abbey in present-day Shangjiluo village, in Hongtong county. One of them, installed in 1335 and titled "A Record of Permanent Monastic Land of the Everlasting-Spring Abbey," offers us a rare glimpse into the changing situation of a village temple in the Huo Spring irrigation system from the early to the late Yuan.[74]

The 1335 inscription describes how a group of Quanzhen Daoists settled in the village in the early Yuan and interacted with villagers to build

---

74. Inscriptions of both steles have been recently published. See Liang Shimeng 梁師孟, "Changchun guan ji" 長春觀記 (precise date unknown, but before 1335); Wang Haogu 王好古, "Changchun guan changzhu tiantu ji" 長春觀常住田土記 (dated 1335), *DQ: Hongtong*, 53 and 77.

the abbey and develop cultivated farmland and watermills, two key resources in an irrigation economy:

> Shangjiluo village is located in a high and mountainous place in the south of Zhaocheng county of Jinning circuit. Mountain mist arises from Huo Mountain on its left, and cultivated lands are irrigated by the Fen River on its right. In front of the village, there is an ancient dragon cave near a cliff gully and a curving stream. Trees are luxuriant, and the cave creek is quiet. Earlier, Daoist Ren Zhijian and his fellows happened to come to this place. They stayed for recreation and enjoyed wonderful views there. They liked the secluded location and sweet spring water so much that they could not bear to leave. So they told each other that "this is precisely the place for us. We should stay and settle down." But they did not obtain any land. At the time, our imperial Yuan dynasty had just been established. The government allowed things to take their natural course. Most cultivated lands were vacant. Folk customs were simple. Everyone was happy to give donations. It happened that villagers including Ren De and others also disliked this world and aspired to immortality. They donated their own land to build a meditation enclosure and a hermitage for the Daoists to reside in permanently. Since then, many people seeking retreat gathered there. The Daoists decided to build halls and to enlarge the hermitage. Day by day, they added to the buildings. Later, Daoist Wang Zhimiao was able to build on the work of his predecessors and led fellow Daoists to collect farm rent, on which they relied to supply the clergy with food.

While the beautiful scenery was perfect for religious contemplation, Ren Zhijian and his colleagues preferred to stay in Shangjiluo village because the fertile irrigated farmland and sweet spring water there made it relatively easy to build and sustain a Daoist institution from scratch. In addition, the villagers welcomed the arrival of Daoist clergy. As chapter 2 discussed, during the Jin-Yuan transition many villagers in north China embraced Quanzhen institutions and invited Quanzhen monks and nuns to their villages. From the villagers' point of view, as the inscription indicates, many local farmlands lay vacant, and new settlers were needed to cultivate them to revive the local agrarian economy. The Everlasting-Spring Abbey served as an institutional base for new settlers, who often came as disciples or acolytes of the Quanzhen abbey. Within a few years, the number of Daoists in the abbey increased from four to more than twenty. These Daoists, according to the earlier stele, "repaired mills powered by water and relied on farming."[75] The first generation of Quanzhen monks in the Daoist community in the Everlasting-Spring Abbey clearly lived by farming the land themselves. In contrast, later generations of monks, as indicated by the story of Wang Zhimiao, gradually became dependent on farm rents collected from local peasants.

The clergy's ownership of water-powered mills and irrigated land in the village thus qualified the Everlasting-Spring Abbey to be a single water household. The 1335 inscription continues, telling how the situation in the abbey changed after the earthquake:

> In the seventh year of the Dade reign [1303], the earth was shaken violently. The abbey, cave, and all buildings were completely destroyed. The number of Daoists declined. Only Wang Daoquan inherited the task of guarding the monastery's holdings. He farmed land for months and years, used the surplus to buy miscellaneous articles, and rebuilt a main hall, a granary, and a kitchen. Everything was completed and entirely new. He was surely able to inherit the enterprise of earlier worthies. This was also because of harvests. One day, Daoquan gathered [words missing] and said, "Daoists gather in spite of differences. The reason they are able to live together and not disperse is because they have enough food to eat and materials to use. Supplies of food and daily use come from [words missing]. The land contracts are still preserved, yet I am worried that they may be damaged or lost. I intend to record the amount of our land on a stone so that they will pass down with no future losses."[76]

The earthquake killed almost all of the Daoists in the abbey. Wang Daoquan, the lone survivor, had to till land, plant crops, and trade for daily supplies and construction materials with surplus from the harvests. If the inscription is true, Wang must have been the abbot of Everlasting-Spring Abbey who served as a ditch head of Shangjiluo village in the 1319 list. Since he still had land contracts and therefore continued to own irrigated land after the earthquake, he was qualified to assume that role. Noticeably, the 1335 inscription does not mention the North Huo Canal Association at all. This is reasonable in that the abbey's primary identity in

75. Liang Shimeng, "Changchun guan ji," *DQ: Hongtong*, 53.
76. Wang Haogu, "Changchun guan changzhu tiantu ji," *DQ: Hongtong*, 77.

the inscription was that of a religious institution, whereas within the North Huo Canal Association it was first and foremost a water household, like peasant water households.

Yet religious establishments were different from their peasant peers because they had separate lineages and networks. The clergy residing in different member villages of the irrigation associations could be connected to each other by religious lineage. The Quanzhen Abbey 全眞觀 at Chai village 柴村, the Lingquan Abbey 靈泉觀 at Daojue village 道覺村, and the Wuji Abbey 無極觀 at Shuangtou village 雙頭村 all belonged to the same Quanzhen lineage. An inscription in Henan province (dated around 1278), titled "Stele of Disciples of Qiyuan Perfected Man," included Quanzhen monks and nuns from twelve Quanzhen abbeys and convents in Hongtong and Zhaocheng villages. Four of the Daoists came from the abbey at Chai village, and one came from the abbey at Daojue village.[77] Quanzhen Daoists traveled to many places and communicated frequently with colleagues from the same lineage. The Daoists from the Quanzhen and Lingquan Abbeys were likely in touch with one another, especially given the close proximity of their residential villages.

In addition, of seven canal supervisors from Guoxia village, three were abbots (from two Daoist abbeys and one Buddhist monastery). The abbot of the Daoist Palace of Heavenly Peace was one of the seven irrigation leaders who visited Wanglahala to ask him to write the 1319 inscription. In the inscription, the Mongol official described these people as the "elderly and virtuous" (*lao er de zhe* 老而德者)—a synonym for local elites in classical Chinese. He also reported that an abbot of the Buddhist Baoyan Monastery 寶嚴寺 participated in installing the stele in the Water

---

77.　"Qiyuan zhenren menzhong bei" 樓元眞人門眾碑, *QSXB*, 173. The stele lists as the master's disciples more than 220 Quanzhen Daoist monks and nuns from about twenty counties and subprefectures in both Henan and Shanxi. This master is most likely Wang Zhijin, also known as the Perfected Man of Qiyun 樓云眞人, the most influential Quanzhen master in Henan during the Jin-Yuan transition period. The author who transcribed the inscription and included it in the 1790 *Local Gazetteer of Meng county* (*Mengxian zhi* 孟縣志)—the original source that preserves the inscription—possibly had mistaken the character "云" for "元." Wang Zhijin was the same Quanzhen master who initiated a large project of conducting water from the Lao River to irrigate massive areas of farmland and power tens of watermills in Shaanxi in 1247 (mentioned earlier in note 14).

God Temple.[78] The involvement of both abbots was related to their service as canal supervisors of the North Huo Canal Association.

Curiously, none of the three religious establishments that provided North Huo canal supervisors were located in Guoxia village. According to a later local gazetteer, these three institutions, all established in earlier periods, were located in urban and suburban areas of Zhaocheng city.[79] These Daoist abbeys and Buddhist monasteries most likely owned considerable amounts of irrigated paddy fields in Guoxia village.[80] Thus, their abbots, as heads of water households and socially elite due to their privileged legal status, became eligible for the position of canal supervisor.

Literacy and education may also have been a factor in the selection of certain individuals, including educated clergy and Confucian scholars, as leaders in irrigation associations.[81] In addition to listing dozens of Buddhist and Daoist monasteries, the 1319 list reveals that irrigation associations integrated a local private school into their collective efforts to rebuild the Huo Spring irrigation system. A director of the Mt. Jin Academy (*Jinshan shuyuan* 晉山書院) acted as a ditch head for Dong village in the North Huo Canal Association. People who lived in such academies were men from Confucian households, including scholars who served as teachers in the Yuan education system and students who

78. Wanglahala, "Chongxiu Mingyingwang dian," *JL*, 16.

79. The Palace of Heavenly Peace (established between 976 and 983) was located in the Guilin district inside the city, and the Woyun Abbey 臥雲觀 (established in 956) and the Buddhist Baoyan Monastery were both about a half-mile east of the city. See *Zhaocheng xianzhi* [1760], 184–85.

80. Religious establishments commonly purchased land in remote villages at the time. For instance, a 1253 inscription reports that a monk from the Buddhist Monastery of Hongyan 洪岩寺 on Huo Mountain bought eleven *mu* of irrigated land at Chai village, a member village of the South Huo Canal Association. See Zhen'an 鴆安, "Hongyan lanruo ji" 洪岩蘭若記, *DQ: Hongtong*, 979.

81. Irrigation communities in an earlier period already considered literacy an important criterion when selecting their leaders. Toyoshima Shizuhide mentions that in 1157, when local residents of Xiaoyi county in Fenzhou subprefecture in Shanxi established an irrigation association, they selected two people as canal supervisors because both could read and had contributed to the development of the canal. One of them came from a local scholarly family, and the other was good at mathematics. See Toyoshima, "Chūgoku hokusei-bu ni okeru suiri," 35.

studied Confucian texts.[82] Scholars and students in local academies usually had higher levels of literacy than did ordinary farmer water users. The Mt. Jin Academy, as a social institution composed of scholars and students, functioned as a single water household, like many Buddhist and Daoist monasteries. Also similar to the clergy, whose webs of connections expanded beyond irrigation communities because of religious ties, the men in the Mt. Jin Academy had their own distinctive social connections bound by the system of official schools and private academies in fourteenth-century Yuan China. For instance, a headmaster of the Mt. Jin Academy later helped the powerful Fan family from neighboring Fenyang county to ask a court official to write an inscription for a private academy. This academy was built based on the Fan family's donation of three hundred *mu* (twenty hectares) of fertile cultivated land and was for educating junior lineage members in their native village.[83]

The appearance of the Mt. Jin Academy in the 1319 list has broader implications: it suggests that academies spread gradually from south to north in Yuan China. Academies originated in the proliferation of private schools in the south and became a central institution by means of which literati formed a community tied together by Neo-Confucian learning, which had coexisted with networks of state schools during the Southern Song period. After the Mongols conquered the south in 1279, the Yuan government integrated academies into the state school system. It appointed and paid salaries to the headmasters, endowed academies with lands, and determined the rent the academies could charge.[84] The number of newly established private academies increased during the fourteenth century, in part because people who donated land to private academies were exempted from labor service.[85] Moreover, the Yuan government reinstated the civil service examinations based on the Neo-Confucian *Four Books* in 1315 during the reign of Ayurbarwada, the only Mongol emperor who favored Confucianism. Scholars and students in the Mt. Jin Academy likely adopted the Neo-Confucian curriculum and

82. For a discussion of the Yuan system of schools and academies, see Xu Zi, *Yuandai shuyuan yanjiu*.

83. "You Yuan chuangjian boshan shuyuan ji" 有元創建卜山書院記, *Fenyang xian jinshi leibian*, 5.325.

84. Bol, *Neo-Confucianism in History*, 229–36.

85. Endicott-West, "The Yüan Government and Society," 6:607.

studied for examinations. Among the 209 irrigation association leaders recorded in the 1319 list, only one was a Confucian scholar. Yet his presence presaged the rise of schoolteachers and students as leading figures in irrigation communities in the aftermath of Mongol rule.[86]

In sum, despite the severe population loss and economic damage caused by the catastrophic 1303 earthquake, the 1319 stele marked the quick revival of the North and South Huo Canal Associations through the cooperation of ordinary villagers, Buddhist and Daoist monastic communities, men from local schools, and local officials. The irrigation associations had to rebuild themselves quickly after a natural disaster because canal water was the most precious resource in the local agrarian economy. The Buddhist and Daoist clergy occupied a unique position from which to lead the postearthquake reconstruction of irrigation systems—not just because of their identity as waster users, but also because of their status as social elite whose members were the beneficiaries of government policies, including those of disaster relief. In other words, relative to ordinary villagers, the clergy still held an advantageous position even in the villagers' own organizations.

Changing Relations between the Clergy and Villagers in the Late Yuan

However, the political conditions that favored organized religions began to change in the last three decades of Yuan rule. Accordingly, relations between villagers and the clergy in irrigation associations also began a significant shift. Starting in the 1330s and continuing until the fall of the Yuan in 1368, it became increasingly difficult to repair damage from earthquakes and other natural disasters.[87] The political chaos of imperial succession between 1320 and 1333 (when seven rulers ascended the throne in

---

86. Morita Akira, "Shindai kahoku ni okeru suiri"; Deng, "Zhuiqiu yongshui zhixu."

87. For a comprehensive survey of natural disasters in North China in the Yuan dynasty, see Wang Peihua, *Yuandai beifang zaihuang.* For a detailed description of the political turbulence in this decade, see Hsiao Ch'i-ch'ing, "Mid-Yüan Politics."

quick succession) caused great social instability throughout the Mongol Empire. Mongol armies traveling between the capital, Dadu, and the steppe went through Shanxi, and some local areas suffered when civil wars broke out each time a ruler was deposed. Local residents dispersed, and many monastic and village communities collapsed.[88] The situation worsened in the reign of the last Yuan monarch, Toghön Temür (Emperor Shundi, r. 1333–68), who ruled China longer than any other Mongol emperor. During his reign, famine and plague caused widespread death in the North China plain. Banditry and rioting broke out in many regions, and the ensuing peasant rebellions that started in the south eventually brought an end to Mongol rule in China.

The lack of sources means that we know little about how the turbulence of the late Yuan period affected the position of the clergy in local irrigation associations. Yet individual examples suggest that in general relations between villagers and the clergy shifted from cooperation to competition and even confrontation. The 1335 inscription about the Everlasting-Spring Abbey at Shangjiluo village in the North Huo Canal Association hints at the declining power of the clergy in rural communities; in the 1330s only the Daoist Wang Daoquan remained and singlehandedly rebuilt the damaged abbey. A few inscriptions from other Shanxi villages demonstrate that, amid the instability, conflicts between the clergy and villagers increased in the 1330s and 1340s, particularly over the management of monastic land. In one case, to control monastic land, a group of villagers from Fenzhou subprefecture skillfully transformed an abbey run by Daoist nuns—which also functioned as a water god temple—into a local temple owned by the village community as a whole.[89] In a 1343 case from Puxian county, members of a local family brought a lawsuit against a Daoist abbey to get back land that had been donated to the Daoist clergy by their ancestors.[90]

This change in the relations between villagers and the clergy corresponded with significant changes in Yuan religious policies during the

---

88.   Wang Fuchu 王復初, "Chongxiu Xingzhen wanshou gong ji" 重修興眞萬壽宮記, in *Shanyou shike congbian*, 38.28b–30a (*SSXB*, ser. 1, 21:15827–28).

89.   "Chongli Miaotang ji" 重理廟堂記, *Fenyang xian jinshi leibian*, 317. For a detailed analysis of this case, see Jinping Wang, "Zongjiao zuzhi yu shuili," 49–52.

90.   "Ligong yiai beiji" 李公遺愛碑記, *Puxian beiming zhi*, 10. 20b–21b (*SSXB*, ser. 3, 31.443–44).

reign of Toghön Temür. In 1334 the central court ordered the reclamation of lands that previous emperors had granted to major Buddhist monasteries and Daoist abbeys.[91] In the same year, the court not only revoked the clergy's tax exemption but also required all Buddhist and Daoist monks to provide labor service just like civilian households.[92] How the local implementation of these policies went is hard to tell. Yet a 1347 imperial-edict stele installed by Quanzhen Daoists at the Palace of Eternal Joy in Ruicheng county is suggestive. The stele is inscribed with two decrees issued by two Mongol princes in 1338 and 1339, respectively. Both decrees emphasized that the clergy were exempted from labor service but did not mention whether the clergy should pay taxes on their land and commercial property.[93] The clergy regained immunity from labor service after gaining patronage from Mongol nobles but likely lost their tax exemption.

In the 1350s and 1360s the central government still controlled many regions in north China, including Shanxi, but it no longer controlled the south. After the outbreak of uprisings by the massive rebel groups known as the Red Turbans in the summer of 1351, the Yuan government could not prevent nationwide popular rebellions any longer. In north China after 1355, administrative and military power devolved to autonomous regional warlords who had been rebels or generals fighting the rebels. However, massive local insurrections did not occur in the Shanxi region. Instead, after 1358 Shanxi became the power base of Chaghan Temür (d. 1362, Chahan Tiemu'er 察罕帖木兒 in Chinese sources), one of the most powerful military leaders who fought actively against rebels. Chaghan Temür relied on the grain collected and the soldiers recruited in Shanxi to supply almost all of his military needs. To ensure the delivery of supplies, he and his successor—his adopted son, Wang Baobao 王保保, later known as Kökö Temür (d. 1375, Kuokuo Tiemu'er 擴廓帖木兒 in Chinese)—retained firm control of Shanxi. They appointed their own local officials there until late 1368, when Kökö Temür was defeated by

91.　Liu Yingsheng, "Yuantong ernian (1334)."

92.　Chen Gaohua, "Yuandai fojiao siyuan fuyi," 14.

93.　"Tuer nian he houer nian lingzhi bei ji" 兔兒年和猴兒年令旨碑記, *Yongle gong bihua*, 69–70.

the armies of Zhu Yuanzhang, the founding emperor of the succeeding Ming dynasty.[94]

The turbulence of the late Yuan period clearly disrupted irrigation associations. Yet we know little about the Huo Spring irrigation system at the end of the Yuan except for a rainmaking prayer delivered by a governor of Jinning circuit named Xiong Zai 熊載 to the Huo Spring temple's water god in the summer of 1367. In this prayer, Xiong presents himself as an official appointed by the Yuan emperor—though it was more likely Kökö Temür—who begged the water god to mercifully rescue local peasants who were suffering from a four-month drought.[95] An extant stele inscription of the prayer mentions four Zhaocheng county officials who accompanied Xiong to make ritual sacrifices to the water god. However, it is unclear whether irrigation associations were still functioning at the end of the Yuan, and whether the Buddhist and Daoist clergy still played leadership roles in these organizations.

Conclusion

In the Mongol-Yuan period, Buddhist and Daoist institutions penetrated remarkably deep into an exclusive territorial village organization in Shanxi: irrigation associations. Irrigation associations were essentially independent local organizations for distributing water and offered a mechanism for structuring local socioeconomic relations. The broad and consistent religious presence in these associations under Mongol rule resulted from two elements: the mechanism of irrigation associations allowed villagers to integrate diverse groups of people and institutions into their organizations, and the extraordinary strength of religious institutions in most of the Mongol era empowered the clergy as influential local elites in local irrigation society.

Irrigation associations were based on locally derived ideas, principles, and regulations, and their members worshipped water gods, as docu-

94. *YS*, 45.952, 141.3386–87, and 207.4601–3; Dardess, *Conquerors and Confucians*, 119–46.

95. Xiong Zai 熊載, "Ji Huoshan Guangsheng si Mingyingwang dian qiyu wen" 祭霍山广胜寺明應王殿祈雨文, *JL*, 31.

mented in irrigation steles and canal registers. The locally derived ideas, principles, and regulations defined water as a gift from a divine power and outlined hierarchical social relations among villages that shared this gift. The formation and operation of an irrigation association was often based on an inherent tension between coordination within the system and competition among member villages. The defined hierarchical order was thus often unstable and continuously redefined in local conflicts, especially in times of water shortage and water disputes. Large external events, such as the Mongol conquest or the great earthquake of 1303, also offered opportunities to create a new hierarchical order, which would be approved by member villages and which made new coordination possible. The imperial state and local officials played an important role in guaranteeing the balance resulting from this process by granting permits to local irrigation associations and recognizing their canal registers. Continuing competition and cooperation restructured and reshaped social relations among the water users in irrigation associations. As a result, the rural socioeconomic order in irrigation communities retained its vitality across generations and dynasties, and the conflicts that framed the conditions of cooperation and competition among villages enforced local identity.

In Shanxi in the thirteenth and fourteenth centuries, the mechanism of irrigation associations allowed them to integrate diverse groups of water users, including Chinese and non-Chinese households, village communities across administrative units, Buddhist and Daoist establishments, and Confucian schools. It also allowed irrigation associations to deal with the multiple providers of authority, including government officials of all ranks as well as Mongol appanage holders and their local agents. These forces worked, sometimes together and sometimes separately, to resolve water disputes, develop irrigation infrastructure and rebuild local society after wars and natural disasters.

Meanwhile, the same mechanism made irrigation associations exclusive in the sense that they did not need the presence, let alone the leadership, of other social institutions. The Mongol-Yuan era was thus a unique episode in the history of irrigation associations due to the extraordinary importance of Buddhist and Daoist institutions in local irrigation society. Buddhist and Daoist monastic communities not only owned massive amounts of irrigated lands and numbers of mills powered by canal water, but the clergy also commonly assumed leadership positions in irrigation associations. The clergy had generally higher levels of literacy than did ordinary peasant water users, and the clergy's broader social and political ties gave them better access to government officials. From the villagers' viewpoint, the religious lineages and networks of the Buddhist and Daoist clergy proved a useful social resource, crucial for villages in their social competition and their relationship with the local government. Some Buddhist institutions even tried to define their relations with temples dedicated to water-providing deities—the ritual and cultural centers of irrigation associations—in Buddhist terms.

The astonishing penetration of Buddhist and Daoist institutions into irrigation associations in Shanxi was not, however, perpetuated in the aftermath of Mongol rule. From the late Yuan period onward, as the clergy began to lose state-backed privileges and elite status, villagers moved to work with other institutions and social groups—such as schools and Confucian literati—that could offer similarly useful social resources. The leadership of local schoolteachers and examination students became a major feature of Shanxi's irrigation associations in the late imperial period. Meanwhile, the clergy and their establishments struggled to survive in the different sociopolitical environment of Ming China.

CHAPTER 5

Continuity and Change in Local Dominance in the Ming Dynasty

In 1607, late in the Ming dynasty (1368–1644), Liu Jiji, a magistrate of Guo county 崞縣 in northern Shanxi, finished compiling a new edition of the county gazetteer. In the section on Buddhist and Daoist establishments, Liu wrote the following:

> In the Jin and Yuan dynasties, there was little restraint on the number of Buddhist and Daoist establishments. Our dynasty made a rule that the number of Buddhists and Daoists could not exceed forty in a prefecture, thirty in a subprefecture, and twenty in a county. Most Buddhist monasteries and Daoist abbeys have been amalgamated. For instance, the following thirteen Buddhist monasteries in this county—Chongfu, Jixiang, Fusheng, Cishi, Futang, Guanyin, Hongfu, Futian, Fotang, two Guangji, and two Fasheng—were all amalgamated into the Chongsheng Monastery. . . . Although our government did not order monks and nuns to resume secular life, or burn their books, or occupy their houses, the two religions have ultimately been weakened.[1]

In his record, Liu painstakingly listed the names of thirty-eight Buddhist monasteries and ten Daoist abbeys that had been amalgamated, respectively, into six and one institutions under an early Ming temple-amalgamation policy. Liu's description unmistakably points to the decline

---

1. *Chongxiu Guoxian zhi* [1607], 8.9.

of Buddhist and Daoist orders in the Ming dynasty, which succeeded the Yuan. And Liu was not alone among Ming Chinese in reporting this phenomenon.

We have two sharply opposing images of the two religions: one, the full flush of their success in the Mongol era; and the other, their decline into shadow in the early seventeenth century. This chapter attempts to explain what happened between these two points: How did Buddhist and Daoist orders lose all the social, political, and economic power they had achieved in the Mongol era? How was the distinctive social order that favored organized religions unmade in the Ming dynasty, and what does history tell us about the legacy of the Mongol era and the new direction of social transformation in north China in the late imperial period?

The first point to make clear is that the decline of Buddhist and Daoist organizations was not the immediate result of the early Ming state's persecution, as Liu's account appears to suggest. Rather, it resulted from enduring competition over power and beliefs among rival local institutions in the context of the state's changing policies. In many localities in Shanxi, the marginalization of the clergy and their establishments took at least the first two hundred years of the dynasty. In those years many Buddhist and Daoist monks, with the support of powerful patrons, continued to play active roles in public affairs. The clergy's social roles and their relationships with new patrons attested to the lasting influence on Ming society of the Mongol-Yuan pattern of local dominance. This chapter examines the transformation of Buddhist and Daoist orders in Ming Shanxi to demonstrate how this influence persisted.

In 1368 Zhu Yuanzhang 朱元璋 (r. 1368–98), a former Buddhist monk and a leader of the Red Turban rebellions in the late Yuan, established the new dynasty of the Great Ming in Nanjing and ended a century of Mongol rule in China. During the thirty years of his reign, Zhu (most often known by his temple name, Taizu 太祖) launched a series of political and social reforms to rectify what he claimed to be the wrongdoings of the Mongols and to restore Han Chinese institutions and culture. These reforms resulted in paradigm changes in political governance and social structure in China.

Above all, Taizu and his advisors reconceived and readjusted state-society relations. The early Ming state mandated the reordering of Chinese society through legislation and the creation of a variety of state institutions. For instance, at the lowest or rural-community level, Taizu issued the *Placard of People's Instructions* (*Jiaomin bangwen* 教民榜文) and invented the crucial *lijia* 里甲 (village tithing) system to re-create a rural social order with the aim of increasing community solidarity and welfare.[2] Moreover, Taizu and his advisors, in contrast to the Mongols, were unwilling to cede de facto administrative functions to large, well-organized nonstate bodies such as the Buddhist and Daoist orders. By legally and politically restraining and even persecuting large organized religions, the Ming state succeeded in eliminating both the legitimacy and capacity of the Buddhist and Daoist orders to assume the same public functions as they had in the Mongol era.

Meanwhile, the early Ming state zealously supported Neo-Confucian calls to reestablish a Confucian social order.[3] In 1384 the new dynasty reinstated civil service examinations that tested candidates on Neo-Confucian texts, and it accorded to all degree holders a permanent sociopolitical status superior to that of commoners.[4] Once again civil service examinations functioned as the key mechanism for recruiting bureaucratic officials among Confucian-educated literati, and examination degrees became a desirable marker of elite social status. In addition, envisaging patrilineal lineages as a major building block of social order, Taizu gave significant legal advantages to lineage organizations over religious organizations and local worship societies. Many families and lineages in the south seized this rare opportunity of state support to take over the management of village worship associations and Buddhist establishments.[5]

Nonetheless, as the Ming historian David Robinson has pointed out, even if Taizu strove to publicly distinguish his new Chinese regime from what he described as the pernicious influence of the Mongols, he retained

2. Farmer, *Zhu Yuanzhang and Early Ming Legislation*, 9–17 and 74–75.

3. Dardess, *Confucianism and Autocracy*, 185–87.

4. In the Ming, a man who passed the local level of civil service examinations received the degree of licentiate (*shengyuan* 生員); he was then exempted from labor service and received a stipend from the state. The two higher degrees were provincial candidate (*juren* 舉人) and presented scholar (*jinshi* 進士), which were given to men who passed the provincial and the national level of civil service examinations, respectively. See Terada, *Mindai kyoshin no kenkyu*, 6–8.

5. McDermott, *The Making of a New Rural Order*, 169–70.

many institutional practices from the Yuan period. Robinson makes two important points in his study of the Ming court. First, the Mongol legacy had a deep influence on the Ming imperial family's identity; and second, decentering literati writings has significant value in uncovering the history of marginalized or neglected groups, ethos, practices, and objects that did not harmonize with literati tastes and perspectives.[6] This chapter echoes both of these claims. It shows how the principalities (*wangfu* 王府, or *zongfan* 宗藩) and garrison units (*weisuo* 衛所) created by Taizu reveal the impact of the Mongol legacy on the regional power structure in the northern province of Shanxi, and how the two institutions—especially the principality—shaped the local social order by patronizing legally marginalized clergy. Sources from Shanxi provide an image of local dominance very different from that portrayed in laws.

The first section of the chapter deals with Ming religious policies and their implementation in Shanxi, sketching an overview of the Buddhist and Daoist orders in local society during and after the early Ming campaigns against the two religions. The second section briefly reviews three official authorities—civil, princely, and military—in the new power structure of Ming Shanxi. The third section discusses how princely institutions served as patrons for religious establishments and established a new patron-client relationship with the clergy. In the fourth section, a case study illustrates this relationship and examines how it helped Buddhist monks maintain the upper hand in their competition with rival village organizations until the mid-sixteenth century. This case also reveals social changes in Shanxi after the mid-sixteenth century. The fifth section summarizes these changes, focusing on the rise of the gentry's local leadership, the increasing significance of community worship associations (*she* 社), and the transformation of Buddhist and Daoist establishments into community temples.

Thus, as the title indicates, this chapter explores both continuity and change in local dominance from the Yuan to the Ming. For continuity, it highlights the social effects of Ming princely and military institutions that, similar to their counterparts in the Yuan, formed centers of legitimate power separate from the civil government and lent strong support to religious establishments up to the mid-sixteenth century. For change,

---

6. Robinson, "The Ming Court and the Legacy of the Yuan Mongols," 407–8.

the chapter emphasizes the fact that after the mid-sixteenth century Buddhist and Daoist establishments were replaced as the institutional center of rural communal life by the temples of local cults. This change attested to the existence of a distinctively northern model of social organization in the late imperial period. In Shanxi, and many other regions of north China as well, it was not kinship but village organizations based on local cults—such as irrigation associations and community worship associations—that eventually replaced Buddhist and Daoist organizations as the dominant intermediary social institutions and the building blocks of rural communities after the mid-sixteenth century. All in all, this chapter completes the central story of this book: New social orders have ends as well as beginnings. The dynamic social practices and structures dominated by organized religions in Shanxi were eventually overturned and overwritten by a new order in the late imperial period.

The Early Ming Religious Policies and Local Responses

In the first few years of the Hongwu reign (1368–98), Taizu's acts reflected his belief in the power of religion both to provide legitimacy to the new emperor and to reestablish symbolic order.[7] Yet after consolidating his rule around 1381, Taizu began to introduce polices that dealt severe blows to both the Buddhist and Daoist orders and aimed to completely subordinate the two religions to the state, as the earlier Song dynasty had done.[8] His religious policies in the 1380s aimed to reduce the clergy's formal political status as well as its numbers. In 1382 he set up a new religious administration in which macroregional Buddhist offices (described in chapter 3), were abolished, although lower-level Buddhist offices survived. In addition, Buddhist and Daoist officials' ranks were downgraded. For

---

7. For instance, Taizu sponsored three Buddhist rites of "Broad Offerings Dharma Assembly" from 1368 to 1372 and established temples on battlegrounds to appease the war dead and thus restore the otherworldly order. See Heller, "From Imperial Glory to Buddhist Piety."

8. He Xiaorong, "Shilun mingtaizu de fojiao zhengce."

instance, a prefectural sangha chancellor (*sengzheng* 僧正) ranked 5a in the Yuan, but his counterpart in the Ming ranked only 9b. Moreover, Taizu restored a Song policy denying government salaries to local Buddhist and Daoist officials. In 1384 he forbade Buddhist and Daoist officials to participate in local official sacrifices and ordered that ordination certificates be issued only once every three years.[9]

The full-fledged campaigns of oppression against Buddhist and Daoist orders began in 1391. Two new state policies were most important: one on temple amalgamation and the other on taxation. They struck at the very core of the two religions' stature—the socioeconomic strength of their institutions. In 1391 Taizu issued an imperial edict that set a strict limit on the number of Buddhist and Daoist monasteries and clergy in every administrative unit: "In all prefectures, subprefectures, and counties, only one big Buddhist and one big Daoist monastery are allowed to exist. We order that all Buddhist and Daoist clergy reside there. The number of Buddhist and Daoist clergy cannot exceed forty in a prefecture, thirty in a subprefecture, and twenty in a county. Neither men younger than forty nor women younger than fifty are allowed to leave their households to join the clergy."[10] This edict, mentioned by Liu Jiji in his 1607 gazetteer, aimed to significantly reduce the number and size of monastic communities at the local level. The lack of systematic statistical data makes it difficult to assess the implementation of this policy nationwide, but regional records suggest that it was largely carried out.[11] Most importantly, this temple-amalgamation policy put most local Buddhist and Daoist institutions in a legally vulnerable position, creating new potential for local appropriation of monastic properties.

Taizu also abolished the critical privilege of tax exemption that Buddhists and Daoists had enjoyed in the Yuan. Each monastery now had to register as one household in the new *lijia* system and to fulfill the corresponding duties, especially paying land taxes.[12] Taizu's reforms even

9. *Ming shilu*, 5:2262–63 and 6:2485 and 2563.

10. *Mingshi*, 74.1818.

11. According to Joseph McDermott's research, the 1391 edict evidently caused the decline of Buddhist establishments throughout Huizhou prefecture (*The Making of a New Rural Order*, 214–17).

12. For studies of the *lijia* system, see Liang, "Lun mingdai lijiafa he junyaofa de guanxi" 論明代里甲法和均徭法的關係, in his *Liang Fangzhong jingjishi lunwen ji*, 577–

stripped monks and nuns of their traditional labor-service exemption. According to another edict that Taizu issued in 1391, all Buddhist and Daoist monks who owned land needed to be registered in the Yellow Register (*huangce* 黄册)—the official Ming record documenting detailed information about every *lijia* household—so that monks could pay land taxes and provide labor service like ordinary *lijia* members did.[13] In 1394 Taizu made another new rule, requiring all large Buddhist and Daoist monasteries to create a position known as land-registry monk (*zhenji daoren* 砧基道人) to take charge of paying taxes and associating with the secular world, while the rest of the monastic community should live a sequestered life.[14]

As a result of these restrictive policies, Buddhist and Daoist monks and nuns in the Ming dynasty no longer enjoyed the state-sanctioned privileges and elite status of their counterparts in the Yuan. The majority of them were not even supposed to interact with lay people. The social perceptions of monks as powerful government officials, good filial sons, and promising husbands described in chapter 3 evaporated in the early Ming. Had all of Taizu's policies been thoroughly implemented, Buddhist and Daoist clergy and their establishments would have been quickly marginalized in Ming society, as the state intended. However, that is not what happened.

The extremely hostile conditions for the two religions did not last very long. Ming historians have pointed out that the political and social reality for both Buddhism and Daoism after Taizu's reign was not as bad as the laws suggest. And Ming emperors in the fifteenth century had already softened a number of Taizu's restrictions on the two religions.[15] The ordination-certificate system that was used to control the numbers of the clerical population broke down after the mid-fifteenth century, and the number of Buddhist and Daoist clergy increased from roughly 120,000 during the Hongwu reign to 300,000 during the Chenghua

603; Hejidra, "The Socio-Economic Development of Rural China during the Ming," 458–64.

13. Liang, "Mingdai de huangce" 明代的黄册, in his *Liang Fangzhong jingjishi lunwen ji jiyi*, 163–84.

14. *Ming shilu*, 8:3372.

15. Gerritsen, "The Hongwu Legacy," 63.

reign (1465–84).[16] Although later Ming rulers did not openly discard Taizu's restrictive policies on temple amalgamation and ordination, they did not consistently implement them either.

However, Taizu's successors did maintain one policy that had a profound impact on the Buddhist and Daoist orders: the abolition of tax and labor-service exemptions. Generally speaking, the Ming dynasty not only brought an end to the days of Buddhist and Daoist establishments as tax shelters for other individuals and institutions, but it also made almost all monastic establishments—excepting those with land granted by Ming emperors—subject to the same taxes as ordinary households. Although Taizu modified the policy in 1394 and allowed residents of permanent monastic land to be exempted from the duty of labor service, the implementation varied among regions. According to Chikusa Masaaki's pioneering study, throughout the dynasty monks in the Jiangnan and Fujian regions were required to perform various types of labor—serving as *lijia* leaders to collect and transport taxes, provisioning soldiers, stationing horses, providing salt workers, and so on—based on the amount of their monastic land. As a result, Buddhist and Daoist establishments often had to pay large sums of money to hire commoners to fulfill the labor-service duties on monks' behalf.[17]

Local data on the implementation of early Ming religious policies in Shanxi is far from satisfying. Local inscriptional sources indicate that the temple-amalgamation policy was implemented in many prefectures and counties. For instance, two steles from Dingxiang county record that only large-scale monasteries—such as the Buddhist Great Monastery of Eternal Peace in Anheng village, mentioned in chapter 3—survived and received monks and nuns from seven abandoned monasteries.[18] Some local gazetteers, like that of Liu Jiji, report the number of amalgamated Buddhist and Daoist monasteries at county and prefectural levels.[19] Yet the majority of local gazetteers compiled in the Ming and Qing periods do not

---

16. Zhao Yifeng, "Mingdai sengdao dudie zhidu."

17. Chikusa Masaaki, "Mindai jiden no fueki."

18. Guo Xuan 郭瑄, "Chongxiu Yong'an si ji" 重修永安寺記 (dated 1429), Qiao Zhen 喬震, "Chongxiu Yong'an si ji" 重修永安寺記 (dated 1491). The inscriptions of the two steles have not been published yet. I transcribed them from the extant steles.

19. For another example, see *Taiyuan xianzhi* [1551], 1.14a–16a (*Tianyige cang Mingdai fangzhi xuankan*, 3:329–31).

mention whether and how many local Buddhist and Daoist establishments were abandoned or amalgamated during the reign of Taizu.

Documentation of the clergy's landholdings and taxation in Shanxi is even patchier. Local inscriptions do demonstrate that some monasteries lost land to rival institutions in the early Ming. A Buddhist monastery in a village of Lingshi 靈石 county, for instance, had more than one hundred *mu* of irrigated farmland in the Yuan period. During the Yongle reign (1401–24), the village's *lijia* organization took some farmland from the monastery in the name of making up a taxation deficit. The monks could do nothing about it.[20] Precisely because Buddhist establishments became the target of official condemnation in the early Ming, requisition of monastic land by the *lijia* was not considered improper in the inscription.[21] A sixteenth-century record mentions that monks at a Buddhist monastery at Mt. Yangtou in southeastern Shanxi paid taxes and provided labor service just like commoners did, which seems to indicate that monks and nuns in Shanxi did assume these duties.[22] It is unclear, however, whether the clergy assumed labor service in person or whether their duties were monetized.

Although far from enough for us to draw a general conclusion about the fate of Buddhist and Daoist establishments in Ming Shanxi, the sources mentioned suggest two important points. First, the immediate situation for Buddhist and Daoist establishments during Taizu's and Yongle's reigns indeed appears to have been problematic. Second, the restrictive religious policies were inseparable from the Ming institutions of enforcing tax and labor service, particularly within the new *lijia* system—the most important state-imposed institution for reordering rural society.

The lack of sufficient sources on the implementation of early Ming religious policies in Shanxi means that we need to look at the issue from different perspectives. One helpful indicator is the number of newly established Buddhist and Daoist monasteries that were recognized by the state. Examining how newly established monasteries in Shanxi gained

20.   "Jian shuilu dian beiji" 建水陸殿碑記, *DQ: Lingshi*, 35.

21.   Such seizures of monastic lands at the local level likely happened in earlier times, too, yet the Yuan sources more commonly cite cases that went the other way, in which monasteries appropriated lands from village communities.

22.   Zhu Zaiyu 朱載堉 (1536–1611), "Yangtoushan xin ji" 羊頭山新記, quoted in Qiu Zhonglin, "Ming Qing Shanxi de shandi," 14–15.

state approval will allow us to glimpse changes in the local power structure in the Ming dynasty. A comprehensive survey of local gazetteers of
Shanxi prefectures suggests that the number of newly established Buddhist and Daoist monasteries during the Ming did not drop dramatically
compared to the number in the Yuan, as we might have assumed. Here I
give the most representative data from Pingyang and Taiyuan prefectures,
two major prefectures in Ming Shanxi (table 1 and table 2).

These numbers are far from accurate; the real totals for both prefectures may have been higher. Yet they are probably the best indication we
have. The data from Pingyang prefecture shows the Yuan as the heyday
of religious establishments between the eleventh and the seventeenth centuries, which is not surprising given the unique proreligion policy that
the Mongol-Yuan state embraced. In contrast, the Taiyuan prefecture data
suggests that the Ming was the peak, which is quite astonishing. Notably, more than one-fifth of all new monasteries in Taiyuan were sponsored by the Jin principality (*Jinfan* 晉藩)—one of the three Ming princely
institutions established in Shanxi—or people affiliated with it.

As the immediate representatives of imperial power, Ming princes had
the capacity to protect Buddhist and Daoist establishments. Most Ming
princes, as Richard Wang has pointed out, enthusiastically patronized
Daoism; 111 princely establishments supported a total of at least 386 known
Daoist temples, not counting temples without names. Ming princes sponsored Daoist ritual practices and the production of Daoist books, and
some even devoted their lives to practicing Daoism.[23] Although most Ming
clergy no longer enjoyed legal and political support from the court, many
of them still benefited from the patronage of powerful figures like Ming
princes.

Indeed, when Buddhists and Daoists lost independent institutional
power in the Ming, they depended heavily on patronage from specific
people in power. The composition of monastic patrons diversified in different regions. In Jiangnan, Timothy Brook has argued, local gentry had
become major patrons for Buddhism by the late Ming.[24] In Beijing and
its environs in the Hebei region, eunuchs and imperial ladies from the

23. Richard Wang, *The Ming Prince and Daoism*, 83.
24. Brook, *Praying for Power*.

Table 1

Numbers of newly established Buddhist monasteries and Daoist abbeys in Pingyang prefecture, based on the 1736 edition of the *Pingyang fuzhi* 平陽府志

County	N. Song	Jin	Yuan	Ming
Linfen	2	6	27	10
Xiangling	4	5	9	2
Hongtong	6	4	24	6
Fushan	1	1	1	0
Zhaocheng	10	2	7	1
Taiping	0	3	3	5
Yueyang	1	1[1]	0	0
Quwo	2	7	3	1
Yicheng	6	3	13	0
Fenxi	1	1[2]	2	0
Lingshi	1	1	2	0
Huozhou	1	2	1	2
Total	35	36	92	27

1. The Yanqing Abbey (founded in 1120) survived the amalgamation policy in the Hongwu era as the site for the Daoist registrar and amalgamated seven local Daoist abbeys. See *Pingyang fuzhi* [1736], 33.16a.

2. As the site of the Daoist registrar, the Chongguan Abbey (founded in 1123) amalgamated three local Daoist abbeys. See ibid., 33.20b.

Table 2

Numbers of newly established Buddhist monasteries and Daoist abbeys in Taiyuan prefecture, based on the 1783 edition of the *Taiyuan fuzhi* 太原府志

County	N. Song	Jin	Yuan	Ming
Yangqu	6	5	20	29
Taiyuan	2	3	9	4
Yuci	8	13	10	10
Taigu	11	31	17	0
Qixian	2	12	15	7
Xugou	8	7	8	18
Jiaocheng	4	1	6	22
Wenshui	2	3	8	24
Kelan zhou	4	2	4	3
Lanxian	1	2	2	2
Xingxian	0	1	2	1
Total	48	80	101	110

inner court sponsored hundreds of Buddhist monasteries.[25] In border provinces like Shanxi, where princely and military institutions were dense, we can expect a different story. Before we try to understand how Buddhist and Daoist establishments in Shanxi operated under the umbrella of powerful patrons, it may be useful to illustrate the official powers with which the clergy (and local society) were dealing by giving a brief account of the political order in Ming Shanxi.

Official Powers in Ming Shanxi

Shanxi province in the Ming dynasty had a structure of local and regional governance divided into three overlapping and crosscutting arenas: civil, military, and princely. For the civil administration, the Ming founder Taizu made Shanxi (once part of the metropolitan area in the Yuan) one of the empire's thirteen provinces, the highest regional administrative units. The province governed three prefectures—Pingyang 平陽 (Pingyang or Jinning circuit during the Yuan), Taiyuan 太原 (Taiyuan or Jining circuit), and Datong 大同 (Xijing circuit)—and five subprefectures.[26] Bureaucratic officials ran the civil administration at provincial, prefectural, and county offices. Most of these officials were recruited via civil service examinations. After 1425, with few exceptions, only *jinshi* degree holders, who had succeeded in all three levels of the civil service examinations, were allowed to fill civil offices ranking above 7b in the bureaucracy.[27]

In addition to the regular civil administration, two distinctive Ming institutions—the military and the princely—had strong presences in Shanxi, and both reflected the role of the Mongol-Yuan legacy in the Ming political and military systems. Although the Mongols withdrew from China to the Mongolian steppe after 1368, their threat to the Ming continued almost throughout the dynasty. Shanxi's vital position made the

25. Chen Yunü, "Mingdai ershisi yamen"; Naquin, *Peking*, 58.

26. These were the subprefectures of Zezhou 澤州, Luzhou 潞州, Fenzhou 汾州, Qinzhou 沁州, and Liaozhou 遼州. In 1595, Lu subprefecture became Lu'an prefecture 潞安府 and Fen subprefecture became Fenzhou prefecture 汾州府.

27. Elman, *Civil Examinations and Meritocracy*, 41.

whole province once again an important buffer zone between China proper and the northern steppe world. The Ming state imposed a heavy military presence on Shanxi, especially in Taiyuan and Datong prefectures. Beginning in 1372, the Ming started to build a series of military cities, towns, passes, and forts throughout the province.[28] Taizu adopted the Mongol-Yuan practice of setting up garrison units known as guards (*wei* 衛; one guard had 5,600 men) and battalions (*suo* 所; one battalion had 1,120 men) and stationed the main Ming forces protecting Beijing and the Nine Frontier Defense Commands (*jiubianzhen* 九邊鎮) along a multilayer defense system along the Great Wall.[29] One of the nine commands was the Defense Command of Datong 大同鎮, due to that prefecture's strategic location on the northern border as it existed at the beginning of the Ming dynasty. After Emperor Yongle moved the capital from Nanjing to Beijing in 1415–21, Datong played a central role in defending Beijing, and Shanxi province as a whole became more important in the national defense. After 1542, Taiyuan also contained the new Defense Command of Shanxi 山西鎮, which controlled a large military force and organized all military affairs in Shanxi province beyond Datong.[30] For instance, in 1569 the Defense Command of Shanxi alone commanded 47,181 soldiers and 14,034 horses that were deployed in areas surrounding three strategically important passes.[31]

Military institutions significantly affected the social fabric in Shanxi province, particularly in Datong and Taiyuan prefectures. To sustain garrison units, the Ming continued the Yuan system of military colonies (*juntun* 軍屯), whose inhabitants—mostly soldiers and their families drawn from hereditary military households (*junhu* 軍戶)—were expected to grow their own food while standing ready to serve in the army. The land of military colonies was exempted from taxation.[32] In heavily militarized border areas, military households and their families constituted most of the population. Many local people preferred military careers to school learning and farming and tended to support religious establishments

---

28. *Ming shilu*, 4:1442–44, 1465–66, 1486, and 1527; Zhao Xianhai, *Mingdai jiubian changcheng*, 76–78.
29. Taylor, "Yuan Origins of the Wei-so System."
30. Zhao Xianhai, *Mingdai jiubian changcheng*, 476–78.
31. Zhang Youting, *Jinfan pinghan*, 129.
32. Serruys, "Remains of Mongol Customs in China," 144–45.

instead of Confucian institutions.[33] Military settlements often became the source of local troubles by sheltering criminals and tax dodgers and appropriating civilians' farmland; even local civil officials did not dare punish them.[34]

The presence of a large number of armies also shaped the economic order of the whole province. Throughout the Ming dynasty, the majority of tax revenue in Shanxi was transported to the border as military supplies. After the military-colony system broke down in the mid-fifteenth century, the increasing burden of transporting military supplies from interior prefectures and counties prompted the monetization of tax in Shanxi—which contributed to the flourishing of Shanxi merchants, who profited from the trade with border armies.[35]

The princely institution constituted the third arena of formal authority in local and regional governance. Taizu enfeoffed his sons in territories located primarily in the western and northern border provinces of the empire and had them command personal armies. This practice was unknown under the Tang or Song dynasties but could be easily explained as a Mongol legacy. As many scholars have concluded, it borrowed directly from the Yuan appanage system of stationing hereditary princes in frontier regions as supreme military leaders.[36] Three imperial principalities were created in Shanxi: Jin 晉, Dai 代, and Shen 沈, which respectively enfeoffed Taizu's third son Zhu Gang 朱棡 (1359–98), thirteenth son Zhu Gui 朱桂 (1374–1446), and twenty-first son Zhu Mo 朱模 (1391–1431). Each imperial princedom had its seat in a city: Jin at Taiyuan after 1378, Dai at Datong after 1391, and Shen at Luzhou (modern-day Changzhi city 長治市) after 1408. According to Ming law, the eldest son of each imperial prince (*qinwang* 親王) inherited his father's title and the main princely estate, while the younger sons of the main house received the lesser title of commandery prince (*junwang* 郡王) and set up smaller-scale commandery principalities (see map 4). In turn, the sons

33. Zhang Youting, *Jinfan pinghan*, 138–40.

34. *Ming shilu*, 94:923–24; Zhao Shiyu, "Weisuo junhu zhidu."

35. Li Sanmou and Fang Peixian, "Ming wanli yiqian Shanxi."

36. Satō Fumitoshi, *Mindai ōfu no kenkyū*, 34–50. For a detailed discussion of the similarities and differences between the Yuan and Ming princely powers, see Zhao Xianhai, *Mingdai jiubian changcheng*, 134–39.

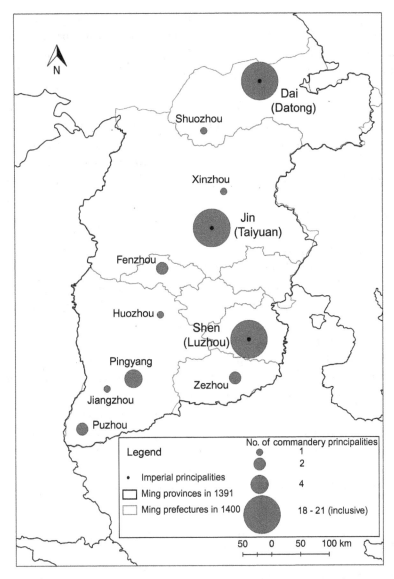

MAP 4 Distribution of imperial and commandery principalities in Shanxi. Map adapted from "Ming Dynasty Provinces in 1391" and "China Prefectures 1400," downloaded from https://worldmap.harvard.edu/data/geonode:ming_dynasty_provinces_in _1391_xdq and https://worldmap.harvard.edu/data/geonode:china_prefectures_1400 _uxo, respectively. Harvard CHGIS.

of commandery princes received still lesser titles.[37] As imperial clansmen (*zongshi* 宗室), titled men and women from the three principalities and many more commandery principalities (around seventy altogether, throughout the Ming) all received annual stipends from the local civil government and had legal immunity for civil crimes.[38] They formed a privileged elite in local society.

Early Ming princes had significant military power, but their descendants gradually lost that power in the fifteenth century. Taizu appointed enfeoffed imperial princes to command the Ming's main forces along the empire's frontiers and granted them considerable autonomy. Zhu Gang, the first prince of the Jin principality, was one of the nine most powerful of them. The political situation changed dramatically in the early fifteenth century. After Taizu died, Zhu Di 朱棣—the prince of Yan, who was stationed in Beijing—used his considerable military power to initiate a four-year civil war and usurp the throne of his nephew, the Jianwen emperor (r. 1398–1402). This political crisis revealed the inherent dangers in granting princes territorial power. Zhu Di became the Yongle emperor and implemented a new policy of restrictions upon princes (*fanjin* 藩禁) to curtail their political and military power. Except for maintaining their squad of bodyguards, Ming princes were legally barred from holding military commands and were forbidden to participate in politics, hold government office, enter the court, engage in friendship with officials, or get together with princes from different locales.[39] In addition, all princes and their titled descendants were forbidden to leave their seat cities without the explicit permission of the reigning emperor.[40] These policies were not implemented without a struggle. It took more than a century, marked by several princely revolts, to render the princely establishments politically

37. The eldest son by the principal wife of a commandery prince inherited his father's title, while other sons received the even lower title of general (*jiangjun* 將軍) or commandant-in-ordinary (*zhongwei* 中尉), comparable to ranks 1b–3b in the civil official ranking system for the former and 4b–6b for the latter. For a more detailed explanation of Ming princely titles, see Richard Wang, *The Ming Prince and Daoism*, 3.

38. For instance, in 1502 a commandery prince from the Jin principality killed someone by beating the victim to death but was punished only by cutting half of his stipend. See *Ming shilu*, 59:3464.

39. Richard Wang, *The Ming Prince and Daoism*, 10.

40. Ray Huang, *1587*, 18.

powerless—which finally happened around the middle of the sixteenth century.[41]

Nevertheless, imperial clansmen still had legal privileges, social prestige, and considerable wealth, positioning them among the most powerful actors in local society.[42] Perhaps because they were denied political and military power, imperial clansmen became increasingly interested in three things: producing more descendants (which increased their stipends from the state), grabbing more wealth, and meddling in nonpolitical affairs in local society. The extremely high birthrate in some principalities in Shanxi—for instance, a Qingcheng commandery prince fathered a hundred sons—worried even the imperial court.[43] As the Ming followed the Song practice of considering all imperial descendants clan members, regardless of their generational remove from the emperor, the number of imperial clan members skyrocketed over the course of the dynasty.[44] By the mid-sixteenth century, there were 9,965 titled individuals of the three imperial lineages in Shanxi, nearly 5,000 of them in the Jin principality alone.[45]

Ming princely establishments owned enormous estates, especially those known as "princely farmland" (*wangzhuang* 王莊)—the taxed income of which went not to the central government but directly to the principalities.[46] By the beginning of the sixteenth century, the Jin principality alone had acquired 72,000 *qing* of princely farmland (since a *qing* is 100 *mu*, this is approximately 5.5 hectares).[47] Yet according to a 1529 court memorial, in the early Ming there were only 410,000 *qing* of taxable farmland in all of Shanxi. To make matters worse, while the

41. Robinson, "Princes in the Polity." As Robinson shows, in the early sixteenth century Ming princes were still able to cultivate ties with members of the officer corps of garrison units and local civil officials, and the prince of Dai from Datong orchestrated the last princely uprising in 1546.

42. Robinson, "Princely Courts of the Ming Dynasty," 1.

43. An, "Mingdai shanxi fanfu," 101.

44. Chaffee, *Branches of Heaven*, 273.

45. Clunas, *Screen of Kings*, 28. By 1610 there were close to 20,000 imperial lineage members in Shanxi, with one-tenth of them living in the city of Taiyuan.

46. For a comprehensive study of princely farmland in the Ming dynasty, see Wang Yuquan, "Mingdai de wangfu zhuangtian" 明代的王府莊田, in his *Laiwu ji*, 110–241.

47. Clunas, *Screen of Kings*, 56.

taxable farmland had decreased to 380,000 *qing* by 1502, by 1529 the government stipends for the Jin principality were eighty-seven times what they had been in Taizu's reign, due to an increase of 2,851 in the number of titled imperial clansmen and clanswomen.[48] The 30,000 *qing* of farmland that disappeared from the government land registers within the first century of the Ming likely had something to do with the appropriation of landholdings by the three principalities (and garrison units). Imperial and commandery princes became the biggest landlords in Shanxi, causing a striking inequality in land and wealth distribution in the province.

In addition, members of the imperial and commandery principalities in Shanxi used a variety of methods to appropriate profits from local society. They forced local irrigation associations to change the order and ratio of water distribution to prioritize princely farmland.[49] They opened princely shops in their fiefs and appealed to the court to grant them countless salt vouchers or let them have the commercial taxes that were collected by local government.[50] Ming emperors showed no mercy to enfeoffed princes involved in political plots but usually tolerated their reckless and rapacious behavior when they committed economic and civil crimes.[51] Local officials often found themselves powerless in dealing with strong imperial clansmen, particularly because they were required by Ming law to pay regular visits to imperial princes and to answer any princely summons.[52] No matter how abusive and debauched imperial clansmen might become, their royal status, material wealth, and legal privileges made them powerful patrons for other social groups. Not only imperial clansmen but also people who were affiliated with principalities—as either sons-in-law, staff members, or clients—became men of influence in local society.[53]

48. *Ming shilu*, 76:2403–4.

49. Hu, "Jinfan yu jinshui."

50. Zhang Dexin, *Mingshi yanjiu lungao*, 128–29.

51. For the economic crimes committed by members of the Ming principalities, see Lei, "Mingdai zongfan jingji fanzui."

52. Zhang Dexin, *Mingshi yanjiu lungao*, 109–10.

53. For instance, Shi Ding 施鼎 (1488–1579), a Yu county native and a staff member in charge of food in the Jin principality, donated a thousand *shi* of food to relieve a severe local famine that lasted four years, from 1548 to 51. Shi's contribution gained him

Representatives of the three arenas of authority took different attitudes toward the clergy and religious establishments in local society. Generally, civil bureaucratic officials, having a Neo-Confucian background, tended to support state initiatives to suppress Buddhism and Daoism and to destroy religious establishments found unorthodox by the state. However, men from garrison units and imperial clansmen were much less concerned about the ideological antagonism and patronized both religions willingly.

In this respect, there were obvious differences across regions in the province. In Pingyang prefecture, the overall impact of princely and military institutions was weak, and Buddhist and Daoist clergy could do little to stop their orders' decline in the new local socioeconomic order restructured by the state. The disappearance of the clergy from local irrigation associations was a small but clear harbinger of an avalanche of change. Consider the Huo Spring irrigation society in Hongtong and Zhaocheng counties discussed in the previous chapter. Local irrigation associations suffered from damages during the Yuan-Ming transition but had begun to function normally again by the end of the fourteenth century. According to a 1392 stele inscription, not one of the recorded irrigation leaders was a Buddhist or Daoist. Except for the Buddhist Monastery of Grand Victory, no Daoist or Buddhist establishments that had been members of the North or South Huo Canal Associations in the Yuan period appeared in the 1392 inscription.[54] The general trend after the fifteenth century was crystal clear: the management teams in local irrigation associations excluded Buddhist and Daoist monks. Throughout the late imperial period, no clergy acted as leaders in the Huo Canal associations. In Hongtong, one version of the *Tongli Canal Register* (*Tongli quce* 通利渠册), based on an old handwritten copy made in 1396 and

---

imperial recognition from the Jiajing emperor, who not only granted Shi an honorific plaque but also exempted his household from labor service. The Yu county magistrate erected a stele praising Shi's righteous behavior. According to Shi's epitaph, from his generation on, the Shis were a great family in local society. Shi's grandson became a son-in-law of the Ninghe commandery principality. See "Jingbiao shangyi dianshanguan Shi Ding shusu jiuhuang beiji" 旌表尚義典膳官施鼎輸粟救荒碑記 and "Shi Ding muzhiming" 施鼎墓誌銘, *DQ: Yuxian*, 98–100 and 107.

54.   Lan Fang 蘭昉, "Chongxiu sanmen ji" 重修三門記, *JL*, 35–36.

reedited in 1907, explicitly forbade the selection of Buddhists or Daoists as canal heads or ditch heads.[55]

In contrast, Datong and Taiyuan prefectures in northern Shanxi experienced the strongest presence, and thus influence, of both military and princely authorities. Not surprisingly, local sources from these two prefectures portray an impressive image of military and princely patronage of Buddhist and Daoist establishments.[56] A Ming gazetteer of Datong prefecture even singled out imperial clansmen and military men as the two wealthiest social groups living in the prefectural city.[57] A recent study by Han Chaojian has demonstrated how military and princely powers from both Datong and Taiyuan prefectures helped Buddhist monks and monasteries at Mt. Wutai resist the control of local civil government in the first two hundred years of the dynasty. According to Han's study, the Jin and Dai principalities, garrison units stationed at the mountain, and Buddhist monastic communities constantly cooperated with each other to control mountain resources—especially the lucrative businesses of lumbering and mining. Garrison units helped Buddhist monasteries avoid paying land taxes to the local county government by accepting monastic land as military colonies, whose land was exempt from taxation. Of course, the clergy, in return, had to give the garrison units a large share of the monastic land's output. In addition to the military forces, both the Jin and Dai principalities sponsored Mt. Wutai monasteries and actively intervened in affairs there. Buddhist monasteries on Mt. Wutai did not fall under the close supervision of local civil administration until the early seventeenth century, when late Ming taxation reforms and the Ming-Qing transition ended military and princely influence at Mt. Wutai and increased the authority of county government.[58]

However, Mt. Wutai was a special case due to its position as one of the empire's top religious centers. From Emperor Yongle's reign on, along with garrison units and principalities, Buddhist monasteries on the moun-

55. *Hongtong xian shuili zhi*, 303.

56. See, for instance, "Longquan si zhongdong beiji" 龍泉寺中洞碑記, "Chongxiu Longquan si qianfodong beiji" 重修龍泉寺千佛洞碑記, "Chongxiu chaoyangdong ji" 重修朝陽洞記, and "Qianfodong huangtu yonggu didao xiachang beiji" 千佛洞皇圖永固帝道遐昌碑記, *DQ: Ningwu*, 14, 18–19, 20, and 22–23.

57. *Datong fuzhi* [1515], 1.25b (*Sikuquanshu cunmu congshu, Shi* 186:221).

58. Han Chaojian, *Siyuan yu guanfu*.

tain received consistent special patronage from the imperial court and powerful eunuchs.[59] The formidable patronage networks that Wutai monks maintained allowed them to remain largely independent from the civil administration for a long time. Their access to considerable tax-free landholdings and the lucrative lumbering and mining businesses, as Han's study shows, also made elite Wutai monks and their monasteries wealthy and influential in local society. In the province's other localities, clergy did not have such favorable conditions, and they had different relations with patrons and rival institutions. The following two sections will concentrate on Taiyuan prefecture—where the Jin principality's presence was strong—to explore how principalities (and occasionally garrison units) patronized religious establishments and how their patron-client relations operated in the tenacious competition between the clergy and village organizations in local society.

Princely Patronage of Religious Establishments in Taiyuan

The Jin principality was a particularly enthusiastic patron of Buddhist and Daoist establishments in Taiyuan prefecture from the days of its first prince, Zhu Gang, the Prince Gong of Jin 晉恭王. Local gazetteers and inscriptional sources record more than thirty Buddist and Daoist establishments in Taiyuan prefecture sponsored by the Jin principality and its affiliated commandery principalities (table 3). In spite of Taizu's policies forbidding the private founding of temples, as Richard Wang observes, the first-generation Ming princes were "politically and militarily powerful enough to elude law enforcement and did as they liked in regard to temple patronage."[60] Soon after he arrived in Taiyuan, Zhu Gang sponsored the building or renovating of a dozen Buddhist and Daoist temples

---

59. For a few examples, see Zhang Jun 張駿, "Zengtuo Puji chansi ji" 增拓普濟禪寺記, "Xiu tongwa dian yuwen" 修銅瓦殿諭文, and "Guangzong si xiu tongwa tongji fodian ji" 廣宗寺修銅瓦銅脊佛殿記, in *Ming Qing Shanxi beike ziliao xuan*, 285–86 and 291–93.

60. Richard Wang, *The Ming Prince and Daoism*, 89.

Table 3

The thirty-two Buddhist and Daoist establishments in Taiyuan prefecture sponsored
by the Jin principality and its affiliated commandery principalities

Establishment	Location	Sponsors
Chongshan Monastery 崇善寺	Prefectural city	Prince Gong of Jin 晉恭王
Wenshu Monastery 文殊寺	Prefectural city	Prince of Jin
Bao'en Monastery 報恩寺	Prefectural city	Commandery prince of Hedong 河東王
Puguang Monastery 普光寺	Prefectural city	The Jin principality
Kaihua Monastery 開化寺	Prefectural city	Commandery prince of Guangchang 廣昌王
Shan'an Monastery 善安寺	Prefectural city	Staff of the Jin principality, prince of Jin, commandery prince of Hedong
Wanshou Hermitage 萬壽庵	Prefectural city	The Jin principality
Baolin Chan Cloister 寶林禪院	Prefectural city	Eunuch of the Jin principality
Baiyi Hermitage 白衣庵	Prefectural city	The Xiping commandery principality 西平王府
Xuantong Abbey 玄通觀	Prefectural city	Prince Gong of Jin and Prince Xian of Jin 晉憲王
Puji Abbey 普濟觀	Prefectural city	The Jin principality
Chunyang Palace 純陽宮	Prefectural city	The Jin principality
Yuantong Monastery 圓通寺	Prefectural city	The Fangshan commandery principality 方山王府
Xingfu Monastery 興復寺	Mt. Juewei, suburb of prefectural city	Prince Gong of Jin
Duofu Monastery 多福寺	Mt. Juewei	Prince Gong of Jin
Maoren Monastery 薹仁寺	Mt. Maoren, northwest of prefectural city	Military officers and sons-in-law of the Jin principality
Tutang Monastery 土堂寺	Northwest of prefectural city	Prince of Jin
Baoning Monastery 保寧寺	Northwest of prefectural city	Clansmen of the Jin principality
Zhenwu Temple 眞武廟	Northwest of prefectural city	Prince of Jin and commandery prince of Ninghua 寧化王
Shenqing Abbey 神清觀	East of prefectural city	Commandery princes of Ninghua and Hedong
Jiaolongdanggu Monastery 蛟龍砦古寺	Southeast of prefectural city	Commandery prince of Ninghua
Longguo Monastery 隆國寺	Northeast of prefectural city	The Jin principality

Hongsheng Monastery 洪聖寺	Yangqu county	The Jin principality and the Ninghua Commandery principality
Fahua Monastery 法華寺	Mt. Meng, south of Taiyuan county	Prince Gong of Jin
Shousheng Monastery 壽聖寺	Mt. Tianlong, southwest of Taiyuan county	Prince Gong of Jin and Prince Zhuang of Jin 晉莊王
Qingju Chan Monastery 清居禪寺	Mt. Matou, south of Ninghua city	Prince Gong of Jin
Baishan Monastery 柏山寺	Lingshi county	The Jin principality
Cangshan Shrine 藏山祠	Mt. Cang, Yu county	The Jin principality and the Ninghua commandery principality
Huayan Monastery 華嚴寺	Yuci county	Wife of a prince of Jin
Jiming Monastery 雞鳴寺	Yuci county	The Jin principality
Zhufo Monastery 諸佛寺	Mt. Xiaoniu in Yuci county	The Jin principality
Lingzhen Abbey 靈真觀	Yuci county	The Jin principality

Sources: Local-gazetteer sources are *Taiyuan fuzhi* [1783], 48.1a–43b; *Taiyuan xianzhi* [1551], in *Tianyige cang Mingdai fangzhi xuankan* 3:329–31; *Yangqu xianzhi* [1843], 1.21a–29a and 2.7a–7b; and *Yuci xianzhi* [1863] 3.9a–14b. Inscriptional sources come from relevant volumes in *DQ*.

in the prefectural city, including the magnificent Monastery of Venerating Goodness (*Chongshansi* 崇善寺), which he built in honor of his deceased mother, Empress Ma, and to which he granted forty *qing* of monastic land.[61] The monastery is still a major monument of Taiyuan today.

Zhu Gang extended his support for local Buddhist establishments in his princedom beyond Taiyuan city. In some cases, he visited well-known Buddhist monasteries and donated money to repair and enlarge them.[62] In other cases, he sent out messengers to inspect famous mountains, looking specifically for ancient monasteries. After the messengers reported their discoveries to him, he made those monasteries clan cloisters (*xianghuoyuan* 香火院) of the Jin principality (clan cloisters often functioned as family shrines at which the members of Ming principalities prayed for divine blessings). In this way, the prince sponsored the rebuilding

61. *Taiyuan fuzhi* [1783], 48.1b–2a.
62. Ren Jiugao 任九臬, "Baofuyan chongjian kongwangfo zhengdian ji" 抱腹岩重建空王佛正殿記, *Ming Qing Shanxi beike ziliao xuan*, 303; Zhu Yinlong 朱胤龍, "Chongxiu tianlongshan Shousheng si diange ji" 重修天龍寺壽聖寺殿閣記, *Ming Qing Shanxi beike ziliao xuan (xu yi)*, 497–98.

of two Buddhist monasteries at Mt. Juewei 崛圍山, north of Taiyuan.[63]
The Chan Buddhist Monastery of Tranquil Residence (*Qingju chansi*
清居禪寺) at Mt. Matou 馬頭山, became a clan cloister of the Jin principality with Zhu Gang's patronage and then enlarged its monastic compound
and gained farm and timber land at the mountain as permanent monastic property. Notably, this monastery had been the clan cloister of the
Mongol prince of Baoning 保寧王 during the Zhizhi reign (1321–23),
indicating that princely institutions in the Yuan were already making
Buddhist establishments their clan cloisters, and the Ming practice
may have been inherited from the Yuan.[64] According to Richard Wang's
study, Ming princes across China commonly built, bought, or designated
certain Daoist temples in their princedoms as their clan cloisters.[65]
Given that princely properties were not subject to regular taxation, clan
cloisters—as private properties of principalities—probably enjoyed the
same tax status.

Indeed, clan-cloister status saved many Buddhist and Daoist monasteries in Shanxi from being destroyed by local officials.[66] Yet as the case
of the Monastery of Tranquil Residence suggests, by using its princely
authority to help the monastery claim local mountain land and timber
as permanent monastic property, the Jin principality gained access to rich
resources on Mt. Matou. This resembled the Mt. Wutai case, showing
that gaining wealth from lucrative mountain resources like timber and
mining was an important factor motivating imperial clansmen.

In addition to Buddhist and Daoist establishments in cities and on
famous mountains, some village temples also received princely patronage. For instance, in 1507 two tenant farmers at Dongluo village in Lingshi county appealed to the prince of Jin and gained from him a decree

63.   "Jueweishan Xingfu si ji" 崛圍山興復寺記 and "Jinsheng xishan juewei Duofu
si bei" 晉省西山崛圍多福寺碑, *DQ: Taiyuan Jiancaoping*, 19–21 and 33.

64.   "Feng lingyu matoushan Qingju chansi songfan shujing ji" 奉令諭馬頭山清居
禪寺送幡輸經記 and "Qingju chansi chuhai chongxiu beiji" 清居禪寺除害重修碑記, *DQ:
Lingshi*, 25 and 27.

65.   Richard Wang, *The Ming Prince and Daoism*, 100–101.

66.   For instance, in 1493 the Luzhou prefect planned to destroy a local Buddhist
monastery. The monastery survived only after the Qinyuan commandery prince 沁源王
requested that the imperial court make the monastery a clan cloister of his principality.
See *Lu'an fuzhi* [1770], 10.33a.

that warned local ruffians not to insult the Baishan Monastery 柏山寺, built at the village by a previous prince of Jin during the Yongle reign. The same decree promoted the two farmers to head all tenants and ordered them to cooperate with five resident monks to take care of the monastery and report to the prince anyone who dared disobey the decree. Later, a commandery principality donated four taels of silver to the monastery, while four imperial clansmen with titles of general and supporter-commandant visited the monastery to offer a stone tablet on which the monks were to inscribe the prince's decree.[67] The prince's decree, his clansmen's visit, and the stele clearly functioned as a signal of princely protection for the monastic community.

Yet why would the noble prince of Jin and his clansmen pay so much attention to a Buddhist temple in a remote village? The decree issued by the prince provided a clichéd explanation: the previous prince had established the Baishan Monastery to pray for the emperor's longevity, blessings on the Jin principality, and the well-being of local people. The good wishes aside, the choice to build a clan cloister in a remote village betrayed the principality's not-so-noble intention of seeking landholdings in rural areas. The direct communication between the prince and the tenants—instead of the monks—indicates that the Jin principality had a stake in the monastic land; it likely received a large share of the profits from the land.[68] Some Dongluo villagers might have "offered" their land to the principality as its clan cloisters' monastic land, and they became the monastery's tenants. "Offering" land to the principality to avoid paying taxes was a common practice in local society at the time.[69] This is not surprising, as the principalities were known for resorting to every conceivable means to appropriate local land in Shanxi. For instance, they commonly chose the taxable land of commoners in different villages as graveyards for their deceased members and in actuality took up more land than they needed for the gravesites. In doing so, the principalities gained profit from the land while making commoners continue to pay taxes.[70]

67. "Lingshi xian Dongluo cun Baishan si jin zuojian beiji" 靈石縣東邏村柏山寺禁作賤碑記, *DQ: Lingshi*, 28.

68. For a similar example, see "Jinfu chengfengsi wei jinyue shi feng lingyu" 晉府承奉司爲禁約事奉令諭, *DQ: Taiyuan xinghualing*, 6.

69. *Songchuang mengyu*, 155; *Ming shilu*, 100:1865.

70. *Mingdai menggu hanji shiliao*, 166.

The lure of land and profits was a powerful magnet drawing the attention of the urban royal elites to rural villages.

In addition, the clergy sought various forms of patronage—monetary, land, and literary—from Ming princes. Some monks requested that a prince instruct others to repair a temple; some asked a prince to write the calligraphy for their monastic plaque or to compose an inscription.[71] The latter was not a new practice. Chinese Buddhist and Daoist institutions had long understood that having a powerful patron write an inscription or monastic plaque was a symbolically meaningful act that heightened the prestige of the institution involved. In exchange, the literary patron—either a prince or a scholar—would increase his own prestige and acquire merit, the reward of a karmic investment.[72]

In short, Ming princes and the clergy, especially those from the princes' clan cloisters, established a mutually beneficial patron-client relationship. This relationship helped imperial clansmen tap into local socioeconomic life far away from where they lived, and it helped monks maintain an edge as players in local public affairs. As we will see below, military officers from garrison units often cooperated with principalities in patronizing the clergy or even took orders from them to do so. We will now turn to a case study concerning the temple of a local cult, for which extraordinarily detailed inscriptional sources allow us to explore how the patron-client relations between Ming princes and monks operated in competitive local affairs.

Case Study of the Cangshan Shrine

The case in question concerns the Cangshan Shrine 葴山祠, located at Mt. Cang in Yu county 盂縣, in Taiyuan prefecture. The shrine was dedicated to three heroic figures in the ancient state of Jin during the Spring and Autumn period (771–476 BCE): the orphan of Zhao 趙孤, Cheng

71. "Tianlong Shousheng si beiji" 天龍壽聖寺碑記, *Ming Qing Shanxi beike ziliao xuan (xu yi)*, 397; Prince Yongnian 永年王, "Chongxiu Lingyan si ji" 重修靈岩寺記, *Jincheng jinshi zhi*, 501.
72. Walsh, "The Economics of Salvation," 358–60.

Ying 程嬰, and Gongsun Chujiu 公孫杵臼.[73] It became a state-supported temple in the Northern Song dynasty after the court granted honorific titles to the three deities, recognized them as a collective god of Mt. Cang, and included them in the official *Canon of Sacrifices*. From then on, the shrine became a must-visit site for local officials in every dynasty needing to pray for divine help, such as in bringing or stopping rain. Later, an official branch temple was built (it was rebuilt around 1200) in the county seat to spare officials and urban residents an arduous journey to the mountain.[74] Over time, villagers in the region built other branch temples. In the Ming, the Cangshan Shrine at the mountain and its branch in the city were recognized as a standard local place of worship and thus continued to receive state support.[75] Meanwhile, the shrine had for centuries been a community temple for an alliance of three neighboring villages—Changchi 萇池, Shenquan 神泉, and Xingdao 興道—which took turns organizing annual temple festivals there.[76] In other words, the shrine was a meeting point of official and local cults, which made it potentially a space of competition for local authority.

The Cangshan Shrine (which hereafter refers only to the mountain shrine, and not its branch, unless otherwise specified) gained extraordinary

---

73. The mountain was later named "Cang" (which means "hiding"), because it was there that Cheng Ying allegedly hid the orphan of Zhao—the posthumous baby son of his master, whose clan had been exterminated—from the Zhaos' enemy, who was searching for the boy. Cheng and Gongsun Chujiu conspired to ensure the survival of the orphaned baby. They presented Cheng's own baby son as the orphan of Zhao to the Zhaos' enemy and denounced Gongsun for hiding the baby. After Gongsun and the imposter baby had been killed, Cheng hid the orphan on the mountain for fifteen years; the grown-up orphan eventually killed his enemy and reclaimed his rights. Cheng then committed suicide to join his friend Gongsun, and both were memorialized as men of loyalty and righteousness—supreme virtues in traditional Chinese culture. The story of these three figures was first recorded in Sima Qian's *Records of the Grand Historian* (*shiji* 史記) and later became an extremely popular theme in dramas after the Yuan dynasty. It has remained a stage favorite up to this day. For the story and the popularity of its drama at the Ming court, see Idema, "The Orphan of Zhao."

74. Pu Ji 蒲機, "Chongxiu Cangshan miaoji" 重修藏山廟記 (dated 1323), *DQ: Yuxian*, 32–33.

75. For the standard local places of worship in the Ming period, see Taylor, "Official Altars, Temples and Shrines."

76. "Chongxiu Shenquan li Cangshan shenmiao ji" 重修神泉里藏山神廟記 (dated 1310), *DQ: Yuxian*, 28.

imperial favor in the mid-fifteenth century when stories of its numinous efficacy in bringing rain spread beyond the county. In 1454, when the neighboring Yangqu 陽曲 county—the seat of Taiyuan prefecture—had a drought, some Yangqu people, under the order of the county magistrate and the prefect, secretly traveled to Yu county and stole the three deities' statues from the Cangshan Shrine. This plan worked marvelously; rain fell immediately wherever the statues passed.[77] The shrine's fame even reached Beijing. Thus, when droughts occurred in Shanxi in 1484 and 1504, the Chenghua (r. 1465–87) and Hongzhi (r. 1488–1505) emperors sent eunuchs to Yu county to pray for rain at the shrine. After the prayer was followed by rain in 1484, the eunuchs collaborated with provincial governors and Yu county officials to repair the shrine. They also made a plaque titled "Clan Cloister of the Court of Ten Thousand Years" (*wansui chaoting xianghuoyuan* 萬歲朝廷香火院) for the shrine, indicating that it now was directly affiliated with the imperial court.[78]

The imperial court's favor sparked a series of actions by different local players rushing to display their support for the shrine. Most interestingly, beginning in 1504, the Jin principality and its collateral branch, the Ninghua commandery principality (*Ninghua wangfu* 寧化王府, established in 1409), appointed not only their staff members but also Buddhist monks as their agents to intervene in shrine affairs. Because monks and local village associations had frequent conflicts in the following decades, the two principalities constantly came to their clerical clients' rescue. Matters even reached the point that the two principalities ordered the inscription of all imperial edicts and princely decrees issued from 1484 to 1526 on a cliff at the mountain, making it clear that they were "imperially ordered proclamations protecting monks (*qinfeng huseng bangwen* 欽奉護僧榜文)."[79] This cliff inscription, which measures 3.52 meters high and 2.55 meters wide, is extraordinarily long and detailed. Together with steles installed inside the shrine, the cliff inscription illustrates the intricate interactions between official powers and local forces, as well as the

77. "Xinjian Cangshan dawang lingyingbei ji" 新建藏山大王靈應碑記 (dated 1455), *DQ: Yuxian*, 58.

78. "Cangshan ci 'Wansui xianghuo yuan' tike" 藏山祠'萬歲香火院'題刻, *DQ: Yuxian*, 68.

79. "Qinfeng huangwang zhi ming chongxiu Cangshan moya tike" 欽奉皇王之命重修藏山摩崖題刻, *DQ: Yuxian*, 84–86.

monks' delicate position when they were caught in the middle. In unfolding the story, the following paragraphs analyze the operation of patron-client relations between imperial clansmen and Buddhist monks at the Cangshan Shrine, as well as the increasing tension between the clergy and villagers.

In 1504 a severe drought hit Shanxi again. The prince of Jin asked local officials to pray for rain and sent a eunuch carrying a golden tablet to the Cangshan Shrine on his behalf. The deities responded to the prayer as desired and sent rain. Since an earlier mountain flood had ruined the majority of the shrine buildings, the prince issued a decree ordering local residents to rebuild the shrine to repay the favor of the deities. Leaders of the three villages (*sancun jiushou* 三村糾首) followed up and reported to the county magistrate, who approved the villagers' temple-building plan and instructed them to select a virtuous and capable man to take charge of the project. This man, who was allegedly recommended by the three villages, turned out to be a Buddhist monk named Pudao 普道 from the Hongsheng Monastery 洪聖寺 at a village in Yangqu county. Not surprisingly, this monastery had become a clan cloister of the Ninghua commandery principality.[80] According to a decree issued by the commandery principality, the search for this "virtuous and capable" leader covered nine subprefectures and counties in northern Shanxi and Hebei, including the famous Mt. Wutai.[81] While serving to emphasize Pudao's qualification, this statement reveals the influence of the princely establishments in making their affiliated monk the final candidate.

The two principalities obviously took the lead in the temple-building project at the Cangshan Shrine. Since Ming princes and titled imperial clansmen were forbidden by law to leave their seat cities, they usually sent their staff members or in-laws as their agents to conduct all kinds of business.[82] They made monks from their clan cloisters their agents as well. Thus, we see that in the project of rebuilding the Cangshan Shrine, the two principalities sent three men to represent them: Pudao as the chief manager; his associate, Monk Wuzhong 悟忠; and a princely staff member as

80. "Chongzeng Cangshan shenci zhi ji" 崇增蔵山神祠之記 (dated 1525), *DQ: Yuxian*, 78–80.

81. "Qinfeng huangwang zhi ming," *DQ: Yuxian*, 85.

82. Lei, "Wangfu jiaren, zongshi yinqin," 204–8.

comanager. In addition, a villager named Liu Rong 劉榮 and his family, from a neighboring county, also received an order from the principalities to donate an incense burner to the shrine, although the nature of the relationship of the villager to the principalities is unclear.[83]

As princely agents, Buddhist monks had very distinctive roles at the shrine. Pudao and Wuzhong not only took charge of the temple-construction project but also tried to institutionalize the shrine as a Buddhist space.[84] In the two decades from 1504 to 1526, Pudao and Wuzhong even reshaped the temple space following Buddhist doctrines. For instance, in 1514 they installed a stone pillar forbidding the killing of animals in the temple. The pillar inscription also made it clear that the Cangshan Shrine was within the compass of the Buddhist Office of Tai-yuan prefecture (*Taiyuanfu senggang si* 太原府僧綱司); four Buddhist officials from the office had their names on the pillar.[85] Monks unmis-takably claimed the shrine's Buddhist affiliation, and the two principali-ties possibly intended, or at least supported, their action. Notably, the Buddhist Office of Taiyuan prefecture was set up within the abovemen-tioned Monastery of Venerating Goodness, the major clan cloister of the Jin principality.[86] While the office was supposedly subject to the prefec-tural government, the Jin principality likely wielded significant, if not greater, clout in the office's affairs. It is suggestive that Pudao and Wuzhao, according to the 1514 inscription, not only belonged to the clan cloister of the Ninghua commandery principality but also acted as staff mem-bers of the Buddhist Office of Taiyuan prefecture. In addition, the 1526 cliff inscription begins with the full text of a monastic precept for Bud-dhist monks (*sengren qinggui* 僧人清規) issued by the Ming founder in

---

83.   He Tiancheng 闔天成, "Cangshan zongsheng lou xiangtai ji" 藏山總聖樓香台記, *DQ: Yuxian*, 77.

84.   Buddhist monks had a long history of building institutional ties with state-supported temples for local gods but seemed particularly eager to do so in the Ming dynasty. For other examples of Buddhist monks initiating or participating in the con-struction of temples dedicated to state-recognized deities, see "Chongxiu Houtu wuyue miaoji" 重修后土五嶽廟記 and Yan Mingtai 閻鳴泰, "Chongxiu Wuyue miao beiji" 重修五嶽廟碑記, *DQ: Ningwu*, 299 and 304. In these two cases, Buddhist monks had sup-port from military officers from the Ningwu garrison 寧武所.

85.   "Cangshan jin zaisha chuangji" 藏山禁宰殺幢記 (dated 1514), *DQ: Yuxian*, 73.

86.   *Taiyuan fuzhi* [1783], 48.2a.

1372 to warn monks at the shrine not to violate the precept—which in turn legitimized the presence of Buddhist monks at the shrine.

Pudao and his associates also consolidated the institutional ties between the Cangshan Shrine and other Buddhist establishments. In 1510 monks from the Xiangyi Monastery 鄉邑寺 in a local village begged Pudao to help them rebuild their dilapidated temple and purchase monastic land. Pudao agreed. But in return, Pudao's disciples became abbots of the Xiangyi Monastery. Pudao and his disciples thus turned the Xiangyi Monastery into a lower temple of Pudao's home institution, the Hongsheng Monastery.[87] According to a 1525 stele that commemorated the enlargement of the Cangshan Shrine, the three temples—the Hongsheng Monastery, the Xiangyi Monastery, and the Cangshan Shrine—rotated abbots, and the two Buddhist monasteries contributed to the large-scale building project at the Cangshan Shrine.[88] This means that monks backed by the Jin and Ninghua principalities not only controlled the shrine but also incorporated it into their Buddhist monastic network. Additionally, Pudao brought more clerical patrons to the shrine. A dozen Buddhist monks from several neighboring Buddhist establishments participated in installing the 1525 stele. All three men who contributed to making the inscription were Buddhist monks: one from a neighboring monastery composed the inscription, and two from a monastery in Dingxiang county wrote, respectively, the seal characters and the calligraphy of the inscription.

Buddhist monks' dominance of the Cangshan Shrine made many local people unhappy, and some responded with violence. The cliff inscription reports that some "ignorant persons" consistently abused the monks and did harm to temple property attached to the shrine; these men removed newly planted seeds from the shrine's farmland, stole harvested crops, damaged farm tools, appropriated temple trees, and destroyed temple archways. The cliff inscription does not indicate the identity of the "criminals" but describes them as only "people traveling between the city and countryside."[89] A close reading of the text suggests that they were most likely members of the three-village association and their urban allies.

87. "Xiangyi chonghui kantu ji" 鄉邑崇繪龕圖記 (dated 1539), *DQ: Yuxian*, 89.
88. "Chongzeng Cangshan shenci," *DQ: Yuxian*, 80.
89. "Qinfeng huangwang zhi ming," *DQ: Yuxian*, 85.

By 1526 the local worship association organized around the Cangshan Shrine had for some time included two parts: the three villages and a group of urban residents, possibly those affiliated with the official branch temple of the shrine in the city.[90] For convenience, we will refer to this urban-rural worship alliance as the Cangshan Association.

Facing hostility from the local communities, the Buddhist monks at the Cangshan Shrine became increasingly worried. They remembered that during an earlier temple-building project in 1484, some aggressive men drove three Buddhist monks to their deaths. Fearful of the increasing harassment, some monks tried to resign their positions and leave the shrine.[91] Upon learning what was happening at the shrine, the prince of Jin issued a decree to local residents, demanding a guarantee that there would be no further crimes targeting the Buddhist monks. The Cangshan Association leaders, known as the Twelve Elders (*shier qilao* 十二耆老), signed the guarantee. The monks thus remained at the shrine.[92] Yet this arrangement was nothing more than a temporary agreement the association made under pressure.

After the crisis, Buddhist monks continued to receive support from authorities. The prince of Jin sent a group of his staff members to bring silver, clothing, food, and other materials to the Cangshan Shrine and to use the money to purchase more land as permanent temple property. Notably, military men from garrison units in Taiyuan also became sponsors of the shrine. More than six men from two garrison units visited the shrine and donated two cows and three taels of silver.[93] Since Pudao's temple-building project operated under the names of the Jin and Ninghua principalities, local officials and literati showed their support as well. According to the 1525 stele, around twenty Yu county officials and clerks, two retired high-ranking officials, and a dozen examination degree holders and students participated in the temple-building project to varying degrees.[94] As a way to demonstrate such connections, in 1526 Pudao installed a new

90.   When it comes to local leaders, existing steles at the shrine erected since the 1526 stele consistently refer to them as "leaders of three villages" and "leaders at the city" (*zaicheng jiushou* 在城糾首).

91.   The sources do not tell us in which year this event happened.

92.   "Chongzeng Cangshan shenci," *DQ: Yuxian*, 80.

93.   "Qinfeng huangwang zhi ming," *DQ: Yuxian*, 85.

94.   "Chongzeng Cangshan shenci," *DQ: Yuxian*, 80.

stele inscribed with poems about Mt. Cang that had been composed by the two retired officials—one of whom, Qiao Yu 喬宇 (1457–1524), was a former minister of personnel at the imperial court and a local literary celebrity who wrote many essays and poems celebrating Shanxi's landscape.[95]

Nevertheless, the tension between villagers and Buddhist monks would not easily dissipate. The two groups had fundamentally different visions about the temple space and different value systems concerning the temple and its deities. As mentioned above, the three villages had a centuries-old tradition of holding annual temple festivals at the mountain shrine, and those festivals often involved animal sacrifices and theatrical performances. In the inscription on the 1514 pillar, monks denigrated such rowdy temple festivals for leaving smelly dung and blood, which drew flocks of chickens, insects, and flies into the temple buildings. Moreover, according to the monks, when people gathered in the temple during festivals, they gave in to alcohol and sexual temptation, committed crimes against sentient beings, and fell into disputes over material things. Instead of killing pigs and sheep to offer animal sacrifices to the deities, the monks suggested, people should donate an equivalent amount of money to the shrine for the expense of temple building and maintenance—a clear expression of the Buddhist concept of the merit field.[96] Buddhist monks had fought against animal sacrifices in local cults for centuries in China yet never won. Pudao and his colleagues surely could not succeed in convincing their village neighbors to give up their tradition. The 1514 pillar might only have intensified the tension between monks and villagers, as the 1526 inscription mentions that those who attacked Buddhist monks hated them for "obstructing sacrifices at the shrine." This accusation most likely referred to the monks' 1514 prohibition of animal sacrifices.[97] Both villagers and monks clearly cared a great deal about what form sacrifices took; animal sacrifices were just as important to commoners as they were anathema to Buddhists.

In addition to the almost unsolvable tension over sacrifices, at the heart of clergy-villager conflicts also lay competition over temple land.

95. "Cangshan lingjing shi bei" 藏山靈境詩碑, *DQ: Yuxian*, 82–83.
96. "Cangshan jin zaisha chuangji," *DQ: Yuxian*, 73.
97. "Qinfeng huangwang zhi ming," *DQ: Yuxian*, 86.

The land was a key concern for all parties involved: during Pudao's building project, a county magistrate surnamed Hou 侯 asked about the temple land when he visited the shrine. The prince of Jin ordered Pudao to present a written document listing all temple land. Most alleged crimes committed by "ignorant persons" involved appropriating temple land and destroying archways that marked its borders. In 1526 Magistrate Wang Liang 汪良 conducted a thorough investigation of the Cangshan Shrine and reclarified the borders of temple land in four directions. In addition, a virtue-promoting poem composed by a monk—presumably Pudao—after agreeing to stay asks people to stop coveting the temple land:

勸君休生毒害心	I encourage you gentlemen not to have poisonous minds;
爲人在世有幾能	How much can you do in this life as a person?
寺廟不了無感應	There will be no divine response if the temple is left uncompleted;
周畢又謗貪嗔化	Yet some people around have made malicious attacks on [us] due to greed and hatred.
賢買地土焚香院	The worthies bought the land and made the temple a place of burning incense;
護持看守住安寧	They made us take care of the temple while living here peacefully.
再休□事胡奪弄	You should stop [making] troubles and seizing [the land] by force;
虧天拔樹□尋根	Otherwise, you'll be in debt to Heaven, [and whatever you do will be like] pulling up the tree in search of the root.[98]

In this poem, the monk made two implicit arguments to appeal to his audience. First, the monks lived in the temple not to benefit from the temple property but to take care of it and to pray for divine blessings, thus doing good for local communities. Second, attacking monks and appropriating the shrine's land would bring retribution in the afterlife for the perpetrators, the "gentlemen" and "people around" in the poem. These men were most likely members of the Cangshan Association. The poem also implies that these men could receive punishment in this life too, as

98. "Qinfeng huangwang zhi ming," *DQ: Yuxian*, 85.

the monks had the support from "the worthies"—that is, imperial clansmen from the two principalities. Nevertheless, the conflicts between the Cangshan Association and the Buddhist monks would not simply go away.

We do not know whether villagers eventually banished all monks from the Cangshan Shrine, but monks clearly lost their position at the shrine within the following few decades.[99] When two magistrates made sacrifices at the shrine and installed new steles in 1548 and 1574, neither stele included the names of Buddhist monks; the 1548 stele bore only the names of local officials and students.[100] Maybe this reflects the new wave of official efforts to suppress Buddhism that arose under Emperor Jiajing (r. 1522–66), who favored Daoism instead. When a new stele was installed at the shrine in 1584, the resident clergy were nine Daoist monks. The major group of lay contributors consisted of twenty-three holders of the licentiate degree (the lowest among the three state-recognized degrees in the civil service examinations); the others included a dozen local officials, one principality-affiliated military degree holder, and two garrison officers.[101] The influence of the Jin and Ninghua principalities at the Cangshan Shrine had apparently faded away, as their names do not appear on steles installed from then on. This probably resulted from the declining strength of principalities themselves. From the Jiajing era on, the court faced extreme financial burdens caused by the enormous expense of the principalities, and it took multiple measures to restrain their expanding population and to cut off their stipends.[102]

While princely and Buddhist influence diminished at the Cangshan Shrine, the power of the Cangshan Association, led by local gentry, increased after the middle of the sixteenth century. According to a 1604 inscription written by a local student named Zhang Shuwen 張淑問, in 1598 he had donated twenty taels of silver and assembled leaders of the Cangshan Association to initiate a new repair project at the shrine. Zhang

99. Monks from Pudao's lineage still controlled the Xiangyi Monastery in 1539. See "Xiangyi chonghui kantu ji," *DQ: Yuxian*, 89.

100. Zhou Mengcai 周夢彩, "Si Cangshan Zhaowengong beiji" 祀藏山趙文公碑記, and Song Shi 宋室, "Si Cangshan dawang shuo" 祀藏山大王説, *DQ: Yuxian*, 94–95 and 106.

101. "Xu Cangshan zhaowang miaoji" 續藏山趙王廟記 (dated 1584), *DQ: Yuxian*, 110.

102. Zhi, "Mingdai zongshi renkou," 123–25.

instructed the association leaders to raise funds from urban and rural residents and personally supervised the repair project.[103] He had authority among the association leaders because his family enjoyed both wealth and official status—his son was a vice prefect at the time.[104]

Daoists were present at the Cangshan Shrine for the rest of the dynastic period, but they no longer received patronage from official powers or exerted the level of influence on temple matters that Buddhist monks had. They were now subject to the authority of the Cangshan Association. According to the 1604 inscription, after two previous resident Daoists had left (or died), association leaders appointed a Daoist named Li Zhenyuan 李真元 as the new abbot of the shrine, with the county magistrate's approval. Li had a reputation for successfully repairing several temples in different places.[105] The inscription stipulates that a fixed amount of crops from the permanent land of the temple was reserved for its daily use. At the end of the 1604 inscription, Li inscribed a record of the new construction he and his associates had completed, the amount of silver used for each project, and the share of crops they received from 1598 to 1604.[106] This detailed expenditure report was meant for members of the Cangshan Association, who now controlled the shrine, managed its property, and oversaw the resident Daoists.

In sum, the clergy—first Buddhists and then Daoists—tenaciously maintained their presence at the Cangshan Shrine for the majority of the Ming dynasty. Yet the Buddhist presence at the shrine before the middle of the sixteenth century and the Daoist presence afterward were very different. With strong support from the Jin and Ninghua principalities,

103. Zhang Shuwen, "Chongxiu Dawang miaoji" 重修大王廟記, *DQ: Yuxian*, 120–21.

104. Zhang Shuwen and his family also sponsored the rebuilding of the Shijiao Monastery 石角寺 in a local village in 1595. See Zhang Shuwen, "Chongxiu Shijiao si beiji" 重修石角寺碑記, *DQ: Yuxian*, 117.

105. We also find records of Daoists from the school of Zhengyi Daoism 正一道 serving as resident clergy at the Cangshan Shrine on five later steles, installed from 1631 to 1644. See Liang Mingqi 梁鳴岐, "Qianyi Xuantian shangdi donglou beizhi" 遷移玄天上帝洞樓碑志, Li Chujing 李儲精, "Dahan zuolin bei xu" 大旱作霖碑敘, Zheng Congren 鄭從仁, "Lingyu zai ji" 靈雨再記, Shi Wenhuan 史文煥, "Cangshan ci xinjian Qizhong ci beiji" 藏山祠新建啟忠祠碑記, Li Fu 李伏 and Shi Chongguang 石重光, "Chongxiu miaobei ji" 重修廟碑記, *DQ: Yuxian*, 136, 38, 140–41, 146, and 151.

106. Zhang Shuwen, "Chongxiu Dawang miaoji," *DQ: Yuxian*, 121.

Buddhist monks, while acting as princely agents, maintained considerable independence from the shrine's local worship association. They also had the upper hand in the competition over the meaning and property of the shrine; the monks not only controlled the shrine and its landholdings but also tried to transform the temple space and ritual practices in Buddhist terms. Daoist monks, in contrast, received little patronage from powerful figures or institutions outside the village world. They lived in the shrine as caretakers and guest managers appointed by the Cangshan Association, which grew stronger—with educated gentry becoming its leaders. The increasing authority of the village organization under the leadership of local gentry marked a new direction for social transformation in Shanxi after the middle of the sixteenth century.

Shanxi Society after the Mid-Sixteenth Century: Gentry, Villagers, and Clergy

The mid-sixteenth century is commonly known as a watershed in Ming history, during which profound change was happening and a new socioeconomic order was emerging. This new order featured the return of literati activism in local society, the extensive spread of literati practices to other social groups, and the dramatic expansion of nationwide commercialization.

In the early Ming, as Peter Bol has argued, the economic downturn and bloody political purges discouraged southern literati from creating Neo-Confucian institutions—such as private academies, community compacts, and granaries—as their Southern Song and Yuan predecessors had done. Instead, the state took on the Neo-Confucian task of reforming local society into a self-supervising moral community by creating a series of village institutions.[107] Yet regardless of Taizu's intentions and tireless efforts, this state-mandated project eventually failed.[108] From the sixteenth century on, significant socioeconomic changes occured nationwide

---

107. Bol, *Neo-Confucianism in History*, 256–61.

108. For Taizu's frequent revisions of policies for governing village society, see Schneewind, "Visions and Revisions" and "Research Note."

and formed favorable conditions for the reemergence of the southern literati as local elites. Meanwhile, more and more members of the educated literati, facing increasing difficulty in earning examination degrees and holding government offices, sought to maintain their perceived elite status by playing moral and social leadership roles in local society.[109] Many led local communities to reestablish earlier Neo-Confucian institutions or to create new social institutions like charity societies as alternatives to state institutions and religious endeavors.[110]

With the breakdown of state institutions and the boom in the commercial economy, the late Ming was the period, using Sarah Schneewind's phrase, when "the locality fights back." Along with the literati, almost all social groups in the late Ming were creating organizations and institutions to suit their interests. As Schneewind rightly argues, the competition among local institutions embodied a debate over "who should direct the organization of society."[111] In addition to asking who directed the social reorganization, we probably should also ask through which institutions local society was organized and integrated.

In the south, literati elite practices, especially creating cooperate lineages, rapidly spread to non-literati social groups and to peripheral regions. By the middle of the Ming dynasty, Neo-Confucian thinkers had absorbed the corporate lineage into their social model fully enough that people increasingly associated lineages with Neo-Confucian institutions. The crucial legal change in ancestral sacrifice during the Great Ritual Controversy in the 1520s accelerated the popular practice of building ancestral halls, contributing to the rapid development of corporate lineages in many regions. In the coastal area of Fujian, for instance, as Michael Szonyi has observed, merchants and moneylenders—who claimed leadership authority in local society on the basis of meritorious deeds supported by their wealth—began to emulate the literati practice of constructing ancestral halls. These non-literati elites initiated the construction of ancestral halls "to demand positions of leadership in the halls and to reshape practices associated with the halls to better serve

109. Terada, *Mindai kyoshin no kenkyu*, 38–40.
110. Bol, *Neo-Confucianism in History*, 261–69.
111. Schneewind, *Community Schools and the State*, 138–39.

their interests."[112] Neo-Confucian ideology, rituals, and institutions also spread rapidly to China's southern peripheries, such as the Pearl River Delta, which had just been integrated into the Chinese imperial state's administration. There, lineage building became the effective and legitimate device through which local society could negotiate with the state, and lineages rose to forcefully dominate local society between the sixteenth and nineteenth centuries.[113] Corporate lineages thus prevailed as the dominant institution in social organization and integration in the south.

In Shanxi, the literati's world also changed significantly around the mid-sixteenth century in a way that brought it into tune with southern literati lifestyles and Neo-Confucian thinking. According to Khee Heong Koh, in the early and middle Ming, Xue Xuan 薛瑄 (1389–1464)—the leading northern Neo-Confucian thinker in the Hedong school (which consisted mostly of scholars from Shanxi and Shaanxi provinces)—and his fellow scholars showed little interest in the southern-style Neo-Confucian program. They relied instead on the state for gaining family honor and on the state-sponsored education system for promoting Neo-Confucianism. After the sixteenth century, however, scholars of the Hedong tradition began to imitate the practices of their southern counterparts, gathering disciples, engaging in public lectures, and building private academies.[114] The north thus increasingly resembled the south within the intellectual world of the Neo-Confucian elite.

The group of degree-holding Neo-Confucian literati, or "gentry," also played leadership roles in social organization and integration in Shanxi after the middle of the sixteenth century.[115] Yet the ways in which local society was organized and integrated were very different than in the south. To begin with, corporate lineages never gained the popularity in Shanxi

112. Szonyi, *Practicing Kinship*, 93.

113. D. Faure, *Emperor and Ancestor*, 105–7.

114. Koh, *A Northern Alternative*, 200.

115. The Chinese terms for the social group of Confucian-educated and exam-taking men (*shi* 士, *shidafu* 士大夫, or *shishen* 士紳) are conventionally translated as "literati" in English-language scholarship on middle-period China and "gentry" in that on Ming and Qing China. While this book has used the term *literati* so far, it will also use the term *gentry* in this section to make it easier to engage the enormous scholarship on gentry in late imperial China.

like they did in the south. Lineage building did occur in Shanxi after the sixteenth century, but only when some individual descent groups success-fully produced *jinshi* degree holders and officials for multiple generations, while steadily earning income from their men's engagement in non-literati careers, especially as merchants.[116] Such lineages were concentrated in southern Shanxi, especially Pingyang prefecture—the region of the province that was most agriculturally productive, commercially wealthy, and culturally flourishing.[117] In most other areas of the province, literati culture was weak, and the growth of degree-holding lineages was limited. Moreover, such lineages often lacked coherent managerial organizations and common property to sustain them over time, and lineage practices hardly ever extended to other local families, which continuously main-tained an indifferent attitude toward lineage organizations.[118]

Instead of reorganizing and integrating local society by building lin-eage organizations, Shanxi gentry played moral and social leadership roles in different ways, one of which was to contribute to organizing local defenses against raiding Mongols. After the 1530s, Shanxi society expe-rienced constant local disorder as the result of frequent natural disasters, local bandits, and most importantly, the repeated Mongol raiding that caused a two-decade border crisis. Starting in 1547, the Eastern Mongols under the leadership of Prince Altan (1507–82, Anda 俺答 in Chinese sources) raided along the Ming's entire northern border every year, usu-ally in the spring and early autumn.[119] People in Shanxi, especially in Datong and Taiyuan prefectures, suffered severely from the Mongol troops' brutality. The crisis raised urgent new issues in local society, with the need to build fortifications, organize defenses, and distribute relief materials. Local gentry and rich merchants took the lead in supporting armies, organizing local militia, and donating food and money to feed refugees.[120] For instance, in 1550 when a Mongol army raided Dingxiang

116.　Chang, *Song yihou zongzu de xingcheng*, 177–244.
117.　*Songchuang mengyu*, 45 and 82.
118.　Du, *Cunshe chuantong*, 189–96.
119.　Geiss, "The Chia-Ching Reign, 1522–1566," 467–68 and 471–77.
120.　For instance, among 646 events of city building in Ming Shanxi, according to Li Ga, all three waves of building happened at the times of the most severe Mongol attacks—the years after the disastrous Tubu Incident in 1449, from 1540 to 1543, and in 1567. While local gentry were hardly mentioned in records of the first wave, they appear

FIGURE 5.1 The high walls of the Expanded-Merit Monastery at Liuhui village, Dingxiang county, Shanxi province. The enlarged monastic space, which now occupies an area of 3,300 square meters, effectively protected villagers from warfare and bandits. Author photo.

county, a retired official living in Liuhui village named Li Dongqu 李東渠 organized his fellow villagers to hold a strategic location at the Expanded-Merit Monastery (*Hongfu si* 洪福寺), which was built on high land outside the village. After the Mongols left, Li led villagers in building walls around the monastery, making a fort of the entire monastic space. The fortified monastery thus became a shelter where Liuhui villagers could survive raids by Mongols or bandits in the following decades. Degree holders from Li's clan continued to play leadership roles in village affairs,

---

frequently in the records of the second and third waves and often paid a large share of the funds. See Li Ga, "Bianfang youjing." For an example of wealthy merchants contributing to local defense, see Ma Li 馬理, "Yishi Yangcheng Wang Hai biao lü ji" 義士陽城王海表閭記 (dated 1542), *Jincheng jinshi zhi*, 512–13.

including the sponsorship of the Expanded-Merit Monastery, which had become critically important to the village's safety (fig. 5.1).[121]

THE RISE OF LOCAL GENTRY IN COMMUNITY
WORSHIP ASSOCIATIONS

In communities spared severe social disorder, local gentry in Shanxi (especially those who held only lower-level examination degrees) characteristically claimed local authority by leading existing local institutions—especially community worship associations that formed around specific community temples (*shemiao* 社廟) for one or more villages. The case of Yuan Yingzhen 原應軫, a native of Yangcheng county in southeastern Shanxi, is suggestive. Yuan held a lower-level examination degree and had served in a lower-ranking government position. After retiring to his native village of Xiajiao, he worked closely with two of his kinsmen from 1510 to 1515 to supervise the construction of a music building (*yuelou* 樂樓) for theatrical performances at the Temple of King Tang (*Tangwang miao* 湯王廟) in the village. In a 1536 inscription, the scholar-official Wang Xuan 王玹, a relative of Yuan, justified Yuan's activity in following words:

> Wenbi [the literary name of Yuan Yingzhen] constructed the building not to please someone or to pray for the god's blessing. Rather, he had a profound intention. He believed that if retired literati only enjoyed gatherings for poetry and alcohol, they were just as dissipated as the Jin-dynasty [266–420] literati and would not do any good in the world. Yet if they use the occasion of making sacrifices to a god as a chance to educate the young people to be virtuous and kind, they could gather their countrymen at the temple to share the god's blessing. Indeed, it is a good thing for a gentleman to serve the god while reading and farming. . . . In doing so, he can encourage the kind-hearted and warn the atrocious, thus alluding to the point of appreciating the righteousness and condemning the evil.[122]

121. Li Nan 李楠, "Chongxiu Hongfu si ji" 重修洪福寺記 (dated 1608), "Chongxiu beishe Hongfu si bei" 重修北社洪福寺碑 (dated 1622). The inscriptions on the fronts and backs of these steles are unpublished. I transcribed the inscriptions from photos I took during a trip to the monastery in July 2014.

122. Wang Xuan, "Chongxiu yuelou zhi ji" 重修樂樓之記, in Feng Junjie, *Shanxi xiqu beike jikao*, 222–23.

Notably, Wang Xuan added a new component of "serving the god" (*shishen* 事神) to the traditional idealized activities of a retired literati scholar, mentioned in chapter 1, of "reading and farming" (*gengdu* 耕讀). The scholar could now, Wang argued, morally transform his village fellows in activities organized in the name of "serving the god."

This discourse became more convincing for local gentry if the locally worshipped god was sanctioned by the Confucian ritual tradition. The god Yuan Yingzhen "served" was King Tang, a sage ruler of the ancient Shang dynasty (ca. 1600–1045 BCE), celebrated in the *Book of Documents* (*Shangshu* 尚書) for his noble action of sacrificing his own life to pray for rain during a severe drought. Because King Tang allegedly died at Mt. Xicheng 析城山, about thirty kilometers southwest of Xiajiao village, a temple dedicated to him was built at the top of the mountain in early times. This temple became the root temple for local worship of King Tang and had received state sanction since the Northern Song dynasty. Villagers in Yangcheng and from many other counties frequently traveled to the root temple to pray for rain, and they built branch temples in their own villages.[123] The temple of King Tang in Xiajiao village, created as early as the twelfth century, was such a branch temple. While ordinary villagers worshipped the god for his alleged power to bring rain, educated gentry, Wang Xuan argued, could use the occasion of making sacrifices to the god to explain inscriptions on old steles installed in the temple. Such inscriptions, often composed by Confucian literati like Wang himself, framed the cult of King Tang in Confucian terms. For instance, in the beginning of his inscription, Wang quoted two Confucian classics— the *Book of Change* and the *Book of Documents*—to legitimize the temple construction and praise the virtues of King Tang. From the perspectives of Yuan Yingzhen and Wang Xuan, Confucian-educated gentry could morally transform local communities by properly directing the worship of popular local deities in tune with Confucian orthodoxy.

---

123. A 1280 stele installed at the Temple of King Tang at Mt. Xicheng recorded a list of all branch temples affiliated with this root temple. The list included more than eighty-six branch temples established in more than twenty-one prefectures and counties in Shanxi and Henan. See "Tangdi xinggong beiji" 湯帝行宮碑記, in Feng Junjie, *Xiju yu kaogu*, 111–15. According to Iguro Shinobu, these branch temples were probably established in the Jin dynasty (*Bunsui to shihai*, 139–47).

More importantly, local gentry like Yuan Yingzhen reformed the community worship associations into tightly organized village institutions. According to another 1536 inscription written for the same Temple of King Tang by a different scholar-official, Yuan had initiated a larger construction project to renovate the whole temple in 1527, and during the project Yuan divided his village fellows into twelve units (*shier jia* 十二甲), a structure likely modeled on the official *lijia* system. Then Yuan wrote the names of each unit's members on two wooden tablets, using one of them for collecting money and resources and the other for allocating labor service for temple affairs. Much like ditch sticks in an irrigation association, discussed in chapter 4, these two tablets represented the authority of association leaders and were given to the accountable person. When a family did not answer Yuan's call to donate food or serve in the temple-construction project, Yuan was said to have responded by visiting the family and kneeling in front of its members until they felt ashamed and agreed to do their part. Yuan's tenacity allegedly convinced Xiaojia villagers to follow his lead in the ten-year renovation project, even during a difficult time of famine.[124] His reform, as Du Zhengzhen has pointed out, increased the authority of the original community association at Xiajiao village, transforming it into an institutionalized village organization with a consistent managerial group that included three chief community heads (*zongli sheshou* 總理社首) and twelve associate community heads (*fenli sheshou* 分理社首). The Yuans, who produced many successful examination degree holders in the middle Ming but fewer after the late Ming, maintained elite status in their village community by dominating the managerial group of the association.[125]

A two-faceted local dominance thus developed in Shanxi society after the mid-sixteenth century. On the one hand, educated gentry increasingly rose to play leadership roles in local society, which resembles the southern phenomena of literati elite localism from the Southern Song onward. On the other hand, instead of using Neo-Confucian ideas, rituals, and institutions to transform local society, these Shanxi gentry chose to seek authority in existing social institutions, most of which were based on re-

124.   Li Han 李瀚, "Chongxiu zhengdian langwu zhi ji" 重修正殿廊廡之記, in Feng Junjie, *Shanxi xiqu beike jikao*, 227–30.
125.   Du, *Cunshe chuantong*, 162–66.

ligious beliefs and practices. Yuan Yingzhen's case illustrates the perspective of many Shanxi gentry, justifying their choice and consolidating their families' local authority by claiming to use community worship associations as an effective platform for transforming local society on Confucian terms.

Community worship associations became increasingly prominent in Shanxi society after the mid-sixteenth century for other reasons, too. First, they were deeply embedded in a strong tradition of local cults. Their development dated back at least to the Northern Song dynasty, when the imperial state authorized the worship of countless local deities in the official *Canon of Sacrifices*. A cradle of ancient Chinese civilization, Shanxi had produced a large number of mythical and historical figures who were commemorated and worshipped as local deities in later times. In many areas of Shanxi, local identity was strongly tied to the cults of such deities, who often were merged with the spirits of local mountains, rivers, and springs to become local tutelary gods. The god of Mt. Cang and King Tang are typical examples.

Worship of these popular deities in Shanxi had profound connections to the local agrarian economy. Climatic and topographical conditions account for the perpetual problem of water scarcity in the majority of the province. The continental monsoon climate brings irregular and deficient annual rainfall and frequent drought. Mountainous land composes 70 percent of the province, and 97.2 percent of the farmland is dry.[126] As discussed in the previous chapter, in areas where irrigation resources such as rivers and springs were available, local people developed canals and organized irrigation associations to distribute water. Yet irrigated agriculture accounted for only a small portion of the economy at the provincial level. Most counties in Shanxi—such as Yu county in the north and Yangcheng county in the southeast—did not have abundant irrigation resources. Peasants in those areas relied entirely on rainfall to water their farmland and thus depended on the mercy of rainmaking deities. Shanxi peasants thus developed a strong tradition of worshipping allegedly efficacious rainmaking deities. Temples dedicated to popular rainmaking deities functioned as important power centers in local societies; almost every county in Shanxi had one or more of these temples, like the

126. Dong Xiaoping and Christian Lamouroux, *Bu guan er zhi*, 3.

Cangshan Shrine and the Temple of King Tang. Villagers organized community worship associations related to such temples to make regular sacrificial offerings, hold temple festivals, and conduct elaborate rituals to pray for rain in times of drought.

The change in who controlled these community temples and worship associations was an indicator of the shifting composition of local elites across dynasties. Branch temples of the Cangshan Shrine served as good examples. While Buddhist monks often played leadership roles in those temples in the Yuan period, local gentry had completely replaced them by the late Ming.[127] For instance, as recorded on a stele, when a four-village association initiated a temple-repair project in 1591 for one branch temple, Liu Sance 劉三策, who held the examination degree of licentiate, acted as the leader. His family, obviously gentry since both Liu's father and his son were licentiates as well, was the major sponsor. The 1591 stele reveals that the branch temple functioned as the community temple for the four villages, which every year held three grand temple festivals of three days each. The repair project was to build a music pavilion (*yueting* 樂亭) for theatrical performances. Although four Daoist monks resided in the temple, they served as mere caretakers and had little authority over temple affairs.[128]

In addition to serving as an important arena in which local people competed for social power, community temples of local popular deities increasingly became an effective instrument for villages in competition over lucrative resources—such as land, water, timber, and mines—in the rapidly commercializing rural economy after the middle of the sixteenth century. The example of Changchi village, a member village of the Cangshan Association described in the case-study above, demonstrates this point. Since the Yuan period, Changchi had allied with Wangjiazhuang village 王家莊 to support a dragon god temple at Mt. Zhijiao 芝角山. The temple connected the two villages, which were located, respectively, north

127.　For instance, when Lizhuang villagers created a branch temple of the Cangshan Shrine in 1356, a Buddhist monk served as its first abbot, and about thirty Buddhist monks contributed to the building project—including two senior monks appointed by an imperial preceptor and one monk from Mt. Wutai appointed by a Mongol emperor. See Gao Yanming 高彥明, "Cangshan ci ji" 藏山祠記 (dated 1356), *DQ: Yuxian*, 49.

128.　"Xinchuang Dawang miao yueting beiji" 新創大王廟樂亭碑記, *DQ: Yuxian*, 112.

and south of the mountain.[129] Most remarkably, sponsoring the dragon god temple allowed the two rural communities to claim ownership of the trees on the local mountain, lucrative resources in a timber trade that was booming at the time. In 1572 Changchi villagers successfully lobbied the county magistrate to announce a ban on cutting pine trees in the vicinity of the temple or damaging the temple and temple steles. Though the ban applied to all local village leaders, it targeted nine local residents, indicating that they might have been the ones who had tried to gain access to the timber business by destroying earlier prescriptive steles installed by Changchi villagers. Changchi villagers justified their need for such a ban by addressing the trees as "sacred pine trees" (*shensongshu* 神松樹), which grew on the dragon god's territory.[130] Such rhetoric was apparently very common in local society. In 1620, the residents of a neighboring village, Baiquan, erected a stele that banned the cutting of local mountain trees near the village's Jade Emperor Temple (*Yuhuang miao* 玉皇廟); they argued that such behavior would disturb the feng shui of the "sacred place" (*shenjing* 神境).[131] According to this logic, villagers who sponsored such a god's temple were the guardians, and by extension owners, of any property in the territory under the god's divine jurisdiction. From the late Ming onward, many similar steles appeared in Shanxi; most of them highlighted the connection between the worship of a specific god and local people's claim to exclusive ownership of profitable resources. Village organizations were often behind these claims.[132]

TURNING BUDDHIST AND DAOIST
ESTABLISHMENTS INTO COMMUNITY TEMPLES

Autonomous village organizations, as historians of late imperial China have amply demonstrated, increasingly became the most important rural institutions in the social, economic, and religious life of Shanxi

129. Wang Huamin 王化民, "Zibai longshen chongxiu beiji" 紫柏龍神重修碑記, *DQ: Yuxian*, 123.

130. Jin Hechuo 近河綽, "Chongxiu zibai longshen miao ji" 重修紫柏龍神廟記, *DQ: Yuxian*, 104.

131. "Baiquan cun shenshan jinyu beiji" 柏泉村神山禁諭碑記, *DQ: Yuxian*, 126.

132. For other examples, see "Chongxiu zhenze gong ji" 重修真澤宮記, *Ming Qing Shanxi beike ziliao xuan*, 451–52.

province after the late Ming.[133] Yet these works have missed an important step in the development of community worship associations: their relationship with Buddhist and Daoist establishments. The rise of community worship associations and the decline of Buddhist and Daoist institutions were interrelated processes of social transformation in Shanxi in the late Ming.

The flourishing of community worship associations went hand in hand with the boom in popular religious beliefs and practices, which developed rapidly at the expense of organized religions in the late Ming. Buddhist and Daoist clergy increasingly faced threats from both the government and local rivals. For instance, a Shanxi provincial censor reported to the court around 1558 that most monastic land had been appropriated or sold off by powerful local people.[134] A 1611 stele from a Buddhist monastery in Xinzhou records that the local government issued an official document to a local village organization, asking it to take charge of overseeing the monks' behavior.[135] While the clergy found it increasingly difficult to hold onto their monastic property, both urban and rural residents constructed more community temples for their favorite deities from all traditions, including Buddhism, Daoism, Confucianism, and local cults. Two local officials in Lu'an prefecture of southeastern Shanxi observed this development and voiced their concern in a new prefectural gazetteer they compiled in 1619:

> Recently, countless people believe in Buddhism and Daoism and establish temple buildings. Everywhere in prefectures, counties, towns, and countryside people are building halls, cloisters, shrines, or pavilions to worship Buddha, Bodhisattva, Daoist lords, and immortals. Some create Halls of the Three Teachings or Cloisters of Ten Directions to integrate those worships. In some places people even created more than ten such buildings simultaneously. Although these practices could transform the stupid and assist the kind, they end up quietly corrupting social customs. This is not

133. Important studies of village organizations in Shanxi include D. Johnson, *Spectacle and Sacrifice*, and Du, *Cunshe chuantong*.

134. *DQ: Qinshui*, 47.

135. The inscription on this stele is not published. I transcribed it from photos taken at the site on July 5, 2014.

a small matter. Maybe even the Buddhist and Daoist sages do not like to hear about it?[136]

Almost all of the temples and shrines were unsanctioned by the government, and most importantly, they were controlled not by the clergy but by the laity. The two officials expressed the same concern about the flourishing of popular religious establishments in another section in the gazetteer on schools. After listing six private academies (two established in the Song-Yuan period and the rest in the Ming) that had been abandoned by 1619, the two officials lamented that no one at the time was carrying on these academies' noble mission of education, as ordinary local people were simply more interested in religion than in Confucian learning.[137] Suffice it to say that temples of popular beliefs were developed at the expense not only of Buddhist and Daoist monasteries but also of Confucian schools in late Ming Shanxi. At this point, we may argue that there was a northern analogue to the "laicization" of religious life that Robert Hymes has demonstrated was prominent in southern Chinese society from the Southern Song onward.[138]

Not all community temples in Shanxi were newly built in the Ming; many of them were transformed Buddhist and Daoist establishments, a process that began as early as the sixteenth century. An important marker of such a transformation was the appearance of permanent buildings for theatrical performances in monastic space, especially in Buddhist monasteries. Such buildings did not appear in Shanxi's Buddhist monasteries until the sixteenth century.[139] From the Yuan period on, theatrical performances became increasingly important in temple festivals at temples of local cults in Shanxi. Local people developed the characteristic liturgical rituals collectively known as "Thank the God with Theatrical Performance" (*choushen saixi* 酬神賽戲). David Johnson shows that these rituals focused on a temple's god and took place during annual festivals

136. *Lu'an fuzhi* [1619], 8.15.
137. Ibid., 7.9a–9b.
138. Hymes, "Sung Society and Social Change," 596.
139. The earliest record of a Buddhist monastery having a theatrical building is dated 1478. The building was constructed in the Guangqing Monastery 廣慶寺 at Ermaying village 二馬營, in Ningwu county. See Feng Junjie, *Shanxi shenmiao juchang kao*, 161–63.

celebrating the god's birthday and other important occasions. The rituals combined food offerings and operas performed by professional groups or by specially trained members of the community with the help of experts.[140] Such temple festivals and rituals had always been concentrated in the temples of local cults. Yet from the sixteenth century onward, many Buddhist monasteries, catering to the interests of their lay neighbors and sponsors, began to hold temple festivals and emphasize the offering of theatrical performances.

The history of the Pure-Belief Monastery (*Jingxin si* 淨信寺), located at Yangyi town in Taigu 太谷 county, attests to this significant change in monastic space and activities. During the Zhengde era (1506–21), local residents and monks cooperated to enlarge the monastery, adding a Temple of Gray Spring and a music pavilion. The Temple of Gray Spring was dedicated to Han Jue 韓厥, a general of the Zhao state in the Spring and Autumn period known for protecting the famous orphan of Zhao, the main deity worshipped at the Cangshan Shrine in Yu county. According to local popular belief, Han discovered the Gray Spring, which irrigated the farmlands of neighboring areas, and he was later worshipped as the spring's deity. During a 1616–19 project of temple enlargement, the music pavilion was removed, causing inconvenience in annual temple festivals dedicated to Han. At the suggestion of a local wine merchant, who raised funds for the temple-building project, neighboring village communities worked together to build a new music pavilion at the monastery in 1623.[141] Local sponsors insisted on the need for a music pavilion at the monastery, indicating the growing importance of temple festivals and the cult of Han Jue at the Pure-Belief Monastery. The theatrical performances in the annual temple festivals at the monastery became so important after the seventeenth century that in 1732 an abbot of the monastery and local community heads (*sheshou* 社首) from Yangyi town cooperated to build a specific community house (*shefang* 社房) inside the monastery, which community leaders could use for managing matters related to temple

140. D. Johnson, *Spectacle and Sacrifice*, 2–3.

141. Yao Zhenyu 姚震宇, "Buxiu Yangyi zhen Jingxin si beiji" 補修陽邑鎮淨信寺碑記 (dated 1622), and Du Jinlei 杜金壘, "Yangyi si xinjian shanting yueting bing zhuan tianwangdian qiang ji" 陽邑寺新建膳亭樂亭並碑天王殿墻記 (dated 1623), in Feng Junjie, *Shanxi xiqu beike jikao*, 354–64.

festivals.[142] From the late Ming on, the Pure-Belief Monastery became the community temple for town residents, who formed a highly organized community worship association around the monastery.

In a similar fashion, many Buddhist and Daoist establishments were gradually transformed into community temples for local sacrifices and entertainment under the control of community worship associations.[143] This transformation revealed a final shift favoring villagers in power relations between the clergy and village organizations in the late Ming and the succeeding Qing dynasty. Consider the example of the Sage-Woman Temple (*Shenggumiao* 聖姑廟) in Gaoping 高平 county of Zezhou subprefecture, in southeastern Shanxi. The temple, built in the Yuan, was controlled by a lineage of Daoist nuns. In the early and middle Ming, to resist pressure from neighboring village communities, the nuns acquired patronage first from a neighboring Ningshan Guard 寧山衛 and then from the Xichuan commandery principality 隰川王府, a branch of the Dai principality that had been relocated from Datong in Zezhou. The temple became a clan cloister of the Xichuan commandery principality in 1506, thanks to a female network of patrons and clients among imperial clanswomen and nuns from the temple. According to a decree issued by the commandery prince of Xichuan, the major patrons of the temple were all of the wives of four commandery princes and three lesser-titled imperial clansmen.[144] The Sage-Woman Temple remained under the control of Daoist nuns in most of the Ming, until the Ming-Qing transition.

In the early Qing period, powerful local people appropriated farmland and mountain trees that had been the temple's property, and the temple fell into disrepair. It was revived only after 1762, when a neighboring seven-village association decided to renovate it. By then, as Zhao Shiyu has argued, the nature of the temple had changed permanently from a religious institution of the clergy to a community temple of the

142. "Jingxin si chongxiu fodian jinzhuang shengxiang zengjian shefang menting ji" 淨信寺重修佛殿金妝聖像增建社房門亭記, *Ming Qing Shanxi beike ziliao xuan*, 373–76.

143. As chapter 4 showed, similar developments had occurred in some local irrigation societies as early as the late Yuan.

144. "Daming zongshi xichuanwang lingzhi" 大明宗室隰川王令旨, *Ming Qing Shanxi beike ziliao xuan*, 434–35.

seven-village association.[145] Similarly, the Palace of Eternal Joy, the center of Quanzhen Daoist order in the Yuan, and the Chan Buddhist Monastery of Tranquil Residence, a clan cloister of the Jin principality in the early Ming, also became the collective property of neighboring village organizations in the Qing period.[146] After the seventeenth century, the paradigm of rural dominance in Shanxi shifted completely, with autonomous village organizations gaining authority and with Buddhist and Daoist establishments becoming utterly powerless in local society.

Conclusion

The Yuan-Ming transition marked important changes in state-religion relations. During the majority of the Mongol-Yuan era, Buddhism and Daoism enjoyed both preferential state policies and the personal patronage of Mongol rulers and nobles. As a result, the two religions acquired considerable institutional power with a strong economic foundation, cross-regional monastic networks, and powerful connections. In the early Ming, under the Ming founder's hostile religious policies, Buddhist and Daoist orders lost the legal and political support of the imperial state and were greatly weakened as social institutions.

Changes in state-religion relations resulted in significant shifts of wealth and power from Buddhist and Daoist establishments to their rival institutions in local society. However, this development had an important twist in Shanxi; it took the first two hundred years of the dynasty for the process to be completed there. In Shanxi, many Buddhist and Daoist establishments survived state suppression and local encroachment on monastic property because they gained new patronage from powerful principalities, and occasionally from garrison units as well. The early Ming inherited an important Yuan element in state building: the court gave princely appanages considerable power in border provinces like Shanxi. Three imperial principalities in Shanxi—Dai, Jin, and Shen—and many

145. Zhao Shiyu, "Shenggu miao."
146. Jiang Rongchang 蔣榮昌, "Yongle gong dimu zuke beiji" 永樂宮地畝租稞碑記, *Yongle gong zhi*, 160; "Chongxiu Qingju chansi jin fashan linzhi bei xu" 重修清居禪寺禁伐山林植碑序, *Ming Qing Shanxi beike ziliao xuan*, 12.

more commandery principalities enjoyed privileged legal status and enormous wealth, and local civil officials were often unable to rein in the excessive power of imperial clansmen. Acting as powerful patrons of religious establishments, Ming imperial and commandery princes formed mutually beneficial patron-client relations with Buddhist and Daoist clergy by adopting the clergy's monasteries as clan cloisters of one or several principalities. The patron-client relationship helped the principalities increase their wealth and expand their influence from their seat cities to broader local societies, and it supported the clergy's continuing to play an active role in local affairs. Thus, while the law was not on the clergy's side during the Ming dynasty, monks and nuns still had powerful patrons from the official world in the early and middle Ming.

This feature of local dominance gradually diminished around the middle of the sixteenth century, when significant political, social, and economic changes occurred. Along with the decline of princely institutions, the imperial state strengthened the power of the civil administration in provinces, prefectures, and counties. Meanwhile, social change took new directions. Local gentry rose to social and moral leadership by organizing local defenses and transforming existing local institutions, especially the increasingly prominent community worship associations. At the expense of organized religions, these associations expanded in Shanxi and encroached on monastic property and space; some even turned Buddhist and Daoist establishments into community temples. In other words, while Buddhists and Daoists subsumed many community temples and worship associations in the Yuan and to some degree in the first half of the Ming, after the mid-sixteenth century community temples subsumed Buddhist and Daoist establishments instead. By the beginning of the seventeenth century, the clergy and their establishments had been severely marginalized in local society. The story of the two religions' leading roles in social organization in Shanxi finally came to a permanent end.

CONCLUSION

In 1211, Mongol armies led by Chinggis Khan and his generals swept into north China and began their conquest of the Jin dynasty. Wiping out nearly half of the population and ruining much of the farmland, the Mongols unleashed a highly destructive war that dismantled the underpinnings of an entire society in north China. How did the Chinese rebuild their society after this extreme devastation? And how did their efforts alter social and economic forces in the succeeding centuries? These are the two key questions this book has raised and sought to answer. Anyone familiar with the basic records of Chinese history would likely say that sufficient evidence to answer these questions survives only in southern China, which was also conquered by the Mongols half a century later in 1279—and particularly in the form of the collected papers of Confucian-educated literati, who formed the backbone of the social reconstruction after the Mongol conquest.

As this book has shown, these assumptions turn out to be mistaken. A surprising number of historical sources survive from the north, particularly Shanxi province, in the form of both existing steles and inscriptions from other steles compiled during and after the nineteenth century. These sources allow this book to tell the riveting story of how northern Chinese men and women adapted to trying circumstances, interacted with alien Mongol conquerors, and created a drastically new social order under the leadership of the clergy, both Buddhist and Daoist.

This new social order endured throughout Mongol rule under the Yuan dynasty and left a lasting impact on the succeeding Ming dynasty. After conquering China, the Mongols did not revive the civil service examinations—the defining Chinese elite institution that since at least the sixth century had recruited Confucian literati to government office—until 1313, and even then they appointed very few officials through the exams. Examination degrees no longer functioned as the key marker of social status. Instead, in addition to relying on Mongols and Central Asians to govern China, the Mongol rulers promoted members of non-literati specialist groups among northerners—military strongmen and clergy in particular—as vital political and social actors. Buddhist and Daoist clergy thus became two of the most powerful social groups in local society. Men and a surprising number of women of varying social status came together in the postconquest years to rebuild society, restart the economy, and reshape values in the Buddhist and Daoist orders. Religious clergy and institutions acquired enough power to dominate the social space between family and state.

Although the new social order that I have described was specific to northern China, it is nevertheless important for our conceptions of middle-period Chinese history. In this period Chinese society in the south saw the emergence of a new elite way of life dominated by Confucian-educated literati, which grew out of changes introduced in the Northern Song dynasty. This southern development was the outcome of the inter-action of a series of state projects—particularly the promotion of literati culture and the civil service examination system—backed by increased wealth and education at all levels of society. Examination degrees provided the desired state sanction for the literati, who more than ever before be-came a self-defining and self-certifying social group. This literati-centered elite lifestyle and the examination-centered state-elite relations marked southern Chinese society in the Northern Song and most subsequent Chinese dynasties. Even under Mongol rule in the Yuan, Chinese literati continued to be the major force in the social transformation of the south.

In the north, however, the major force in social transformation was not Confucian degree holders but rather the newly powerful social group of clergy. Yuan Haowen, the most famous literati scholar in the late Jin and early Mongol period, experienced this transformation. He saw the

Confucian order fall apart, numerous literati die at the hands of the Mongols, and many more northerners—including his good friends among the literati and even his own daughter—become Quanzhen monks and nuns. Yuan had to wonder whether Heaven had mandated that Quanzhen Daoism and its clergy replace Confucianism and the literati to save countless lives and souls from violence, ignorance, and complete chaos in north China, the homeland that he barely recognized after the Mongol conquest. Whether or not the clergy had Heaven's mandate, they replaced Confucian literati and led the social reconstruction of north China out of the ashes of the Jin-Mongol war.

This book has traced the development of this new social order in the northern province of Shanxi under Mongol rule and its unmaking in the Ming dynasty. The full course of this order's rise and fall in Shanxi represented the distinctive northern path of social transformation. This northern path differs significantly from the south-centered narrative of social change, which so far has dominated our understanding of middle-period Chinese history to the extent that north China is rarely discussed in influential accounts of Chinese social history.

The Northern Path of Social Transformation

The terms *northern* and *southern* as used here are, of course, notional, and they risk neglecting the great local diversity within both the northern and southern regions. The use of these terms here does not mean that all northern and southern localities fell neatly into the two proposed patterns. Instead, it aims to emphasize the overall divergence in the patterns of social change and social order that emerged in the south and the north under different historical circumstances in middle-period China. The southern pattern represents the trajectory of historical development in a society where literati (whose status was partly independent of the state) and a set of institutions shaped by Neo-Confucian ideology dominated. The northern pattern represents a very different society. While literati, their social institutions, and Neo-Confucian ideology were significantly weaker in the north, alternative traditions and institutions—especially those of religions—were consistently robust.

Dominant social elites and leading social institutions thus marked the difference between north and south China. During the Northern Song and Jin dynasties, a Confucian-educated elite had come to dominate both parts of the country. However, the Mongol invasion disrupted that order profoundly, especially in the north. In south China, the Confucian-educated elite continued to shape society, while in the north, non-literati elites maintained a strong presence as Confucian literati were far fewer and far less active. This was true in the Mongol era but became less so after the Ming dynasty restored the civil service examinations nationwide. Nonetheless, religion-based institutions—including the temples of popular cults and, for a time, Buddhist monasteries and Daoist abbeys—served as focal points of social organization and integration in the north.

THE MONGOL ERA

The Mongol conquest provided the most important catalyst for the emergence of the northern pattern of social transformation. Unprecedented destruction caused severe economic collapse, population loss, and the meltdown of political and social institutions in north China. In this war-torn society, the people's suffering surpassed their imagination. With their teachings of universal salvation, both Buddhist and Daoist organizations were inherently concerned with public welfare and were able to provide effective linkages to create community solidarity when people's kinship and territorial ties were repeatedly disrupted by unremitting military destruction and natural disasters. Thus, the two religions each played a leading role in helping northern refugees survive the chaos and rebuild postwar northern society.

Buddhist and Daoist orders were able to perform this role because of the remarkable political connections and institutional strength they achieved in the new Mongol-Yuan regime. The two religious orders benefited from three types of political resources available to them. First, the Mongol khans granted extensive tax exemptions to the two religions and showered them with imperial patronage. Second, Mongol princes and nobles, as appanage holders with considerable autonomy, patronized clerical figures and religious establishments in their fiefs in north China. Third, the Yuan regime turned religious institutions into new centers of

legitimate political power paralleling those in the secular civilian government. Notably, this practice differed sharply from that of the previous
Song and Jin dynasties, which had kept religious institutions under the
close supervision of civil officials. In other words, whereas in earlier dynasties the decision to enter religious life closed off all possibilities of
pursuing a political career, it now opened up opportunities for clergy to
participate in a new political system in which religious administration
played a critical part.

With strong political support from the Mongol state and Mongol
nobles, the Quanzhen Daoist order, under the headship of Qiu Chuji,
provided leaders and inclusive institutions that dramatically restructured
local communities during the Jin-Yuan transition. Its promise of personal
cultivation and social salvation appealed to lay followers and sponsors
across class, gender, and ethnic boundaries. Through numerous large-scale
Quanzhen projects such as printing a new Daoist canon and building regional Quanzhen centers, eminent Quanzhen masters like Song Defang
in Shanxi led their male and female disciples in establishing extensive monastic networks that penetrated almost every city, town, and village
throughout north China. The Quanzhen order provided desperate local
residents with material, organizational, and ideological support. It helped
rebuild infrastructure and local communities badly damaged by the Mongol conquest. Its lay associations and subordinate temples created links
between these communities and regional Quanzhen centers such as the
Palace of Eternal Joy, in southern Shanxi. The Quanzhen order thus built
a congregational type of religion at the local level, with local people affiliated with their local Quanzhen abbeys and convents. This contrasted
starkly with the role of Daoist clerics from the Northern Song onward in
the south, where local laypeople engaged with Daoists to meet specific
needs on specific occasions—such as by hiring them as rite masters or
exorcist healers—and maintained no long-term ties with them.[1]

The unprecedented institutional strength of the Quanzhen Daoist order in north China allowed its clergy to incorporate new social groups,
most notably women. The Quanzhen order took a large number of women
into Quanzhen monasteries during the Jin-Mongol war and promoted

1. Hymes, "Sung Society and Social Change," 608.

women's participation in rebuilding postwar local communities. Quan-zhen nuns played particularly important roles in sheltering homeless widows and orphaned girls in their Daoist convents. The Quanzhen order empowered women to choose an alternative monastic lifestyle and encour-aged them to take on broader social responsibilities. Many Quanzhen nuns earned respect for their contributions in rebuilding local communities. Some, such as the Jurchen nun Aodun Miaoshan, even achieved fame and honor as abbots in famous Quanzhen institutions or through their association with noble Mongol men and women.

In contrast, southern Confucian teachings encouraged abandoned or widowed women to remain loyal to their male family members by re-maining chaste or even committing suicide. In the Southern Song, both literati and the state held up heroic female martyrs as models for male loyalty to the state. Southern literati in the Yuan, as Beverly Bossler has demonstrated, continued to "fuel the production of texts celebrating faith-ful widows" to "promote Confucian virtue, and to participate in the preservation of Han civilization."[2] Southern literati also skillfully used Yuan law to restrict women's property rights and remarriage, which con-sequently strengthened the Chinese patrilineal tradition and facilitated the development of lineage organizations endorsed by Neo-Confucian thinkers.[3] The comparison between the northern and southern strategies for women reflects the different ways in which northern and southern Chinese societies reacted to the Mongol conquest by restructuring the existing gender arrangements—in the north, putting women outside the family system into nunneries, and in the south, keeping them within families.

In addition to accommodating numerous homeless men and women, both the Quanzhen Daoist and Buddhist orders integrated the monas-tery and the family in new ways. They flexibly adapted the popular Chinese ethic of filial piety to underscore the obligations that religious clergy had to both their religious masters and their lay families. In doing so, they gained acceptance from lay Chinese who had embraced the ideal of filial piety since birth. The Quanzhen communities also creatively invented

2. Bossler, *Courtesans, Concubines, and the Cult of Female Fidelity,* 414–15.
3. Birge, *Women, Property, and Confucian Reaction,* 253–82.

the ritual of regular assembly at a famous master's graveyard by all his disciples, which strengthened the internal cohesion of Quanzhen religious lineages that spanned generations. They even took on their members' familial obligations by helping take care of the graves of a member's lay family (in the case of a widowed nun, often the graves of the members of both her natal family and her deceased husband's family).

Although looking after the souls of dead ancestors was common in earlier Buddhist discourse on filial piety, granting secular honors to living relatives was not. Monk administrators, as the compelling story of the Mt. Wutai monk Zhang Zhiyu showed in chapter 3, used their official status in the Mongol-Yuan regime's powerful Buddhist bureaucracy to provide economic advantages and social prestige to their lay kin. Many Chinese men, especially those from families that never or no longer had official status, took steps that their counterparts in the Northern Song or Jin would not have seriously contemplated: receiving ordination as a Buddhist monk and using success in the Buddhist bureaucracy to help their natal families achieve upward social mobility in the secular world.

Monks' new familial responsibilities extended even from families of their parents to families of their own. Clerical marriage in Yuan China differed significantly from the isolated cases of corrupt monks who had wives and fathered sons in almost every dynasty after Buddhism was introduced to China in the first millennium. The Mongol-Yuan state politicized the clergy by granting them elite legal status and by creating powerful religious bureaucracies in which they could serve. The usual Buddhist rhetoric of leaving the family and maintaining an appropriate distance from lay society barely applied.[4] Buddhists and Daoists in Yuan China were so close to the secular world that some contemporaries complained. Monks, they said, were no different from the laity in their lifestyle and pursuit of worldly profit. Clerical marriages reflected less a moral crisis—though they were certainly still in violation of Confucian ethics, Buddhist *vinayas*, and Yuan law—and more an acute awareness of the structural difficulty in achieving honor and wealth in traditionally proper ways. The blurring or eroding of boundaries between the secular and the religious in familial matters was thus inextricably tied to a critical social reality in Mongol-Yuan China. The clergy as a whole enjoyed extraordinary

---

4. Robson, "'Neither Too Far, nor Too Near.'"

privileges, status, and wealth at the same time that upward social mobility for the laity had stagnated due to the Mongol-Yuan regime's rigid hereditary household system and its discrimination against Chinese in official recruitment.

In addition to the institution of the family, Buddhist and Daoist organizations reshaped other existing social institutions, especially territorial village organizations, to play important roles in rebuilding local communities. Territorial village organizations, with locally oriented concerns, had for centuries fostered local identity in rural communities. Most of them sought divine aid. Even irrigation associations, which functioned primarily to regulate and allocate canal water, fostered the shared belief among water households in specific water gods. This belief brought people together in ritual and cultural activities. The changing power dynamic between organized religious institutions and territorial village organizations altered social organization in Shanxi after the thirteenth century. In the Mongol era, Buddhist and Daoist organizations were dominant. Monks and nuns commonly occupied leadership positions in villagers' organizations, including the most independent and exclusive irrigation associations.

In everyday life, the relations between the clergy and their village neighbors might not always have been as congenial as portrayed in contemporary inscriptional sources. The happy acceptance by local people of clerical dominance in the Yuan is an artifact first of the sources and second of the clergy's very special political privileges. It would have been natural for local people, especially those engaged in other kinds of associations, to resist clerical penetration of their localities or even to resent growing clerical authority over local affairs. Thus, we should not take Yuan-era inscriptions at face value when they claim that local people spontaneously asked monks and nuns to do various things in their localities. Whether local laypeople took on the role of supplicant partly because of coercion or because they really did need the clergy's connections and resources, the social reality was the same: monks and nuns had the upper hand in their competition with local rivals.

Religious organizations, especially those of Buddhism, also expanded in the south after 1279 and competed with existing social institutions in local society, but they did not achieve the success that their northern counterparts did. In the south, literati families sought leadership in local society by presenting themselves as exemplars of family morality and by establishing patrilineal lineages and voluntary Neo-Confucian institutions such as private academies and community compacts. These literati institutions continued to maintain a strong position in the Yuan in spite of threats from powerful religious institutions. For instance, immediately following the Mongol conquest, many Buddhist institutions tried to occupy the lands and even the buildings of Confucian academies in the south. Yet the academies fought back. They received support not only from local Chinese families but also from the Yuan state, which recognized academies and absorbed them into the official network of education institutions for Confucian households.[5] In contrast to the overwhelming dominance of Buddhist and Daoist organizations in the north, literati institutions remained powerful in the south.

In sum, powerful Quanzhen Daoist and Buddhist organizations were instrumental in creating the new social order in north China under Mongol rule. Notably, the two religious orders were dominant not just in Shanxi but also in Shandong, Hebei, Henan, and Shaanxi. In this distinctive social order, Buddhist and Daoist clergy acted as local elites. They received imperial patronage. They interacted with the Mongol state. They organized postwar community-building projects. They held government positions. As landlords and business owners, they controlled considerable tax-exempt wealth. And as leaders of village organizations, they had the authority to manage critical resources for agricultural production.

THE POST-MONGOL ERA

The distinctive social order that took shape under Mongol rule first broke down in the fighting and destruction of the Yuan-Ming transition. It completely lost its legal and political foundations in the succeeding Ming dynasty, as the Ming founder made new laws and launched campaigns to suppress organized religions. Buddhist and Daoist establishments were gradually marginalized in local society with the slow but steady disappearance of the political, social, and economic conditions that had favored organized religions.

5. Walton, "Academies in the Changing Religious Landscape," 1254–59.

The unmaking of the distinctive social order in Shanxi, which occupied the first two hundred years of the Ming, sheds light on two previously overlooked northern changes in local dominance. First, the powerful institution of principalities, which were fiefs granted to imperial princes by Ming emperors, greatly influenced the competition between organized religions and their local rivals. Second, territorial village organizations based on local cults turned against organized religious institutions, their longtime partners, and turned Buddhist and Daoist monasteries into community temples.

The presence or absence of principalities had a meaningful impact on regional divergence in Ming China. Principalities stationed in border provinces, as legitimate power centers separate from the local government, were a key Mongol legacy in the Ming political system. In addition to Shanxi, princely institutions were strong in most northern provinces, including Shandong, Henan, and Shaanxi. The only exception was Hebei, which was in the immediate environment of the capital, Beijing. In contrast, the three most studied southern regions—the Lower Yangzi Delta or Jiangnan, the coastal province of Fujian, and the Pearl River Delta or Guangdong—had no principalities.[6] The development of these regions has shaped the traditional view of Chinese society in the late imperial period as having a strong civil government run by scholar-officials educated in the Neo-Confucian tradition, with corporate lineages in many places being the dominant social institution in local society.

Take Huizhou in the uplands of lower Yangzi valley as an example. According to Joseph McDermott's landmark study, lineages came to dominate their rival institutions in the Huizhou countryside in the early and

---

6. Notably, three interior southern provinces in the Ming—Jiangxi, Huguang, and Sichuan—had princely institutions throughout the dynasty. Both scholarly studies of princely institutions in Huguang and those of the socioeconomic history of the Jianghan Plain demonstrate that principalities and their agents there also acted as powerful forces in local society, appropriating land and other economic resources, hijacking local tax revenues, and forcing local peasants to become tenants of princely estates. See Satō, *Mindai ōfu no kenkyū*, 303–55; Lu, *Changjiang zhongyou de rendi guanxi*, 234–39, 242–45, and 390–94. Clearly, more empirical studies on these regions are needed to demonstrate whether their trajectories of social change in the Ming are similar to or significantly different from those in Jiangnan, Fujian, and the Pearl River Delta.

middle Ming by effectively capitalizing on government policies.[7] Lineage members took the opportunity to organize when the early Ming government supported Neo-Confucian calls for stronger kinship institutions. After the government's efforts to integrate village worship associations into the *lijia* (the village tithing system) had failed, people in Huizhou lineages stepped in. They transformed village worship associations from those based on territorial cults to those dominated by lineages, and they pressed hard to control the shrines of village alliances. The organization and activities of local cults thus came to rest on a foundation of lineages.[8] As Buddhist establishments declined under attacks by government authorities at both the central and local levels, groups in Huizhou lineages appropriated monks' landholdings and rebuilt Buddhist monasteries as lineages' ancestral halls. Although village worship associations and Buddhist establishments persistently resisted the expansion of lineages, both lost the battle. From the mid-sixteenth century onward, corporate lineages rapidly became the dominant institution in Huizhou villages. Their newly established ancestral halls helped members of some lineages attain a collective preeminence as the wealthiest regional group of merchants in Ming China.

For Shanxi, it was a different story. The protracted competition among rival local institutions exhibited distinctive features both before and after the mid-sixteenth century. In the early and middle Ming, wealth and power were concentrated in one special category of lineages, the imperial and commandery principalities—which lent crucial support to the clergy and their establishments. By making Buddhist and Daoist establishments their clan cloisters, the princes formed patron-client relations with the clergy, in which the clergy acted as the agents of one or several affiliated principalities to occupy and manage local temples, landholdings, and other resources within the principalities. In return, the clergy and their establishments received princely patronage, which helped them resist the attacks of local civil government and rival institutions, including the state-mandated *lijia* organizations and village organizations based on local cults. This suggests that many competitions among rival local institutions

7. McDermott, *The Making of a New Rural Order*, 169–234.

8. This trend also occurred in Fuzhou, in Fujian province. See Szonyi, *Practicing Kinship*, 199.

in the early Ming were struggles among state-imposed institutions that represented the interests of, respectively, the civil government and the regionalized princely houses.

Only in the mid-sixteenth century, after the strength of princely institutions waned and the authority of local civil government increased, did organized religions ultimately lose the battle. Yet the outcome of the battle was different from that in the south: it was not corporate lineages but territorial village organizations based on local cults that claimed the final victory.[9] These organizations, as the major rival of lineages and organized religions, had existed in Shanxi at least since the Northern Song dynasty. Their formation was profoundly embedded in local socioeconomic life, characterized by a chronic shortage of water—the resource vital for agriculture. Local traditions interpreted access to water, either in the form of canal water or natural rainfall, in an overwhelmingly religious framework: one or more local deities provided irrigation water or brought rainfall.

Cults of these local deities constituted the ideological repertoire for rural social organizations in Shanxi across dynasties, and the cult organizations provided permanent arenas for different individuals and forces to compete for local authority. While the relationship between territorial village organizations and Buddhist and Daoist organizations remained more or less cooperative in the Mongol era, with the clergy being supreme, the dynamic of power relations changed fundamentally in the post-Mongol era. The top-down social reconfiguration imposed by the state in the early Ming obscured a deep undercurrent of changes in local society, in which village organizations absorbed local Buddhist and Daoist establishments and turned them into community temples. Remember that Buddhist and Daoist organizations built very dense monastic networks that penetrated into almost every village in north China in the

---

9. Historians of late imperial China have provided various explanations for why corporate lineages were weak in the north. Some scholars emphasize that most northern lineages were economically poor. For instance, Li Wenzhi and Jiang Taixin have argued that while the lineages in the Pearl Delta, Fujian, and Jiangnan regions held 10–50 percent of the overall landholdings in the Qing period, northern lineages held less than 1–2 percent (*Zhongguo zongfa zongzuzhi*, 190–98). Some scholars shed light on the distinctive northern styles of lineage practices. See Cohen, *Kinship, Contract, Community, and State*; Han Chaojian, "Huabei de rong yu zongzu."

Mongol era. And a relatively cheap and common way for villagers to create a new temple was to use an already standing building. From the Yuan-Ming transition onward, villagers quietly transformed many monastic establishments into community temples of popular deities.

After the mid-sixteenth century, this undercurrent of social change turned into a visible one, and its confluence with other trends of changes contributed to the indisputable rise in Shanxi of territorial village organizations based on local cults. Many local inscriptions celebrated villagers' successful efforts to integrate Buddhist and Daoist institutions into villagers' practice of popular cults. In some cases, villagers created buildings for theatrical performances—the architectural marker of community temples—in Buddhist or Daoist monastic space. In other cases, community worship associations controlled Buddhist and Daoist establishments, monopolizing their property and taking charge of temple affairs. With the rampant commercialization of the rural economy, territorial village organizations based on local cults grew stronger, as they often won rural community competitions for new lucrative resources such as mountain timber and mines. Meanwhile, a gentry class whose power was based on the civil service examinations reemerged (one can say reemerged insofar as a similar group of local literati had existed in the Northern Song and Jin). Local gentry and wealthy merchants strategically chose to support and transform these village organizations as a way of claiming local authority, and their participation brought in leadership, funding, and helpful social resources.

As with the Yuan inscriptions, we should not take at face value the local laypeople's exultant rejection of clerical influence that we find in Ming sources. Ming inscriptions grew out of processes in which the voices competing with the clergy had access to power, and thus the existence of those voices increasingly emerges in the inscriptions. Nonetheless, the dominance of such voices in Ming inscriptions corresponds to a new pattern of social change in Shanxi after the middle of the sixteenth century: territorial village organizations that were based on local cults and controlled by the laity and often led by local gentry became the dominant social institution in the rest of the late imperial period. It is probably only at this point that we might begin to speak of a convergence of northern and southern social orders in terms both of lay-clerical relations and of the local elite's lifestyle and relationship to local communities.

Regional Diversity in Social Change

We have seen how and why northern and southern China differed in their social transformations in the four centuries following the Mongol conquest. However, the contrast between the north and the south raises new questions. Did other less-studied Chinese regions fall into either of these two patterns, or did they develop their own distinctive ones? Methodologically, how should we study regional diversity in middle-period China, when available local sources are so much scarcer than those from the late imperial period?

Emphasizing what he calls the village quartet, McDermott has provided a helpful conceptual framework for analyzing various paths of social and economic transformation in rural China since the Northern Song.[10] As he argues, by no later than the eleventh century, four different kinds of village institutions—village worship associations, Buddhist and Daoist temple communities, popular cult shrines, and large kinship associations—had begun to compete for wealth and influence, with different kinds of institutions becoming dominant from region to region. The outcome was the coexistence throughout the Chinese empire of a variety of social orders composed of similar if not identical components. After the mid-Ming, market-driven social and economic changes encouraged a nationwide integration in late imperial China. However, this integration consisted not of the spread or repetition of a single form of social order but rather of a great range of regional variations in the arrangement and hierarchy of these four types of institutions.

While this book is consistent with McDermott's framework in explaining the historical formation of the rural order in Shanxi by the mid-Ming, it differs in using for its analytical setting not the village but a broader macroregional level. This approach brings intraregional and cross-regional networks of people and institutions into an analytical framework. It allows us to see the changes in social order at both a horizontal level (the development of large translocal organizations such as literati societies and organized religions in a given dynasty) and a vertical level (the long-lasting competition among different institutions in a given

10. McDermott, "The Village Quartet."

locality across dynasties). By exploring both horizontal and vertical levels of change, and particularly their interactions, we can gain a more comprehensive understanding of why and how diverse social transformations took place in different macroregions. At both levels, as this book shows, northern Chinese elites and their institutions relied heavily on state patronage for legitimacy, foregrounding the role of the imperial state in long-term social transformation.

I argue that we need to approach the question of regional diversity by studying the interplay of two simultaneous processes that shaped social change in middle-period China. From the top down, we witness a profound restructuring of state-society relations. From the bottom up, in contrast, we see a dramatic reconfiguration of the hierarchy of local institutions that constituted a particular region's social order. Top-down action, either as a direct outcome of the governing political system or as a state response to social pressures, delineated the parameters of the state-sanctioned power that was legally enjoyed by social actors. And the bottom-up change determined the participants in and the platforms for enduring local competition over power, beliefs, and wealth. Local elites were often involved in both processes and helped integrate them in shaping local norms and practices—the changes in which ultimately transformed the fabric of local society.

In terms of the top-down restructuring of state-society relations, the Mongol conquest marked a critical moment in the second millennium of Chinese imperial history. During the reigns of the first four Mongol khans, the Mongols willingly delegated much local governance to influential and compliant leaders of Chinese local groups, as long as the latter paid the tribute levies and organized labor service for specific tasks and military duty for the Mongols' campaigns. As a result, the Mongols yielded significant administrative authority and responsibility to autonomous local groups like organized religious institutions. Khubilai Khan created a more centralized bureaucratic government and reclaimed some autonomous power from local institutions, but he did not fundamentally change the Mongols' practice of decentralized rule. The Yuan emperors and other Mongol nobles continuously granted authority to a variety of actors and let those actors compete among themselves, with the result being many different forms of local society.

It is worth pointing out that what happened in China was one facet of a Eurasian-wide pattern of governance and administration under the Mongol empire. The generally decentralized nature of the political order in the Mongol state in Greater Iran, for instance, was even more obvious than in Yuan China. Before Hülegü's creation of the Persian Ilkhanate in 1256, the Mongol state in Greater Iran also followed the traditional steppe pattern of rule by entrusting administration to various local notables who had submitted to the Great Khan and sent yearly tribute to the Mongol court. Like Yuan China, the Ilkhanate built a relatively effective central government mainly by implementing a unified fiscal policy to bring lucrative local taxes into the state coffers. Yet the general political order was still decentralized, as evidenced by the continued existence of tributary local dynasties or hegemony that retained political autonomy.[11]

Equally important, the early Ming drastically redefined and reconfigured state-society relations, tightening the administrative power of the state apparatus and returning to the Chinese imperial tradition of centralized rule. Furthermore, the early Ming embarked on what Peter Bol describes as a "statist enterprise" to mandate social transformation, aiming to create a country of "largely self-sufficient rural communities whose moral, cultural, and social existence would be organized by state institutions under the tutelage of an all-powerful ruler."[12]

There is, however, an overlooked piece in this narrative of state activism: the multiplicity of state institutions. In addition to state institutions—such as the well-studied *lijia* organizations, community schools, and city-god temples—that were supervised by the regular government, the Ming also inherited the Mongol legacy of creating state institutions like principalities that were given legitimacy and power due to their personal relations with the emperor. The Ming allowed these institutions to continue to pursue their private interests at the cost of local government's administrative authority and the well-being of local people. As this book has shown, some local forces allied themselves with one state institution against another. We must revise our picture of an overwhelming

11. See Kolbas, *The Mongols in Iran*, 375–80; Aigle, "Iran under Mongol Domination."

12. Bol, "The 'Localist Turn,'" 2.

early-Ming state that transformed all of Chinese society. From the six-teenth century on, the early-Ming statist activism, as Bol points out, ceased to exist, and a localist turn took over. This shift saw the burgeon-ing of all kinds of bottom-up social institutions and subsequently the emergence of a new social order—or, more precisely, new social orders—in different regions depending on the result of competition among vari-ous institutions.[13]

From a bottom-up perspective, this book provides an important guide for understanding the social transformations of China across dynasties. In short, victorious institutions often functioned as social mechanisms for generating and redistributing wealth on a broad scale. Many of these institutions had one thing in common: they were tax havens, thanks to the imperial state's grant of tax-exempt status. In north China under the Song and Jin, the literati class had access through civil service examina-tions to a state-based wealth-redistribution system. In this system, the of-ficial schools generated wealth from tax-free landholdings granted by the state, and this wealth was redistributed among teachers and students in form of annual stipends. Also, literati who passed the examinations and became officials received salaries from the state and were exempt from the duty of labor service, which enabled their families to accumulate much agricultural wealth. While these families occasionally contributed to local public services, they redistributed their wealth mostly among their kin or peers by donating land to local schools.

After the Mongols ended this Song-Jin practice, state-sanctioned religions quickly rose as new social mechanisms for circulating and dis-tributing wealth in the north. Both Buddhist and Daoist monasteries controlled substantial landholdings, industries, and businesses, all of which generated considerable tax-free income. Some of their wealth came di-rectly from state actors—including Mongol rulers, nobles, and local gov-ernors—in the form of grants; some came from the two religions' own economic enterprises and mutual appropriations; and some came from local people's donations, often given for the sake of avoiding heavy tax

13. Bol's study focuses on literati-centered institutions. In contrast, Kishimoto Mio points out that all types of vertical associations (based on relations of people's de-pendence on the personal authority of officials or gentry) and horizontal associations (based on relations of equality among people who formed an alliance) spread widely among both elites and commoners (*Min Shin kōtai to kōnan shakai*, 4–10).

burdens. Extensive wealth thus came under the control of the two religions and was redistributed to men and women belonging or attached to their institutions, including many former Jin literati.

The clergy's social activism in north China under Mongol rule greatly resembled local literati activism in the south in the Southern Song, Yuan, and late Ming periods, though with a critical difference. While the clergy's social activism in the north depended heavily on formal governmental authorization and financial support, local literati activism in the south was largely autonomous, both ideologically and economically. Ideologically, it was endorsed and justified by the increasingly influential Neo-Confucianism. Economically, it relied much less on input from the state and more on commercial and agricultural wealth in private hands.

Due to the lack of sustainable and independent wealth, most northern literati in the Ming continued to rely on the revived state-based wealth-redistribution system through schools, exams, and families, unlike their southern counterparts. Meanwhile, principalities (and, in some places, military institutions) replaced monasteries as powerful wealth-gathering institutions as well as tax shelters for other social groups in many northern provinces. Yet principalities in general were not concerned with public welfare, unlike the literati and clergy. The principalities functioned much less as a wealth-redistributing system to provide public services for local society than they did as a system for extracting extensive wealth and resources from local society primarily for the sake of their private interests—particularly for supporting a lifestyle of luxury among imperial clansmen and clanswomen.

Only after the sixteenth century did increasing commercialization allow many northerners, especially merchant and literati families, to accumulate considerable private commercial and agricultural wealth as southerners had been doing for centuries. In this context we see the emergence of village organizations based on local cults, especially those institutions sponsored or directly led by local gentry and increasingly powerful merchant groups, as a new wealth-distributing system in Shanxi's rural society. While this book has briefly touched on this emerging order in the late imperial period, it is essentially a story for another monograph.

At this point, it is natural to ask whether, in addition to the activism of the state, literati, and clergy, other major patterns of social dominance existed in middle-period Chinese society (for instance, activism on the

part of the military and merchants). Of course, social dominance does
not necessarily mean that one pattern excludes the others. We need to
ask how different forms of social activism interacted with one another to
shape the formation of similar or diverse social orders in different regions.
Answers to these questions must await more extensive local and regional
research. Given the multifaceted nature of regional diversity, this book
calls for future synthetic analysis to draw on not one or two but a wide
range of regional narratives, including but not limited to perspectives such
as north and south, heartlands and hinterlands, and Han majority and
minority regions.

APPENDIX I

List of Unpublished Stele Inscriptions Used in This Book

I. From the Palace of Eternal Joy, Ruicheng
county, Shanxi province

1. Rear side of the stele "Chongxiu da chunyang wanshou gong bei" 重修大純陽萬壽宮碑, dated 1262.
2. Rear side of the stele "Piyun Song zhenren citang beiming" 披雲宋真人祠堂碑銘, dated 1263.
3. Rear side of the stele "Yuan huang baofeng wuzu qizhen zhici bei" 元皇褒封五祖七真之辭碑, dated 1317.
4. "Chunyang wanshou gong tidian xiayuan tiandi changzhuhu ji" 純陽萬壽宮提點下院田地常住戶記, dated 1324.

II. Others

1. Wang Liyong 王利用, "Xuantong hongjiao piyun zhenren daoxing zhi bei" 玄通弘教披雲真人道行之碑, dated 1320. A transcription from its rubbing, which is preserved at the Chinese National Library in Beijing.
2. "Gu ronglu dafu dasitu Da chengtian husheng si zhuchi qian Wutai Da wansheng youguo si zhuchi Baoyun pumen zongzhu Guanghui miaobian shuzong hongjiao dashi Yingong beiming" 故榮祿大夫大司徒大承天護聖寺住持前五臺大萬聖佑國寺住持寶雲普門宗主廣慧妙辯樹宗弘教大師印公碑銘, dated 1339. Yamamoto Meishi 山本明志 generously shared his transcription with the author.

3. "Da Yong'an si ji" 大永安寺記, dated 1349. Now at the Monastery of Eternal Peace, Hengshan village, Dingxiang county, Shanxi province.

4. Guo Xuan 郭瑄, "Chongxiu Yong'an si ji" 重修永安寺記, dated 1429. Now at the Monastery of Eternal Peace.

5. Qiao Zhen 喬震, "Chongxiu Yong'an si ji" 重修永安寺記, dated 1491. Now at the Monastery of Eternal Peace.

6. Li Nan 李楠, "Chongxiu Hongfu si ji" 重修洪福寺記, dated 1608. Now at the Hongfu Monastery at Liuhui village, Dingxiang county, Shanxi province.

7. "Xinzhou jiuyuan xiang wencun Chongming si tiewen bei" 忻州九原鄉溫村崇明寺帖文碑, dated 1611. Now at the Chongming Monastery at Wen village, Xinzhou, Shanxi province.

8. "Chongxiu beishe Hongfu si bei" 重修北社洪福寺碑, dated 1622. Now at the Hongfu Monastery.

APPENDIX 2

Translation of Inscriptions on the 1300 Liang Stele and the 1310 Miaoyan Stele

I. "The Stele of Master Liang's Filial Conduct"
亮公孝行之碑

I have heard about a precious Buddhist place that is well known in China and documented in sutras. This place is where the wondrous Bodhisattva Mañjuśrī resides. At this place lived my father named Liang, who has an honorary title of Master Tongli [comprehending the principle], and my mother Lady Guo. The master bows down to Earth and looks up to Heaven with great respect. He humbly rectifies his mind and carefully cultivates his conduct. He has no confusion internally nor heretical behaviors externally. His morality has impressed Heaven and Earth, and he has received responses from divine powers. This is the morality of the master. Once upon a time when the master was about to fall asleep, a monastic tutelary deity came to say the following words aloud to him, "You have morality and filial conduct. I thus grant you a miraculous turtle." The master consented happily and thanked the deity with deep gratitude. Then the master woke up in awe. This is indeed a wonder. The master followed the instruction of the deity and visited the foot of Dragon Mountain in person. There, he found a miraculous turtle emerging from the earth. The turtle prophesied the long-lasting honor and prosperity [of the family] as well as the birth of a dharma child [meaning a child who will later become a Buddhist monk]. The master's father told him, "It is hard for a son to repay his parents' hardship. If you do not practice

Buddhism in this life, how can you repay your parents?" The master then donated his wealth to hire skilled craftsmen to carve a stone stele to repay the abundant favor of his parents. The master was blessed and his filial conduct completed. He then fathered three sons and a daughter. 竊聞佛堂寶地，名喧震旦神洲，有經爲證。妙吉祥文殊菩薩居住處，恭惟父諱亮，號曰通理大師。母曰郭氏。俯懷翼翼，仰叩蒼蒼。肅恭其心，慎修其行。內不回惑，外無異妄。動天地，應神明，師之道德也. 師之欲寢，朗然伽藍報曰：「汝有道德孝行，賜汝神龜。」師之允諾懽然，則禮深若賀謝。悚然而覺，誠可奇哉。師依教訓，親詣龍山之麓，果然地涌神龜，爲萬載之榮昌，更爲法子之後記。父謂子曰「父母苦勞，難可報耳。今世若不修持，異日將何報答？」由是特捨己財，專命良工刊石鐫碑□ 酬厚德。神明加祐，孝行廣備。遂生三子一女。

The eldest son is Zhongyu, who married Lady Li. Their daughter married Tan Derang. Zhongyu had a reputation for his filial conduct, and he read broadly. He was benevolent, righteous, wise, and kind. He was as kindhearted as Yanzi, yet did not have the longevity of Daozhi. He died early like Yanzi, but committed no evils like Daozhi did.[1] 長曰仲遇，妻李氏。女適檀德讓。孝行揚名，廣涉典文。有仁有義，智慧溫良。有顏子之惠，無盜跖之壽。有顏子之夭，無盜跖之惡。

The second son is Zhiyu, whose honorary title is Master Bianyi [eloquence and righteousness]. Zhiyu is naturally strict with himself and lenient to others. He hands out alms to show sympathy for the widowed and orphaned. He comprehends the Three Teachings [Confucianism, Buddhism, and Daoism] and profoundly understands the Five Vehicles.[2] He handles disputes with rewards and punishments like Gaotao did, and

---

1. Yanzi and Daoizhi were two historical figures living in the same era in ancient China. Yanzi was a virtuous student of Confucius and died young. Daozhi was a rebel known for doing evil things, but he lived a long time. The contrast in the fates of Yanzi and Daozhi was a classic allusion used to explain the unfairness in life.

2. The "Five Vehicles 五乘" is a Buddhist term, referring to five kinds of teaching that bring people to particular stages of attainment. The Five Vehicles are the vehicles of humans 人乘 (enabling the rebirth among men conveyed by observing the five precepts), gods 天乘 (rebirth among the gods by the ten forms of good action), obedient disciples 聲聞乘 (rebirth among Buddhist disciples by adherence to the four noble truths), self-enlightened ones 緣覺乘 (rebirth among self-englightened ones by contemplation of twelvefold dependent arising), and bodhisatta 菩薩乘 (rebirth among the buddhas and bodhisattvas by the practice of the six perfections).

his filial conduct resembles that of Zengcan.[3] His heart is like a precious mirror that reflects shades and forms of everything. His deeds and accomplishments have brought him the official rewards of a seal and a silk ribbon attached to the seal. Zhiyu repaired Buddhist halls, enlarged monastic buildings, . . . [4] murals and statues. As a result, it was as if the Buddha and the lotus world had been moved to the World of Clearness and Coolness [that is, Mt. Wutai]. Everyone was surprised and happy. In the year of Jiashen [1284], Zhiyu built a multistory stupa and named it "Tall and Magnificent." The stupa connects to the golden water below and the blue clouds above. The dust touches . . . ascend to Heaven. In the Yuanzhen reign [1295–97], Zhiyu received two golden decrees from Prince Babusha. Zhiyu is like a talented gentleman and a loyal general in the Buddhist order. As to his literary talent, he has long comprehended the nature and outward manifestation of everything. As to his military talent, he is a person of outstanding ability in the world. In . . . year during the Dade era [1297–1307], Zhiyu donated his private wealth to the Monastery of Eternal Peace specifically to remake an ancestral tablet. He also donated a gold-plated Buddha image. In doing so, he intended to repay the favor of his parents who gave birth to him and raised him. Then, in the fourth year of the Dade era [1300], Master Zhiyu was specially appointed the sangha chancellor of Fenzhou subprefecture and occupied an official position of rank 5a. His family's reputation is celebrated. [It is] rich and titled, [it merits] songs of splendor, and ballads tell of its pleasure upon pleasures. His fame extends across the whole country. In the same year [1300], Zhiyu hired people to cut a stone and inscribe the stele. Auspicious signs appeared. There were more than ten thousand contributors, and the stele cost more than fifty ingots. People tried to carry the stone stele yet failed to move it. Zhiyu then stepped forward. He burned incense and prayed, "I pray for a blessing from the saint and the eight groups of spiritual beings [Buddhist tutelary deities]." Suddenly, a sound like thunder came from the sky. Clouds and fog emerged from nowhere. The stele was lifted up in the air and moved to the Merit-Worship Chapel by the working of supernormal powers. People called it "the miraculous

---

3. Gaotao was a well-known judge in ancient legends, and Zengcan was a student of Confucius known for filial piety.

4. Ellipsis points indicate that some text is no longer present on the stele.

stele." Zhiyu's profound merit also elicited the appearance of a miraculous turtle and five-colored lights with immeasurable magnificence. Two miraculous and auspicious turtles were born in the same cave. Zhiyu fulfilled the good omen of Master Liang's dream. No one had seen such a thing before. Isn't it rare? Isn't it extraordinary? [Zhiyu's merit] will exist forever and facilitate the prosperity of his descendants until the stele falls and his name disappears. 次曰智裕，號曰辯懿大師，天然賦性，克己安人。賑恤鰥寡，孤獨矜憐，深通三教，義□　五乘。有賞有罰兮，似臬陶理訟。有孝有行兮，猶若曾參。心同寶鏡，窺影窺形。舉措建功，有印有綬。由是修葺殿宇廣廈□廡於□　繪塑，有若金山華藏移來清凉世界。人人驚□　，個個歡心。甲申之歲，建層層萃堵波，號曰高顯。下連金水，上聳青云，塵沾離□□　影生天後。至元貞特授八不砂□□　金寶令旨二道。釋門奇士，將帥忠良。論文則久韜性相，論武則蓋世英才。大德□　年特捨己財，請永安寺內重建祖宗牌額一面，渾金聖像一堂。欲報出世恩，當酬養育德。復於大德四年特授汾州僧正，官□　五品之余，門闌有慶，富貴榮歌，謠盡喜喜，邂逅懼心，名傳四海，聲震八方。同年刊石鐫碑，現祥奇瑞。論功則萬有馀人，論賄則五十馀錠。欲行運載，全然不動。師乃向前焚香禱曰："願聖如持，龍天護佑。"駭然空中作嚮，有若天雷，雲生霧長，從空而起。神功運轉，斯者還歸。號曰神碑。師之恩厚，感得靈龜。五色光生，燦爛萬種。奇祥二龜，同生一穴。師乃應夢之祥。具眼未聞，可不希哉？　可不罕哉？欲留永播後代之榮昌，石隕名毀纔然□　矣.

The third son is Zhize, whose honorary title is Master Guanghui [extensive kindness]. His reputation spreads far, and his outstanding wisdom is like the jade from Zhong Mountain and fine stones from the Si River . . . not make jade in the mountain more, and quarrying chime stones from the river does not make fine stones less. He is benevolent and virtuous. He respects his parents and maintains harmony with others. He is capable of setting up family property and being lavish in his [patronage of] ritual and music. He has great wisdom but conceals it like the guard of the stone gate.[5] It is the ultimate attainment. 次三曰智澤，號曰廣慧大師，

---

5. "The guard of the stone gate" is a classical allusion to the *Analects* 14:38. The passage says, "Zilu stayed for the night at the Stone Gate. The gatekeepers said, 'Where are you from?' Zilu said, 'I am from Confucius's household.'—'Oh, is that the one who keeps pursuing what he knows is impossible?'" The phrase has been used to refer to someone who is worthy. See Confucius, *The Analects of Confucius*, 72.

弘名遠播，智群猶鐘山之玉，泗濱之石。行道□　不爲之盈，采浮磬不爲之索。
有仁有義，敬親和睦，能置家業，禮樂豐焉。有智潛形，石門晨守，可爲至也.

Grandsons: Daoyin, Daoqi, Daojie, Daofa 孫道印　道玘　道傑　道法

Great-grandsons: Decai, Deli 重孫德才　德禮

County-recommended scholar: Liu Haoran, Li Jujing, Wang Gongguan 鄉貢進士劉浩然　李局敬　王恭觀

Composed by Monk Fu, Master Hui'an [kindness and peace], who
has received the imperial bestowal of a Red Cassock, Lecturer of
Sutras, *Vinayas*, and Commentaries at the Cloister of True Countenance of the Great Garland Monastery on Mt. Wutai 五臺山大華嚴
寺眞容院講經律論、賜紅沙門惠安大師福吉祥撰

Calligraphy by Monk Chao, Master . . . who has received the imperial bestowal of a Red Cassock, Lecturer of Sutras, *Vinayas*, and
Commentaries, Chief Sangha Judge on Mt. Wutai 五臺山都僧判、
講經律論、賜紅沙門□□　大師潮吉祥書

Edited by Monk Jiao, Master Fazhao [Dharma illumination] who has
received the imperial bestowal of a Red Cassock, Lecturer of Sutras,
Vinayas, and Commentaries, Senior Monk who confers precepts
for bodhisattvas and monks in the world, Chief Supervisor of the
Buddhist Supervisory Office at Mt. Wutai and Other Circuits
Appointed by the Emperor 宣授五臺等路釋教都總攝、天下臨壇大
德、傳大乘戒、講經律論、賜紅沙門法照大師教吉祥校正

Calligraphy of the stele title written by Monk Zhi, Master Miaoyan
[wonderful and glorious], who has received the imperial bestowal of
a Red Cassock, Lecturer of Sutras, *Vinayas*, and Commentaries,
Senior Monk who confers precepts for bodhisattvas and monks in
the world, Chief Supervisor of the Buddhist Supervisory Office at
Mt. Wutai and Other Circuits Appointed by the Emperor 宣授五臺
等路釋教都總攝、天下臨壇大德、傳大乘戒、講經律論、賜紅沙門妙嚴
大師志吉祥篆

Stone erected on the fifteenth day of the eighth leap month in 1300 by
Monk Yu, Master Bianyi from the Cloister of True Countenance of
the Great Garland Monastery at Mt. Wutai, Acting Sangha Chancellor of Fenzhou subprefecture 大德四年閏八月望日五臺山大華嚴寺
眞容院行汾州僧正辯懿大師裕吉祥立石

II. "The Stele of Kind Conduct to Master
Miaoyan, the Chief Supervisor of the Buddhist
Supervisory Office at Mt. Wutai and Other
Circuits Appointed by the Emperor"
宣授五臺等處釋教都總攝妙嚴善行之碑

> Calligraphy by Xing Yunxiu, Head Instructor of Confucian School,
> County-Recommended Scholar in Dingxiang county, Xinzhou
> subprefecture, Jining circuit 冀寧路忻州定襄縣鄉貢進士、管領儒學
> 教諭邢允修書
>
> Composed by Monk Fu, Master Yuanzhao [perfect illumination]
> who has received the imperial bestowal of a Red Cassock, Lec-
> turer of Sutras, *Vinayas*, and Commentaries, Monk who confers
> precepts for bodhisattvas and monks at the Cloister of True Coun-
> tenance of the Great Garland Monastery on Mt. Wutai 五臺山大華
> 嚴寺菩薩眞容院傳大乘戒、講經律論、賜紅沙門圓照大師福吉祥撰
>
> Calligraphy of the stele title by Monk Yan of Moon-Rock, Master of
> Xuanjiao-guangguo [propagating the Buddhist teaching and glori-
> fying the state] who has received the imperial bestowal of a Red
> Cassock, Lecturer of Sutras, *Vinayas*, and Commentaries, Monk
> who confers precepts for bodhisattvas and monks, Abbot of the
> Great Buddhist Monastery of Myriad Sacred Beings that Support
> the Kingdom, Chief Supervisor of the Buddhist Supervisory Office
> at Mt. Wutai and Other Circuits Appointed by the Emperor 宣授五
> 臺等處釋教都總攝、大萬聖佑國寺住持、傳大乘戒、講經律論、賜紅沙
> 門宣教光國大師月岩嚴吉祥篆

The fathomless ocean of enlightenment is clear and still. Thoughts shape
the enlightenment like the wind causes waves. One's mind is like a gem,
which is originally translucent and bright yet loses its glory because of the
passion of desire. If one expects to return to the original state of his
mind, he must restore the light. Previously, on the day of the summer
solstice in the third year of the Zhida reign [1310], Zhiyu, whose honorary
title is Master Bianyi, wanted to repay the endless favor he had received
from Heaven. The teaching of the Buddha has spread everywhere in the
world and embraced everything. Its great power is unfathomable, and its
virtuous wisdom is limitless. It is oriented toward compassion and realized

through expedient means. The ferry of Buddha-truth saves all sentient beings, and the great all-round mirror illuminates the four directions. The Great Guide [Buddha] helps those who are lost escape from the ford of delusion; the Great Lord of Healing offers remedy for all suffering. The Buddha's treasury of light can destroy the chain of transmigration . . . [6] clean up the love and desire of all sentient beings. Precious flowers in the Pure Land can gather all the fragrance of wonderful offerings, and the Pure Lotus Land is enough . . . the joyful kingdom for human beings and heavenly gods. 覺海澄源，因識風而鼓浪。心珠朗耀，由愛水以沉輝。欲期返本，須要回光。昔歲在庚戌至大三年季夏至□ 有辯義大師智裕，欲酬無窮之恩，用荷昊天之德。惟大雄氏之教，瀰漫六合，包括萬有。威神莫測，福慧無方。以慈悲爲主，方便爲門。以法航兼濟一切，以大圓鏡遍照四方。脫穎迷津，則爲大導來。總藥諸苦，則爲大醫王。其光明藏足以破無始之□□　其□□□　足以滌有生之愛欲。其寶林花足以集眾香之妙供，其清蓮花蚸足以□人天之樂圈.

Thereby, Zhiyu responded to the profound grace of his father Master Liang, an eminent monk, who raised Zhiyu with hardship . . . and whose great virtue was like that of Heaven. Zhiyu embraced all monastic precepts. He read golden sutras widely and achieved extensive learning and wonderful knowledge. He probed morality and rose above the common herd. His moral conduct was ultimately pure, and . . . fortunate. Zhiyu thought that since he intended to free himself from any cause of worries, he should give up karmic relations that had tied him down. He was ultimately respectful and reliable. With a solemn rite, Zhiyu became a disciple of Master Fazhao, the Chief Supervisor of the Buddhist Supervisory Office at Mt. Wutai and Other Circuits. The master and the disciple suited each other perfectly. Both the clergy and the laity were infinitely blessed. The bright mind became translucent again, and the Buddhist teaching was restored. He spared no trouble to harmonize his heart and rode on the ferry of Buddha-truth. Zhiyu then left the sea of worries and gained the happiness of emptiness. His achievement was due to the vast favor of instructions by his teachers. Zhiyu has expounded and propagated his teachers' grace, and his own excellent integrity has also been exhibited. 由是荅荷深恩者，亮公大德和尚劬勞□ 厚德類昊天。受具足戒。金文廣覽，博學妙聞，研精道德，出俗超群。節行至潔□ 之幸也。□ 自行

---

6. Ellipsis points indicate that some text is no longer present on the stele.

思將欲脫塵勞之因，當舍系縛之緣。高崇至極，難足緣付。恭惟禮到五臺等處釋教都總攝法照大師爲受業師。師□　　相契，眞俗俱福。無斁融心，重明佛理。再整法航，出煩惱海，得無爲樂。蓋因師長教誨之鴻恩也。師恩既闡，至節洪彰.

At sometime between nine and eleven o'clock in the morning on the twentieth day of the fifth month in 1309, Monk Zhiyu paid his respects to a chief manager of governmental affairs at the Hall of Mashela [Mashal-lah?] of the Great Buddhist Monastery of Myriad Sacred Beings that Support the Kingdom. From Monk Yan, the chief supervisor and lecturer of this monastery, Zhiyu received a special decree from the crown prince. The decree says, "Zhang Zhiyu is the current sangha registrar of the Cloister of True Countenance at Mt. Wutai. Let him be the new sangha registrar of Mt. Wutai. You give this order to Zhiyu. This has been said." The chief supervisor [Monk Yan] handed this official document over to the sangha registrar [Monk Zhiyu] and completed his duty. Merit and karma crowded together, and the crown prince's favor was evident. Then, on the twenty-second day of the sixth month, Manager of Governmental Affairs (rank 1b) Anjing reported to carry out the crown prince's special decree, which says, "Summon Sangha Registrar Zhang Zhiyu and meet him at the Round Hall. Give him the original copy of this decree as well as a guarantee signed by monks from all monasteries at Mt. Wutai. Personally deliver a Buddhist garment to the sangha registrar. [To Zhiyu]: You wear it. This has been said." On the seventh day of the seventh month, Anjing— Grand Master of Imperial Entertainments with Silver Seal and Blue Ribbon, Manager of Governmental Affairs, and Commissioner of the Bureau of Gathering Merits—and Misami, Assistant Administrator of Jinjienu [meaning unknown], carried out the emperor's edict that reflected a decree issued by the empress dowager, which says, "Send Manager of Governmental Affairs Mangwuan to ride on a post-horse rushing to the Upper Capital to report to the emperor [things about Zhiyu], and let the emperor issue an edict." Thus, Zhiyu received the emperor's edict, which says, "Zhiyu is to be supervised under Monk Hai's name on Mt. Wutai, and be made the sangha registrar. This has been said." The grace of dharma . . . people from far and near all heard it. Zhiyu's fame has thus spread across the whole world. Everyone admires him and everywhere . . . is clear . . . fragrant. Externally, he has been known for his loyalty and filial piety; internally, he has expounded the . . . of Mahayana teaching . . . the greatest moral integrity. Zhiyu has protected the dharma sincerely and diligently. Both monks and the laity admire and respect him. He explores fundamental principles. His mind is in wonderful harmony with the original purity. He is intelligent by natural endowment, and is distinguished from others. . . . He numbers the first among all Buddhist monks for never slacking off on monastic laws. 是以歲在己酉至大二年五月二十日巳時，就大萬聖佑國寺馬舍剌殿前拜都平章，於本寺都總攝大師講主嚴吉祥根底特奉皇太子特旨：“五臺山菩薩眞容院見任僧錄張智裕，五臺山做嘗川僧錄者。你與□ 會者。麼道。” 總攝折遍時將照會文字與了僧錄。俱得圓備，福緣既奏，恩意彌彰。又至六月二十二日有安晉平章奏奉皇太子特旨：“宣至僧錄張智裕於圓殿內見了，親教元授到聖旨宣命幷臺山諸寺院師德保狀，將親教禪衣直裰僧錄。你披着。麼道。” 七月初七日，銀青榮祿大夫、平章政事、會福院使安晉，幷迷撒密同知金界奴奉御批奏皇太后懿旨：“遣使平章政事忙兀安馳驛赴上都聞奏皇帝，頒降宣諭。” 得聖旨：“這智裕根底但屬五臺山和尚根底管着，交做僧錄者。麼道。” 法恩□□ 遐邇咸聞。名傳四海□ 振八方。名傳四海□ 人人□ 仰□ 振八方□ 處處□ 折□□ 清激行□ 芬芳。外揚忠孝之名，內閣大乘之□□ 爲至節。精勤護法，僧俗欽崇。研窮理性，妙契本源。天資穎悟，毅然不群□□ 操而策□ 紀綱不爲懈倦，而釋門第一.

Zhiyu inherited the favor from Monk Zhi, Master Miaoyan, with granted . . . Cassock, the Chief Supervisor of the Buddhist Supervisory Office at Mt. Wutai and Other Circuits. Master Miaoyan was granted an official post that ranked at the second grade. He was an excellent monk in the Buddha Land and . . . in the Buddhist order. His knowledge of monastic precepts was profound, his appearance excelled all, and his complete sincerity influenced others. People came to provide offerings and donate money to him every day. Master Miaoyan's compassion protected the Buddha-truth unprecedentedly. He raised donations to repair halls and pavilions, paint and mold Buddha statues, carve statues of five hundred Arhats, and create a library with a gold-plated precious canon. He also contributed to building more than one hundred wing-rooms. 今則相承恩惠，緣有賜□ 衣□ 師五臺等處釋教都總攝妙嚴大師志吉祥，官封二品，禪門□□ 寶地芝蘭，深通戒律。顏息出群，至誠感格。送供者遂逐朝恒有，施賄者□ 日不絕。慈悲護法，邁古超今，未之有也。□□ 募緣大殿重閣，繪塑佛像，創刻五百羅漢，渾金妝飾寶藏，以成丈室。廊廡百十餘間，師之力也。

Emperor Yuzong (posthumous title of Crown Prince Zhenjin, Khubilai's eldest son) sent Commissioner Youlinzhen (Tibetan lama

Rin-cen-rgyal-mtshan) to visit Mt. Wutai to offer incense. Master Miaoyan was appointed as chief sangha registrar at Mt. Wutai because of his fine Buddhist cultivation. Soon, Emperor Shizu (Khubilai), who was holy and mighty in civil and military capacity, issued an edict, granting him the honorary title "Master Miaoyan" and again appointed him to the formal post. The master was generous and lenient; he broadly disseminated the Buddha's teaching for three years. The master had profound views on Buddhism and required extraordinarily strict discipline among his disciples. In the thirty-first year of Shizu (1294), the emperor (Temür, Emperor Chengzong) ascended the throne and received the mandate of Heaven. He issued an edict that ordered Monk Zhi, Master Miaoyan, from the Diamond Monastery . . . sangha registrar. In the second year of the Yuanzhen reign (1296), the empress dowager made a personal visit to Mt. Wutai. Master Miaoyan led monks from the Schools of Doctrines and Chan Buddhism to perform rites and chant sutras ceaselessly to expound the teaching of the sutras. A vision of lights like a bell appeared. Thus, the empress dowager issued a special decree, ordering monks to spread the dharma. At that time the Fourfold Assembly were happy.[7] In the third month of spring in the first year of the Dade reign (1297–1307), the emperor appointed Master Miaoyan to establish a Buddhist Supervisory Office over Zhending, Ping [Pingyang, southern Shanxi], Shaan [Shaanxi], Taiyuan, Datong, and Mt. Wutai. Master Miaoyan became the head of the office and was granted a silver seal by the emperor. Master Fazhao [Monk Jiao], the supervisor of Buddhist monasteries on two of the five terraces and the Cloister of True Countenance, also joined the office. 裕宗皇帝毓德春宮遣使有璘眞總管任侯詣臺山降香，師以行道精嚴□ 臺山都僧錄之職任焉。未幾世祖皇帝聖神文武，旨詔賜號妙嚴大師，復署前職。以師寬厚，廣演三季，見深玄敎，門軌則清潔甚奇。三十一年，皇帝嗣登寶位，體握乾符。有旨以五臺山金阹寺妙嚴大師志吉祥□□ 僧錄。元貞二年夏六月皇太后車駕親幸五臺。師仍率領敎禪師德禮念不暇，闡揚經敎，現鐘光相。由是特降懿旨，命僧傳法。爾時四眾懽喜。大德元年春三月，以眞定、平、陝、太原、大同、五臺等處用師創立釋敎總攝所，以師爲首。特賜銀印，兩臺與眞容總攝法照大師敎吉祥，皆篳也。

---

7. The "Fourfold Assemby" (*sizhong* 四眾) is a Buddhist term, referring to the four groups of Buddhist community, including monks, nuns, and male and female devotees.

At that time, the outstanding monk Zhiyu, son of Master Liang (Master Tongli) from Anheng village of Dingxiang county, built a Buddhist chapel, erected a stupa, and carved a filial-piety stele for his ancestors with dedication and diligence. Zhiyu used his own money to hire fine craftsmen to reinstall an ancestral tablet in the Great Monastery of Eternal Peace and donated a gold-plated Buddha image to the monastery. In the seventh year of the Dade reign (1303), Chief Supervisor of Diamond Monastery, Master Miaoyan, granted Zhiyu the honorary title "Bianyi" and named him Lecturer Yu Jixiang. Zhiyu's capacity promotes the Buddhist teaching in a splendid manner and helps those who were lost return to the proper path immediately. He propagates the teaching of the Three Vehicles and opens the eyes of wisdom to guide those who are blind (to the great vehicle).[8] He sits in meditation everywhere . . . and enters the mental state of concentration. Zhiyu wanted to repay the favor of his teacher, Master Miaoyan. He then carved a stone from Tuo Mountain at the Merit-Worship Chapel. The stele exalts only one of ten thousand achievements and virtues of the master. The master's name is Zhi, Miaoyan is his honorary title, and Yin his family name. His karma in this life was completed, and he entered nirvana permanently. . . . His wonderfulness is enduring and will not be lost. He is like the wise and the blessed yet little known among the venerated. It is no different from the bright lights that shine permanently without wonderful wisdom. It is also like the lovely moonlight, which could match the pure fire of the sun. In his whole day [of Buddhist cultivation] among monastic bells, how many of the sounds brought him a receptive audience? In his whole night [of Buddhist cultivation] among light and moon, who had a sharp eye [for his virtue]? When I asked Zhiyu about Master Miaoyan's deeds, he told me everything he knew. 是時定襄安橫里通理大師亮公子男智裕，僧中妙行，精勤建庵立塔，鐫刊祖宗孝行之碑。特捨己財，命良工重立大永安寺祖宗牌額一面。施到渾金佛像一堂。大德七年春三月，金吩總攝妙嚴大師賜法曰辯義大師講主裕吉祥。隨機沛教□ 迷途於目下。法演三乘，開慧目而誘引群盲。刹刹坐坐頭頭□□ 入三昧相。欲報師恩，於崇福庵匹佗山之石，發揚功行之萬一。云爾師諱志，妙嚴其號，殷氏其姓也。因緣既備，永附涅槃□然妙湛恒常不遁。如智福者，老耆無聞。何異燈光燦爛，豈透妙慧以恒明，月

---

8. The term "Three Vehicles" refers to the last three vehicles of the "Five Vehicles," including the vehicle of obedient diciples, self-enlightened ones, and bodhisatta.

色嬋□　　，敢對太陽眞火。盡日鐘魚間，嚮幾箇知音。通宵燈月交輝，何人具
眼。今者予叩妙嚴大師宗跡，知而不盡也。

I thus wrote the following inscription:
Buddhism is popular;
Monks come together in crowds.
The profound contemplation unfolds upon requiring;
. . . concentration.
Transform without being confined;
And move about freely.
The sound of the Buddha's teaching is spreading;
And people are free from worry everywhere.
A profoundly enlightened mind is noble;
An unstrained mind roams freely.
The glory of wisdom never dies;
It is manifested in the master's . . . profound practice.
Discuss extensively the absolute truth of the universe;
There is neither inside nor outside, and the truth is great.
Transcend the false . . . ;
This is the karma of doing something big.
His cultivation is unhindered;
His achievement cannot be concealed but is to be propagated.
Carve the stone to inscribe the inscription;
[He is] commemorated forever.

遂爲之銘曰：
　玄教風行　緇徒雲會　一叩禪開　□□　三昧　變動不拘　縱橫自在　雷音方馳
　　到處通泰　巍巍之寂靜妙明　心境之自在遊戲　莊嚴功成之不壞　顯現師
　　□　之妙用　廣談一眞之法吶　無內無外　其眞愈大　透脫虛□　是美作一
　　大事之因緣　煉無窒礙　闡揚功力難掩　勒石刊銘　萬世永賴

The formal Gentleman for Managing Affairs, Magistrate of Dingxiang
   county, the Adjunct Manager of Auruq and Agriculture Intendant
   Zhao Dewen 前承事郎、定襄縣尹、兼管諸軍奧魯、勸農事趙德溫
Monk Jiao, Master Fazhao, who has received the imperial bestowal of
   a Red Cassock, Lecturer of Sutras, *Vinayas*, and Commentaries,

Senior Monk who confers precepts for bodhisattvas and monks in the world, Chief Supervisor of the Buddhist Supervisory Office at Mt. Wutai and Other Circuits Appointed by the Emperor 宣授五臺等路釋教都總攝、天下臨壇大德、傳大乘戒、講經律論、賜紅沙門□師法照大師教吉祥

Monk Liang, Master Tongli 通理大師亮吉祥

Grandfather Zhang Weihai; Grandmothers Lady Dong and Lady Yang 祖父張文海祖母董　楊氏

Four sons: eldest son, formal . . . Wen; the next son, Monk Liang (Master Tongli); . . . ; the next son, formal clerk Zhang Zihao; the next son, Lay Buddhist Zhang Zi . . . 四男長前經□□□　溫次通理大師亮吉祥□　前司吏張子浩次安居士張子□

Grandsons: Zhongwei; Zhi . . . ; Zhongyi; Zhongkang; Formal Chief . . . Zhize; . . . Zhong . . . ; Zhongmin; . . . 孫仲威智□仲懿仲康前都□智澤□仲□仲珉□

Great-grandsons: . . . Zhixuan . . . Ding . . . 重孫□□□智宣□□定□□

Monk Jun, Master of Pine-Moon, Monk who confers precepts for bodhisattvas and monks, Master Xuanmi Chief Sangha Judge of Ten Monasteries at Mountain Gate of the Cloister of True Countenance on Mt. Wutai 五臺山眞容院前山門十寺僧統判、宣密大師、傳大乘戒、祖師松月道人俊吉祥

More than ten disciples . . . 門資降龍大□　正□□□　十餘人

Yang Anjing, Grand Master of Imperial Entertainments with Silver Seal and Blue Ribbon, Manager of Governmental Affairs, . . . Bureau of Buddhist and Tibetan Affairs, Bureau of Gathering Merits, Director of . . . 銀青榮祿大夫平章政事□　政院會福□□　領□□事楊安晉

Mangwua, Manager of Governmental Affairs 平章政事□　兀安

[Misami], Grand Master for Palace Attendance, Grand Academician Shanzhen . . . 中奉大夫□□　館大學士善珍司□□□　密□□　奉御□□□

In the third year of Zhida reign, the year of Gengxu (1310) . . . Zhiyu, a monk from the Cloister of True Countenance of the Great Garland Monastery on Mt. Wutai and the Chief Sangha Registrar

Appointed by the Emperor, erected the stone 昔大元至大三年歲次
上章閹茂南呂月□□□□ 人大華嚴寺菩薩眞容院僧、宣授五臺山都僧錄
辯義大師裕吉祥立石

　　The eldest son, formal Sangha Chancellor of Xinzhou subprefecture;
the next son, formal Chief . . . of Dingxiang county 長子前忻州僧正□　提
□□□ 次前定襄縣都□□□□□ 志

　　Grandson . . . 孫□□□□

Bibliography

Primary sources are listed by titles, and secondary sources are listed by author or editor.

Primary Sources

Caomu zi 草木子. Ye Ziqi 葉子奇 (fl. 1378). Beijing: Zhonghua shuju, 1959.

Chongxiu Guoxian zhi 重修崞縣志 [1607]. Liu Jiji 劉輯濟 et al. Facsimile copy held in the Kyoto University Institute for Research in Humanities Library.

Cunfuzhai ji 存復齋集. Zhu Derun 朱德潤 (1294–1365). Taipei: Xuesheng shuju, 1973.

Daojia jinshi lüe 道家金石略. Compiled by Chen Yuan 陳垣. Edited and supplemented by Chen Zhichao 陳智超 and Zeng Qingying 曾慶瑛. Beijing: Wenwu chubanshe, 1988.

Daoyuan xuegu lu 道園學古錄. Yu Ji 虞集 (1272–1348). Shanghai: Zhonghua shuju, 1936.

Datong fuzhi 大同府志 [1515]. Zhang Qin 張欽 et al. In *Sikuquanshu cunmu congshu* 四庫全書存目叢書, *Shi* 史, vol. 186. Jinan: Qilu shushe, 1996.

Dingxiang jinshi kao 定襄金石考 [1932]. Niu Chengxiu 牛誠修. 4 vols. Manuscript held in Sterling Memorial Library, Yale University, New Haven, CT.

Donglu Wangshi nongshu 東魯王氏農書. Wang Zhen 王禎 (fl. 1333). Annotated by Miao Qiyu 繆啓愉 and Miao Guilong 繆桂龍. Shanghai: Shanghai guji chubanshe, 2008.

Fenyang xian jinshi leibian 汾陽縣金石類編. Compiled by Wang Yuchang 王堉昌. Annotated by Wu Yuzhang 武毓章, Wang Xiliang 王希良, and Zhang Yuan 張源. Taiyuan: Shanxi guji chubanshe, 2000.

Fozu lidai tongzai 佛祖歷代通載. Nianchang 念常 (b. 1282). 1347. Reprinted in *Zhonghua zaizao shanben* 中華再造善本. Beijing: Beijing tushuguan chubanshe, 2005.

Guangshengsi zhi 廣勝寺志. Compiled by Hu Shixiang 扈石祥. Beijing: Zhongyang minzu xueyuan chubanshe, 1988.

Guiqian zhi 歸潛志. Liu Qi 劉祁 (1203–50). Edited by Cui Wenyin 崔文印. Beijing: Zhonghua shuju, 1983.

Hedong shuili shike 河東水利石刻. Compiled by Zhang Xuehui 張學會. Taiyuan: Shanxi renmin chubanshe, 2004.

Hongtong Jiexiu shuili beike jilu 洪洞介休水利碑刻輯錄. Compiled and edited by Huang Zhusan 黃竹三 and Feng Junjie 馮俊傑. Beijing: Zhonghua shuju, 2003.

Hongtong xian shuili zhi 洪洞縣水利志. Edited by Zheng Dongfeng 鄭東風. Taiyuan: Shanxi renmin chubanshe, 1993.

Hongtong xian shuili zhi bu 洪洞縣水利志補. Sun Huanlun 孫煥侖. Taiyuan: Shanxi renmin chubanshe, 1992.

Huoshan zhi 霍山志. Compiled by Shi Likong 釋力空. Taiyuan: Shanxi renmin chubanshe, 1986.

Jin Yuan Quanzhenjiao shike xinbian 金元全真教石刻新編. Compiled by Wang Zongyu 王宗昱. Beijing: Peking University Press, 2005.

Jincheng jinshi zhi 晉城金石志. Jinchengshi difangzhi congshu bianweihui 晉城市地方志叢書編委會. Hainan: Haichao chubanshe, 1995.

Jinshi 金史. Tuotuo 脫脫 (1313–55). Beijing: Zhonghua shuju, 1975.

Jinshi cuibian buzheng 金石萃編補正. Compiled by Fang Lüjian 方履籛. In *SSXB*, series 1, vol. 5.

Jinwen zui 金文最. Compiled by Zhang Jinwu 張金吾 (1787–1829). Taipei: Chengwen chubanshe, 1967.

Jiu Tangshu 舊唐書. Liu Xu 劉昫 (887–946). Beijing: Zhonghua shuju, 1975.

Liao Jin Yuan shike wenxian quanbian 遼金元石刻文獻全編. Compiled by the Beijing tushuguan shanben jinshizu 北京圖書館善本金石組. Beijing: Beijing tushuguan chubanshe, 2003.

Lingchuan xianzhi 陵川縣志 [1779]. Cheng Dejiong 程德烱 et al. Manuscript held in the Toyo Bunko, Tokyo.

Linxian guji kao 臨縣古蹟考. Compiled by Wu Mingxin 吳命新. In *SSXB*, series 3, vol. 31.

Lu'an fuzhi 潞安府志 [1619]. Hong Liangfan 洪良範 et al. Facsimile copy held in the Kyoto University Institute for Research in Humanities Library.

Lu'an fuzhi 潞安府志 [1770]. Zhang Shuqu 張淑渠 et al. In *SFJ*, vol. 30.

Mingdai menggu hanji shiliao huibian: Volume 5 明代蒙古漢籍史料彙編 (第五輯). Compiled by Wang Xiong 王雄. Huhehaote: Neimenggu daxue chubanshe, 2009.

Ming Qing Shanxi beike ziliao xuan 明清山西碑刻資料選. Compiled by Zhang Zhengming 張正明 and David Faure. Taiyuan: Shanxi guji chubanshe, 2005.

Ming Qing Shanxi beike ziliao xuan (xu yi) 明清山西碑刻資料選續一. Compiled by Zhang Zhengming, David Faure, and Wang Yonghong 王勇紅. Taiyuan: Shanxi guji chubanshe, 2007.

Mingshi 明史. Zhang Tingyu 張廷玉 (1672–1755). Beijing: Zhonghua shuju, 1974.

Ming shilu 明實錄. Zhongyang yanjiuyuan lishi yuyan yanjiusuo 中央研究院歷史語言研究所. 100 vols. Taipei: Academia Sinica, 1962.

Mu'an ji 牧庵集. Yao Sui 姚燧 (1238–1313). In *Congshu jicheng chubian* 叢書集成初編, vols. 2101–07. Shanghai: Shangwu yinshuguan, 1936.

Nancun chuogeng lu 南村輟耕錄. Tao Zongyi 陶宗儀 (1329–ca. 1412). Beijing: Zhonghua shuju, 1959.

Pingyang fuzhi 平陽府志 [1615]. Fu Shuxun 傅淑訓 et al. Facsimile copy held in the Kyoto University Institute for Research in Humanities Library.

Pingyang fuzhi 平陽府志 [1736]. Ting Gui 廷珪 et al. Manuscript held in Sterling Memorial Library, Yale University, New Haven, CT.

Puxian beiming zhi 蒲縣碑銘志. Compiled by Wang Juzheng 王居正. In *SSXB*, series 3, vol. 31.

Qingliangshan zhi 清涼山志. Zhencheng 鎮澄 (1546–1617). Edited by Li Yumin 李裕民. Taiyuan: Shanxi renmin chubanshe, 1989.

Qinshui beike soubian 沁水碑刻蒐編. Compiled by Jia Zhijun 賈志軍. Taiyuan: Shanxi renmin chubanshe, 2008.

Quan Liao Jin wen 全遼金文. Edited by Yan Fengwu 閻鳳梧. 3 vols. Taiyuan: Shanxi guji chubanshe, 2002.

Quan Yuan wen 全元文. Edited by Li Xiusheng 李修生. Nanjing: Jiangsu guji chubanshe, 1999–2001.

Ruicheng xianzhi 芮城縣志 [1764]. Yan Rusi 言如泗 et al. Manuscript held in the Toyo Bunko, Tokyo.

Ruicheng xianzhi 芮城縣志 [1997]. Compiled by Ruicheng xianzhi bianzuan weiyuanhui 芮城縣志編纂委員會. Xian: Sanqin chubanshe, 1997.

Sanjin shike daquan 三晉石刻大全. Liu Zeming 劉澤明 et al. Taiyuan: Sanjin chubanshe, 2009–2012.

———. *Jincheng shi Qinshui xian juan* 晉城市沁水縣卷. 2012. *DQ: Qinshui.*

———. *Jinzhong shi Lingshi xian juan* 晉中市靈石縣卷. 2010. *DQ: Lingshi.*

———. *Linfen shi Hongtong xian juan* 臨汾市洪洞縣卷. 2009. *DQ: Hongtong.*

———. *Linfen shi yaodu qu juan* 臨汾市堯都區卷. 2011. *DQ: Linfen yaodu.*

———. *Taiyuan shi jiancaoping qu juan* 太原市尖草坪區卷. 2012. *DQ: Taiyuan jiancaoping.*

———. *Taiyuan shi xinghualing qu juan* 太原市杏花嶺區卷. 2011. *DQ: Taiyuan xinghualing.*

———. *Xinzhou shi Ningwu xian juan* 忻州市寧武縣卷. 2010. *DQ: Ningwu.*

———. *Yangquan shi Yuxian juan* 陽泉市盂縣卷. 2010. *DQ: Yuxian.*

Sanjin shike zongmu: Yuncheng diqu juan 三晉石刻總目：運城地區卷. Wu Jun 吳均. Taiyuan: Shanxi guji chubanshe, 1998.

Shanxi dizhen beiwen ji 山西地震碑文集. Compiled by Wang Rudiao 王汝鵰. Taiyuan: Beiyue wenyi chubanshe, 2003.

Shanyou shike congbian 山右石刻叢編. Hu Pinzhi 胡聘之 (1840–1912). In *SSXB*, series 1, vols. 20–21.

Shike shiliao xinbian 石刻史料新編. Edited by the Xinwenfeng chuban gongsi bianjibu. 4 series. Taipei: Xinwenfeng, 1982–2006.

Song huiyao jigao 宋會要輯稿. Xu Song 徐松 (1781–1848). Beijing: Zhonghua shuju, 1957.

Songchuang mengyu 松窗夢語. Zhang Han 張瀚 (1510–1593). Edited by Sheng Dongling 盛冬鈴. Beijing: Zhonghua shuju, 2007.

Taiyuan fuzhi 太原府志 [1783]. Tan Shangzhong 譚尚忠 et al. In *SFJ*, vols. 1–2.

Taiyuan xianzhi 太原縣志 [1551]. Gao Ruxing 高汝行 et al. In *Tianyige cang Mingdai fangzhi xuankan* 天一閣藏明代方志選刊, vol. 3. Taipei: Xinwenfeng, 1985.

Tang huiyao 唐會要. Wang Pu 王溥 (922–82). Shanghai: Zhonghua shuju, 1955.

Tongzhi tiaoge jiaozhu 通制條格校注. Edited and annotated by Fang Linggui 方齡貴. Beijing: Zhonghua shuju, 2001.

Xinxiu Quwo xianzhi 新修曲沃縣志 [1758]. Zhang Fang 張坊 et al. Facsimile copy held in the Kyoto University Institute for Research in Humanities Library.

Yangqu xianzhi 陽曲縣志 [1843]. Li Peiqian 李陪謙 et al. In *SFJ*, vol. 2.

Yongle gong bihua 永樂宮壁畫. Edited by Xiao Jun 蕭軍. Beijing: Wenwu chubanshe, 2008.

Yongle gong zhi 永樂宮志. Zhang Yinong 張亦農 and Jing Kunjun 景昆俊. Taiyuan: Shanxi renmin chubanshe, 2006.

Yuan dianzhang 元典章. Edited by Chen Gaohua 陳高華, Zhang Fan 張帆, Liu Xiao 劉曉, and Dang Baohai 黨寶海. 4 vols. Tianjin: Zhonghua shuju, 2011.

Yuan Haowen quanji 元好問全集. Yuan Haowen 元好問 (1190–1257). Edited by Yao Dianzhong 姚奠中 and Li Zhengmin 李正民. Taiyuan: Shanxi guji chubanshem 2004.

Yuandai baihuabei jilu 元代白話碑集錄. Cai Meibiao 蔡美彪. Beijing: Kexue chubanshe, 1955.

Yuandai zouyi jilu 元代奏議集錄. Edited by Qiu Shusen 邱樹森 and He Zhaoji 何兆吉. 2 vols. Hangzhou: Zhejiang guji chubanshe, 1998.

Yuanshi 元史. Song Lian 宋濂 (1310–81). Beijing: Zhonghua shuju, 1976.

Yuanshi shifan 袁氏世範. Yuan Cai 袁采 (fl. 1140–95). Southern Song edition. Reprinted in *Zhonghua zaizao shanben* 中華再造善本. Beijing: Beijing tushuguan chubanshe, 2003.

Yuci xianzhi 榆次縣志 [1862]. Yu Shiquan 俞世銓 et al. In *SFJ*, vol. 16.

Zengding Hushan leigao 增訂湖山類稿. Wang Yuanling 汪元量 (1241–ca. 1318). Edited by Kong Fanli 孔凡禮. Beijing: Zhonghua shuju, 1984.

Zhaocheng xianzhi 趙城縣志 [1760]. Li Shengjie 李昇階 et al. In *Xijian Zhongguo difangzhi huikan* 稀見中國地方志彙刊. Beijing: Zhongguo shudian, 1992.

Zhaocheng xianzhi 趙城縣志 [1827]. Yang Yanliang 楊延亮 et al. In *SFJ*, vol. 52.

Zhongguo difangzhi jicheng: Shanxi fuxianzhi ji 中國地方志集成: 山西府縣志輯. Edited by Fenghuang chubanshe bianxuan 鳳凰出版社編選. 70 vols. Nanjiang: Fenghuang chubanshe, 2005.

Zhongzhou ji 中州集. Yuan Haowen. Beijing: Zhonghua shuju, 1959.

Secondary Sources

Aigle, Denise. "Iran under Mongol Domination: The Effectiveness and Failings of a Dual Administrative System." *Bulletin d'études orientales* 57, supplement (2006–7): 65–78.

Amano Motonosuke 天野元之助. "Chūgoku ni okeru suiri kankō" 中國における水利慣行. *Shirin* 38, no. 6 (1955): 123–49.

An Jiesheng 安介生. "Mingdai shanxi fanfu de renkou zengzhang yu shuliang tongji" 明代山西藩府的人口增長與數量統計, *Shixue yuekan* 5 (2004): 97–104.

Araki Toshikazu 荒木一敏. *Sōdai kakyo seido kenkyū* 宋代科舉制度研究. Kyoto: Dōhōsha, 1969.

Atwood, Christopher P. "Buddhists as Natives: Changing Positions in the Religious Ecology of the Mongol Yuan Dynasty." In *The Middle Kingdom and the Dharma Wheel: Aspects of the Relationship between the Buddhist Samgha and the State in Chinese History*, edited by Thomas Jülch, 278–321. Leiden, the Netherlands: Brill, 2016.

———. *Encyclopedia of Mongolia and the Mongol Empire*. New York: Facts On File, 2004.

———. "Mongols, Arabs, Kurds, and Franks: Rashīd al-Dīn's Comparative Ethnography of Tribal Society." In *Rashīd al-Dīn: Agents and Mediator of Cultural Exchanges in Ilkhanid Iran*, edited by Anna Akasoy, Charles Burnett, and Ronit Yoeli-Tlalim, 223–51. London: The Warburg Institute, 2013.

———. "Validation by Holiness or Sovereignty: Religious Toleration as Political Theology in the Mongol World Empire of the Thirteenth Century." *International History Review* 26, no. 2 (2004): 237–56.

Bai Wengu 白文固. "Lidai sengdao renshu kaolun" 歷代僧道人數考論. *Pumen xuebao* 9 (2002): 1–15.

Baldrian-Hussein, Farzeen. "Lü Tung-pin in Northern Song Literature." *Cahiers d'Extrême-Asie* 2 (1986): 133–69.

Baldwin, Michelle. "Wall Paintings of the Assembly of the Buddha from Shanxi Province: Historiography, Iconography, Three Styles, and a New Chronology." *Artibus Asiae* 54, nos. 3–4 (1994): 241–67.

Bira, Sh. "Qubilai Qa'an and 'Phags-pa La-ma." In Reuven and Morgan, *The Mongol Empire and Its Legacy*, 240–49.

Birge, Bettine. *Women, Property, and Confucian Reaction in Sung and Yuan China, 960–1368*. Cambridge: Cambridge University Press, 2002.

Bo Yongjian 卜永堅. "Yuandai de fodao chongtu: Yi Hebei weixian futu cun yuquan si bei wei zhongxin" 元代的佛道衝突: 以河北蔚縣浮圖村玉泉寺碑爲中心. *Huanan yanjiu ziliao zhongxin tongxun* 35 (2004): 17–31.

Bol, Peter. "Chao Ping-wen (1159–1232): Foundations for Literati Learning." In Tillman and West, *China under Jurchen Rule*, 115–44.

———. "The 'Localist Turn' and 'Local Identity' in Later Imperial China." *Late Imperial China* 24, no. 2 (2003): 1–50.

———. *Neo-Confucianism in History*. Cambridge, MA: Harvard University Asia Center, 2008.

———. "Seeking Common Ground: Han Literati Under Jurchen Rule." *Harvard Journal of Asiatic Studies* 47, no. 2 (1987): 461–538.

Boltz, Judith. *A Survey of Taoist Literature, Tenth to Seventeenth Centuries.* Berkeley, CA: Institute of East Asian Studies, 1987.

Bossler, Beverly. *Courtesans, Concubines, and the Cult of Female Fidelity: Gender and Social Change in China, 1000–1400.* Cambridge, MA: Harvard University Asia Center, 2013.

———. "'A Daughter Is a Daughter All Her Life': Affinal Relations and Women's Networks in Song and Late Imperial China," *Late Imperial China* 21, no. 1 (2000): 77–106.

———. *Powerful Relations: Kinship, Status, and the State in Sung China.* Cambridge, MA: Harvard University Asia Center, 1998.

Brook, Timothy. *Praying for Power: Buddhism and the Formation of Gentry Society in Late-Ming China.* Cambridge, MA: Harvard University Council on East Asian Studies and the Harvard-Yenching Institute, 1993.

Cai Meibiao 蔡美彪. *Basibazi beike wenwu jishi* 八思巴字碑刻文物集釋. Beijing: Zhongguo shehui kexue chubanshe, 2011.

———. *Liao Jin Yuan shi kaosuo* 遼金元史考索. Beijing: Zhonghua shuju, 2012.

Chaffee, John W. *Branches of Heaven: A History of the Imperial Clan of Sung China.* Cambridge, MA: Harvard University Asia Center, 1999.

———. "Chu Hs'i and the Revival of the White Deer Grotto Academy, 1179–1181 AD." *T'oung Pao* 71 (1985): 40–62.

———. *The Thorny Gates of Learning in Sung China: A Social History of Examinations.* Albany: State University of New York Press, 1995.

Chan, Hok-Lam 陳學霖. "From Tribal Chieftain to Sinitic Emperor: Leadership Contests and Succession Crises in the Jurchen-Jin State, 1115–1234." *Journal of Asian History* 33, no. 2 (1999): 105–41.

———. "Liu Ping-chung 劉秉忠 (1216–74): A Buddhist-Taoist Statesman at the Court of Khubilai Khan." *T'oung Pao* 53, nos. 1–3 (1967): 98–146.

———. "The Organization and Utilization of Labor Service under the Jurchen Chin Dynasty." *Harvard Journal of Asiatic Studies* 52, no. 2 (1992): 613–64.

Chang Jianhua 常建華. *Song yihou zongzu de xingcheng ji diyu bijiao* 宋以後宗族的形成及地域比較. Beijing: Renmin chubanshe, 2013.

Chao, Shin-Yi. "Daoist Examinations and Daoist Schools during the Northern Song Dynasty." *Journal of Chinese Religions* 31 (2003): 1–38.

———. "Good Career Moves: Life Stories of Daoist Nuns of the Twelfth and Thirteenth Centuries." *Nan nü* 10 (2008): 121–51.

Chen Gaohua 陳高華. "Yuandai chubanshi gaishu" 元代出版史概述. *Lishi jiaoxue* 11 (2004): 13–18.

———. "Yuandai de liumin wenti" 元代的流民問題. *Yuanshi luncong* 4 (1992): 132–47.

———. "Yuandai fojiao siyuan fuyi de yanbian" 元代佛教寺院賦役的演變. *Beijing lianhe daxue xuebao (renwen shehui kexueban)* 11, no. 3 (2013): 5–15.

———. "Yuandai nüxing de jiaoyou he qianxi" 元代女性的交遊和遷徙. *Zhejiang xuekan* 1 (2010): 80–84.

———. "Yuandai xinjian fosi lüelun" 元代新建佛寺略論. *Zhonghua wenshi luncong* 1 (2015): 31–65.

———. *Yuanshi yanjiu xinlun* 元史研究新論. Shanghai: Shanghai shehui kexueyuan chubanshe, 2005.

Chen Gaohua 陳高華, Zhang Fan 張帆, and Liu Xiao 劉曉. *Yuandai wenhuashi* 元代文化史. Guangzhou: Guangdong jiaoyu chubanshe, 2009.

Chen Guang'en 陳廣恩. "*Chang'an zhitu* yu Yuandai Jingqu shuili jianshe" 《長安志圖》 與元代涇渠水利建設. *Zhongguo lishi dili luncong* 1 (2006): 88–94.

Chen Guofu 陳國符. *Daozang yuanliu kao* 道藏源流考. Beijing: Zhonghua shuju, 1963.

Chen, Jinhua. "The Birth of a Polymath: The Genealogical Background of the Tang Monk-Scientist Yixing (673–727)." *Tang Studies* 18–19 (2001–2): 1–39.

———. "Family Ties and Buddhist Nuns in Tang China: Two Studies." *Asia Major* 3rd ser., 15, no. 2 (2002): 51–85.

Ch'en, Kenneth K. S. "Buddhist-Taoist Mixtures in the Pa-shih-i-hua T'u." *Harvard Journal of Asiatic Studies* 9, no. 1 (1945): 1–12.

Chen Wenyi 陳雯怡. *You guanxue dao shuyuan: Cong zhidu yu linian de hudong kan Songdai jiaoyu de yanbian* 由官學到書院: 從制度與理念的互動看宋代教育的演變. Taipei: Lianjing, 2004.

Chen Yuan 陳垣. *Nansong chu hebei xindaojiao kao* 南宋初河北新道教考. 1941. Reprint, Beijing: Zhonghua shuju, 1962.

Chen Yunü 陳玉女. "Mingdai ershisi yamen de fojiao xinyang" 明代二十四衙門的佛教信 仰. *Chenggong daxue lishi xuebao* 25 (1999): 173–236.

Chen Zhichao 陳智超. "Jin Yuan Zhendadao jiaoshi bu" 金元真大道教史補. *Lishi yanjiu* 6 (1986): 129–44.

Chia, Lucille. "The Uses of Print in Early Quanzhen Daoist Texts." In *Knowledge and Text Production in an Age of Print: China, 900–1400*, edited by Lucille Chia and Hilde de Weerdt, 167–213. Leiden, the Netherlands: Brill, 2011.

Chikusa Masaaki 竺沙雅章. *Chūgoku bukkyō shakaishi kenkyū* 中國佛教社會史研究. Kyoto: Dōhōsha, 1982.

———. "Mindai jiden no fueki ni tsuite" 明代寺田の賦役について. In *Min Shin jidai no seiji to shakai* 明清時代の政治と社會, edited by Ono Kazuko 小野和子, 489–512. Kyoto: Kyoto daigaku Jimbun kagaku kenkyūjo, 1983.

———. *Sō Gen bukkyō bunka shi kenkyū* 宋元佛教文化史研究. Tokyo: Kyūko shoin, 2001.

Cho, Wonhee. "Beyond Tolerance: The Mongols' Religious Policies in Yuan-Dynasty China and Il-Khanate Iran, 1200–1368." PhD diss., Yale University, 2014.

Clark, Hugh R. *Portrait of a Community: Society, Culture, and the Structures of Kinship in the Mulan River Valley*. Hong Kong: Chinese University Press, 2007.

Clarke, Shayne. *Family Matters in Indian Buddhist Monasticisms*. Honolulu: University of Hawai'i Press, 2014.

Cleaves, Francis Woodman. "The Sino-Mongolian Inscription of 1240." *Harvard Journal of Asiatic Studies* 23 (1960–61): 62–73.

Clunas, Craig. *Screen of Kings: Royal Art and Power in Ming China*. Honolulu: University of Hawai'i Press, 2013.

Cohen, Myron L. *Kinship, Contract, Community, and State: Anthropological Perspectives on China*. Stanford, CA: Stanford University Press, 2005.

Confucius. *The Analects of Confucius*. Translated by Simon Leys. New York: Norton, 1997.

Dardess, John W. *Confucianism and Autocracy: Professional Elites in the Founding of the Ming Dynasty*. Stanford, CA: Stanford University Press, 1983.

———. *Conquerors and Confucians: Aspects of Political Change in Late Yuan China*. New York: Columbia University Press, 1973.

———. *Governing China, 150–1850*. Indianapolis, IN: Hackett, 2010.

———. *A Ming Society: T'ai-ho County, Kiangsi, in the Fourteenth to Seventeenth Centuries*. Berkeley: University of California Press, 1996.

De Rachewiltz, Igor. "Personnel and Personalities in North China in the Early Mongol Period." *Journal of the Economic and Social History of the Orient* 9, nos. 1–2 (1966): 88–144.

———. "Some Remarks on Töregene's Edict of 1240." *Papers on Far Eastern History* 23 (1981): 38–63.

———. "Ye-lü Chu-ts'ai (1189–1243): Buddhist Idealist and Confucian Statesman." In Wright and Twitchett, *Confucian Personalities*, 189–216.

De Rachewiltz, Igor, Hok-lam Chan, Hsiao Chi'i-chi'ing, and Peter W. Geier, eds. *In the Service of the Khan: Eminent Personalities of the Early Mongol-Yüan Period*. Wiesbaden, Germany: Harrassowitz, 1993.

De Rachewiltz, Igor, and T. Russell. "Ch'iu Ch'u-chi, 1148–1227." *Papers on Far Eastern History* 29, no. 3 (1984): 1–26.

Dean, Kenneth, and Zheng Zhenman. *Ritual Alliances of the Putian Plain, Volume 1, Historical Introduction to the Return of the Gods*. Leiden, the Netherlands: Brill, 2010.

Deng Xiaonan 鄧小南. "Zhuiqiu yongshui zhixu de nuli: Cong qian jindai Hongtong de shuiziyuan guanli kan 'minjian' yu 'guanfang'" 追求用水秩序的努力: 从前近代洪洞的水资源管理看"民间"与"官方." *Jinan shixue* 3 (2005): 75–91.

———. *Zuzong zhifa: Beisong qianqi zhengzhi shulüe* 祖宗之法: 北宋前期政治述略. 2nd ed. Beijing: Sanlian shudian, 2014.

Deng Xiaonan 鄧小南 and Christian Lamouroux. "The 'Ancestors' Family Instructions': Authority and Sovereignty in Song China." *Journal of Song-Yuan Studies* 35 (2005): 79–97.

Despeux, Catherine, and Livia Kohn. *Women in Daoism*. Cambridge, MA: Three Pines Press, 2004.

Dien, Albert E. *Six Dynasties Civilization*. New Haven, CT: Yale University Press, 2007.

Dong Xiaoping 董曉萍 and Christian Lamouroux 藍克利. *Bu guan er zhi: Shanxi sishewucun shuili wenxian yu minsu* 不灌而治: 山西四社五村水利文獻與民俗. Beijing: Zhonghua shuju, 2003.

Dong Xinlin 董新林. "Beisong Jin Yuan muzang bishi suojian ershisi xiao gushi yu gaoli *Xiaoxing lu*" 北宋金元墓葬壁飾所見"二十四孝"故事與高麗《孝行錄》. *Huaxia kaogu* 2 (2009): 141–52.

Du Zhengzhen 杜正貞. *Cunshe chuantong yu mingqing shishen: Shanxi Zezhou xiangtu shehui de zhidu bianqian* 村社傳統與明清士紳: 山西澤州鄉土社會的制度變遷. Shanghai: Shanghai cishu chubanshe, 2007.

Elliot, Mark. *The Manchu Way: The Eight Banners and Ethnic Identity in Late Imperial China*. Stanford, CA: Stanford University Press, 2001.

Elman, Benjamin A. *Civil Examinations and Meritocracy in Late Imperial China*. Cambridge, MA: Harvard University Press, 2013.

Endicott-West, Elizabeth. *Mongolian Rule in China: Local Administration in the Yuan Dynasty*. Cambridge, MA: Council on East Asian Studies, Harvard University, 1989.

———. "The Yüan Government and Society." In Franke and Twitchett, *The Cambridge History of China*, 6:587–615.

Eskildsen, Stephen. *The Teachings and Practices of the Early Quanzhen Taoist Masters*. Albany: State University of New York Press, 2004.

Farmer, Edward L. *Zhu Yuanzhang and Early Ming Legislation: The Reordering of Chinese Society Following the Era of Mongol Rule*. Leiden, the Netherlands: Brill, 1995.

Faure, Bernard. *Chan Insights and Oversights: An Epistemological Critique of the Chan Tradition*. Princeton, NJ: Princeton University Press, 1993.

Faure, David. *Emperor and Ancestor: State and Lineage in South China*. Stanford, CA: Stanford University Press, 2007.

Feng Chengjun 馮承鈞. *Yuandai baihua bei kao* 元代白話碑考. Taipei: Taiwan shangwu yinshuguan, 1962.

Feng Junjie 馮俊傑. *Shanxi shenmiao juchang kao* 山西神廟劇場考. Beijing: Zhonghua shuju, 2006.

———. *Shanxi xiqu beike jikao* 山西戲曲碑刻輯考. Beijing: Zhonghua shuju, 2002.

———. *Xiju yu kaogu* 戲劇與考古. Beijing: Wenhua yishu chubanshe, 2002.

The Four Books: The Basic Teachings of the Later Confucian Tradition. Translated with introduction and commentary by Daniel K. Gardner. Indianapolis, IN: Hackett, 2007.

Franke, Herbert. *From Tribal Chieftain to Universal Emperor and God: The Legitimation of the Yuan Dynasty*. Munich, Germany: Bayerische Akademie der Wissenschaften München, 1978.

———. "Tibetans in Yuan China." In *China under Mongol Rule*, edited by John D. Langlois Jr., 296–328. Princeton, NJ: Princeton University Press, 1981.

Franke, Herbert, and Denis Twitchett, eds. *The Cambridge History of China, Volume 6: Alien Regimes and Border States, 907–1368*. Cambridge: Cambridge University Press, 1994.

Fu Haichao 符海潮. *Yuandai hanren shihou qunti yanjiu* 元代漢人世侯群體研究. Baoding: Hebei daxue chubanshe, 2008.

Fujishima Kenju 藤島建樹. "Zenshinkyō no tenkai: Mongoru seikanka no katō no baai" 全真教の展開: モンゴル政権下の河東の場合. In *Dōkyō to shūkyō bunka* 道教と宗教文化, edited by Akizuki Kan'ei 秋月觀暎, 425–38. Tokyo: Hirakawa, 1987.

Funada Yoshiyuki 船田善之. "Semuren yu Yuandai zhidu shehui: Chongxin tantao menggu, semu, hanren, nanren huafen de weizhi" 色目人與元代制度、社會: 重新探討蒙古、色目、漢人、南人劃分的位置. *Yuanshi luncong* 9 (2004): 162–74.

Geiss, James. "The Chia-Ching Reign, 1522–1566." In Twitchett and Mote, *The Cambridge History of China*, 7:440–510.

Gernet, Jacques. *Buddhism in Chinese Society: An Economic History from the Fifth to the Tenth Centuries.* Translated by Franciscus Verellen. New York: Columbia University Press, 1995.

Gerritsen, Anne. "The Hongwu Legacy: Fifteen-Century Views on Zhu Yuanzhang's Monastic Policies." In *Long Live the Emperor! Uses of the Ming Founder Across Six Centuries of East Asian History,* edited by Sarah Schneewind, 55–72. Minneapolis: Society for Ming Studies, 2008.

Gimello, Robert M. "Chang Shang-ying on Wu-t'ai Shan." In *Pilgrims and Sacred Sites in China,* edited by Susan Naquin and Chün-fang Yü, 89–149. Berkeley: University of California Press, 1992.

Goossaert, Vincent. "The Invention of an Order: Collective Identity in Thirteenth Century Quanzhen Taoism." *Journal of Chinese Religion* 29 (2001): 111–38.

Gregory, Peter N. *Tsung-mi and the Sinification of Buddhism.* Princeton, NJ: Princeton University Press, 1991.

Gu Yinsen 顧寅森. "Shilun Yuandai huangjia fosi yu zangchuan fojiao de guanxi: Yi da huguo renwang si wei zhongxin" 試論元代皇家佛寺與藏傳佛教的關係: 以大護國仁王寺爲中心. *Zongjiaoxue yanjiu* 1 (2014): 103–9.

Hachiya Kunio 蜂屋邦夫. *Kindai Dōkyō no kenkyū: Ou Chōyō to Ba Tanyō* 金代道教と研究: 王重陽と馬丹陽. Tokyo: Tōkyō daiyigaku Tōyō bunka kenkūjo hōkoku, 1992.

———. *Kin Gen jidai no Dōkyō: Shichishin kenkyū* 金元時代の道教: 七真研究. Tokyo: Tōkyō daiyigaku Tōyō bunka kenkūjo hōkoku, 1998.

Halperin, Mark. "Buddhists and Southern Literati in the Mongol Era." In Marsone and Largerwey, *Modern Chinese Religion I,* 2:1433–92.

———. *Out of the Cloister: Literati Perspectives on Buddhism in Sung China, 960–1279.* Cambridge, MA: Harvard University Asia Center, 2006.

Han Chaojian 韓朝建. "Huabei de rong yu zongzu: Yi Shanxi Daixian wei zhongxin" 華北的容與宗族: 以山西代縣爲中心. *Minsu yanjiu* 5 (2012): 32–55.

———. *Siyuan yu guanfu: Ming Qing Wutaishan de xingzheng xitong yu difang shehui* 寺院與官府: 明清五臺山的行政系統與地方社會. Beijing: Renmin chubanshe, 2016.

Han Zhiyuan 韩志远. "Yuan Haowen zai Jin Yuan zhiji de zhengzhi huodong" 元好問在金元之際的政治活動. *Yuanshi luncong* 5 (1993): 282–94.

Hansen, Valerie. *Changing Gods in Medieval China, 1127–1276.* Princeton, NJ: Princeton University Press, 1990.

Harrison, Henrietta. "Daode, quanli yu jinshui shuili xitong" 道德、權力與晉水水利系統. *Lishi renlei xuekan* 1 (2003): 97–113.

Hartwell, Robert. "Demographic, Political, and Social Transformations of China, 750–1550." *Harvard Journal of Asiatic Studies* 42, no. 2 (1982): 365–442.

He Xiaorong 何孝榮. "Shilun mingtaizu de fojiao zhengce" 試論明太祖的佛教政策. *Shijie zongjiao yanjiu* 4 (2007): 19–30.

Hejidra, Martin. "The Socio-Economic Development of Rural China during the Ming." In Twitchett and Mote, *The Cambridge History of China,* 8:417–578.

Heller, Natasha. "From Imperial Glory to Buddhist Piety: The Record of a Ming Ritual in Three Contexts." *History of Religions* 51, no. 1 (2011): 59–83.

Hong Jinfu 洪金富. "Yuan 'Xijinzhi yuanmiao xingxiang' pian shuzheng" 元《析津志原廟行香》篇疏證. *Zhongyang yanjiuyuan lishi yuyan yanjiusuo jikan* 79 (2009): 1–40.

Hou Huiming 侯慧明. "Yuan kan *Xuandu baozang* keju yu Xuandu guan kao" 元刊《玄都寶藏》刻局與玄都觀考. *Xinan daxue xuebao* 35, no. 1 (2009): 92–96.

Hu Yingze 胡英澤. "Jinfan yu jinshui: Mingdai Shanxi zongfan yu difang shuili" 晉藩與晉水: 明代山西宗藩與地方水利. *Zhongguo lishi dili luncong* 4 (2014): 122–35.

Huang Kuanchong 黃寬重. *Songdai de jiazu yu shehui* 宋代的家族與社會. Beijing: Guojia tushuguan chubanshe, 2009.

Huang Qinglian 黄清連. *Yuandai huji zhidu yanjiu* 元代户計制度研究. Taipei: National Taiwan University, 1977.

Huang, Ray. *1587: A Year of No Significance*. New Haven, CT: Yale University Press, 1981.

Huang, Shih-Shan Susan. "Summoning the Gods: Painting of Three Officials of Heaven, Earth and Water and Their Association with Daoist Ritual Performance in the Southern Song Period (1127–1279)." *Artibus Asiae* 61, no. 1 (2001): 5–52.

Hymes, Robert. *Statesmen and Gentlemen: The Elite of Fu-chou, Chiang-hsi, in Northern and Southern Sung*. New York: Cambridge University Press, 1986.

———. "Sung Society and Social Change." In *The Cambridge History of China, Volume 5: Sung China, 960–1279, Part 2*, edited by John W. Chafee and Denis Twitchett, 526–664. Cambridge: Cambridge University Press, 2015.

———. *Way and Byway: Taoism, Local Religion, and Models of Divinity in Sung and Modern China*. Berkeley: University of California Press, 2002.

Idema, Wilt. L. "The Orphan of Zhao: Self-Sacrifice, Tragic Choice and Revenge and the Confucianization of Mongol Drama at the Ming Court." *Cina* 21 (1988): 159–90.

Iguro Shinobu 井黒忍. *Bunsui to shihai: Kin mongoru jidai kahoku no suiri to nōgyō* 分水と支配: 金モンゴル時代華北の水利と農業. Tokyo: Waseda University Press, 2013.

Iiyama Tomoyasu 飯山知保. "A Career between Two Cultures: Guo Yu, a Chinese Literatus in the Yuan Bureaucracy." *Journal of Song-Yuan Studies* 44 (2014): 471–501.

———. "Genealogical Steles in North China during the Jin and Yuan Dynasties." *International Journal of Asian Studies* 13, no. 2 (2016): 151–96.

———. *Kin Gen jidai no kahoku shakai to kakyo seido: Mō hitotsu no shijinsō* 金元時代の華北社會と科舉制度: もう一つの士人層. Tokyo: Waseda University Press, 2011.

———. "'Sonkōryō hikokugun' no kenkyū: 12 kara 14 seiki kahoku ni okeru seneihi no shutsugen to keihu denshō no hensen '孫公亮墓' 碑刻群の研究: 12–14 世紀華北における "先塋碑" の出現と系譜傳承の變遷. *Ajiaahurika gengo bunka kenkyū* 85 (2013): 62–170.

Irinchen 亦鄰真. "Du 1276 nian Longmen yuwang miao basiba zi lingzhi bei: Jian ping Nigula Baopei de yizhu" 讀1276 年龍門禹王廟八思巴字令旨碑: 兼評尼古拉鮑培的譯注. *Neimenggu daxue xuebao (shehui kexue)* 1 (1963): 113–23.

Jackson, Peter. "From Ulus to Khanate: The Making of the Mongol State c. 1220–c. 1290." In Reuven and Morgan, *The Mongol Empire and Its Legacy*, 12–38.

Jan, Yun-hua. "Hai-Yün (1203–57)." In De Rachewiltz, Chan, Hsiao, and Geier, *In the Service of the Khan*, 224–42.

Jing, Anning (景安寧). *Daojiao quanzhenpai gongguan zaoxiang yu zushi* 道教全眞派宮觀、造像與祖師. Beijing: Zhonghua shuju, 2012.

——. "The Longshan Daoist Cave." *Artibus Asiae* 68, no. 1 (2008): 7–56.

——. *The Water God's Temple of the Guangsheng Monastery: Cosmic Function of Art, Ritual, and Theater*. Leiden, the Netherlands: Brill, 2002.

——. *Yuandai bihua: Shenxian fuhui tu* 元代壁畫：神仙赴會圖. Beijing: Peking University Press, 2002.

Johnson, David. *Spectacle and Sacrifice: The Ritual Foundations of Village Life in North China*. Cambridge, MA: Harvard University Asia Center, 2009.

Johnson, Linda Cooke. *Women of the Conquest Dynasties: Gender and Identity in Liao and Jin China*. Honolulu: University of Hawai'i Press, 2011.

Kang Le 康樂. "Zhuanlunwang guannian yu Zhongguo zhonggu de fojiao zhengzhi" 轉輪王觀念與中國中古的佛教政治. *Zhongyang yanjiuyuan lishi yuyan yanjiusuo jikan* 67, no. 1 (1996): 109–42.

Katz, Paul R. *Images of the Immortal: The Cult of Lü Dongbin and the Palace of Eternal Joy*. Honolulu: University of Hawai'i Press, 1999.

——. "Writing History, Creating Identity: A Case Study of Xuanfeng qinghui tu." *Journal of Chinese Religions* 29 (2001): 161–78.

Keika Atsushi 桂華淳祥. "Kindai no jikan meigaku hatsubai ni tsuite: Sansei no seikoku shiryō o tegakari ni" 金代の寺観名額発賣について: 山西の石刻資料を手がかりに. *Ōtani daigaku Shinshū Sōgō Kenkyūjō Kiyō* 1 (1983): 25–41.

Kieschnick, John. *The Impact of Buddhism on Chinese Material Culture*. Princeton, NJ: Princeton University Press, 2003.

Kishimoto Mio 岸本美緒. *Min Shin kōtai to kōnan shakai: Juunana seiki Chūgoku no chitsujo mondai* 明清交替と江南社會：17 世紀中國の秩序問題. Tokyo: Tōkyō daigaku shuppankai, 1999.

Koh, Khee Heong. *A Northern Alternative: Xue Xuan (1389–1464) and the Hedong School*. Cambridge, MA: Harvard University Asia Center, 2011.

Kohn, Livia. *Laughing at the Tao: Debates among Buddhists and Daoists in Medieval China*. Princeton, NJ: Princeton University Press, 1995.

Kolbas, Judith. *The Mongols in Iran: Chingiz Khan to Uljaytu, 1220–1309*. London: Routledge, 2006.

Komjathy, Louis. *Cultivating Perfection: Mysticism and Self-Transformation in Early Quanzhen Daoism*. Leiden, the Netherlands: Brill, 2007.

——. "Sun Buer: Early Quanzhen Matriarch and the Beginning of Female Alchemy." *Nan Nü* 16, no. 2 (2014): 171–238.

Lai Tianbing 賴天兵. "Guanyu Yuandai sheyu Jianghuai/Jiangzhe de shijiao duzongtong suo" 關於元代設於江浙/江淮的釋教都總統所. *Shijie zongjiao yanjiu* 1 (2010): 55–68.

Lamouroux, Christian. Review of *The Song-Yuan-Ming Transition in Chinese History*, edited by Paul Jakov Smith and Richard von Glahn. *Journal of Song-Yuan Studies* 35 (2004): 177–89.

Lei Bingyan 雷炳炎. "Mingdai zongfan jingji fanzui shulun" 明代宗藩經濟犯罪述論. *Jinan shixue* 6 (2009): 257–67.

———. "Wangfu jiaren, zongshi yinqin yu mingdai zongfan fanzui" 王府家人、宗室姻靚與明代宗藩犯罪. *Hunan shehui kexue* 1 (2011): 204–8.

Li Ga 李嘎. "Bianfang youjing: Menggu lüejin yu Mingdai Shanxi de zhucheng gaochao" 邊方有警: 蒙古掠晉與明代山西的築城高潮. *Mingda yanjiu* 21 (2013): 31–74.

Li Sanmou 李三謀 and Fang Peixian 方配賢. "Ming wanli yiqian Shanxi nongye huobishui de tuixing wenti" 明萬歷以前山西農業貨幣稅的推行問題. *Zhongguo shehui jingjishi yanjiu* 1 (1999): 22–29.

Li Suping 李素平. "Nüguan Yuan Yan kao" 女冠元嚴考. *Zhongguo Daojiao* 4 (2006): 48–50 and 54.

Li Wenzhi 李文治 and Jiang Taixin 江太新. *Zhongguo zongfa zongzuzhi he zutian yizhuang* 中國宗法宗族制和族田義莊. Beijing: Shehui kexue wenxian chubanshe, 2000.

Li Xiusheng 李修生. "Yuandai de ruhu: Yuandai wenhuashi biji zhiyi" 元代的儒户: 元代文化史筆記之一. In *Yuandai wenxian yu wenhua yanjiu* 元代文獻與文化研究, edited by Han Geping 韓格平 and Wei Chongwu 魏崇武, 1–17. Beijing: Zhonghua shuju, 2012.

Li Zhi'an 李治安. "Liangge Nanbeichao yu zhonggu yilai de lishi fazhan xiansuo" 兩個南北朝與中古以來的發展線索. *Wen shi zhe* 6 (2009): 5–19.

———. *Yuandai fenfeng zhidu yanjiu* 元代分封制度研究. Beijing: Zhonghua shuju, 2007.

Liang Fangzhong 梁方仲. *Liang Fangzhong jingjishi lunwen ji* 梁方仲經濟史論文集. Beijing: Zhonghua shuju, 1989.

———. *Liang Fangzhong jingjishi lunwen ji jiyi* 梁方仲經濟史論文集集遺. Guangzhou: Guangdong renmin chubanshe, 1990.

Liu Jingzhen 劉靜貞. "Nü wu wai shi?—muzhiming zhong suojian Beisong shidafu shehui zhixu linian" 女無外事?—墓誌銘中所見北宋士大夫社會秩序理念. *Funü yu liangxing guanxi* 4 (1993): 21–46.

Liu Pujiang 劉浦江. *Ershi shiji liaojinshi lunzhu mulu* 二十世紀遼金史論著目錄. Shanghai: Shanghai cishu chubanshe, 2003.

———. *Liaojinshi lun* 遼金史論. Shenyang: Liaoning daxue chubanshe, 1999.

Liu Yingsheng 劉迎勝. "Yuantong ernian (1334) chaoting shouhuan tianchan shijian yanjiu: Guojia yu guizu, siyuan zhengduo tudi douzheng de beihou" 元統二年朝廷收還田產事件研究: 國家與貴族、寺院爭奪土地鬥爭的背後. *Yuanshi ji minzu yu bianjiang yanjiu jikan* 24 (2012): 1–45.

Lu Xiqi 魯西奇. *Changjiang zhongyou de rendi guanxi yu diyu shehui* 長江中游的人地關係與地域社會. Xiamen: Xiamen daxue chubanshe, 2016.

Makino Shūji 牧野修二. "Transformation of the *Shi-jên* in the Late Chin and Early Yüan." *Acta Asiatica* 45 (1983): 1–26.

Marsone, Pierre. "Accounts of the Foundation of the Quanzhen Movement: A Hagiographic Treatment of History." *Journal of Chinese Religion* 29 (2001): 95–110.

———. "Daoism under the Jurchen Jin Dynasty." In Marsone and Largerwey, *Modern Chinese Religion I*, 2:1111–59.

Marsone, Pierre, and John Largerwey, eds. *Modern Chinese Religion I: Song-Liao-Jin-Yuan (960–1368 AD)*. 2 vols. Leiden, the Netherlands: Brill, 2015.

McDermott, Joseph P. *The Making of a New Rural Order in South China, Volume 1, Village, Land, and Lineage in Huizhou, 900–1600*. New York: Cambridge University Press, 2013.

————. "The Village Quartet." In Marsone and Largerwey, *Modern Chinese Religion I*, 2:1433–92.

McGee, Neil E. "Questioning Convergence: Daoism in South China during the Yuan Dynasty." PhD diss., Columbia University, 2014.

Mikami Tsugio 三上次男. *Kinshi kenkyu III: Kindai seiji shakai no kenkyu* 金史研究三: 金代政治社會の研究. Tokyo: Chūō-kōron bijutsu shuppan, 1973.

Morgan, David. *The Mongols*. 2nd ed. Malden, MA, and Oxford: Blackwell Publishing, 2007.

Morita Akira 森田明. "Shindai kahoku ni okeru suiri soshiki to sono seikaku: Sanseishō tsūri-kyo no baai" 清代華北における水利組織とその性格: 山西省通利渠の場合. *Rekishigaku kenkyū* 450 (1977): 27–37.

Morita Kenji 森田憲司. "Gencho ni okeru daishi ni tsuite" 元朝における代祀について. *Tōho shūkyo* 98 (2001): 17–32.

Muraoka Hitoshi 村岡倫. "Mongoru jidai shoki no kasei sansei chiho uyoku urusu no bunchi seiritsu o megutte" モンゴル時代初期の河西・山西地方右翼ウルスの分地成立をめぐって. *Ryukoku shitan* 117 (2001): 1–22.

Nagase Mamoru 長瀬守. *Sō-Gen suirishi kenkyū* 宋元水利史研究. Tokyo: Kokusho kankōkai, 1983.

Nakamura Jun 中村淳. "Mongoru jidai no Dōbutsu ronsō' no jitsuzō—Kubilai no Chūgoku shihai he no michi" モンゴル時代の道佛論爭の實像: クビライの中國支配への道. *Tōyō gakuhō* 75, nos. 3–4 (1994): 33–63.

Naquin, Susan. *Peking: Temples and City Life, 1400–1900*. Berkeley: University of California Press, 2000.

Nishio Kenryū 西尾賢隆. *Chūgoku kinsei ni okeru kokka to Zenshū* 中国近世における国家と禅宗. Kyoto: Shibunkaku, 2006.

Nogami Shunjō 野上俊靜. *Genshi Shaku Rō den no kenkyū* 元史釋老傳の研究. Kyoto: Hatsubai Hōyū Shoten, 1978.

Oda Yaichirō 太田彌一郎. "Gen Daitoku shichinen Sansei dai shisai shimatsu: Genchō suibo e no tenkanten" 元大德七年 (1303) 山西大震災始末: 元朝衰亡への転換点. *Tōhoku daigaku tōyōshi ronshū* 10 (2005): 267–84.

Ong, Chang Woei. *Men of Letters within the Passes: Guanzhong Literati in Chinese History, 907–1911*. Cambridge, MA: Harvard University Asia Center, 2008.

Otagi Matsuo 愛宕松男. *Tōyō shigaku ronshū* 東洋史學論集. Vol. 4. Tokyo: Sanichi shobō, 1988.

Ōyabu Masaya 大藪正哉. *Gendai no hosei to shūkyo* 元代の法制と宗教. Tokyo: Shūei Shuppan, 1983.

Petech, Luciano. "'Phags-pa (1235–1280)." In De Rachewiltz, Chan, Hsiao, and Geier, *In the Service of the Khan*, 646–54.

————. "Tibetan Relations with Sung China and with the Mongols." In *China Among Equals: The Middle Kingdom and Its Neighbors, 10th–14th Centuries*, edited by Morris Rossabi, 173–203. Berkeley: University of California Press, 1983.

Qiu Yihao 邱軼浩. "Wudao: sanjiao beijing xia de Jindai ruxue" 吾道: 三教背景下的金代儒學. *Xin shixue* 20, no. 4 (2009): 59–113.

Qiu Zhonglin 邱仲麟. "Ming Qing Shanxi de shandi kaifa yu senlin kanfa: Yi Jinzhon, Jinnan wei zhongxin de kaocha" 明清山西的山地開發與森林砍伐: 以晉中、晉南為中心的考察. In *Shanxi shuili shehui shi* 山西水利社會史, edited by the Shanxi daxue zhongguo shehuishi yanjiu zhongxin, 7–39. Beijing: Peking University Press, 2012.

Reuven, Amitai-Press, and David O. Morgan, eds. *The Mongol Empire and Its Legacy.* Leiden, the Netherlands: Brill, 1999.

Robinet, Isabelle. *Taoism: Growth of a Religion.* Translated by Phyllis Brooks. 2nd ed. Stanford, CA: Stanford University Press, 1997.

Robinson, David M. "The Ming Court and the Legacy of the Yuan Mongols." In *Culture, Courtiers, and Competition: The Ming Court (1368–1644)*, edited by Robinson, 365–421. Cambridge, MA: Harvard University Asia Center, 2008.

———. "Princely Courts of the Ming Dynasty." *Ming Studies* 65 (2012): 1–12.

———. "Princes in the Polity: The Anhua Prince's Uprising of 1510." *Ming Studies* 65 (2012): 13–56.

Robson, James. "'Neither Too Far, nor Too Near:' The Historical and Cultural Contexts of Buddhist Monasteries in Medieval China and Japan." In *Buddhist Monasticism in East Asia: Places of Practice*, edited by James A. Benn, Lori Meeks, and James Robson, 1–17. London: Routledge, 2010.

Rossabi, Morris. "Khubilai Khan and the Women in His Family." In *Studia Sino-Mongolica: Festschrift für Herbert Franke*, edited by Wolfgang Bauer, 153–58. Wiesbaden, Germany: Franz Steiner Verlag, 1979.

———. *Khubilai Khan: His Life and Times.* Berkeley: University of California Press, 1988.

———. "The Reign of Khubilai Khan." In Franke and Twitchett, *The Cambridge History of China*, 6:414–89.

Sakurai Satomi 櫻井智美. "Gendai shyukenyin no setsuritsu" 元代集賢院の設立. *Shirin* 83, no. 3 (2000): 115–43.

Sakurai Satomi 櫻井智美 and Yao Yongxia 姚永霞. "Gen shigen kyunen kotaishi en'ō shikō hi o megutte" 元至元9 年「皇太子燕王祠香碑」をめぐって. *Sundai shigaku* 145 (2012): 23–49.

Satō Fumitoshi 佐藤文俊. *Mindai ōfu no kenkyū* 明代王府の研究. Tokyo: Kenbun shuppan, 1999.

Schipper, Kristofer, and Franciscus Verellen, eds. *Taoist Canon: A Historical Companion to the Daozang.* Chicago: University of Chicago Press, 2004.

Schneewind, Sarah. *Community Schools and the State in Ming China.* Stanford, CA: Stanford University Press, 2006.

———. "Research Note: The Village-Level Community Libation Ceremony in Early Ming Law." *Ming Studies* 1 (2005): 43–57.

———. "Visions and Revisions: Village Policies of the Ming Founder in Seven Phases." *T'oung Pao* 87, nos. 4–5 (2001): 317–59.

Schneider, Julia. "The Jin Revisited: New Assessment of Jurchen Emperors." *Journal of Song-Yuan Studies* 41 (2011): 343–404.

Schopen, Gregory. *Bones, Stones and Buddhist Monks: Collected Papers on the Archaeology, Epigraphy, and Texts of Monastic Buddhism in India*. Honolulu: University of Hawai'i Press, 1997.

———. "Filial Piety and the Monk in the Practice of Indian Buddhism: A Question of 'Sinicization' Viewed from the Other Side." *T'oung Pao* 70 (1984): 110–26.

Scott, James C. *Weapons of the Weak: Everyday Forms of Peasant Resistance*. New Haven, CT: Yale University Press, 1985.

Serruys, Henry. "Remains of Mongol Customs in China during the Early Ming Period." *Monumenta Serica* 16, nos. 1–2 (1957): 137–90.

Shi Guoqi 施國祁. *Yuan Yishan nianpu* 元遺山年譜. Taipei: Shijie shuju, 1954.

Shinno, Reiko. "Medical Schools and the Temples of the Three Progenitors in Yuan China: A Case of Cross-Cultural Interaction." *Harvard Journal of Asiatic Studies* 67, no. 1 (2007): 89–133.

Shinohara, Koichi. "Stories about Asoka Images." In *Speaking of Monks: Religious Biographies in India and China*, edited by Koichi Shinohara and Phyllis Granoff, 210–18. Oakville, ON: Mosaic Press, 1992.

Smith, Paul Jakov. "Fear of Gynarchy in an Age of Chaos: Kong Qi's Reflections on Life in South China under Mongol Rule." *Journal of the Economic and Social History of the Orient* 41, no. 1 (1998): 1–95.

Smith, Paul Jakov, and Richard von Glahn, eds. *The Song-Yuan-Ming Transition in Chinese History*. Cambridge, MA: Harvard University Asia Center, 2003.

Spence, Jonathan. *Return to Dragon Mountain: Memories of a Late Ming Man*. New York: Viking, 2007.

Stevenson, Daniel B. "Visions of Mañjuśrī on Mount Wutai." In *Religions of China in Practice*, edited by Donald S. Lopez Jr., 203–22. Princeton, NJ: Princeton University Press, 1996.

Su Li 蘇力. *Yuandai difang jingying yu jiceng shehui: Yi Jiangnan diqu wei zhongxin* 元代地方精英與基層社會: 以江南地區為中心. Tianjing: Tianjing guji chubanshe, 2009.

Szonyi, Michael. *Practicing Kinship: Lineage and Descent in Late Imperial China*. Stanford, CA: Stanford University Press, 2002.

Tackett, Nicolas. *The Destruction of the Medieval Chinese Aristocracy*. Cambridge, MA: Harvard University Asia Center, 2014.

Takahashi Bunji 高橋文治. "Gen Yisan to tōsō" 元遺山と黨爭. *Otemon gakuin dayigaku bungakubu kiyō* 22 (1987): 247–64.

Tan Xiaoling 譚曉玲. *Chongtu yu qixu: Yuandai nüxing shehui juese yu lunli guannian de sikao* 衝突與期許: 元代女性社會角色與倫理觀念的思考. Tianjin: Nankai University Press, 2009.

Tao Jinsheng (Jing-shen Tao) 陶晉生. "Jindai de zhengzhi jiegou" 金代的政治結構. *Lishi yuyan yanjiusuo jikan* 41, no. 4 (1969): 567–93.

———. "Political Recruitment in the Chin Dynasty." *Journal of the American Oriental Society* 94, no. 1 (1974): 24–34.

———. "Public Schools in the Chin Dynasty." In Tillman and West, *China under Jurchen Rule*, 50–67.

Taylor, Romeyn. "Official Altars, Temples and Shrines Mandated for All Counties in Ming and Qing." *T'oung Pao* 83 (1997): 93–125.

———. "Yuan Origins of the Wei-so System." In *Chinese Government in Ming Times: Seven Studies*, edited by Charles Hucker, 23–40. New York: Columbia University Press, 1969.

Teiser, Stephen. *The Ghost Festival in Medieval China*. Princeton, NJ: Princeton University Press, 1988.

Ter Haar, Barend J. "Newly Recovered Anecdotes from Hong Mai's (1123–1202) *Yijian zhi*." *Journal of Sung-Yuan Studies* 23 (1993): 19–41.

———. *The White Lotus Teachings in Chinese Religious History*. Leiden, the Netherlands: Brill, 1992.

Terada Takanobu 寺田隆信. *Mindai kyoshin no kenkyu* 明代鄉紳の研究. Kyoto: Kyoto University Press, 2009.

Tillman, Hoyt Cleveland. "An Overview of Chin History and Institution." In Tillman and West, *China under Jurchen Rule*, 23–38.

Tillman, Hoyt Cleveland, and Stephen H. West, eds. *China under Jurchen Rule: Essays on Chin Intellectual and Cultural History*. Albany: State University of New York Press, 1995.

Toyoshima Shizuhide 豐島靜英. "Chūgoku hokusei-bu ni okeru suiri kyōdōtai ni tsuite" 中國北西部における水利共同体について. *Rekishigaku kenkyū* 201 (1956): 24–35.

Twitchett, Denis, and Frederick W. Mote, eds. *The Cambridge History of China, Volume 7: The Ming Dynasty, 1368–1644, Part I*. Cambridge: Cambridge University Press, 1998.

———. *The Cambridge History of China, Volume 8: The Ming Dynasty, 1368–1644, Part II*. Cambridge: Cambridge University Press, 1998.

Walsh, Michael J. "The Buddhist Monastic Economy." In Marsone and Largerwey, *Modern Chinese Religion I*, 2:1270–1303.

———. "The Economics of Salvation: Toward a Theory of Exchange in Chinese Buddhism." *Journal of the American Academy of Religion* 75, no. 2 (2007): 353–82.

Walton, Linda. "Academies in the Changing Religious Landscape." In Marsone and Largerwey, *Modern Chinese Religion I*, 2:1235–69.

———. "Song-Yuan zhuanbian de hanren jingying jiazu: Ruhu shenfen, jiaxue chuantong yu shuyuan" 宋元轉變的漢人精英家族: 儒户身份、家學傳統與書院. *Zhongguo shehui lishi pinglun* 9 (2008): 78–88.

Wang, Jinping 王錦萍. "Clergy, Kinship, and Clout in Yuan Dynasty Shanxi." *International Journal of Asian Studies* 13, no. 2 (2016): 197–228.

———. "Rujia zi, daozhe shi: Jin Yuan zhiji quanzhen jiaotuan zhong de rudao shiren" 儒家子, 道者師: 金元之際全真教團中的入道士人. *Xin shixue* 24, no. 4 (2013): 55–92.

———. "A Social History of the *Treasured Canon of the Mysterious Capital* in North China under Mongol Rule." *East Asian Publishing and Society* 4 (2014): 1–35.

———. "Zongjiao zuzhi yu shuili xitong: Mengyuan shiqi shanxi shuili shehui zhong de sengdao tuanti tanxi" 宗教組織與水利系統: 蒙元時期山西水利社會中的僧道團體探析. *Lishi renlei xuekan* 1 (2011): 25–60.

Wang Peihua 王培華. *Yuandai beifang zaihuang yu jiuji* 元代北方災荒與救濟. Beijing: Beijing shifan daxue chubanshe, 2010.

Wang, Richard. *The Ming Prince and Daoism: Institutional Patronage of an Elite*. Oxford: Oxford University Press, 2012.

Wang Yuquan 王毓銓. *Laiwu ji* 萊蕪集. Beijing: Zhonghua shuju, 1983.

Wang Zongyu 王宗昱. "Quanzhenjiao de rujiao chengfen" 全真教的儒教成份. *Wenshi zhishi* 12 (2006): 4–13.

Wen, Xin. "The Road to Literary Culture: Revisiting the Jurchen Language Examination System." *T'oung Pao* 101, no. 3 (2015): 130–67.

Wittfogel, Karl August. *Oriental Despotism: A Comparative Study of Total Power*. New Haven, CT: Yale University Press, 1957.

Wright, Arthur F., and Denis Twitchett, eds. *Confucian Personalities*. Stanford, CA: Stanford University Press, 1962.

Wu Pei-Yi. "Yang Miaozhen: A Woman Warrior in Thirteenth-Century China." *Nan nü* 4, no. 2 (2002): 137–69.

Wu Songdi 吳松弟. *Zhongguo renkou shi: Liao Song Jin Yuan shiqi* 中國人口史：遼宋金元時期. Shanghai: Fudan daxue chubanshe, 2005.

Xiao Qiqing 蕭啓慶 (Hsiao Ch'i-ch'ing). "Mid-Yüan Politics." In Franke and Twitchett, *The Cambridge History of China*, 6:490–560.

———. *Nei beiguo er wai zhongguo: Mengyuanshi yanjiu* 內北國而外中國：蒙元史研究. Beijing: Zhonghua shuju, 2007.

———. *Yuanchao shi xinlun* 元朝史新論. Taipei: Yunchen wenhua, 1999.

———. *Yuandai shi xintan* 元代史新探. Taipei: Xinwenfeng chubangongsi, 1983.

———. *Yuandai zuqun wenhua yu keju* 元代族群文化與科舉. Taipei: Lianjing, 2008.

Xie Chongguang 謝重光 and Bai Wengu 白文固. *Zhongguo sengguan zhidushi* 中國僧官制度史. Xining: Qinghai renmin chubanshe, 1990.

Xu Pingfang 徐蘋芳. "Guanyu Song Defang he Pan Dechong mu de jige wenti" 關於宋德方和潘德沖墓的幾個問題. *Kaogu* 8 (1960): 42–54.

Xu Zhenghong 許正弘. "Lun Yuanchao Kuokuozhen taihou de chongfo" 論元朝闊闊真太后的崇佛. *Zhonghua foxue yanjiu* 16 (2015): 73–103.

Xu Zi 徐梓. *Yuandai shuyuan yanjiu* 元代書院研究. Beijing: Shehui kexue wenxian chubanshe, 2000.

Xue Ruizhao 薛瑞兆. *Jindai keju* 金代科舉. Beijing: Zhongguo shehui kexue chubanshe, 2004.

Yang Ne 楊訥. "Yuandai nongcun shezhi yanjiu" 元代農村社制研究. *Lishi yanjiu* 4 (1965): 117–22.

Yang Qingchen 楊慶辰. "Yiwei zhijian: Cui Li gongdebei shijian zhongde Yuan Haowen" 依違之間：崔立功德碑事件中的元好問. *Wenshi zhishi* 2 (2007): 89–93.

Yao Congwu 姚從吾. "Yuan Haowen duiyu baoquan zhongyuan chuantong wenhua de gongxian" 元好問對於保全中原傳統文化的貢獻. *Dalu zazhi shixue zongshu*, 2nd ser., 3 (1967): 41–52.

Yao, Tao-chung. "Buddhism and Taoism under the Chin." In Tillman and West, *China under Jurchen Rule*, 145–80.

———. "Ch'iu Ch'u-chi and Chinggis Khan." *Harvard Journal of Asiatic Studies* 40, no. 1 (1986): 201–19.

Ye Changchi 葉昌熾. *Yu shi* 語石. Taipei: Tanwan shangwu yinshuguan, 1980.

Yoshikawa Tadao 吉川忠夫. "Waki wa seki ni itarazu: Zenshinkyō to Zen o megutte" 脇は席に至らず—全眞教と禅をめぐって. *Zenbunka kenkyūsho kiyō* 15 (1988): 449–72.

You Biao 游彪. *Songdai siyuan jingji shigao* 宋代寺院經濟史稿. Baoding: Hebei daxue chubanshe, 2002.

Yu, Anthony C. *State and Religion in China: Historical and Textual Perspectives.* Chicago: Open Court, 2005.

Yüan Ts'ai. *Family and Property in Sung China: Yüan Ts'ai's Precepts for Social Life.* Translated with annotations and an introduction by Patricia Buckley Ebrey. Princeton, NJ: Princeton University Press, 1984.

Zhang Boquan 張博泉 and Wu Yuhuan 武玉環. "Jindai de renkou yu huji" 金代的人口與戶籍. *Xuexi yu tansuo* 2 (1989): 135–40.

Zhang Dexin 張德信. *Mingshi yanjiu lungao* 明史研究論稿. Beijing: Shehui kexue chubanshe, 2011.

Zhang Fan 張帆. "Jindai difang guanxue lüelun" 金代地方官學略論. *Shehui kexue jikan* 1 (1993): 83–88.

Zhang Guangbao 張廣保. *Jin Yuan Quanzhenjiao shi xin yanjiu* 金元全眞教史新研究. Hong Kong: Qingsong chubanshe, 2008.

Zhang Guowang 張國旺. "Yuandai Wutaishan fojiao zaitan: Yi Hebei sheng Lingshou xian Qilin yuan shengzhibei wei zhongxin" 元代五台山佛教再探: 以河北省靈壽縣祈林院聖旨碑爲中心. *Shoudu shifan daxue xuebao: Shehui kexue ban* 1 (2008): 27–31.

Zhang Junfeng 張俊峰. *Shuili shehui de leixing: Ming Qing yilai Hongtong shuili yu xiangcun shehui bianqian* 水利社會的類型: 明清以來洪洞水利與鄉村社會變遷. Beijing: Peking University Press, 2012.

Zhang Qiaogui 張橋貴. "Daojiao chuanbo yu shaoshu minzu guizu dui hanwenhua de rentong" 道教傳播與少數民族貴族對漢文化的認同. *Shijie zongjiao yanjiu* 2 (2002): 102–10.

Zhang Xiumin 張秀民. *Zhongguo yinshua shi* 中國印刷史. Hangzhou: Zhejiang guji chubanshe, 2006.

Zhang Youting 張友庭. *Jinfan pinghan: Shanxi Ningwu guancheng de lishi renleixue kaocha* 晉藩屏翰: 山西寧武關城的歷史人類學考察. Shanghai: Shanghai shehui kexueyuan chubanshe, 2012.

Zhao Gaiping 趙改萍. *Yuan Ming shiqi zangchuan fojiao zai neidi de fazhan ji yingxiang* 元明時期藏傳佛教在內地的發展及影響. Beijing: Zhongguo shehui kexue chubanshe, 2009.

Zhao Shiyu 趙世瑜. "Shenggu miao: Jin Yuan Ming bianqian Zhong de yijiao mingyun yu jindongnan shehui de duoyangxing" 聖姑廟: 金元明變遷中的 "異教" 命運與晉東南社會的多樣性. *Qinghua daxue xuebao: Zhexue shehui kexueban* 4 (2009): 5–15.

———. "Weisuo junhu zhidu yu Mingdai zhongguo shehui: shehuishi de shijiao" 衛所軍戶制度與明代中國社會: 社會史的視角. *Qinghua daxue xuebao: Zhexue shehui kexue ban*, 3 (2015): 114–27.

Zhao Xianhai 趙現海. *Mingdai jiubian changcheng junzhen shi: Zhongguo bianjiang jiashuo shiye xia de changcheng zhidu shi yanjiu* 明代九邊長城軍鎮史: 中國邊疆假說視野下的長城制度史研究. Beijing: Shehui kexue wenxian chubanshe, 2012.

Zhao Yifeng 趙軼峰, "Mingdai sengdao dudie zhidu de bianqian" 明代僧道度牒制度的變遷. *Gudai wenming* 2, no. 2 (2008): 72–87.

Zheng Suchun 郑素春. "Yuandai Quanzhen jiaozhu yu chaoting de guanxi" 元代全真教主與朝廷的關係. In *Meng Yuan de lishi yu wenhua: Meng Yuan shi xueshu yantaohui lunwenji* 蒙元的歷史與文化: 蒙元史學術研討會論文集, edited by Xiao Qiqing, 703–35. Taipei: Xuesheng shuju, 2001.

Zhi Fucheng 智夫成. "Mingdai zongshi renkou de xunmeng zengzhang yu jiezhi cuoshi" 明代宗室人口的迅猛增長與節制措施. *Zhongzhou xuekan* 4 (1990): 121–26.

Zu Shengli 祖生利 and Funada Yoshiyuki 船田善之. "Yuandai baihua beiwen de tili chutan" 元代白話碑文的體例初探. *Zhongguoshi yanjiu* 3 (2006): 117–35.

Zürcher, Erik. *The Buddhist Conquest of China: The Spread and Adaptation of Buddhism in Early Medieval China.* 2 vols. Leiden, the Netherlands: Brill, 1972.

Index

Page numbers for maps, figures, and tables are indicated in italics.

Harvard-Yenching Institute Monograph Series

(titles now in print)